Compiled and Edited by Reg Cade & Barry Gallafent

Advertising Sales Manager Andrew Wiltshire Tel: (01908) 643022

Published by
Marwain Publishing Limited,
Marwain House, Clarke Road, Mount Farm, Milton Keynes MK1 1LG

Designed by
Pepberry Limited,
Marwain House, Clarke Road, Mount Farm, Milton Keynes MK1 1LG

Repro by
HiLo Offset, Colchester, Essex

Printed by
HiLo Offset, Colchester, Essex

Distributed by (Booktrade)
Springfield Books Limited,
Springfield House, Norman Road, Denby Dale, Huddersfield HD8 8TH

(Camping and Caravan Trade)
Marwain Publishing Limited

ISBN 0 - 905377 - 73 - 7

FOREWORD

Welcome to the West Country and the South West, commonly referred to as the playground of Britain. Wherever you travel you will find plenty to do, the contrasting culture and history of the region brings alive local places of interest.

For instance you can choose to tour Devon's English Riviera, find Cornwall's mysterious 'God's Country', sample Somerset's famous ciders, see the Roman artifacts and natural hot springs in Bath, consider Dorset's outstanding natural beauty and the land that inspired Thomas Hardy to write so many novels.

Bigger and better than before and fact packed with the most detailed, essential and up to date information, this new revised edition promises to be the leading guide for touring the South West of England in 1997.

CADE'S WEST COUNTRY CARAVAN AND CAMPING SITE GUIDE will direct you to the best sites to stay and present a varied selection of places of interest to visit in County order. Also the guide is illustrated with a series of maps and useful descriptions of towns and villages throughout the region.

To save money on your holiday, simply look for the ◨ sign and see which parks will give you and your family 50p per night upon redemption of the money off vouchers in the back section of this guide. Use one voucher per night and save up to £10 off the cost of your site fees.

Local Government reorganisation started again in 1996 and many more changes are planned for April 1997. We for this year have chosen to use our traditional method of displaying holiday parks using the old county system, we shall of course be modifying the system when Government reorganisation is finished.

Like all other **"CADE'S"** guides, the information is carefully researched and as accurate as possible as we go to press. We must, however, point out that we are not agents of the sites and publish only such information as is supplied to us by the owner or operator in good faith. Therefore we cannot be responsible for any conditions or facilities that differ from those published. For this reason it is always advisable to check directly with the site before booking.

It is our aim in the publication of this guide to enable you to plan your holiday in advance. Remember that booking is advisable especially in the peak season. It would help us to continue providing this information if you could mention **"CADE'S"** when replying to advertisers.

Meanwhile, may I wish you the best of holidays in 1997.

REG CADE
(MANAGING DIRECTOR, MARWAIN PUBLISHING LIMITED)

INDEX

SYMBOLS

- ⋏ Tents
- 🚐 Motor Caravans
- 🚙 Touring Caravans
- ⇌ Nearest Station
- ♿ Facilities for Disabled
- ⚡ Electricity Hook-ups
- 🚽 Flush Toilets
- 🚰 Water
- ⌂ Showers
- ⊙ Shaver Points
- Washing Facilities
- Ironing Facilities
- Launderette
- Chem. Toilet Disposal
- S₷ Site Shop
- M₷ Mobile Shop
- L₷ Local Shop
- Gas
- ☎ Public Telephone
- ✘ Café Restaurant
- ♀ Licensed Club
- TV T.V.
- Games Room
- Childs Play Area
- Swimming Pool
- ⊛ Sports Area
- No Dogs Allowed
- Parking by Unit
- Money-Off Vochers Accepted

Nearby Facilities

- ⌂ Golf
- Fishing
- ⊥ Sailing
- Boating
- U Riding
- Water Ski-ing
- ♀ Tennis
- Climbing

Avon	Sites	5
	Places of Interest	6
Cornwall	Sites	10
	Places of Interest	32
Devon	Sites	38
	Places of Interest	60
Dorset	Sites	68
	Places of Interest	78
Hampshire	Sites	83
	Places of Interest	86
Isle Of Wight	Sites	91
	Places of Interest	94
Somerset	Sites	96
	Places of Interest	106
Wiltshire	Sites	111
	Places of Interest	112
Money Off Vouchers		115

PRICE BANDS
Please note that these are intended to be a guide only. They are based on a Non-Electric Caravan Pitch, 2 Adults, 1 Child and a Car - for one night. You should always verify the current charges directly with the site before travelling.

Band A up to £4.99   **Band B** up to £7.99   **Band C** over £8.00

CADE'S WEST COUNTRY CAMPING, TOURING & MOTOR CARAVAN SITE GUIDE 1997

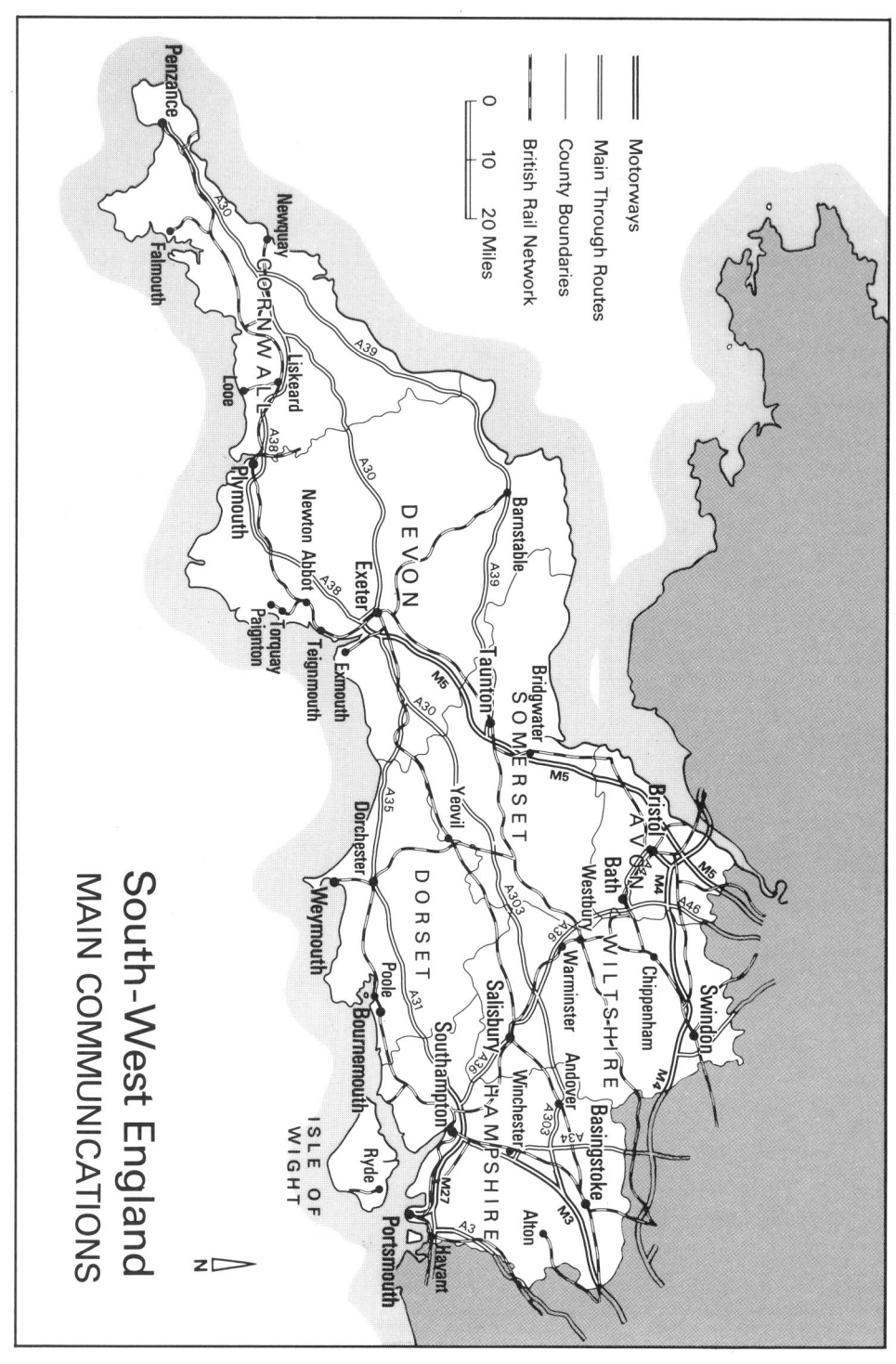

AVON

BATH
Bath Marina & Caravan Park, Brassmill Lane, Bath, Avon, BA1 3JT.
Tel: **428778** Std: 01225
Fax: **428778** Std: **01225**
Nearest Town/Resort Bath
Directions 2 miles west of Bath on the A4 at Newbridge, turn left at the Murco garage into Brassmill Lane, take the first turning on the right.
Acreage 4 **Open** All Year
Access Good **Site** Level
Sites Available ⛺ 🚐 **Total** 88
Low Season Band C
High Season Band C
Facilities ♿ ƒ ✗ 🚻 ♨ ☎ ⦿ ⌁ ♻ ⎙ ⬛
🍴 🅿 🛒 🎮 🍽
Nearby Facilities ┌ ✓ ⌇ ∪ ♞
⚡ Bath
Alongside a river, picturesque. 3 min walk from park and ride bus.

BATH
Bury View, Corston Fields, Bath, Avon, BA2 9HD.
Tel: 873672 Std: 01225.
Nearest Town/Resort Bath.
Directions 5 miles from Bath, situated on A39 Wells road.
Acreage 1¼ **Open** All Year
Access Good **Site** Level
Sites Available ⛺ ⛺ 🚐 **Total** 15
Low Season Band A
High Season Band A
Facilities ƒ 🚻 ♨ ⦿ ☎ ⎙ ⬛
Nearby Facilities ┌
⚡ Bath
Quiet countryside site, close to Bath.

BATH
Newton Mill Camping, Newton Road, Bath, North East Somerset, BA2 9JF.
Tel: 333909 Std: 01225
Fax: **461556** Std: **01225**.
Nearest Town/Resort Bath.
Directions Take the A4 to Bristol, turn left at the Globe Pub roundabout, then turn left onto the B3110. We are 1 mile on the left.
Acreage 22 **Open** All Year
Access Good **Site** Level
Sites Available ⛺ ⛺ 🚐 **Total** 250
Low Season Band B
High Season Band C
Facilities 🛁 ♿ ƒ 🚻 ♨ ⦿ ☎ ⎙ ⬛
🍴 🅿 🛒 🎮 🍽 ⛲ 🚲 ⬛
Nearby Facilities ┌ ✓ ⌇ ∪ ♞ ▲
⚡ Bath.
Wooded valley with our own trout stream. Buses to Bath every 10 minutes.

BRISTOL
Baltic Wharf Caravan Club Site, Cumberland Road, Bristol, Avon, BS1 6XG.
Tel: 268030 Std: 01179
Nearest Town/Resort Bristol
Directions Any direction in Bristol follow signs to S.S. Great Britain, continue on to Baltic Wharf.
Acreage 2½ **Open** All Year
Access Good **Site** Level
Sites Available ⛺ ⛺ 🚐 **Total** 58
Facilities ƒ 🚻 ♨ ⦿ ☎ ⎙ ⬛
🍴 🅿 🛒
Nearby Facilities ┌ ✓ ∪
⚡ Bristol Temple Meads
Within easy reach of Bath, Wells and Cheddar. Floating harbour - S.S. Great Britain. Water ferry to the city centre. Assistance for walking disabled.

BRISTOL
Salthouse Farm Touring Park, Severn Beach, Pilning, Avon.
Tel: 632274 Std: 01454
Nearest Town/Resort Bristol.
Directions M48 junction 1 take the A403 for 3 miles. At traffic lights turn right onto the B4055 1 mile to Severn Beach, site is on the right. M5 junction 17 take the B4055 to traffic lights.
Acreage 2 **Open** April to October
Access Good **Site** Level
Sites Available ⛺ ⛺ 🚐 **Total** 40
Low Season Band B
High Season Band C
Facilities ♿ ƒ 🚻 ♨ ⦿ ☎ ⎙ ⬛
🍴 🅿 🛒 🎮 🍽 ⛲ ⬛
Nearby Facilities ┌ ✓
Alongside an estuary and the New Severn Bridge. Ideal touring.

CLEVEDON
Warrens Holiday Park, Colehouse Lane, Clevedon, Avon, BS21 6TQ.
Tel: 871666 Std: 01275
Nearest Town/Resort Weston-super-Mare.
Directions M5 junction 20, follow road towards Congresbury for 1 mile.
Acreage 8 **Open** March to January
Access Good **Site** Level
Sites Available ⛺ ⛺ 🚐 **Total** 100
Facilities 🛁 ƒ 🚻 ♨ ⦿ ☎ ⎙ ⬛
🍴 🅿 🛒 🎮 🍽 ⛲
Nearby Facilities ┌ ✓ ⌇ ∪ ♞ ▲
⚡ Yatton
Fishing.

CONGRESBURY
Oak Farm Touring Park, Weston Road, Congresbury, Avon, BS19 5EB.
Tel: 833246 Std: 01934
Nearest Town/Resort Weston-super-Mare
Directions 4 miles from junc. 21 on M5, on the A370 midway between Bristol and Weston Super Mare.
Open 31st Mar to October
Access Good **Site** Level
Sites Available ⛺ ⛺ 🚐 **Total** 27
Facilities ƒ 🚻 ♨ ⦿ ☎ ⎙ ⬛
Nearby Facilities ┌ ✓ ⌇ ∪ ♞ ▲
⚡ Yatton

REDHILL (BRISTOL)
Brook Lodge Touring Caravan & Camping Park, Brook Lodge, Cowslip Green, Redhill, Nr. Bristol, Avon, BS18 7RD.
Tel: 862311 Std: 01934
Nearest Town/Resort Bristol/Bath
Directions From the historic city of Bristol take the A38 south west for 9 miles, park is signposted on the left. From the M5 junction 19 take the A369, then the B3129, then the B3130, then right onto the A38, 6 miles. From the south on the A38, 3½ miles beyond the traffic lights at Churchill.
Acreage 3½ **Open** March to October
Access Good **Site** Mostly Level
Sites Available ⛺ ⛺ 🚐 **Total** 29
Low Season Band B
High Season Band C
Facilities ⬛ ƒ 🚻 ♨ ⦿ ☎ ⎙ ⬛
🍴 🅿 🛒 ⚜ ⬛
Nearby Facilities ┌ ✓ ∪ ▲
Beautiful grounds with trees, lawns and garden. Stream for trout fishing nearby. Bird life and walks. Rural non-tourist area. Ideal for touring.

WESTON-SUPER-MARE
Ardnave Holiday Park, Kewstoke, Weston-super-Mare, Somerset, BS22 9XJ.
Tel: 622319 Std: 01934
Nearest Town/Resort Weston-super-Mare.
Directions Off motorway M5 at junction 21 follow signs to Kewstoke.
Acreage ½ **Open** March to October
Access Good **Site** Level
Sites Available ⛺ 🚐 **Total** 12
Low Season Band B
High Season Band C
Facilities ƒ ✗ 🚻 ♨ ⦿ ☎ ⎙ ⬛
⚡ 🅿 🛒 ⬛
Nearby Facilities ┌ ✓ ⌇ ∪ ♞ ♞
⚡ Weston-super-Mare.
Near Beach, Graded 4 Ticks.

WESTON-SUPER-MARE
Purn International Holiday Park, A370 Bridgwater Road, Bleadon, Weston-super-Mare, Somerset, BS24 0AN.
Tel: 812342 Std: 01934
Nearest Town/Resort Weston Super Mare
Directions From North leave M5 at junction 21 A370 into Weston A370 out of Weston - park 2 miles on right next to Anchor Inn, signposted. From South leave M5 junction 22 take signs for Weston on left next to Anchor Inn on A370.
Acreage 3 **Open** March to 7th Nov
Access Good **Site** Level
Sites Available ⛺ ⛺ 🚐 **Total** 60
Low Season Band B
High Season Band C
Facilities 🛁 ♿ ƒ 🚻 ♨ ⦿ ☎ ⎙ ⬛
🍴 🅿 🛒 ⚜ 🍽 ⛲ ⬛
Nearby Facilities ┌ ✓ ⌇ ∪ ♞
⚡ Weston Super Mare
Nearest Park to Weston, Licensed club and our own traditional country pub, The Anchor Inn with restaurant and family room, entertainment and dancing. Childrens Bouncing Robin Club with Uncle Darren. RAC appointed 4 Ticks and AA 3 Pennants.

WINSCOMBE
Netherdale Caravan & Camping Site, Bridgwater Road, Sidcot, Winscombe, North Somerset, BS25 1NH.
Tel: 3481/3007 Std: 0193 484.
Nearest Town/Resort Cheddar.
Directions From Weston-super-Mare follow A371 to join A38 at Sidcot corner, site ¼ mile south. From Wells and Cheddar follow A371 westwards to join A38 a mile south of site.
Acreage 3½ **Open** March to October
Access Good **Site** Lev/Slope
Sites Available ⛺ ⛺ 🚐 **Total** 25.
Low Season Band B
High Season Band C
Facilities ƒ 🚻 ♨ ⦿ ☎ ⚡ 🅿 ✗ ⬛
Nearby Facilities ┌ ✓ ⌇ ∪ ♞ ▲
⚡ Weston-super-Mare.
Excellent walking area, footpath from site to valley and Mendip Hills adjoining. Good views. Ideal touring centre for Somerset. Many historical places and beaches within easy reach of site. Only individual motorcycles accepted, not groups. Dry ski slope - 3 miles.

CADE'S WEST COUNTRY CAMPING, TOURING & MOTOR CARAVAN SITE GUIDE 1997

PLACES OF INTEREST

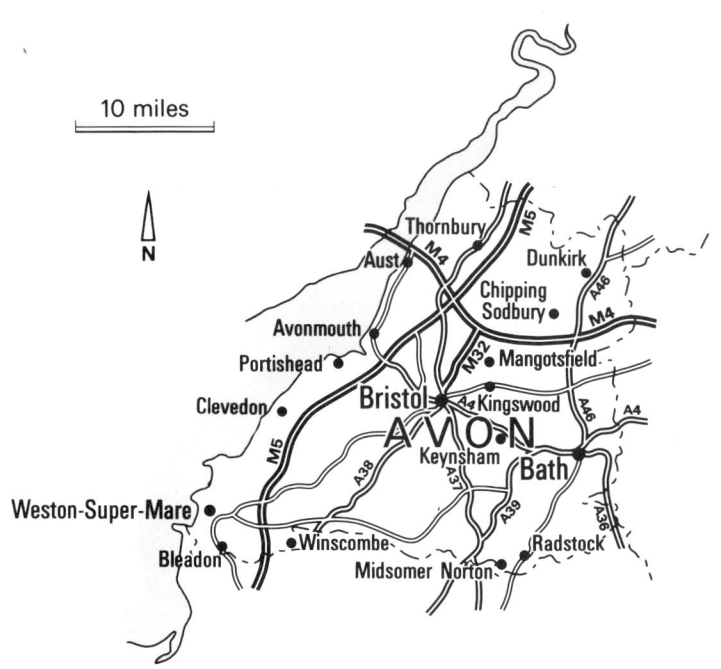

BATH
Regarded as the most elegant city in England, Bath is famous for its history, architecture, roman artifacts, natural hot springs and culture.

The largest of Avons principal cities, Bath was founded circa 44 AD and as a Roman camp was first named "Acquae Sullis" - the waters of Sull, (a Celtic Goddess). An important ecclesiastical centre, Bath was the seat of The Bishop of Wells (909-1088), the seat of The Bishop of Bath (1088-1192), the seat of Bath and Glastonbury (1192-1244) and finally, on the seat of The Bishop of Bath and Wells (1244-To Present).

The English King Edgar was crowned at Bath in 973 at the Saxon Abbey, situated closely to the now Norman Minster which replaced it.

At one time Bath was a thriving centre of the early wool manufacturing industry, but now Bath is mostly famous for its architecture which attracts thousands of visitors annually and is mandatory for budding architects, artists, engineers and the like. Development of Bath commenced in the eighteenth century and is attributed to the work of John Wood and his son, Robert Master and Thomas Baldwin. Motivated originally by Ralph Allen an eighteenth century Cornishman who quarried stone locally, supplying many of the important buildings. The best of the Roman structures are the Spa Baths and huge reservoir laid down by Roman plumbers 2000 years ago. The reservoir is still in working order providing up to half a million gallons of water each day at a constant 125 degrees fahrenheit.

Above the reservoir the pump room is a centre where townspeople and tourists can meet for coffee and music. Annual festivals of music, poetry, dance and contemporary art are held here.

Other notable places of interest to be found in Bath include the famous Museum of Costume founded by Mrs Dorothy Langley Moor and the lesser known but equally extensive collections of silver, paintings, porcelain and pottery.

If you appreciate horticulture, many varied flowers and trees are a common feature of the city and the Royal Victoria Park covers fifty acres of ground and houses the Botanical Gardens in which over five thousand varieties are grown.

BATH
AMERICAN MUSEUM : Claverton Manor, Bath, Avon, BA2 7BD. Tel : 01225 460503.
Nearest Railway Station : Bath Spa. Location : 2.5 miles from Bath and 3.5 miles south-east of Bath off the A36 (Warminster road). Open: 2pm - 5pm every day (except Monday) from end March to end October. **Special Attractions:** 18 period furnished rooms from 17th/19th Centuries. Galleries of pewter, glass, textiles, folk art and maps. Many exhibits in beautiful gardens. American Arboretum. Seasonal exhibitions. Teas with American cookies.

BATH
BATH POSTAL MUSEUM : 8 Broad Street, Bath, Avon, BA1 5LJ. Tel : 01225 460333.
Nearest Railway Station : Bath. Location : In the city centre near the post office. Open : All Year. Monday to Saturday 11am-5pm, Sunday (March to December) 2pm-5pm. **Special Attractions:** Displays the story of written communication from the days of Papyrus and clay tablets to the present time. Changing exhibitions, Airmail room, model Victorian Post Office, video, tea room and gift shop.

BATH
BECKFORD'S TOWER & MUSEUM : Lansdown, Bath, Avon, BA1 9BH. Tel : 01225 338727. Fax : 01225 481850.
Nearest Railway Station : Bath Spa. Location : On top of Lansdown, 2 miles from City Centre. Within easy reach of M4 and A4. Open : Saturdays, Sundays, Bank Holiday Mondays 2pm - 5pm. Closed November to February. **Special Attractions:** Built in 1825 for William Beckford, with panoramic views from the Belvedere (up 156 easy steps). Two museum rooms illustrating - with prints, pictures and models - Beckford's life at Fonthill and Bath.

BATH
THE BUILDING OF BATH MUSEUM : The Countess of Huntingdon's Chapel, The Vineyards, The Paragon, Bath, Avon, BA1 5NA. Tel : 01225 333895. Fax : 01225 445473.
Nearest Railway Station : Bath Spa. Location : Junction 18 off the M4, bottom of Lansdown Hill. 10 minute walk from Royal Crescent and Abbey. Open : 11th February to 30th November, Tuesday to Sunday including Bank Holiday Mondays, 10.30am-5pm. **Special Attractions:** This new museum tells the fascinating story of how Georgian Bath was built. The exhibition depicts resort life in the time of 'Beau' Nash and explains house construction from the laying of the first foundation stone to the last coat of paint. Exhibits include a spectacular illuminated model of Bath.

BATH
DYRHAM PARK : Chippenham, Wiltshire, SN14 8ER. Tel : 0117 937 2501.
Nearest Railway Station : Bath. Location : A46, Bath/Stroud Road 2 miles south of junction 18 on M4. Open : Park - All year, daily 12pm-5.30pm, last admission 5pm or dusk if earlier (closed christmas day). House and Garden - April to October, daily except Wednesday and Thursday, 12pm - 5.30pm, last admission 5pm or dusk if earlier. Park and Garden - April to October, 11am-5.30pm. Except Wednesday and Thursday when Park only 12pm-5.30pm. Restaurant and Shop - As House.

BATH
HERSCHEL HOUSE & MUSEUM : 19 New King Street, Bath, Avon. Tel : 01225 311342.
Nearest Railway Station : Bath Spa. Location : A short walk from the SW Corner of Queens square via Charles Street. Open : 2pm-5pm daily March to October, also Saturdays and Sundays 2pm-5pm November to February and at other times by booking. **Special Attractions:** The home of Sir William Herschel and his sister Caroline. A Georgian House with period furniture and musical instruments, astronomical exhibits, workshop, kitchen and interesting small garden. Restored 18th Century Town Garden.

BATH
HOLBURNE MUSEUM & CRAFTS STUDY CENTRE : Great Pulteney Street, Bath, Avon, BA2 4DB. Tel : 01225 466669. Fax : 01225 333121.
Nearest Railway Station : Bath Spa. Location : Situated in a lovely garden at the end of historic Great Pulteney Street, five minutes' walk from the city centre. Open : February to Mid-December weekdays 11am - 5pm, Sundays 2.30pm - 5.30pm. Closed Mondays November to Easter. Licensed Teahouse serving coffee, lunches and teas. **Special Attractions:** Permanent collection of Old Master paintings, silver, porcelain, etc. Crafts Study Centre showing 20th Century pottery, textiles, furniture, calligraphy. Frequent temporary exhibitions and events. Free Parking.

BATH
MUSEUM OF COSTUME : Bennett Street, Bath, Avon, BA1 2QH. Tel : 01225 477785.
Nearest Railway Station : Bath Spa. Location : 10 minutes walk from the city centre. Open : All year (except 25th and 26th December), Monday to Saturday 10am-5pm, Sunday 11am-5pm. **Special Attractions:** One of the largest collections of costume in the UK. It covers the history of fashion from the late 16th Century to the present day. Special exhibition of 200 Years of Wedding Dress until January 1998.

BATH
THE MUSEUM OF EAST ASIAN ART : 12 Bennett Street, Bath, Avon, BA1 2QL. Tel : 01225 464640. Fax : 01225 461718.
Nearest Railway Station : Bath Spa. Open : April to October - Monday to Saturday 10am-6pm, Sunday 10am-5pm. November to March - Monday to Saturday 10am-5pm, Sunday 12noon-5pm. **Special Attractions:** A unique museum housing a collection of Chinese, Japanese, Korean and South East Asian artefacts. Objects range in date from C. 5000BC to C. 20th and reveal the finest achievements in East Asian crafts. Introductory video (6 languages), gallery guides and childrens quizzes. Shop selling a wide range of East Asian gifts and crafts.

BATH
NORWOOD FARM : Bath Road, Norton St. Philip, Near Bath, Avon, BA3 6LP. Tel : 01373 834356. Fax : 01373 834765.
Nearest Railway Station : Frome, Trowbridge or Bath. Location : 6 miles south of Bath on the B3110. Open : Easter holidays to the end of September, 10.30am-6pm. **Special Attractions:** Unique organic rare breeds farm, rearing over 30 breeds of old British sheep, cattle, pigs, goats, ponies and poultry. Working in harmony with nature producing quality food in a quality environment. Farm shop, picnic and play area, cafe with home-made food, Farmwalk and a free car park. Entrance fee charged.

BATH
ROMAN BATHS MUSEUM : Pump Room, Stall Street, Bath, Avon, BA1 1LZ. Tel : 01225 477785.
Nearest Railway Station : Bath Spa. Location : Central Bath. Open : All year (except 25th and 26th December). April to September 9am-6pm, August 9am-6pm and 8pm-10pm, October to March 9.30am-5pm. Sunday 10.30am-5pm. **Special Attractions:** Visit the world-famous Roman Baths in Bath. Built 2000 years ago around the only hot springs in Great Britain and still remarkably intact.

BATH
THEATRE ROYAL BATH : Sawclose, Bath, Avon, BA1 1ET. Tel : 01225 448844.
Nearest Railway Station : Bath Spa. Bus service every ten minutes Wed - Sun. Location : Central Bath. Open : Monday to Wednesday 7.30pm, Thursday to Saturday 8pm, Wednesday Matinee 2.30pm, Saturday Matinee 2.30pm. **Special Attractions:** One of Britain's oldest and most beautiful theatres, presenting a weekly changing programme of top quality touring productions including many prior to West End shows. Also houses the Vaults Restaurant, Garrick's Head Pub, backstage tours, art gallery and Ustinov Studio.

BATH
VICTORIA ART GALLERY : Bridge Street, Bath, Avon, BA2 4AT. Tel : 01225 477772. Fax : 01225 477231.
Nearest Railway Station : Bath Spa. Location : Opposite Pulteney Bridge. Open : Monday to Friday 10am-5.30pm, Saturday 10am-5pm. Closed Sunday and Bank Holidays. **Special Attractions:** Bath and North East Somerset's free public art gallery with a permanent collection of over 600 oil paintings and 5000 watercolours, drawings and prints. The gallery is also a venue for major touring exhibitions.

BRISTOL
This famous old city has been a port for over eight hundred years and was the first country borough. It is now a resort and manufacturing centre, the seat of a University and the seat of a Bishop. It has imported wine from Bordeaux and Spain since the middle ages and has traded with America since the 17th century.

The impressive Cathedral received its Charter from Henry VIII in 1542, although it was originally the church of an Abbey founded in 1148.

Bristol is also the home of Isombard Kingdom Brunel's most famous monuments, namely the Clifton Suspension Bridge and the iron clad ocean liner S.S. Great Britain. One of the most exciting spectacles to witness in Bristol is the Grand Prix World Power Boat Championship, which takes place in late May or early June every year and is held at Bristol City Docks.

Many fine historic buildings can be viewed in Bristol, including The Lord Mayors Chapel, The Corn Exchange, The Theatre Royal which dates from 1766, The Methodist Chapel built by John Wesley in 1743 and Temple Church a 14th century ruin which has a leaning tower. In the Kingdom district many restored Georgian houses can be seen.

Finally the notable natural phenomena of the Bristol Channel is the Severn Bore. The Bore is a tidal wave which sweeps in from the sea for several days each month, but is at its strongest and most dangerous in Spring and Autumn. It drags a tidal wave of up to 16 knots on its wake and at its most placid the Bore can be around 9 feet high although it has reached heights of over 30 feet.

BRISTOL
ASHTON COURT ESTATE : Long Ashton, Bristol, Avon, BS18 9JN. Tel : 0117 963 9174. Fax : 0117 953 2143.
Nearest Railway Station : Bristol Temple Meads. Location : 2 miles from Bristol City centre, off the A369 to Portishead. Open : 8am till dusk. **Special Attractions:** 850 acre Historic Estate with woodlands and grasslands to explore. Visitor Centre, pitch & putt golf and special events.

BRISTOL
BLAISE CASTLE HOUSE MUSEUM : Henbury, Bristol, BS10 7QS. Tel : 0117 950 6789. Fax : 0117 959 3475.
Nearest Railway Station : Bristol Temple Meads. Open : 10am-1pm and 2pm-5pm Tuesday to Sunday inclusive, closed Monday. **Special Attractions:** A late 18th Century house containing Bristol's Museum of Everyday Life. The picturesque grounds include remains of an Iron Age hill fort and a id 18th Century Gothic Castle which gives Blaise its name.

BRISTOL
BRISTOL INDUSTRIAL MUSEUM : Princes Wharf, City Docks, Bristol, BS1 4RN. Tel : 0117 925 1470. Fax : 0117 929 7318.
Nearest Railway Station : Bristol Temple Meads. Location : In the heart of Bristol, alongside the Historic harbour. Open : All Year, Tuesday to Sunday 10am-5pm. Closed Mondays except Bank Holidays. **Special Attractions:** Industrial and transport history of the Bristol region, including the World's first touring caravan "Wanderer". Steam Railway and Steam Tug offering trips on Summer weekends.

BRISTOL
BRISTOL OLD VIC THEATRE : King Street, Bristol, Avon, BS1 4ED. Tel : 0117 949 3993. Fax : 0117 949 3996.
Nearest Railway Station : Bristol Temple Meads. Location : City centre, 15 minutes from the station. Open : Monday to Saturday, 10am-8pm. **Special Attractions:** The Country's oldest working repertory theatre, Bristol Old Vic has a remarkable reputation for classical plays and new writing. Apart from memorable theatre, visitors can enjoy fascinating backstage tours, Director's Previews, Playdays and Aftershow Talkarounds. Plus great meals in our Siddons Bar and Buttery.

BRISTOL
THE BRISTOL PACKET BOAT TRIPS : Wapping Wharf, Gas Ferry Road, Bristol, Avon, BS8 1AW. Tel : 0117 926 8157 or 0117 973 5315.
Location : S.S. Great Britain car and coach park off Cumberland Road. Open : Every day, March to September. **Special Attractions:** Boat trips around the City Docks. To Beeses Tea Gardens for tea and the Chequers Hanham for lunch. Avon Gorge cruises under the suspension bridge. Ferrying around the City Docks, able to pick up at one place and drop off at another. Private charters, public and educational trips. Evening river cruises.

BRISTOL
BRISTOL ZOO GARDENS : Clifton, Bristol, BS8 3HA. Tel : 0117 973 8951. Fax : 0117 973 6814.
Location : Bristol Zoo is on the A4176. From the M5, exit at junction 17 Southbound or junction 18 Northbound. The Zoo is well signposted from both junctions. From Bristol city centre follow the signs to the Zoo. Open : Every day from 9am. Closing time approx 5.30pm (Summer), and 4.30pm (Winter). Closed Christmas Day. **Special Attractions:** Enjoy a real life experience in beautiful gardens! Don't miss the new Bug World which is full of fascinating invertebrates and Twilight World - a fantastic new nocturnal house. There's also an Aquarium, Reptile House, monkeys on lake islands, a Zoolympics trail, animal encounters and more. Remember your visit will support our important conservation work. Registered Charity Number 203695.

BRISTOL
CITY MUSEUM & ART GALLERY : Queens Road, Bristol, BS8 1RL. Tel : 0117 922 3571. Fax : 0117 922 2047.
Nearest Railway Station : Temple Meads. Open : Daily, seven days a week, 10am-5pm. **Special Attractions:** There is plenty to see - The Mineral Collection, The Mysteries of Ancient Egypt, Bristol Ceramics. Victorian paintings, watercolours and an oustanding collection of Oriental art, native birds, mammals, animals from other lands and the long extinct "Sea Dragons" Also a variety of temporary exhibitions. Restricted access to some galleries.

BRISTOL
CLIFTON OBSERVATORY, CAMERA OBSCURA & CAVE : Clifton Suspension Bridge, Clifton, Bristol, Avon, BS8 3TY. Tel : 01275 393798.
Location : Bristol side of the Clifton Suspension Bridge. Open : All Year, Summer 11am-6pm, Winter 11am-4pm. **Special Attractions:** The only camera obscura open to the public in England. "Giants Cave" with extended platform enabling panoramic views of Avon Gorge and the Suspension Bridge. A most unusual attraction.

BRISTOL
THE EXPLORATORY HANDS-ON SCIENCE CENTRE : Bristol Old Station, Temple Meads, Bristol, Avon, BS1 6QU. Tel : 0117 907 9000. Fax : 0117 907 8000.
Nearest Railway Station : Bristol Temple Meads. Location : Next to Temple Meads Railway Station in the centre of Bristol. Open : Every day, 10am-5pm. **Special Attractions:** Britain's first and largest hands-on science centre with over 150 different exhibitions, all hands-on.

8 *CADE'S WEST COUNTRY CAMPING, TOURING & MOTOR CARAVAN SITE GUIDE 1997*

BRISTOL
THE GEORGIAN HOUSE : 7 Great George Street, Bristol, BS1 5RR. Tel : 0117 921 1362.
Nearest Railway Station : Temple Meads. Open : Tuesday to Saturday, 1pm-5pm. **Special Attractions:** No.7 Great George Street was built between 1787 and 1791 for John Pinney, a Bristol merchant. Here you can explore upstairs and down, from the fine drawing room with its elegant furniture and delicate plaster work ceiling, to the basement kitchen complete with roasting spit, oven and pots and pans.

BRISTOL
HARVEY'S WINE CELLARS : 12 Denmark Street, Bristol, BS1 5DQ. Tel : 0117 927 5036. Fax : 0117 927 5002.
Location : Denmark Street is one way. Coaches can drop passengers outside Bristol Hippodrome. Access by coach is from Park Street. Open : Monday to Saturday, 10am-5pm. **Special Attractions:** Medieval Cellars beneath 12 Denmark Street, Harvey's Wine Museum and Harvey's Restaurant. Museum contains a unique collection of antiques; corkscrews, bottles, decanters, silverware and 18th Century drinking glasses. Visitors over 18 are welcome to join pre-arranged guided group tours and tutored tastings. The cellars were the birthplace of Harvey's Bristol Cream Sherry in the 1880's.

BRISTOL
MARITIME HERITAGE CENTRE : Wapping Wharf, Gas Ferry Road, Bristol, BS1 6TY. Tel : 0117 926 0680.
Nearest Railway Station : Bristol Temple Meads. Open : Seven days a week, 10am-6pm Summer, 10am-5pm Winter. **Special Attractions:** The story of ship building in Bristol and an introduction to one of the most famous ships of all, The S.S. Great Britain. Combine a visit to the Bristol Industrial Museum and travel by train between the two on the Bristol Harbour Railway.

BRISTOL
OLDOWN COUNTRY PARK : Tockington, Bristol, Avon, BS12 4PG. Tel : 01454 413605. Fax : 01454 413955.
Nearest Railway Station : Bristol Parkway. Location : Follow the brown tourist signs for "Oldown" from the A38 at Alveston. Near Thornbury. Open : Every day except Mondays. March to September, 10am-6pm. October to February, 10am-4pm. **Special Attractions:** Farm and forest open to the public. Walks, adventure playground, farmyard animals, trailer rides and other activities. Farm shop, pick-your-own fruit, delicatessen and gifts. Restaurant and gardens, picnic area and ample car parking. Facilities for the disabled.

BRISTOL
THE RED LODGE : Park Row, Bristol, BS1 5LJ. Tel : 0117 921 1360.
Nearest Railway Station : Temple Meads. Open : Tuesday to Saturday, 1pm-5pm. **Special Attractions:** The Elizabethan Red Lodge housed successive local families and later the first girls' reformatory in this country. Now furnished as a family home; the great oak room panelling is magnificent and adjoining smaller bedroom a place to ponder past lives. The Knot Garden offers tranquility in our busy city.

BRISTOL
WILLSBRIDGE MILL : The Wildlife Trust, Willsbridge Hill, Bristol, Avon, BS15 6EX. Tel : 0117 932 6885.
Nearest Railway Station : Keynsham. Location : Free car park signposted off the A431 at Longwell Green, 6 miles from the city centres of Bristol and Bath. Open : Easter to October 31st. Every day 2pm-5pm except Mondays and Saturdays, however open Bank Holiday Mondays. **Special Attractions:** South Gloucestershire's unique wildlife visitor centre, Willsbridge Mill, an impressive Corn Mill houses a range of 'hands on' wildlife and historical exhibits. Set in Willsbridge Valley, a wooded nature reserve with nature trail, streamside board walk. Demonstration wildlife garden and ponds. Cafe, wildlife gift shop and toilets. Wheelchair access to exhibition, garden, ponds and part of valley.

CLEVEDON
A quiet seaside resort on the Severn estuary, Clevedon lies at the junction of two low hill ranges and is a good walking centre. It was the birth place of Hartley Coleridge.

Arthur Hallam - who's death inspired the poet Tennyson's "In Memoriam" lived in 14th century Clevedon Court and his body is buried at St Andrews Church. This attractive court was also the working place of Thackeray and part of Vanity Fair was written here.

CLEVEDON
CLEVEDON COURT : Near Clevedon, Bristol. Tel : 01275 872257.
Location : 1.5 miles East of Clevedon on the Bristol Road (B3130). Open : April to the end of September. Wednesday, Thursday, Sunday and Bank Holiday Monday 2pm-5pm. Last admission 4.30pm. **Special Attractions:** Built about 1320 and altered throughout the centuries, the house, with its great hall remains substantially a medieval Manor House. There is a 14th century chapel and 18th century terraced gardens. Collection of Nailsea Glass and Eltonware. Tea, coffee and home made cakes in the old kitchen.

RADSTOCK
RADSTOCK MUSEUM : Barton Meade House, Haydon, Radstock, Bath, BA3 3QS. Tel : 01761 437722.
Nearest Railway Station : Bath. Location : 1 mile from the centre of Radstock on the Kilmersdon road. Open : Saturday 10am-4pm, Sunday and Bank Holiday Mondays 2pm-5pm. Closed all of December. **Special Attractions:** Local history museum depicting the history of coalmining in North Somerset and the lves of Miners. See a Victorian miners cottage room, a Victorian schoolroom, a 1930's Co-Op shop, the areas connection with Wesley and Nelson and much more.

WESTON-SUPER-MARE
INTERNATIONAL HELICOPTER MUSEUM : The Airport, Locking Moor Road, Weston-super-Mare, Avon, BS24 8PP. Tel : 01934 635227. Fax : 01934 822400.
Nearest Railway Station : Weston-super-Mare. Location : On the A368/371 Weston-super-Mare to Wells road, 3 miles from the sea front and 2 miles from the M5 junction 21. Open : Summer 10am-6pm every day. Winter 10am-4pm. **Special Attractions:** There is plenty to see in Britain's only Helicopter and Autogyro Museum. Discover how helicopters work, see the World's fastest helicopter and the unique 'Hind' Russian Attack Helicopter. Explore the restoration hanger. A fascinating place to visit. Cafeteria, shop and simulator ride.

WESTON-SUPER-MARE
WESTON HERITAGE CENTRE : 3-6 Wadham Street, Weston-super-Mare, Avon, BS23 1JY. Tel : 01934 412144.
Nearest Railway Station : Weston-super-Mare. Location : Between the sea front and North High Street, opposite Grove Park. Open : All Year, Monday to Saturday, 10am-5pm. **Special Attractions:** The story of the resort and the North Somerset countryside in displays and models - the sites and subjects to explore. Information point sells trails and guides. Coffee shop, local souvenirs and gifts.

**PLEASE MENTION
CADE'S
WHEN REPLYING
TO ADVERTISERS**

CADE'S WEST COUNTRY CAMPING, TOURING & MOTOR CARAVAN SITE GUIDE 1997

CORNWALL

CORNWALL

BODMIN
Glenmorris Park, Longstone Road, St. Mabyn, Bodmin, Cornwall, PL30 3BY.
Tel: 841677 Std: 01208
Fax: 841677 Std: 01208
Nearest Town/Resort Bodmin/Wadebridge.
Directions ½ mile south west of Camelford on the A39, turn left signposted B3266 for 6 miles. Turn right signposted St. Mabyn, ¼ mile to site. 5½ miles north of Bodmin.
Acreage 10 **Open** Easter to October
Access Good **Site** Level
Sites Available A ⊕ ⊟ **Total** 100
Low Season Band A
High Season Band B
Facilities ∫ ⅏ ⚹ ∩ ⊙ ⌐ ⌑ ⊟ ✿
೫ ╠ ⊙ ❀ ∩ ⋇ ❋ ⊟
Nearby Facilities ୮ ✓ ⊥ ⋇ ∪ ℛ
⇌ Bodmin Parkway.
Quiet and secluded, 4 Tick Graded site. Centrally located for touring and beaches.

BODMIN
Ruthern Valley Holiday Park, Ruthernbridge, Nr. Bodmin, Cornwall, PL30 5LU
Tel: 831395 Std: 01208
Nearest Town/Resort Bodmin
Directions Through Bodmin on A389 towards St. Austell, on outskirts of Bodmin Ruthernbridge signposted right. Follow signs for Ruthern or Ruthernbridge.
Acreage 2 **Open** April to October
Access Good **Site** Level
Sites Available A ⊕ ⊟ **Total** 30
Low Season Band C
High Season Band C
Facilities ∫ ⅏ ⚹ ∩ ⊙ ⌐ ⌑ ⊟ ✿
೫ ⊙ ❀ ∩ ⊟
Nearby Facilities ୮ ✓ ⊥ ∪ ℛ
⇌ Bodmin Parkway
Quiet peaceful wooded location centrally based for touring.

BOSCASTLE
Lower Pennycrocker Farm, St. Juliot, Boscastle, Cornwall.
Tel: 250257 Std: 01840
Nearest Town/Resort Boscastle
Directions 2½ miles north of Boscastle on B3263, turn left signposted Pennycrocker.
Acreage 4 **Open** Easter to September
Access Good **Site** Level
Sites Available A ⊕ ⊟ **Total** 40
Low Season Band A
High Season Band A
Facilities ⊟ ∫ ⅏ ⚹ ∩ ⊙ ೫ ╠ ⊟
Nearby Facilities ✓ ∪
⇌ Bodmin
Scenic views, ideal touring.

BOSCASTLE

West End Camping Site, West End Farm, Tresparrett, Camelford, Cornwall.
Tel: 261612 Std: 01840
Nearest Town/Resort Boscastle
Directions On coastal road between Bude and Boscastle. A39 onto the B3263.
Acreage 1 **Open** Easter to September
Access Good **Site** Level
Sites Available A ⊕ ⊟ **Total** 25
Low Season Band A
High Season Band A
Facilities ⅏ ∩ ✿
Nearby Facilities
⇌ Bodmin

BUDE

Budemeadows Touring Holiday Park, Poundstock, Bude, Cornwall, EX23 0NA.
Tel: 361646 Std: 01288
Nearest Town/Resort Bude
Directions From Bude take A39 south for 3 miles.
Acreage 9 **Open** All Year
Access Good **Site** Level
Sites Available A ⊕ ⊟ **Total** 100
Low Season Band C
High Season Band C
Facilities ⊟ ∫ ⅏ ⚹ ∩ ⊙ ⌐ ⌑ ⊟ ✿
೫ ⊙ ❀ ⅏ ∩ ⋇ ❋ ⊟
Nearby Facilities ୮ ✓ ⊥ ⋇ ∪ ℛ
⇌ Exeter
1 mile from sandy beaches, cliff walks and rolling surf of Widmouth Bay. Spectacular coastal scenery.

BUDE

Cornish Coasts Caravan Park, Middle Penlean, Poundstock, Bude, Cornwall, EX23 0EE.
Tel: 361380 Std: 01288
Nearest Town/Resort Bude/Widemouth Bay
Directions On seaward side of A39 Bude to Camelford road, 5 miles south of Bude.
Acreage 3 **Open** Easter to October
Access Good **Site** Lev/Slope
Sites Available A ⊕ ⊟ **Total** 78
Low Season Band B
High Season Band B
Facilities ⊟ ∫ ⅏ ⚹ ∩ ⊙ ⌐ ⌑ ⊟ ✿
೫ ⊙ ❀ ∩ ⊟
Nearby Facilities ୮ ✓ ⊥ ⋇ ∪ ℛ ⊹
⇌ Exeter
Peaceful, friendly site. Superb views over countryside and coast line. Ideal touring location with many beaches nearby. Good base for spectacular coastal path, walking groups transport arranged. Holiday caravans to let.

BUDE

Penhalt Farm Holiday Park, Widemouth Bay, Nr. Bude, Cornwall.
Tel: 361210 Std: 01288
Nearest Town/Resort Bude
Directions 5 miles south of Bude to Widemouth Bay, then on the Millook road.
Acreage 8 **Open** Easter to October
Access Good **Site** Level
Sites Available A ⊕ ⊟
Low Season Band A
High Season Band B
Facilities ∫ ⚹ ⅏ ⚹ ∩ ⊙ ⌐ ⌑ ⊟ ✿
೫ ╠ ⊙ ❀ ∩
Nearby Facilities ୮ ✓ ⋇ ∪ ℛ
⇌ Exeter
Family camp site, overlooking sea, Widemouth Bay. 2 x 6 berth caravans and 1 x 4 berth caravan to let.

BUDE

Upper Lynstone Camping & Caravan Park, Upper Lynstone Farm, Bude, Cornwall.
Tel: 352017 Std: 01288
Nearest Town/Resort Bude
Directions ½ mile south of Bude on Widemouth Bay road.
Acreage 5 **Open** Easter to October
Access Good **Site** Lev/Slope
Sites Available A ⊕ ⊟ **Total** 90
Facilities ∫ ⅏ ⚹ ∩ ⊙ ⌐ ⊟ ✿
೫ ⊙ ❀ ∩ ⊟
Nearby Facilities ୮ ✓ ⋇ ∪ ℛ
⇌ Exeter
Within easy reach of good surfing beaches. Access to cliff walks. Only individual motorcycles accepted, not groups. E.T.B. 4 Tick Grading.

BUDE

Widemouth Bay Caravan Park, John Fowler Holidays, Widemouth Bay, Nr. Bude, Cornwall, EX23 0DF.
Tel: 361208 Std: 01288
Nearest Town/Resort Widemouth/Bude
Directions 2 miles south of Bude, just off the A39.
Acreage 50 **Open** March to October
Access Good **Site** Level
Sites Available A ⊕ ⊟ **Total** 300
Low Season Band A
High Season Band C
Facilities ⊟ ⚹ ∫ ⅏ ⚹ ∩ ⊙ ⌐ ⌑ ⊟ ✿
೫ ⊙ ❀ ✕ ⅏ ❀ ∩ ⋇ ❋ ⊟
Nearby Facilities ୮ ✓ ⊥ ⋇ ∪ ℛ
Adjacent to an excellent surfing beach.

BUDE - CORNWALL
LUXURY HOLIDAY HOMES.
EXCELLENT FACILITIES FOR
CAMPING & TOURING

✱ Set in 12 acres of landscaped parkland overlooking Bude Bay.
✱ Beaches one and a half miles.
✱ Splash indoor pool nearby.
✱ Local village inn 5 mins walk.
✱ Woodland walks. ✱ Children's adventure park.
✱ Own coarse fishing.✱ Fun golf course.
✱ Small farm museum ✱ FREE Showers ✱ Laundry
MAIN SEASON
✱ Archery ✱ Clay pigeon shooting.
✱ Pony trekking & rides. ✱ Tractor & trailer rides.
✱ Licensed Restaurant & Bar

For brochure please write phone or fax to:-
Mrs. Q. Colwill, Wooda Farm, Poughill, Bude,
Cornwall, EX23 9HJ. TEL: 01288 352069
FAX: 01288 355228

A.N.W.B.-B.H.&H.P.A
ALAN ROGERS GOOD CAMPS GUIDE
RECOMMENDED

CORNWALL

BUDE
Willow Valley Camping Park, Dye House, Bush, Bude, Cornwall. EX23 9LB
Tel: 353104 Std: 01288
Nearest Town/Resort Bude
Directions On A39, 1 mile from Stratton on the Stratton to Bideford road. Do not go into Bude.
Acreage 4 **Open** April to October
Access Good **Site** Level
Sites Available ▲ ⊕ ⊟ **Total** 43
Low Season Band B
High Season Band C
Facilities
Nearby Facilities
⇌ Exeter
Picturesque, friendly family site, sheltered in beautiful Strat Valley. 2 miles to sandy, surfing beaches, or small quiet coves. Ideal touring centre.

BUDE
Wooda Caravan Park, Poughill, Bude, Cornwall.
Tel: 352069 Std: 01288
Nearest Town/Resort Bude
Directions Take road to Poughill 1¼ miles, go through village. At crossroads turn left. Site 200yds along road on right hand side.
Acreage 12 **Open** April to October
Access Good **Site** Lev/Slope
Sites Available ▲ ⊕ ⊟ **Total** 160
Low Season Band B
High Season Band C
Facilities
Nearby Facilities
⇌ Exeter
Overlooks sea and coastline, woodland walks, coarse fishing, large childrens play area, dog exercise field, short golf course, contact Mrs Q. Colwill ETB grading Excellent 5 Ticks. Sandy beaches 1½ miles. Licensed farm restaurant.

CAMBORNE
Magor Farm Caravan Site, Tehidy, Camborne, Cornwall, PR14 0GS.
Tel: 713367 Std: 01209
Nearest Town/Resort Camborne
Directions Take the third exit off the Camborne/Redruth by-pass, turn right taking you over the by-pass. The site is approx. 1¼ miles straight on. Site entrance is on the left hand side when taking a sharp right hand bend. From Portreath follow the coast road (West) along the B3301, take left hand turn signposted Camborne, after 1 mile turn left at T-Junction, caravansite is ½ mile on the left.
Acreage 7½ **Open** Easter to September
Access Good **Site** Level
Sites Available ▲ ⊕ ⊟ **Total** 164
Facilities
Nearby Facilities
⇌ Camborne
Country park, a short distance from towns, miles of beaches and cliffs. Leisure centre.

CAMELFORD
Juliots Well Holiday Park, Camelford, Cornwall.
Tel: 213302 Std: 01840
Nearest Town/Resort Tintagel
Directions Leave Camelford on A39 Wadebridge Road. 1 mile out turn right at Valley Truckle, then first left towards Lanteglos, site 400 yards on right.
Acreage 8¼ **Open** March to October
Access Good **Site**
Sites Available ▲ ⊕ ⊟ **Total** 60

Low Season Band B
High Season Band C
Facilities
Nearby Facilities
⇌ Bodmin
National grading scheme 5 ticks, AA 4 Pennants.

CAMELFORD
Lakefield Caravan Park, Lower Pendavey Farm, Camelford, Cornwall, PL32 9TX.
Tel: 213279 Std: 01840
Nearest Town/Resort Camelford/Tintagel.
Directions 1¼ miles north of Camelford on the B3266 - Boscastle road.
Acreage 5 **Open** Easter to October
Access Good **Site** Level
Sites Available ▲ ⊕ ⊟ **Total** 30
Low Season Band A
High Season Band B
Facilities
Nearby Facilities
⇌ Bodmin.
Scenic views, own lake. Ideal for touring Cornwall. Farm animals to feed and pet, Pony rides on site.

CARBIS BAY
Chy an Gweal Caravan Park, Carbis Bay Road, St. Ives, Cornwall.
Tel: 796257 Std: 01736
Nearest Town/Resort St. Ives
Directions Site is on the main St. Ives A3074 road, less than 1 mile from town centre.
Acreage 4 **Open** May to September
Access Good **Site** Level
Sites Available ▲ ⊕ ⊟ **Total** 50
Facilities

Carlyon Bay
Caravan & Camping Park
AA ▶ **RAC APPOINTED**

SUPERB LOCATION WITH FOOTPATH TO BLUE FLAG BEACH

★ **AA Britain's Best Sites**
★ **Practical Caravan Top 35 Video**
★ **England For Excellence Award nomination**
★ **AA Outstanding Environment Award 1992, 93 & 94/95**
★ **Children's entertainment in peak season**
★ **Run by the same Cornish family for 3 generations**

'A Family Affair!'

Carlyon Bay Camping Park, Cypress Avenue, Carlyon Bay, St. Austell, Cornwall PL25 3RE
TEL: 01726 - 812735

CORNWALL

RAC Selected Site **Hedley Wood Caravan & Camping Park** AA ►
Bridgerule, Holsworthy, Devon EX22 7ED Tel & Fax 01288 381404
16 acre woodland family run site with outstanding views, where you can enjoy a totally relaxing holiday with a ' laid back' atmosphere, sheltered & open camping areas. Just 10 minutes drive from the beaches, golf coarses, riding stables & shops. On site Facilities include: Children's adventure areas, Bar's, Clubroom's, Shop, Laundry, Meals & all amenities. Free Hot showers & water. Nice dogs/pets are welcome. Daily kennelling facility Dog walks/Nature trail. Clay pigeon shoot. Static caravans for hire, caravan storage available. Open All Year.

Nearby Facilities Γ ✈ ⏚ U ℛ
⇌ Carbis Bay
Superb location, less than ½ mile to beach. The only park in St. Ives area that does not accept dogs. Static vans also available. Bar on site.

CARLYON BAY
Carlyon Bay Camping Park, Cypress Avenue, Carlyon Bay, St. Austell, Cornwall, PL25 3RE.
Tel: 812735 Std: 01726 Fax: 815496 Std: 01726
Nearest Town/Resort St. Austell
Directions From St Austell head east on the A390 to the Britannia Inn and the roundabout, turn onto the A3082 and follow the Carlyon Bay signs.
Acreage 32 **Open** April to September
Sites Available Å ⊕ ⊛ **Total** 180
Low Season Band B
High Season Band C
Facilities ∤ ⌸ ♣ ᚏ ⊙ ⏚ ⛾ ⌷ ♆
♒ ⏦ ☰ ♨ ✕ ⎏ ⌁ ⚘ ❄ 🄿
Nearby Facilities Γ ✈ ⏚ U ↝
⇌ Par
Within walking distance of the beach and an 18 hole golf course.

COVERACK
Little Trevothan Caravan Park, Coverack, Helston, Cornwall, TR12 6SD.
Tel: 280260 Std: 01326
Nearest Town/Resort Helston
Directions A39 to Helston, follow B3083 to Culdrose, turn left B3293 signposted to Coverack. Go past BT Goonhilly, turn right before Zoar Garage, third turning on left, 300yds on the right.
Open April to October
Access Good **Site** Level
Sites Available Å ⊕ ⊛ **Total** 30
Low Season Band B
High Season Band B
Facilities ∤ ⌸ ♣ ᚏ ⊙ ⏚ ⌷ ♆
♒ ⏦ ☰ ♨ ✕ ⎏ ⌁ ⚘ ❄ 🄿
Nearby Facilities Γ ✈ ⏚ U ↝ ℛ ↯
⇌ Redruth
Beach nearby, flat meadows, off road.

COVERACK
Penmarth Farm Camp Site, Coverack, Helston, Cornwall.
Tel: 280389 Std: 01326
Nearest Town/Resort Helston
Directions 10 miles from Helston.
Acreage 2 **Open** March to October
Access Good **Site** Level
Sites Available Å ⊕ ⊛ **Total** 28
Facilities ⎇ ⌸ ♣ ᚏ ⊙ ⏚ ⛾ ⌷
Nearby Facilities Γ ✈ ⏚ U
⇌ Cambourne
¼ mile to beach and walks. Milk, cream and eggs at farm.

CRACKINGTON HAVEN
Hentervene Caravan & Camping Park, Crackington Haven, Nr. Bude, Cornwall, EX23 0LF.
Tel: 230365 Std: 01840 Fax: 230514 Std: 01840
Nearest Town/Resort Bude
Directions 10 miles southwest of Bude, turn off A39 opposite Otterham Garage (Esso), signed Crackington Haven. After 2½ miles turn left onto Crackington Road at Hentervene sign, park is ½ mile on right - 2 miles from beach.
Acreage 8¼ **Open** All Year
Access Good **Site** Level
Sites Available Å ⊕ ⊛ **Total** 35
Low Season Band B **High Season Band** B
Facilities ∤ ⌸ ♣ ᚏ ⊙ ⏚ ⛾ ⌷ ♆
♒ ⏦ ☰ ♨ ✕ ⎏ ⌁ ⚘ ❄ 🄿
Nearby Facilities Γ ✈ ⏚ U ↝ ℛ
⇌ Bodmin
Ideal touring centre, scenic views, 2 miles to beach. Pets Welcome. Off licence, take away meals in season. Vans for sale.

CRANTOCK
Treago Farm Camping & Caravan Park, Treago Farm, Crantock, Newquay, Cornwall, TR8 5QS.
Tel: 830277 Std: 01637 Fax: 830277 Std: 01637
Nearest Town/Resort Newquay
Directions 1 mile south west of Newquay on the A3075, turn right signposted to Crantock. Do not enter the village, follow signposts to West Pentire.

Acreage 4 **Open** March to November
Access Good **Site** Level
Sites Available Å ⊕ ⊛ **Total** 100
Low Season Band B **High Season Band** C
Facilities ⎇ ∤ ⌸ ♣ ᚏ ⊙ ⏚ ⛾ ⌷ ♆
♒ ⏦ ☰ ♨ ✕ ⎏ ⌁ ⚘ ❄ 🄿
Nearby Facilities Γ ✈ ⏚ U ℛ
⇌ Newquay
Surrounded by National Trust land and cliff walks. Foot path to Crantock and Polly Joke sandy beaches.

FALMOUTH
Tremorvah Tent Park, Swanpool, Falmouth, Cornwall.
Tel: 312103 Std: 01326
Nearest Town/Resort Falmouth
Directions Follow international camping signs around Falmouth to Swanpool Beach.
Acreage 3 **Open** Mid May to October
Access Fair **Site** Terraced
Sites Available Å ⊕ **Total** 72
Facilities ⌸ ♣ ᚏ ⊙ ⏚ ⛾
⌷ ♒ ⏦ ☰ ♨
Nearby Facilities Γ ✈ ⏚ U ↝ ℛ
⇌ Falmouth
Family site on hillside to rear of Swanpool beach on coastal footpath.

FOWEY
Penhale Caravan & Camping Park, Fowey, Cornwall, PL23 1JU.
Tel: 833425 Std: 01726
Nearest Town/Resort Fowey
Directions 1 mile west of Lostwithiel on the A390, turn onto the B3269. After 3 miles turn right at the roundabout onto the A3082. Penhale is 500yds on the left.
Acreage 5 **Open** April to October
Access Good **Site** Lev/Slope
Sites Available Å ⊕ ⊛ **Total** 56
Low Season Band B **High Season Band** B
Facilities ⌸ ♣ ᚏ ⊙ ⏚ ⛾ ⌷ ♆ ♒ ⏦ ☰ ♨
Nearby Facilities Γ ✈ ⏚ U ↝ ℛ
⇌ Par
Splendid views, close to sandy beaches with many lovely walks nearby. Central for touring.

CARAVANS • CHALETS • CAMPING

HOLIDAY PARK
FALMOUTH • CORNWALL • TR11 5BJ

Situated in a tranquil, sheltered, well wooded valley. Ideal touring centre and within walking distance to safe sandy beaches. Sailing, golf and other amenities.

- **MODERN HOLIDAY CARAVANS & CHALETS FOR HIRE**
- **HOLIDAY CAMPING AREAS WITH ELECTRICAL HOOK-UPS**
- **CARAVAN RALLIES WELCOME**

Ring or write for FREE colour brochure (24 hrs): **01326 312190**

CORNWALL

FOWEY
Polruan Holiday Centre, Polruan-by-Fowey, Cornwall, PL23 1QH.
Tel: 870263 Std: 01726
Fax: 870263 Std: **01726**
Nearest Town/Resort Fowey.
Directions From Plymouth A38 to Dobwalls, left onto A390 to East Taphouse, then left onto B3359. After 4¼ miles turn right signposted Polruan.
Acreage 2 **Open** April to September
Access Good **Site** Lev/Slope
Sites Available A ⊕ ⊟ **Total** 32
Low Season Band B
High Season Band C
Facilities ⊠ ∫ ⊞ ♠ ⌐ ⊙ ⌐ ⊟ ☎
⊠ ⊙ ⊜ ⋒ ⊟
Nearby Facilities ✓ ⊥ ↘ ∪
≠ Par
Coastal park surrounded by sea, river and National Trust farmland.

FOWEY
Yeate Farm Camp and Caravan Site, Bodinnick-by-Fowey, Cornwall.
Tel: 870256 Std: 01726
Nearest Town/Resort Fowey
Directions A38 Liskeard by-pass, fork left A390. Left at East Taphouse B3359 follow signs to Bodinnick. Site on right of Bodinnick ferry road.
Acreage 1 **Open** April to October
Access Good **Site** Level
Sites Available A ⊕ ⊟ **Total** 30
Low Season Band B
High Season Band C
Facilities ⊠ ∫ ⊞ ♠ ⌐ ⊙ ⌐ ⊞ ☎ ⊠ ⊙ ⊟
Nearby Facilities ✓ ⊥ ↘ ∪
≠ Par/Lostwithiel
Private quay, slip and storage for small boats. Good walks over mainly National Trust Land. Only individual motorcycles accepted not groups.

GORRAN HAVEN
Trelispen Caravan and Camping Park, Gorran, St. Austell, Cornwall.
Tel: 843501 Std: 01726.
Nearest Town/Resort Gorran Haven.
Directions From A390 at St. Austell take B3293 for Mevagissey, nearing Mevagissey take road for Gorran Haven, nearing Gorran Haven look for Trelispen Camping Park signs.
Acreage 1½ **Open** April to October
Access Good **Site** Level
Sites Available A ⊕ ⊟ **Total** 40.
Facilities ∫ ⊞ ♠ ⌐ ⊙ ⌐ ⊠ ☎ ⊠ ⊟ ⊟
Nearby Facilities ✓ ⊥ ↘ ∪ ⌐
≠ St. Austell.
Small site in pleasant rural surroundings near impressive cliff scenery and several safe sandy beaches.

HAYLE
Atlantic Coast Park, 53 Upton Towans, Gwithian, Hayle, Cornwall, TR27 5BL.
Tel: 752071 Std: 01736
Nearest Town/Resort Hayle
Directions When entering Hayle from Camborne by-pass (A30), turn right at the double roundabout onto the B3301, Atlantic Coast Park is approx. 1 mile on the left.
Acreage 4½ **Open** April to October
Access Good **Site** Level
Sites Available A ⊕ ⊟ **Total** 32
Low Season Band A
High Season Band C
Facilities ∫ ⊞ ♠ ⌐ ⊙ ⌐ ⊠ ☎
⊠ ⊙ ⊜ ♠ ⋒ ⊟
Nearby Facilities ⌐ ✓ ⊥ ↘ ∪ ⌐ ⌐ ≹
≠ Hayle
Situated in sand dunes close to a bathing and surfing beach, excellent walks.

HAYLE
Higher Trevaskis Caravan & Camping Park, Station Road, Connor Downs, Hayle, Cornwall, TR22 5DQ.
Tel: 831736 Std: 01209
Nearest Town/Resort Hayle/St Ives.
Directions At Hayle roundabout (Little Chef) on A30 take the first exit (signposted Connor Downs). After 1 mile turn right to Carnhell Green. Park is on the right in ¾ of mile.
Acreage 5¼ **Open** April to October
Access Good **Site** Level
Sites Available A ⊕ ⊟ **Total** 75
Low Season Band B
High Season Band B
Facilities ∫ ⊞ ♠ ⌐ ⊙ ⌐ ⊠ ☎
⊠ ⊙ ⊜ ⋒ ⊛ ⊟
Nearby Facilities ⌐ ✓ ⊥ ↘ ∪ ⌐ ⌐
≠ Hayle
Pleasant, secluded, family run, countryside park with good clean facilities. Sheltered fields. Some facilities for the disabled.

HAYLE
Parbola Holiday Park, Wall, Gwinear, Cornwall, TR27 5LE.
Tel: 831503 Std: 01209
Nearest Town/Resort Hayle
Directions Travel on A30 to Hayle, at roundabout leave first exit to Connor Downs. At end of village turn right to Carnhell Green, right at T-Junction, Parbola is 1 mile on the left.
Acreage 17 **Open** April to September
Access Good **Site** Level
Sites Available A ⊕ ⊟ **Total** 115
Facilities ⊠ ♠ ∫ ♠ ⊞ ♠ ⌐ ⊙ ⌐ ⊠ ☎
⊠ ⊠ ⊙ ⊜ × ⊞ ♠ ⋒ ⋈ ⊛ ⊟
Nearby Facilities ⌐ ✓ ⊥ ↘ ∪ ⌐
No dogs allowed July/August.

Beachside
HOLIDAY CHALET & TOURING CARAVAN PARK
Beside golden sandy beach in St.Ives Bay

A family holiday chalet, bungalow & touring caravan park amidst sand dunes, and with our own access on to the beach.

- Children's adventure playground
- Bar with evening entertainment
- Heated swimming & paddling pool
- Free Hot Showers ■ Launderette
- Shop ■ Electric Hook-ups
- Ideal for Touring

01736 753080
FREE BROCHURE

BEACHSIDE HOLIDAY PARK,
Dept. CC
Hayle, Cornwall TR27 5AW

CADE'S WEST COUNTRY CAMPING, TOURING & MOTOR CARAVAN SITE GUIDE 1997

CORNWALL

AWARD WINNING PARK
VOTED TOP 100

An extensively landscaped and superbly equipped park catering for couples and families looking for somewhere to get away to the peace and quiet of beautiful countryside, yet only a few minutes from lovely Praa Sands and many other beaches and attractions. All our luxury holiday homes have shower, toilet, colour television, fridge etc. Large games area for children. New touring and camping facilities, many electric hook-ups. Ideal area for walking, coarse and fishing, birdwatching etc. No clubhouse or bar.

Ashton, Nr Helston, Cornwall TR13 9TG Tel: **(01736) 762231**

HAYLE
Sunny Meadow Holiday Park, Lelant Down, Hayle, Cornwall.
Tel: 752243 Std: 01736
Nearest Town/Resort Hayle/St Ives.
Directions Take the Hayle by-pass, turn off for St Ives to the mini roundabout. Take the first left onto the B3311. We are ¼ mile up on the left.
Acreage 1 **Open** March to November
Access Good   **Site** Level
Sites Available ▲ ⊕ ⊟ **Total** 10
Facilities ∮ ⊞ ▲ Γ ⊙ ⌐ ▄ ⊡ ☻
⚐ ⊙ ⊡ ⊡
Nearby Facilities Γ ✓ ⊥ ↘ U ⋧ ✗
⇌ St Erth
A few miles from both north and south coasts offering ideal opportunity to tour the Peninsula.

HELSTON
Boscrege Caravan Park, Ashton, Helston, Cornwall.
Tel: 762231 Std: 01736
Fax: **762231** Std: **01736**
Nearest Town/Resort Praa Sands.
Directions From Helston follow Penzance road (A394) to Ashton, turn right by post office along road signposed to Godolphin and continue about 1½ miles to Boscrege Park.
Acreage 7 **Open** Easter/1 April to October
Access Good   **Site** Level
Sites Available ▲ ⊕ ⊟ **Total** 50
Low Season Band B
High Season Band C
Facilities ⊟ ∮ ⊞ ▲ Γ ⊙ ⌐ ☻
⚐ ⊡ ⊙ ⊟ ⊡ ▲ ⊡ ⊟
Nearby Facilities Γ ✓ ⊥ ↘ U ⋧
⇌ Penzance.
Quiet family park in garden setting. No club. Near sandy beaches. Ideal for exploring West Cornwall. Microwave for campers.

HELSTON
Franchis, Cury Cross Lanes, Helston, Cornwall, TR12 7AZ.
Tel: Mullion 240301 Std: 01326.
Nearest Town/Resort Mullion/Helston.
Directions From Helston take the A3083 (Helston to The Lizard road). Franchis 6 miles on from Helston.
Acreage 4 **Open** Easter to October
Access Good   **Site** Level
Sites Available ▲ ⊕ ⊟ **Total** 70.
Low Season Band B
High Season Band C
Facilities ⊟ ∮ ⊞ ▲ Γ ⊙ ⌐ ☻
⚐ ⊡ ⊙ ⊟ ⊡
Nearby Facilities Γ ✓ ⊥ ↘ U ⋧
⇌ Redruth.
Only individual motorcycles accepted, not groups. Sport diving air to 3500 P.S.I. Rose Award Park. Licensed shop on site.

HELSTON
Gunwalloe Caravan Park, Helston, Cornwall, TR12 7QP.
Tel: 572668 Std: 01326
Nearest Town/Resort Helston
Directions Take the A3083 from Helston

towards Lizard for 2 miles, turn right to Gunwalloe for 1 mile, signposted.
Acreage 2½ **Open** April to October
Access Good   **Site** Level
Sites Available ▲ ⊕ ⊟ **Total** 40
Low Season Band A
High Season Band B
Facilities ∮ ⊞ ▲ Γ ⊙ ⌐ ☻ ⊙ ⊟ ⊡
Nearby Facilities Γ
⇌ Redruth
Farm site, near to beaches (1 mile), coastal walk. Central for all Lizard Peninsular.

HELSTON
Lower Polladras Camping & Caravan Park, Carleen, Nr. Helston, Cornwall, TR13 9NX.
Tel: 762220 Std: 01736
Nearest Town/Resort Helston.
Directions From Helston take the A394 to Penzance and turn right at the B.P. Garage along the B3302. After ½ mile turn left to Carleen village. From the A30 turn left in Camborne along the B3303, then take the first right turning after junction of 3303 and 3302.
Acreage 4 **Open** April to October
Access Good   **Site** Level
Sites Available ▲ ⊕ ⊟ **Total** 60
Facilities ⊟ ∮ ⊞ ▲ Γ ⊙ ⌐ ▄ ⊡ ☻
⚐ ⊡ ⊙ ⊡ ⊛ ⊡
Nearby Facilities Γ ✓ ⊥ ↘ U ⋧
⇌ Camborne.
Pleasant views of surrounding hills. Ideal touring situation. Childrens adventure playground.

HELSTON
Poldown Caravan & Camping Site, Carleen, Breage, Helston, Cornwall.
Tel: 574560 Std: 01326
Nearest Town/Resort Helston.
Directions Take A394 (signed Penzance) from Helston. At top of the hill on outskirts of Helston take the B3303 signed Hayle/St Ives. Take the second left on this road and we are ¼ mile along.
Acreage 1¼ **Open** April to October
Access Good   **Site** Level
Sites Available ▲ ⊕ ⊟ **Total** 10
Low Season Band A
High Season Band B
Facilities ∮ ⊞ ▲ Γ ⊙ ⌐ ▄ ⊡ ☻
⚐ ⊡ ⊡ ⊡
Nearby Facilities Γ ✓ ⊥ ↘ U ⋧
⇌ Penzance
Ideal for touring West Cornwall. Small, secluded, pretty site.

HELSTON
Retanna Holiday Park, Edgcumbe, Helston, Cornwall, TR13 0EJ.
Tel: 340042 Std: 01326.
Nearest Town/Resort Falmouth.
Directions On A394 betwixt Falmouth and Helston (5 miles).
Acreage 8 **Open** April to October
Access Good   **Site** Lev/slope
Sites Available ▲ ⊕ ⊟ **Total** 17
Low Season Band B
High Season Band B

Facilities ⊟ ∮ ⊞ ▲ Γ ⊙ ⌐ ▄ ⊡ ☻
⚐ ⊡ ⊙ ⊟ ⊛ ⊡
Nearby Facilities Γ ✓ ⊥ ↘ U ⋧ ✗
⇌ Falmouth.
Scenic views. Ideal centre for touring West Cornwall.

INDIAN QUEENS
Gnome World Tourist Park, Indian Queens, Nr. St Columb, Cornwall, TR9 6HN.
Tel: 860812 Std: 01726
Nearest Town/Resort Newquay/St Austell
Directions Mid Cornwall, just off the A30 at Indian Queens. Follow Gnome World Camp Site signs for approx ½ mile.
Acreage 4½ **Open** March to October
Access Good   **Site** Level
Sites Available ▲ ⊕ ⊟ **Total** 50
Low Season Band A
High Season Band B
Facilities ∮ ⊞ Γ ☻ ⚐ ⊡ ⊡ ⊡ ⊡
Nearby Facilities Γ ✓ ⊥ ↘ U ⋧ ⋧ ✗
⇌ Newquay/St Austell
Gnome World Gardens. Spacious, level site with scenic views and a nature trail. Near beaches. Ideal for cycling, walking and especially relaxing. Map of interesting places to visit in Cornwall available free of charge. Ideal touring.

ISLES OF SCILLY
Jenford, Bryher, Isles of Scilly, Cornwall.
Tel: 422886 Std: 01720.
Nearest Town/Resort Penzance.
Directions
Acreage 1 **Open** April to October
Site Level
Sites Available ▲ **Total** 37.
Low Season Band A
High Season Band A
Facilities ⚲ ⊞ ▲ Γ ⚐ ⊡ ⊙ ☻ ↳
Nearby Facilities Γ ✓ ⊥ ↘

ISLES OF SCILLY
Troytown Campsite, Troytown Farm, St. Agnes, Isles of Scilly, Cornwall, TR22 OPL.
Tel: 422360 Std: 01720
Nearest Town/Resort Hugh Town/St Marys
Directions Ship or helicopter from Penzance or plane from Lands End to St Mary's. 15 minute boat trip to St Agnes, tractor for luggage from quay to the site. No cars/caravans. Trailers accepted.
Acreage 1¾ **Open** March to October
Site Lev/Slope
Sites Available ▲ **Total** 38
Facilities ⚲ ⊞ ▲ Γ ⊙ ⌐ ⊡ ⊡
Nearby Facilities ⋧
⇌ Penzance.
Small island site on the shoreline with a beach. Sea views to Bishop Rock Lighthouse. Britain's most southerly-westerly site, family run. Spin and tumble drier available for use.

KILKHAMPTON
East Thorne Touring Park, Kilkhampton, Bude, Cornwall, EX23 9RY.
Tel: 321618 Std: 01288
Nearest Town/Resort Bude
Directions North on the A39, 5 miles from Bude.

14   CADE'S WEST COUNTRY CAMPING, TOURING & MOTOR CARAVAN SITE GUIDE 1997

CORNWALL

Acreage 2½ **Open** March to October
Access Good **Site** Level
Sites Available 🅰 ⛺ 🚐 **Total** 29
Facilities ⚡ 🚿 🧺 ☎ ⛽ ...
... 🛒 ...
Nearby Facilities 🎣 ✓ ⚵ ≽ ∪

LANDS END
Cardinney Caravan & Caravan Park, Main A30, Lands End Road, Crows-An-Wra, Lands End, Cornwall, TR19 6HJ.
Tel: 810880 Std: 01736
Nearest Town/Resort Sennen Cove
Directions From Penzance follow Main A30 to Lands End, approx 5¼ miles. Entrance on right hand side on Main A30, large name board at entrance.
Acreage 5 **Open** Wk before Easter to October
Access Good **Site** Level
Sites Available 🅰 ⛺ 🚐 **Total** 105
Low Season Band B
High Season Band B
Facilities ⚡ 🚿 🧺 ☎ ⛽ ...
... 🛒 🍴 ...
Nearby Facilities 🎣 ✓ ⚵ ≽ ∪ ⌘ ✈
≠ Penzance
Sennen Cove Blue Flag, scenic coastal walks, ancient monuments, scenic flights, Minack Ampitheatre, trips to the Isles of Scilly. Ideal for touring Lands End Peninsula. Hard standings.

LANDS END
Lower Treave Caravan Park, Crows-an-Wra, St. Buryan, Penzance, Cornwall, TR19 6HZ.
Tel: 810559 Std: 01736
Nearest Town/Resort Penzance
Directions On A30 Penzance/Lands End road, ½ mile west of Crows-an-Wra.
Acreage 4½ **Open** April to October
Access Good **Site** Level
Sites Available 🅰 ⛺ 🚐 **Total** 80.
Low Season Band B
High Season Band B
Facilities ⚡ 🚿 ☎ ⛽ ...
... 🛒 ...
Nearby Facilities 🎣 ✓ ⚵ ∪ ✈
≠ Penzance.
An ideal centre for exploring the Lands End Peninsula.

LAUNCESTON
Chapmanswell Caravan Site, St. Giles on the Heath, Launceston, Cornwall, PL15 9SG.
Tel: 211382 Std: 01409
Nearest Town/Resort Launceston.
Directions Chapmanswell Caravan Park is situated 6 miles from Launceston along the A388 on your left hand side going towards Holsworthy, just past the pub and garage in Chapmanswell.
Acreage 12 **Open** 15th March to 5th November
Access Good **Site** Level
Sites Available 🅰 ⛺ 🚐 **Total** 81.
Low Season Band B
High Season Band B
Facilities ⚡ 🚿 ☎ ⛽ ...
... 🍴 ...
Nearby Facilities 🎣 ✓ ∪ ✈
≠ Exeter
Very central for Cornwall and Devon, easy reach of North Devon beaches, Dartmoor and Cornish resorts. Village pub meals 200 yards.

LEEDSTOWN
Calloose Caravan and Camping Park, Leedstown, Hayle, Cornwall.
Tel: 850431 Std: 01736.
Fax: 850431 Std: **01736**
Nearest Town/Resort Hayle.
Directions Take B3302 from Hayle to Helston for 4 miles to Leedstown. Site signposted in village.
Acreage 12½ **Open** April to October
Access Good **Site** Level
Sites Available 🅰 ⛺ 🚐 **Total** 120
Low Season Band B
High Season Band B
Facilities ⚡ 🚿 🧺 ☎ ⛽ ...
... 🛒 🍴 ...
Nearby Facilities 🎣 ✓ ✻
≠ Hayle.
Centrally situated for West Cornwall. Sheltered valley site. Skittle alley, crazy golf and takeaway. New bike track and recreation field.

LISKEARD
Pine Green Caravan Park, Double Bois, Liskeard, East Cornwall.
Tel: Std:
Nearest Town/Resort Liskeard.
Directions 3 miles from Liskeard towards Bodmin. Just off the main A38 at Double Bois.
Acreage 3 **Open** April to October
Access Good **Site** Level
Sites Available 🅰 ⛺ 🚐 **Total** 50
Low Season Band B
High Season Band B
Facilities ⚡ 🚿 ☎ ⛽ ...
Nearby Facilities 🎣 ✓ ⚵ ≽ ∪ ✈
≠ Liskeard
Overlooking beautiful wooded valley and open countryside.

LISKEARD
Trenant Chapel House, Trenant Caravan Park, St Neot, Liskeard, Cornwall.
Tel: 320896 Std: 01579
Nearest Town/Resort Liskeard
Directions Take St Cleer road off A38 at Dobwalls, 1 mile left SP St. Neot, 1 mile right SP Trennant, ½ mile right SP Trennant.
Acreage 1 **Open** April to October
Site Level
Sites Available 🅰 ⛺ 🚐 **Total** 8
Facilities 🚿 ☎ ⛽ ...
Nearby Facilities ✓ ⚵ ∪
≠ Liskeard
Siblyback and Colliford Reservoirs close, fishing, boardsailing and bird watching..Site in sheltered corner upper Fowey valley bounded by tributary of Fowey river, close Bodmin moor, ideal walking, touring.

LIZARD
Gwendreath Farm Caravan Park, Kennack Sands, Helston, Cornwall, TR12 7LZ.
Tel: 290666 Std: 01326
Nearest Town/Resort The Lizard
Directions A3083 from Helston, left on B3293 after R.N.A.S. Culdrose. After Goonhilly Earth Station, take the first right then first left. At end of lane go through Seaview Caravan Park.
Acreage 3 **Open** Easter to October
Access Good **Site** Level
Sites Available 🅰 ⛺ 🚐 **Total** 30
Facilities ⚡ 🚿 ☎ ⛽ ...
... 🛒 ...
Nearby Facilities 🎣 ✓ ≽ ∪
≠ Redruth
Attractive, peaceful family site overlooking the sea in an area of outstanding natural beauty. Short woodland walk to safe sandy beaches.

LIZARD
Silver Sands Holiday Park, Kennack Sands, Gwendreath, Ruan Minor, Helston, Cornwall, TR12 7LZ.
Tel: 290631 Std: 01326
Nearest Town/Resort Helston.
Directions On entering Helston take the A3083 Lizard road, pass R.N.A.S. Culdrose then turn left at roundabout onto the B3293 signposted St Keverne. In 4 miles, immediately past Goonhilly Satellite Station, turn right to Kennack. After 1 mile turn left.
Acreage 6 **Open** May to September
Access Good **Site** Lev/Slope
Sites Available 🅰 ⛺ 🚐 **Total** 34
Low Season Band B
High Season Band B
Facilities ⚡ 🚿 🧺 ☎ ⛽ ...
... 🛒 ...
Nearby Facilities 🎣 ✓ ⚵ ≽ ∪ ✈
≠ Redruth
800mts to safe sandy beach, ideal touring and walking. Quiet, family site in area of outstanding natural beauty.

LONGDOWNS
Calamankey Campsite, Calamankey Farm Campsite, Longdowns, Penryn, Cornwall TR10 9DL.
Tel: 860314 Std: 01209
Nearest Town/Resort Falmouth
Directions A394 from Penryn, 2½ miles.
Acreage 2½ **Open** Easter to October
Access Good **Site** Sloping
Sites Available 🅰 ⛺ 🚐 **Total** 60
Facilities 🚿 ☎ ⛽ ...
Nearby Facilities 🎣 ✓ ⚵ ≽ ✈
≠ Penryn
Beach 4½ miles. Ideal touring. Farming area.

LOOE
Camping Caradon, Trelawne, Looe, Cornwall, PL13 2NA.
Tel: 272388 Std: 01503
Nearest Town/Resort Polperro/Looe
Directions From Looe on the A387, take right turn onto B3359. First turning on the right, approx 200yds on the left.
Acreage 2¼ **Open** April to October
Access Good **Site** Level
Sites Available 🅰 ⛺ 🚐 **Total** 85.
Facilities ⚡ 🚿 🧺 ☎ ⛽ ...
... 🛒 🍴 ...
Nearby Facilities 🎣 ✓ ⚵ ≽ ∪ ✈
≠ Looe.
Friendly, family run park with rural surroundings.

LOOE
Polborder House Caravan and Camping Park, Bucklawren Road, St. Martin, Looe, Cornwall, PL13 1QR.
Tel: 240265 Std: 01503
Nearest Town/Resort Looe.
Directions 2¼ miles esat of Looe off B3253, follow signs for Polborder and Monkey Sanctuary.
Acreage 3 **Open** April to October
Access Good **Site** Level
Sites Available 🅰 ⛺ 🚐 **Total** 36
Low Season Band B
High Season Band C
Facilities ⚡ 🚿 🧺 ☎ ⛽ ...
... 🛒 ...
Nearby Facilities 🎣 ✓ ⚵ ≽ ∪ ✈
≠ Looe.
Peaceful, select, AA Award park, set in beautiful countryside.

CADE'S WEST COUNTRY CAMPING, TOURING & MOTOR CARAVAN SITE GUIDE 1997

CORNWALL

LOOE
Talland Barton Caravan Park, Talland Bay, Looe, Cornwall, PL13 2JA.
Tel: 72429 Std: 01503
Nearest Town/Resort Looe.
Directions Take A387 from Looe towards Polperro. After 1 mile turn left. Follow this road for 1½ miles. The site is on the left hand side by Talland Church.
Acreage 1¼ Open Easter to October
Access Poor   Site Lev/Slope
Sites Available ▲ ⌺ ⌻ Total 30
Low Season Band A
High Season Band B
Facilities ƒ ▯ ▴ ⌐ ⊙⌐ ▨
▯ ⊕ ◓ ⊗ ▾ ▯ ⊟
Nearby Facilities ⌐ ✎ ⊥ ⋎ ∪ ⌡
≠ Looe.
Between Looe and Polperro, near a beach. Peaceful countryside, ideal touring.

LOOE
Tencreek Caravan & Camping Park, Looe, Cornwall, PL13 2JR.
Tel: 262447 Std: 01503
Nearest Town/Resort Looe
Directions 1½ miles west of Looe on the A387 Looe to Polperro road.
Acreage 14 Open All Year
Access Good   Site Level
Sites Available ▲ ⌺ ⌻ Total 250
Facilities ▣ ▴ ƒ ▯ ▴ ⌐ ⊙⌐ ▨ ⊟
▯ ▯ ⊕ ◓ ⊗ ▾ ▯ ⊛ ▯ ⊟
Nearby Facilities ⌐ ✎ ⊥ ⋎ ∪ ⌡ ⌡
≠ Looe.
Extensive coastal and countryside views. The nearest park to Looe. Free use of all facilities. Practical Caravan Top 100, E.T.B. 4 Tick Grading and Rose Award.

LOOE
Treble B Holiday Centre, Polperro Road, Looe, Cornwall, PL13 2JS.
Tel: 262425 Std: 01503
Fax: 262425 Std: 01503
Nearest Town/Resort Looe.
Directions 2 miles west Looe on A387 midway between Looe/Polperro.
Acreage 20 Open May to September
Access Good   Site Lev/Slope
Sites Available ▲ ⌺ ⌻ Total 450.
Low Season Band B
High Season Band C
Facilities ▣ ƒ ▯ ▴ ⌐ ⊙⌐ ▨ ▯ ⊟
▯ ▯ ⊕ ⊗ ▾ ▯ ▴ ⌐ ⊛ ▯
Nearby Facilities ⌐ ✎ ⊥ ⋎ ∪ ⌡ ⌡ ⌡
≠ Looe.
Family site, ideal base for touring all Cornwall. A.A. graded 5 Pennant site and R.A.C. appointed. Free coloured brochure. Enquiries to Dept. 06. Free showers.

LOOE
Tregoad Farm Touring Caravan & Camping Park, St. Martins, Looe, Cornwall, PL13 1PB.
Tel: 262718 Std: 01503
Fax: 262718 Std: 01503
Nearest Town/Resort Looe.
Directions Situated approx. 1½ miles from Looe and 200yds off the Plymouth to Looe road (B3253).
Acreage 10 Open April to October
Access Good   Site Level
Sites Available ▲ ⌺ ⌻ Total 150
Low Season Band B
High Season Band B
Facilities ƒ ▯ ▴ ⌐ ⊙⌐ ▨ ▯ ⊟
▯ ▯ ⊕ ⊗ ▾ ▯ ▯
Nearby Facilities ⌐ ✎ ⊥ ⋎ ∪ ⌡ ⌡

≠ Looe/Liskeard
Ideally situated on southerly slopes with magnificent views to Looe Bay and the rolling Cornish Hinterland.

LOOE
Trelawne Manor Holiday Village, Looe, Cornwall, PL13 2NA.
Tel: 272151 Std: 01503
Nearest Town/Resort Looe.
Directions A38 from Liskeard through Dobwalls, turn left onto the A390 for St. Austell. Go through Taphouse, then turn left onto the B3359. Trelawne is on the left after 8¼ miles.
Open 13 April to 7 October
Access Good   Site Level
Sites Available ▲ ⌺ ⌻
Facilities ƒ ▴ ▯ ▴ ⌐ ⊙⌐ ▨ ▯
▯ ▯ ⊕ ◓ ⊗ ▾ ▯ ▴ ⌐ ⊛ ▯
Nearby Facilities ⌡
≠ Liskeard
Centred around a stately manor house (former home of Lady Jane Grey). Just 1¼ miles from the sea.

LOOE
Trelay Farmpark, Pelynt, Looe, Cornwall, PL13 2JX.
Tel: 220900 Std: 01503.
Nearest Town/Resort Looe/Polperro.
Directions From Looe take the A387 towards Polperro. After 2 miles turn right onto the B3359. Trelay Farmpark is clearly signed ¾ mile on the right.
Acreage 3 Open Easter to October
Access Good   Site Level
Sites Available ▲ ⌺ ⌻ Total 55
Facilities ▴ ƒ ▯ ▴ ⌐ ⊙⌐ ▨ ▯
▯ ⊕ ⊟ ▯
Nearby Facilities ⌐ ✎ ⊥ ⋎ ∪ ⌡ ⌡

Tencreek Holidays
LOOE, CORNWALL

FREE family facilities include:
★ Modern toilets & showers
★ Heated swimming pool ★ Launderette
★ Adventure park ★ Shop ★ Licensed club with nightly entertainment
★ Two bars ★ Cafe/take-away
★ Apartments available in Looe
★ Dog exercise area
★ Golf ★ Sea ★ Coarse & shark fishing
★ Boating ★ Horse riding etc. all nearby

Panoramic views of sea & countryside.
Perfectly situated, for Looe & Polperro.
The nearest park to Looe Beach.
Tents, Touring Caravans and Motor Caravans very welcome.
Electric hook-ups available.
Also fully equipped Rose Award Caravans, sleep 6-8.
Families and couples only. Rallies welcome.

OPEN ALL YEAR The nearest park to Looe!
FREE BROCHURE
☎ Tel: (01503) 262447/262757

Tencreek Caravan & Camping Park, Looe, Cornwall PL13 2JR.

CORNWALL

PENGRUGLA

MEVAGISSEY • CORNWALL

Your Garden Caravan & Camping Park in the Heart of Cornwall

WHY COMPROMISE ON QUALITY & LUXURY
FOR BOOKING INFORMATION & COLOUR BROCHURE

TELEPHONE 01726 842714

A quiet, uncommercialised park surrounded by farmland. Wide views over open countryside. Large pitches on a gentle south facing slope.

LOSTWITHIEL
Downend Camp, Lostwithiel, Cornwall.
Tel: 872363 Std: 01208
Nearest Town/Resort Lostwithiel.
Directions On the A390.
Acreage 5 Open April to October
Access Good   Site Level
Sites Available ▲ ⌴ ⛺ Total 30
Facilities ƒ ⌸ ♨ ♿ ⊙ ⌁ ♿ ⛁ ⊘ ⊟
Nearby Facilities ┌ ✓
⛴ Lostwithiel.
Ideal touring. ½ mile to woods.

LOSTWITHIEL
Powderham Castle Tourist Park, Lanlivery, Nr. Fowey, Cornwall.
Tel: 872277 Std: 01208.
Nearest Town/Resort Fowey/St. Austell.
Directions 1½ miles southwest Lostwithiel on A390, turn right at signpost for Lanlivery/Luxulyan, up road 400 yards.
Acreage 10 Open April to October
Access Good   Site Level
Sites Available ▲ ⌴ ⛺ Total 75
Low Season Band B
High Season Band C
Facilities ⬚ ƒ ⌸ ♨ ♿ ⊙ ⌁ ⊟ ⊙ ♿
⛺ ⌁ ⊘ ⊟ ♨ ⌴ ✻ ⊟
Nearby Facilities ┌ ✓ ⌁ ∪ ⌒ ♞ ♣
⛴ Lostwithiel.
Quiet uncrowded site, uncommercialised. Central touring position. Canoe and boat hire. Battery charging, freezer pack service. Dish washing and vegetable preparation facilities. Indoor Badminton and soft tennis court, putting green, childrens pool. Winner AA Award for Sanitation and Environmental Facilities. ETB 5 Tickets.

MARAZION
Trevair Touring Site, South Treveneague Farm, St. Hilary, Penzance, Cornwall, TR20 9BY.
Tel: 740647 Std: 01736
Nearest Town/Resort Marazion
Directions 3 miles from Marazion, B3280 through Goldsithney signposted South Treveneague.
Acreage ½ Open End March to October
Access Good   Site Level
Sites Available ▲ ⌴ ⛺ Total 35
Facilities ƒ ⌸ ♨ ♿ ⊙ ⌁ ⌂ ⊟
Nearby Facilities ┌ ✓ ⌁ ∪
⛴ St Erth
Set in the peace and quiet of a secluded sunny valley, clean and friendly. Goats, donkey and tame birds.

MARAZION
Wheal Rodney Carapark, Marazion, Cornwall.
Tel: 710605 Std: 01736.
Fax: 710605 Std: 01736
Nearest Town/Resort Marazion.
Directions ½ mile north Marazion.
Acreage 4¼ Open 1 April or Easter to October
Access Good   Site Level
Sites Available ▲ ⌴ ⛺ Total 45
Low Season Band A
High Season Band B
Facilities ƒ ⌸ ♨ ♿ ⊙ ⌁ ⊟ ♨ ⊙ ♿ ⊘ ⊟
Nearby Facilities ┌ ✓ ⌁ ∪ ⌒
⛴ Penzance.
½ mile from safe beach. Sauna, solarium, spa bath on site.

MAWGAN PORTH
Magic Cove Touring Park, Mawgan Porth, Newquay, Cornwall, TR8 4BZ.
Tel: 860263 Std: 01637.

Nearest Town/Resort Newquay
Directions A30 Bodmin by-pass, turn right 4¼ miles from the end. At the roundabout take the second left (Newquay) then right 400yds past Shell Garage. Pass the airport, T-Junction right to Mawgan Porth. Right after BP Garage and Magic Co
Acreage 1 Open Easter to October
Access Good   Site Level
Sites Available ▲ ⌴ ⛺ Total 26
Low Season Band A
High Season Band C
Facilities ƒ ⌸ ♨ ♿ ⊙ ⌁ ♿ ⛁ ⊟
Nearby Facilities ┌ ✓ ∪ ⌒
⛴ Newquay
300yds from beach, ideal for touring Cornwall. Water and drainage on each pitch, hook-ups include T.V. point.

MAWGAN PORTH
Sun Haven Valley Holiday Park, Mawgan Porth, Newquay, Cornwall, TR8 4BQ.
Tel: 860373 Std: 01637
Fax: 860373 Std: 01637
Nearest Town/Resort Mawgan Porth
Directions On the B3276 coast road between Newquay and Padstow. Signposted from the garage at Mawgan Porth ¾ mile inland.
Acreage 5 Open May to September
Access Good   Site Level
Sites Available ▲ ⌴ ⛺ Total 118
Low Season Band C
High Season Band C
Facilities ⚹ ƒ ⌸ ♨ ♿ ⊙ ⌁ ⊟ ⊘ ♿
⛺ ⌁ ⊘ ⊟ ♨ ⌴ ⊟
Nearby Facilities ┌ ✓ ∪ ⌒
⛴ Newquay
Sheltered site in beautiful countryside. AA Award Winning site with excellent facilities.

We have - NO CLUB - NO BAR - NO BINGO
But offer you a family run park with:

Free hot water for showers, personal & dish washing - Hair & hand dryers - Shaver points - Launderette - Shop with off-licence - Electric hook-ups - Swimming and paddling pools - Children's play areas - Write or phone (24 hours) for brochure -

(4) TREGARTON FARM TOURING PARK
Gorran, St Austell, Cornwall PL26 6NF.
Tel: (01726) 843666

CADE'S WEST COUNTRY CAMPING, TOURING & MOTOR CARAVAN SITE GUIDE 1997   17

CORNWALL

MEVAGISSEY
Pengrugla Caravan Park, Mevagissey, Cornwall, PL26 6EL.
Tel: 842714 Std: 01726
Nearest Town/Resort Mevagissey.
Directions
Acreage 20 **Open** All Year
Access Good **Site** Lev/Slope
Sites Available ▲ ⚏ ⛟ **Total** 120
Facilities ⚿ ∱ ⌸ ♨ ⌒ ⊙ ↵ ▄ ☑ ☎
ⓈⓏ ◐ ☎ ✗ ♠ ⋒ 🅿
Nearby Facilities ┌ ✓ ⊥ ⌇ ∪ ⚲ 🅿 ⚹
⚹ St Austell
Site is next door to Heligan Gardens. 5 Tick Graded Excellence, Rose Award Caravans and Top 100 Parks in the UK.

MEVAGISSEY
Seaview International, Boswinger, Gorran, St. Austell, Cornwall, PL26 6LL.
Tel: 843425 Std: 0172.
Fax: **843358** Std: **01726**
Nearest Town/Resort Mevagissey.
Directions From St. Austell take B3273 to Mevagissey, prior to village turn right. Then follow signs to Gorran.
Acreage 16 **Open** April to September
Access Good **Site** Level
Sites Available ▲ ⚏ ⛟ **Total** 165
Low Season Band B
High Season Band C
Facilities ⚿ ∱ ⚲ ⌸ ♨ ⌒ ⊙ ↵ ▄ ☑ ☎
ⓈⓏ ◐ ☎ ♠ ⋒ ⚲ 🅿
Nearby Facilities ✓ ⊥ ⌇ ∪ 🅿 🎣
⚹ St Austell.
Beautiful level park overlooking the sea, surrounded by sandy beaches graded among cleanest in Britain, nearest ½ mile. Free sports and pastimes on site. Holiday caravans also for hire. AA Best Campsite of the Year 1995/6.

MEVAGISSEY
Tregarton Farm Touring Park, Gorran, St. Austell, Cornwall. PL26 6NF
Tel: 843666 Std: 01726.
Fax: **843666** Std: **01726**
Nearest Town/Resort Mevagissey.
Directions From St Austell south on B3273 signposted Mevagissey. Afetr Pentewan turn right signposted Gorran. Park is on right after 4 miles.
Acreage 8 **Open** April to October
Access Good **Site** Lev/Slope
Sites Available ▲ ⚏ ⛟ **Total** 150
Low Season Band C
High Season Band C
Facilities ⚲ ∱ ⌸ ♨ ⌒ ⊙ ↵ ▄ ☑ ☎
ⓈⓏ ◐ ☎ ⋒ ⚲ ☀ 🅿
Nearby Facilities ┌ ✓ ⊥ ⌇ ∪ ⚲ 🅿
⚹ St. Austell.
Quiet family park. Beach 1¼ miles. Ideal for touring Cornwall.

MULLION
Mullion Holiday Park, Mullion, Nr. Helston, Cornwall, TR12 7LJ.
Tel: 240000 Std: 01326
Fax: **445202** Std: **01392**
Nearest Town/Resort Mullion
Directions Follow the A3083 from Helston to the Lizard for approx. 5 miles, we are on the left.
Acreage 10 **Open** May to September
Access Good **Site** Level
Sites Available ▲ ⚏ ⛟ **Total** 150
Facilities ∱ ⌸ ♨ ⌒ ⊙ ↵
 ⓈⓏ ☎ ✗ ♨ ⋒ ⚲ ☀
Nearby Facilities ┌ ✓ ⊥ ⌇ ∪
⚹ Redrath.
In an area of outstanding natural beauty on the Lizard Peninsula, within easy reach of the beautiful Helford River, Kynance Cove, other sandy beaches and top attractions.

MULLION
Teneriffe Farm Caravan Site, A.B. Thomas, Teneriffe Farm, Mullion, Helston, Cornwall TR12 7EZ.
Tel: 240293 Std: 01326
Fax: **240293** Std: **01326**
Nearest Town/Resort Helston.
Directions 10 miles Helston to The Lizard, turn right for Mullion. Take Mullion Cove road, turn left Predannack.
Acreage ½ **Open** Easter to October
Access Good **Site** Lev/Slope
Sites Available ▲ ⚏ ⛟ **Total** 20.
Facilities ∱ ⚲ ⌸ ⌒ ⊙ ↵ ☎ ◐ ☎ 🅿
Nearby Facilities ┌ ✓ ⌇ ∪ 🅿 ⚹
⚹ Redruth.
Views of sea. S.A.E. required. Tumble drying facility.

NEWQUAY
Cottage Farm Touring Park, Treworgans, Cubert, Newquay, Cornwall, TR8 5HH.
Tel: 831083 Std: 01637.
Nearest Town/Resort Newquay.
Directions Newqauy to Redruth road A3075, turn right onto High Lanes. Follow signs to Cubert, before Cubert Village turn right signposted Crantock-Wesley road. Down the lane for ¼ mile then turn left signposted Tresean and Treworgans.
Acreage 2 **Open** April to October
Access Good **Site** Level
Sites Available ▲ ⚏ ⛟ **Total** 45
Facilities ∱ ⌸ ♨ ⌒ ⊙ ↵ ▄ ☑ ☎
 ⓘ ◐ ☎ ⋒ 🅿
Nearby Facilities ┌ ✓ ⌇ ∪ 🅿
⚹ Newquay.
Within easy reach of three National Trust beaches. Small, family site, peaceful and in a rural location.

18 CADE'S WEST COUNTRY CAMPING, TOURING & MOTOR CARAVAN SITE GUIDE 1997

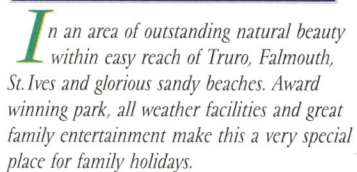

CORNWALL

Newquay Holiday Parks

JUST WHAT YOU'RE LOOKING FOR!

If you want a high quality Holiday Park in a beautiful country setting or close to a glorious sandy beach then Newquay Holiday Parks are just what you're looking for...

For more information or a Free copy of our brochure...

  Telephone 01637 871111 (ext.24)

Our friendly staff will be pleased to help you
or write to 24 Newquay Holiday Park, Newquay, Cornwall TR8 4HS

NEWQUAY
Hendra Holiday Park, Newquay, Cornwall, TR8 4NY.
Tel: 875778 Std: 01637
Nearest Town/Resort Newquay.
Directions A30 to Cornwall to Indian Queens, turn right on the A392 Newquay road at Quintrell Downs. Hendra is 1¼ miles before Newquay Town Centre.
Acreage 36 **Open** April to October
Access Good **Site** Lev/Slope
Sites Available ▲ ⊞ ⊟ **Total** 600
Low Season Band B
High Season Band C
Facilities
Nearby Facilities ✝
‡ Newquay.
Scenic country views. Waterslide and train rides. Brochure Line - FREEPHONE 0500 242523.

NEWQUAY
Newperran Tourist Park, Rejerrah, Newquay, Cornwall, TR8 5QJ.
Tel: 572407 Std: 01872
Nearest Town/Resort Newquay.
Directions Take A30 turn right 2½ miles past the village of Mitchell. On reaching A3075 at Goonhaven turn right and after ¼ mile, sign on righthand side turning on left.
Acreage 25 **Open** Mid May to Mid Sept
Access Good **Site** Level
Sites Available ▲ ⊞ ⊟ **Total** 270
Low Season Band B
High Season Band C
Facilities
Nearby Facilities ✝
‡ Newquay.
Concessionary green fees, own fishing lake nearby, scenic views and central to nine golden beaches. AA 5 Pennants.

NEWQUAY
Newquay Holiday Park, Newquay, Cornwall, TR8 4HS.
Tel: 871111 Std: 01637
Fax: 850818 Std: **01637**
Nearest Town/Resort Newquay
Directions East of Newquay on the A3059 towards St Columb. .
Open Mid May to End September
Access Good **Site** Sloping
Sites Available ▲ ⊞ ⊟ **Total** 259
Facilities
Nearby Facilities ✝
‡ Newquay
South facing park, 2 miles outside of Newquay. Free entertainment.

NEWQUAY
Porth Beach Tourist Park, Porth, Newquay, Cornwall, TR7 3NH.
Tel: 876531 Std: 01637
Fax: **871227** Std: **01637**
Nearest Town/Resort Newquay.
Directions Out of Newquay onto the B3276.
Acreage 6 **Open** End March to October
Access Good **Site** Level
Sites Available ▲ ⊞ ⊟ **Total** 201.
Facilities
Nearby Facilities ✝
‡ Newquay.
200yds from sandy Porth beach, with meandering trout stream on site.

NEWQUAY
Resparva House Camping & Caravanning, Summercourt, Newquay, Cornwall, TR8 5AH.
Tel: 510332 Std: 01872
Nearest Town/Resort Newquay.
Directions From east on A30, ¼ mile west of Summercourt turn left signposted Chapel Town/Summercourt. Site entrance is on the right.
Acreage 1 **Open** Easter to October
Access Good **Site** Level
Sites Available ▲ ⊞ ⊟ **Total** 15
Facilities
Nearby Facilities ✝
‡ Truro
Ideal touring.

NEWQUAY
Rosecliston Park, Trevemper, Newquay, Cornwall.
Tel: 830326 Std: 01637
Nearest Town/Resort Newquay
Directions Take A3075 from Newquay, Rosecliston is 1 mile on left.
Acreage 8 **Open** Whitsun to September
Access Good **Site** Lev/Slope
Sites Available ▲ ⊞ ⊟ **Total** 130
Facilities
Nearby Facilities ✝
‡ Newquay
Family site with many facilities on the outskirts of Newquay.

NEWQUAY
Summer Lodge Holiday Park, Whitecross, Newquay, Cornwall, TR8 4LW.
Tel: 860415 Std: 01726
Fax: **860490** Std: **01726**
Nearest Town/Resort Newquay
Directions A30 turn right at Indian Queens onto A392. Approx 2 miles along the A392 you come to Whitecross, holiday park signposted left.
Acreage 10 **Open** Easter to September
Access Good **Site** Level
Sites Available ▲ ⊞ ⊟ **Total** 50
Facilities

Away from the mainstream - next to the trout stream overlooking the golden beach

- Luxury caravans to let plus level pitches with full hook-ups for touring caravans or campers.
- AA assessment for quality.
- Only 200 yards from the rockpools and beautiful sandy beach.
- Peaceful parkland with its meandering trout stream.
- The bustling seaside resort of Newquay is just a short drive away.
- Free entry to the fabulous entertainments at our Hendra Holiday Park.

Porth Beach Tourist Park caters exclusively for families and mixed couples

Free colour brochure from:
Porth • Newquay • TR7 3NH • Tel: (01637) 876531

CADE'S WEST COUNTRY CAMPING, TOURING & MOTOR CARAVAN SITE GUIDE 1997

CORNWALL

Nearby Facilities
☦ Newquay
Set in beautiful countryside and ideally situated for touring. Short distance from beach and main town of Newquay.

NEWQUAY

Sunnyside Holiday Park, Quintrell Downs, Newquay, Cornwall.
Tel: 873338 Std: 01637
Fax: **851403** Std: **01637**
Nearest Town/Resort Newquay
Directions From Newquay take the A392. Site is situated at Quintrell Downs, 2¼ miles from the town centre.
Acreage 11 **Open** April to 30 October
Site
Sites Available Å ⊕ **Total** 100
Low Season Band C
High Season Band C
Facilities
Nearby Facilities
☦ Quintrell Downs
Cornwalls leading site for 18-35 age group. On site night club plus a minibus service to town.

NEWQUAY

Trebarber Farm, St. Columb Minor, Newquay, Cornwall, TR8 4JT.
Tel: 873007 Std: 01637
Fax: **873007** Std: **01637**
Nearest Town/Resort Newquay.
Directions 3 miles from Newquay on A3059, Newquay to St. Columb Major road.
Acreage 5 **Open** June to September
Access Good **Site** Level
Sites Available Å ⊕ ⊟
Low Season Band B
High Season Band B
Facilities

Nearby Facilities
☦ Newquay.
Quiet Ideal family centre for touring, beaches. Walking distance to Porth reservoir (coarse fishing) and to Golf course.

NEWQUAY

Trekenning Tourist Park, St Columb, Newquay, Cornwall, TR8 4JF.
Tel: 880462 Std: 01637
Fax: **880462** Std: **01637**
Nearest Town/Resort Newquay.
Directions On junction A30/A39 adjacent to St Columb Major roundabout.
Acreage 6½ **Open** April to October
Access Good **Site** Lev/Slope
Sites Available Å ⊕ ⊟ **Total** 75
Low Season Band C
High Season Band C
Facilities
Nearby Facilities
☦ Newquay.
Family run park set in beautiful countryside but minutes from sandy beaches and all of Cornwalls attractions.

NEWQUAY

Treloy Tourist Park, Newquay, Cornwall, TR8 4JN.
Tel: 872063 Std: 01637
Nearest Town/Resort Newquay.
Directions 5 minutes from Newquay on the A3059 Newquay to St Columb Major Road
Acreage 11¼ **Open** April to September
Access Good **Site** Lev/Slope
Sites Available Å ⊕ ⊟ **Total** 141
Facilities
Nearby Facilities
☦ Newquay.
Ideal site for touring the whole of Cornwall. Coarse fishing nearby. Own golf course

½ mile, concessionary Green Fees.

NEWQUAY

Trencreek Holiday Park, Trencreek, Newquay, Cornwall, TR8 4NS.
Tel: 874210 Std: 01637
Nearest Town/Resort Newquay.
Directions A392 to Quintrell Downs, turn right Newquay East/Porth, at Porth crossroads, ¾ mile outside Newquay, turn left to Trencreek.
Acreage 10 **Open** April to September
Access Good **Site** Level
Sites Available Å ⊕ ⊟ **Total** 150
Facilities
Nearby Facilities
☦ Newquay.
Coarse fishing on site, 15 minutes footpath walk to Newquay, 1 mile by road.

NEWQUAY

Trethiggey Touring Park, Quintrell Downs, Newquay, Cornwall. TR8 4LG
Tel: 877672 Std: 01637
Nearest Town/Resort Newquay
Directions Follow main route signposted to Newquay and turn left onto the A3058 at Quintrell Downs, the site is in ¼ mile.
Acreage 15 **Open** 1st March to 1st January
Access Good **Site** Level
Sites Available Å ⊕ ⊟ **Total** 157
Low Season Band A
High Season Band B
Facilities
Nearby Facilities
☦ Quintrell Downs
Peaceful location with scenic views, close to several sandy beaches. English Tourist Board Graded 4 Tick (very good). NO overcrowding. Caravan storage. 12 static caravans to let. Take-away food available.

SELF CATERING AND CAMPING HOLIDAYS

All you need for a fabulous family holiday!

✓ LICENCED CLUB
✓ CABARET NIGHTLY
✓ TAKEAWAY
✓ AMUSEMENTS
✓ POOL TABLES
✓ HEATED POOLS
✓ MINI FLUME SLIDE
✓ SURFRIDER RESTAURANT
✓ MINI-MARKET
✓ LAUNDERETTE
✓ PLAY AREAS
✓ FREE HOT SHOWERS
✓ MODERN TOILETS

Summer Lodge
NEWQUAY CORNWALL

Where sea and country meet...

NEWQUAY CORNWALL TR8 4LW

TELEPHONE:
01726 860415

FACSIMILE:
01726 861490

CADE'S WEST COUNTRY CAMPING, TOURING & MOTOR CARAVAN SITE GUIDE 1997

CORNWALL

NEWQUAY

Trevella Park, Crantock, Newquay, Cornwall, TR8 5EW.
Tel: 830308 Std: 01637
Nearest Town/Resort Newquay.
Directions 2 miles south of Newquay on the A3075, turn right signposted Crantock.
Acreage 15 **Open** Easter to October
Access Good **Site** Level
Sites Available ▲ ⊕ ♛ **Total** 270
Low Season Band B
High Season Band C
Facilities
Nearby Facilities ┏ ✔ ⊥ ⇲ ∪ ≯ ♪
⇌ Newquay.
½ mile from the beach, concessionary green fees, own fishing lake. AA 5 Pennants.

NEWQUAY

Trevornick Holiday Park, Holywell Bay, Newquay, Cornwall, TR8 5PW.
Tel: 830531 Std: 01637
Fax: **830531** Std: **01637**
Nearest Town/Resort Newquay.
Directions Take Newquay to Perranporth A3075 road. Take turning for Cubert/Holywell.
Acreage 30 **Open** Easter to September
Access Good **Site** Level
Sites Available ▲ ⊕ ♛ **Total** 500
Low Season Band B
High Season Band C
Facilities
Nearby Facilities ┏ ✔ ⊥ ⇲ ∪ ≯ ♪ ✝
⇌ Newquay.
Next to the beach, stunning sea views. Tourers and static tents. Golf, fishing, tennis and riding on site.

NEWQUAY

Watergate Bay Holiday Park, Watergate Bay, Newquay, Cornwall.
Tel: 860387 Std: 01637
Fax: **860387** Std: **01637**
Nearest Town/Resort Newquay
Directions 4 miles north of Newquay on the B3276 Coast Road to Padstow. Follow directions shown from Watergate Bay.
Acreage 15 **Open** March to November
Access Good **Site** Level
Sites Available ▲ ⊕ ♛ **Total** 171
Low Season Band B
High Season Band C
Facilities
Nearby Facilities ┏ ✔ ⊥ ⇲ ∪ ≯ ♪
⇌ Newquay
½ mile from Watergate Bay in a rural location in an area of outstanding natural beauty.

TRETHIGGEY TOURING PARK

QUINTRELL DOWNS, NEWQUAY, CORNWALL TEL: 01637 877672

A friendly, family-run rural site for touring caravans, tents and dormobiles. Easy access from main road, approx. 2 miles from Newquay centre and several sandy beaches. Modern facilities inc. ample clean showers, toilets, laundry, shop, off licence, electric hook-ups, children's play area.

Caravan Club, Caravan and Camping Club approved.

FROM £4.20 A NIGHT **Please write or phone for free colour brochure**

DISCOVER CORNWALL

VOTED IN TOP 100 PRACTICAL CARAVAN MAGAZINE '96

A warm friendly welcome awaits you from the Seery family as we live up to our reputation of being one of the South West's top family holiday parks.

White Acres Country Park

- TOURING AND CAMPING WITH SUPER NEW LEVEL PITCHES
- THE FINEST FACILITIES WITH HOSPITALITY & FRIENDLINESS ASSURED
- LUXURY HOLIDAY HOMES. NEW FOR '97 CASTLE ADVENTURE PLAY AREA!

✳ SAUNA ✳ SOLARIUM ✳ HEATED INDOOR POOL COMPLEX ✳ NIGHTLY CABARET ✳
✳ GYMNASIUM ✳ SUPERMARKET ✳ THREE CHILDRENS PLAY AREAS ✳ FOUR LAKES ✳
✳ ON-SITE TACKLE & BAIT SHOP ✳ LAUNDERETTE ✳ SPA BATH ✳ POOL TABLES ✳
✳ TABLE TENNIS ✳ EXCLUSIVE CLUB & SALOON BAR ✳ RESTAURANT & TAKEAWAY ✳

**Voted Nationally in Top 100 Practical Caravan Magazine
ALSO ..... Cornwall's Top Regional Park in 1996!**

ALL THIS ..... AND LOTS MORE!
Write, 'Phone or Fax now for your
FREE COLOUR BROCHURE

White Acres Country Park, White Cross, Newquay, Cornwall TR8 4LW

Tel: 01726 860220 Fax: 01726 860877

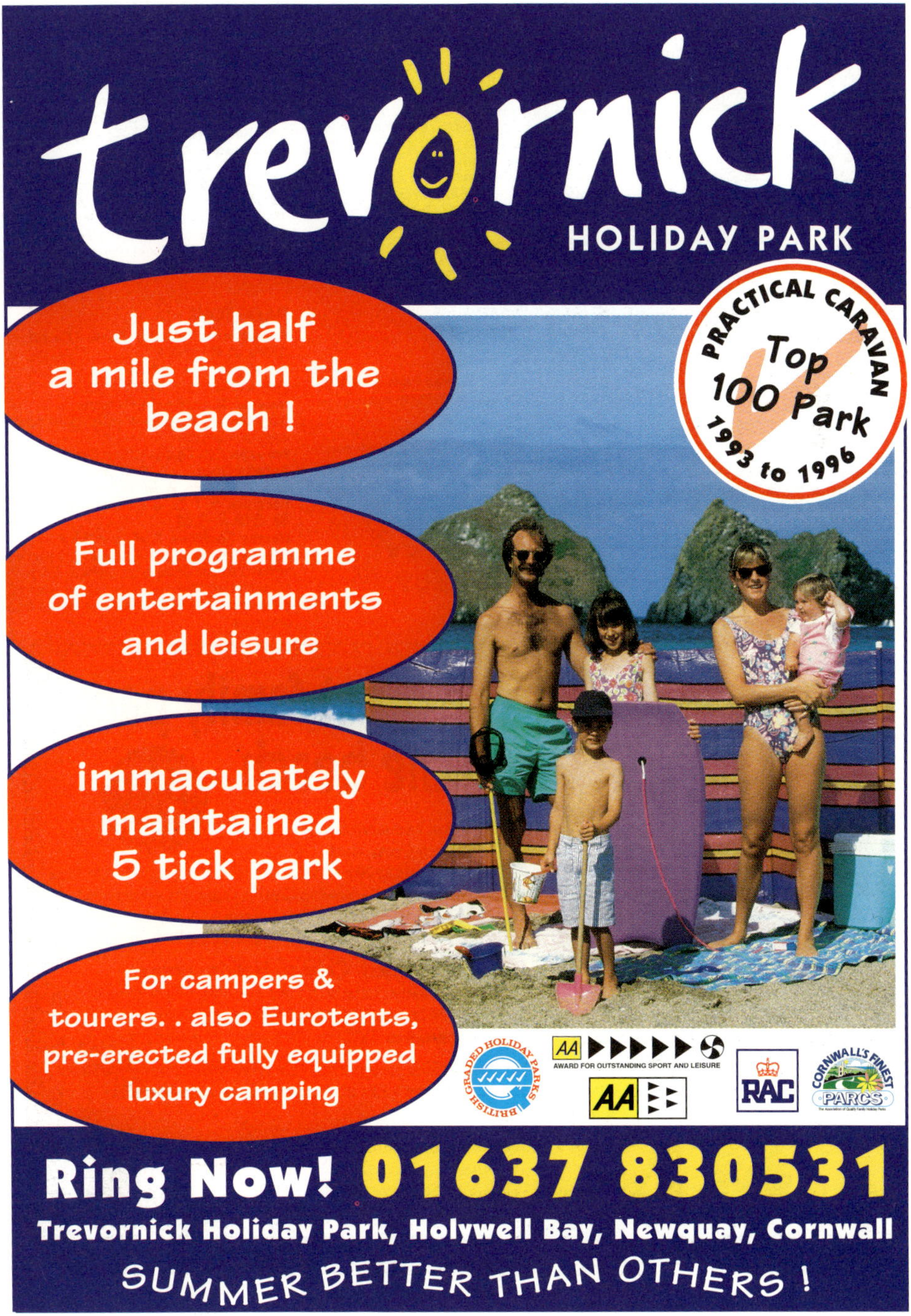

trevornick
HOLIDAY PARK

PRACTICAL CARAVAN Top 100 Park 1993 to 1996

- Just half a mile from the beach !
- Full programme of entertainments and leisure
- immaculately maintained 5 tick park
- For campers & tourers.. also Eurotents, pre-erected fully equipped luxury camping

Ring Now! 01637 830531
Trevornick Holiday Park, Holywell Bay, Newquay, Cornwall

SUMMER BETTER THAN OTHERS !

CORNWALL

PADSTOW
Carnevas Farm Holiday Park, Carnevas Farm, St. Merryn, Padstow, Cornwall, PL28 8PN.
Tel: 520230 Std: 01841.
Nearest Town/Resort Padstow.
Directions Take Newquay coast road from Padstow, turn right at Tredrea Inn just before getting to Porthcothan Bay. Site ¼ mile up road on right.
Acreage 8 **Open** April to October
Access Good **Site** Lev/Slope
Sites Available A ⊕ ⊟ **Total** 198
Low Season Band B
High Season Band C
Facilities ∮ ⊞ ♨ ⌈ ⊙ ⌐ ⊿ ⊙ ⊛
⊠ ⌘ ⊙ ⊜ ♨ ⌂ ⊟
Nearby Facilities ⌈ ✓ ⊥ ↘ ∪ ⇗ ⌱
≢ Newquay
Near numerous sandy beaches in lovely rural position, ideal touring, well run family park. AA 3 Pennant site, Rose Award Park 1996, English Tourist Board Grading system 5 ticks.

PADSTOW
Dennis Cove Camping, Dennis Cove, Padstow, Cornwall, PL28 8DR.
Tel: 532349 Std: 01841
Nearest Town/Resort Padstow
Directions Signposted off A389 on outskirts of Padstow Town.
Acreage 5 **Open** Easter to September
Access Good **Site** Lev/Slope
Sites Available A ⊕ ⊟ **Total** 62
Low Season Band B
High Season Band C
Facilities ⊞ ♨ ⌈ ⊙ ⌐ ⊿ ⊙ ⊛
⌘ ⌱ ⊙ ⊜ ⊛ ⊠ ⊓ ⋜ ⊟
Nearby Facilities ⌈ ✓ ⊥ ↘ ∪ ⇗ ⌱
≢ Bodmin Parkway
Site adjoins Camel Estuary and town of Padstow. Scenic views and ideal base for variety of watersports. 5 Touring caravan pitches only. No large groups without prior reservation.

PADSTOW
Harlyn Sands Holiday Park, Lighthouse Road, Trevose Head, Nr. Padstow, Cornwall.
Tel: 520720 Std: 01841
Fax: **521251** Std: **01841**
Nearest Town/Resort Padstow
Directions From Padstow take the B3276 Newquay coast road. After 1 mile follow signs for Harlyn Sands.
Open April to October
Access Good **Site** Level
Sites Available A ⊕ ⊟ **Total** 100
Low Season Band B
High Season Band C
Facilities ∮ ⊞ ♨ ⌈ ⊙ ⌐ ⊿ ⊙ ⊛
⊠ ⌘ ⊙ ⊜ ⊓ ♨ ⌂ ⊟
Nearby Facilities ⌈ ✓ ⊥ ↘ ∪
≢ Bodmin Parkway
300 yards from the beach.

PADSTOW
Mother Iveys Bay Caravan Park, Trevose Head, Padstow, Cornwall. PL28 8SL
Tel: 520990 Std: 01841
Nearest Town/Resort Padstow
Directions Padstow to Newquay coast road B3276 4 miles west of Padstow pick up Mother Iveys signs.
Acreage 1½ **Open** Easter to October
Access Busy **Site** Lev/Slope
Sites Available A ⊕ ⊟ **Total** 100
Facilities ⊕ ∮ ♨ ⊞ ♨ ⌈ ⊙ ⌐ ⊙ ⊛
⌘ ⊙ ⊜ ♨ ⊟
Nearby Facilities ⌈ ✓ ⊥ ∪ ⌱
≢ Bodmin Parkway
Own private sandy beach.

PADSTOW
Music Water Touring Park, Rumford, Wadebridge, Cornwall, PL27 7SJ.
Tel: 540257 Std: 01841
Nearest Town/Resort Padstow.
Directions Wadebridge A39 to roundabout take B3274 signposted Padstow. Turn left, 2 miles 500yds Park on right.
Acreage 7 **Open** April to October
Access Good **Site** Level
Sites Available A ⊕ ⊟ **Total** 145
Low Season Band B
High Season Band C
Facilities ∮ ⊞ ♨ ⌈ ⊙ ⌐ ⊿ ⊙ ⊛
⊠ ⌘ ⊙ ⊜ ♨ ⌂ ⋜
Nearby Facilities ⌈ ✓ ∪
≢ Bodmin.
Scenic views, ideal walking, clean friendly family site, splash pool.

PADSTOW
Trerethern Touring Park, Padstow, Cornwall, PL28 8LE.
Tel: 532061 Std: 01841
Fax: **532061** Std: **01841**
Nearest Town/Resort Padstow
Directions On A389 1 mile south south west of Padstow
Acreage 13¼ **Open** April to October
Access Good **Site** Level
Sites Available A ⊕ ⊟ **Total** 90
Facilities ⊕ ∮ ⊞ ♨ ⌈ ⊙ ⌐ ⊙ ⊛
⊠ ⌘ ⊙ ⊜ ⊓ ⊛ ⊟
Nearby Facilities ⌈ ✓ ⊥ ↘ ∪ ⇗ ⌱
Panoramic views, several sandy beaches within 3 miles. Extra large pitches, footpath to padstow. Winter storage, no statics, separate dog exercise area. 4 Ticks, free brochure.

The quiet family park on the beach

PHONE FREE COLOUR BROCHURE
01726 812868

Next to large, safe sandy beach
• Lots of open grassy space
• Fascinating wildlife lake • Indoor heated swimming pool with Aqua Slide • Tennis Courts • Bowling Green • Crazy Golf • Playground
• Amusements • Cycle hire • Cafe & Shop • Laundrette • Pets welcome • Adjacent to Par Village • Perfect base for touring Cornwall.

Choice of Modern Caravan Holiday Homes
• Extra wide luxury caravan homes available • Fully fitted kitchen with fridge • Lounge with colour T.V. • Separate bedrooms
• Shower and flush W.C.

Tent & Touring Park • Level grass pitches • Excellent toilet & shower facilities • Pot wash • Babies bathroom • Electric hook-ups some with water & TV connections.

Free colour brochure from: Par Sands Holiday Park, St. Austell Bay Cornwall PL24 2AS.
Telephone St. Austell (01726) 812868.

EXCELLENT

CORNWALL

PAR
Par Sands Holiday Park, Par Beach, St. Austell Bay, Cornwall, PL24 2AS.
Tel: 812868 Std: 01726.
Fax: **817899** Std: **01726**
Nearest Town/Resort St. Austell/Fowey.
Directions 4 miles east of St Austell on road to Fowey A3082.
Acreage 12 **Open** April to October
Access Good   **Site Level**
Sites Available ▲ ⊕ ⊟ **Total** 200
Low Season Band B
High Season Band C
Facilities ▣ ♿ / ▥ ♨ ⌂ ⊙ ⌐ ⌘ ◻ ✆
♒ ❍ ⊛ ✕ ♠ ⋈ ⤳ ✳ ▣
Nearby Facilities ┌ ⁄ ⊥ ↳ ∪ ⌇ ⌐
✚ Par.
Alongside safe sandy beach and freshwater wildlife site. Indoor heated swimming pool with aquaslide. ETB Rose Award 4 Ticks.

PENTEWAN
Pentewan Sands Holiday Park, Pentewan, St. Austel, Cornwall, PL26 6BT.
Tel: Mevagissey 843485 Std: 01726
Nearest Town/Resort Pentewan.
Directions From A390 at St. Austell take B3273 south towards Mevagissey. Entrance is 4 miles on left.
Acreage 27 **Open** April to October
Access Good   **Site Level**
Sites Available ▲ ⊕ ⊟ **Total** 470
Low Season Band B
High Season Band C
Facilities ▣ / ▥ ♨ ⌂ ⊙ ⌐ ⌘ ◻ ✆
♒ ❍ ⊛ ✕ ♀ ▥ ♠ ⌇ ✳ ⋈ ▣
Nearby Facilities ┌ ⁄ ⊥ ↳ ∪ ⌇ ⌐
✚ St. Austell.
Large individual marked pitches (many with electric hook-ups) on well equipped site with own safe sandy beach.

PENZANCE
Boleigh Farm Site, Boleigh Farm, Lamorna, Penzance, Cornwall.
Tel: 810305 Std: 01736
Nearest Town/Resort Penzance.
Directions Site is 4½ miles southwest of Penzance on the B3315, first on the right after turn to Lamorna Cove.
Acreage 1½ **Open** March to October
Access Good   **Site Level**
Sites Available ▲ ⊕ ⊟ **Total** 30
Low Season Band B
High Season Band B
Facilities ▥ ♨ ⌂ ⊙ ⌐ ✆ ⋈ ⊙ ▣
Nearby Facilities ┌ ⁄ ⊥ ↳ ∪ ⌇ ⌐ ✳
✚ Penzance.
Local Prehistoric Stones, Pipers and Merry Maidens, etc. Sea 1 mile. Coastal walks. Spin dryer. 7 miles to Lands End, 5 miles Minac (open air) theatre.

PENZANCE
Bone Valley Caravan Park, Heamoor, Penzance, Cornwall, TR20 8UJ.
Tel: 60313 Std: 01736
Nearest Town/Resort Penzance
Directions Follow A30 (Penzance Bypass) to roundabout signposted Heamoor follow road straight through village, next right at caravan/camping sign, to next caravan/camping sign, turn left.
Acreage 1 **Open** March to 7th January
Access Good   **Site Level**
Sites Available ▲ ⊕ ⊟ **Total** 17
Low Season Band B
High Season Band C
Facilities ♨ ⌂ ⊙ ⌐ ⌘ ◻ ✆
♒ ▣ ❍ ⋈ ▣
Nearby Facilities ┌ ⁄ ⊥ ↳ ∪ ⌇ ⌐ ✳
✚ Penzance
Clean, friendly, family park, very sheltered with guaranteed personal 24 hour service.

PENZANCE
Garris Farm, Gulval, Penzance, Cornwall, TR20 8XD.
Tel: 365806 Std: 01736
Fax: **365806** Std: 01736
Nearest Town/Resort Penzance
Directions Leave A30 turning right at Growlas on road to Luogvan B3309 to Castlegate. Follow road to Chysauster ancient village.
Acreage 8 **Open** May to October
Access Good   **Site Sloping**
Sites Available ▲ ⊕ ⊟
Low Season Band A
High Season Band B
Facilities ▥ ❍ ✆
Nearby Facilities ⊥ ↳ ∪
✚ Penzance.

PENZANCE
River Valley Caravan Park, Relubbus, Marazion, Penzance, Cornwall, TR20 9ER.
Tel: 763398 Std: 01736
Nearest Town/Resort Marazion.
Directions From Hayle B3302 to Leedstown, turn right onto B3280 to Townsend and straight on to Relubbus.
Acreage 18 **Open** March to 5th Jan
Access Good   **Site Level**
Sites Available ▲ ⊕ ⊟ **Total** 90
Low Season Band B
High Season Band C
Facilities ▣ / ▥ ♨ ⌂ ⊙ ⌐ ⌘ ◻ ✆
♒ ❍ ⊛ ▣
Nearby Facilities ┌ ⁄ ⊥ ↳ ∪
✚ Penzance.
Quiet park, no clubhouse, in sheltered valley. Top grade toilets. £1 discount every night to Cade's readers. Tourist Board Graded 5 Tick "Excellent".

PENZANCE
Wayfarers Camping Site, St. Hilary, Penzance, Cornwall, TR20 9EF.
Tel: Penzance 763326 Std: 01736
Nearest Town/Resort Marazion.
Directions 2 miles east of Marazion on B3280.
Acreage 4 **Open** March to November
Access Good   **Site Level**
Sites Available ▲ ⊕ ⊟ **Total** 60
Facilities / ▥ ♨ ⌂ ⊙ ⌐ ◻ ✆
♒ ❍ ⊛ ▣ ⋈ ▣
Nearby Facilities ┌ ⁄ ⊥ ↳ ∪ ⌇ ⌐ ✳
✚ Penzance.
Quiet, family site. Easy reach Mounts Bay and beaches. Central for West Cornwall touring. Holiday Caravans for hire.

PERRANPORTH
Penrose Farm Touring Park, Goonhavern, Truro, Cornwall, TR4 9QF.
Tel: 573185 Std: 01872
Nearest Town/Resort Perranporth.
Directions Leave A30 onto the B3285 signed Perranporth, site 1¼ miles on the left.
Acreage 9 **Open** April to October
Access Good   **Site Level**
Sites Available ▲ ⊕ ⊟ **Total** 100
Low Season Band B
High Season Band C
Facilities ▣ / ▥ ♨ ⌂ ⊙ ⌐ ⌘ ◻ ✆
♒ ❍ ⊛ ▣
Nearby Facilities ┌ ⁄ ⊥ ↳ ∪ ⌇ ⌐
✚ Newquay/Truro
Quiet, clean and sheltered park with animal centre and adventure play area. Good spacing. Close to Perranporth beach. 4 Tick Graded.

PERRANPORTH
Perran Sands Holiday Centre, Perranporth, Cornwall, TR6 0AQ.
Tel: 573551 Std: 01872
Nearest Town/Resort Perranporth.
Directions Take the A30 through Cornwall. 3 miles after Mitchell turn right onto the B3285 towards Perranporth. Perran Sands is on the right just before Perranporth.
Acreage 25 **Open** 6 May to 7 October
Access Good   **Site Level**
Sites Available ▲ ⊕ ⊟ **Total** 450
Facilities ♿ / ⚐ ▥ ♨ ⌂ ⊙ ⌐ ⌘ ◻ ✆
♒ ❍ ⊛ ✕ ♀ ▥ ♠ ⌇ ▣
Nearby Facilities ┌ ⁄ ∪
✚ Truro.
On a cliff top amid dunes and grassland. A short walk from the beach.

Perranporth Camping & Touring Park

The park, within easy walking distance (approx. 5 minutes) of beach and town, comprises seven acres of well drained sheltered grass land with tarmacadam access roads and all modern facilities.

Mini Supermarket · Swimming Pool · Launderette · Showers and Washrooms · Six berth luxury flats above 'Failte Club' with licensed bar, overlooking heated swimming pool and children's paddling pool.

Budnick Road, Perranporth, Cornwall   Telephone: Perranporth **(0187257) 2174**
AA Camping Club Caravan Club   British Tourist Authority listed site

CORNWALL

PERRANPORTH
Rosehill Farm Tourist Park, Goonhavern, Cornwall, TR4 9LA.
Tel: 572448 Std: 01872
Nearest Town/Resort Perranporth
Directions 200 yds from The New Inn in Goonhavern on the B3285 Perranporth road.
Acreage 6 **Open** Easter to October
Access Good   **Site** Lev/Slope
Sites Available A ⊕ ⊜ **Total** 65
Low Season Band B
High Season Band C
Facilities ƒ ⊞ ⚲ ⌐ ⊙ ⌐ ⚌ ⎵
⛛ ⊙ ⊜ ⊞ ⚿ ⌂ ⎵
Nearby Facilities ⌐ ⁄ ⊥ ⅄ U ⏎
⇌ Truro & Newquay
Quiet family site, 1¼ miles from Perranporth beach, ideal touring base. Free hot showers, separate dog walking field. Cleanliness insured by resident owners. Booking is essential July and August, discount for advance bookings.

POLPERRO
Killigarth Manor Caravan Park, Polperro, Looe, Cornwall.
Tel: 272216 Std: 01503.
Fax: **272218** Std: **01503**.
Nearest Town/Resort Polperro.
Directions From Looe take the A387, after approx 4 miles turn left, signposted Killigarth. Park is about 400yds on the left.
Acreage 7 **Open** Easter to October
Access Good   **Site** Level
Sites Available A ⊕ ⊜ **Total** 202
Low Season Band B
High Season Band C
Facilities & ƒ ⊞ ⚲ ⌐ ⊙ ⌐ ⚌ ⎵
⛛ ⊙ ⊜ ⚿ ⚆ ⊞ ⌂ ⏁ ⎵
Nearby Facilities ⌐ ⁄ ⊥ U ⏎ ⏎

⇌ Looe.
Set in an area of outstanding natural beauty. Indoor swimming pool.

POLZEATH
South Winds, Old Polzeath Road, Polzeath, Near Wadebridge, Cornwall. PL27 6QU.
Tel: 863267 Std: 01208.
Fax: **862080** Std: **01208**
Nearest Town/Resort Wadebridge.
Directions
Acreage 7 **Open** Easter to October
Access Good   **Site** Level
Sites Available A ⊕ ⊜ **Total** 100
Low Season Band B
High Season Band C
Facilities ƒ ⊞ ⚲ ⌐ ⊙ ⌐ ⚌ ⎵
⛛ ⊙ ⊜ ⊛ ⎵
Nearby Facilities ⌐ ⁄ ⊥ ⅄ U ⏎ ⏎ ⏎
⇌ Bodmin Road.
Outstanding views of countryside and sea.

POLZEATH
Tristram Caravan & Camping Park, Polzeath, Nr Wadebridge, Cornwall, PL27 6SR.
Tel: 863267/862215 Std: 01208
Fax: **862080** Std: **01208**
Nearest Town/Resort Wadebridge
Directions
Acreage 5 **Open** Easter to October
Access Good   **Site** Level
Sites Available A ⊕ ⊜ **Total** 130
Low Season Band C
High Season Band C
Facilities ƒ ⊞ ⚲ ⌐ ⊙ ⌐ ⚌ ⎵
⛛ ⛛ ⊙ ⊜ ⚿ ⌂ ⛛ ⎵
Nearby Facilities ⌐ ⁄ ⊥ ⅄ U ⏎ ⏎ ⏎
⇌ Bodmin Parkway
Cliff top site. Direct access onto Polzeath beach.

POLZEATH
Valley Caravan Park, Polzeath, Wadebridge, Cornwall, PL27 6SS.
Tel: 862391 Std: 0208.
Nearest Town/Resort Wadebridge
Directions From Wadebridge take the B3314 to Polzeath (7 miles), enter the village. Our entrance is opposite the beach between the post office and Spar shop.
Acreage 7 **Open** All Year
Access Fair   **Site** Level
Sites Available A ⊕ ⊜ **Total** 65
Low Season Band B
High Season Band C
Facilities & ƒ ⊞ ⚲ ⌐ ⊙ ⌐ ⚌ ⎵
⛛ ⊙ ⊜ ⚿ ⛛ ⌂ ⎵ ⎵
Nearby Facilities ⌐ ⁄ ⊥ ⅄ ⏎ ⏎
⇌ Bodmin Parkway
Near the beach.

PORTREATH
Cambrose Touring Park, Portreath Road, Redruth, Cornwall.
Tel: Porthtowan 890747 Std: 01209
Nearest Town/Resort Redruth/Portreath.
Directions From Redruth, B3300 (Portreath road) north.
Acreage 3 **Open** Easter to October
Access Good   **Site** Level
Sites Available A ⊕ ⊜ **Total** 50
Facilities & ƒ ⊞ ⚲ ⌐ ⊙ ⌐ ⚌ ⎵
⛛ ⊙ ⊜ ⌂ ⎵
Nearby Facilities ⌐ ⁄ ⊥ U ⏎ ⏎
⇌ Redruth.
1½ miles sandy beaches, centrally situated as a base from which to tour. Under the personal supervision of the resident proprietors - R.G. & J. Fitton.

We are a friendly, quiet, family park, offering spacious level pitches and exceptional, high quality amenities. Situated in a pleasant countryside valley, only a few minutes from the sand and surf of Perranporth Beach and the holiday resort of Newquay.

CORNWALL

Perran Springs
TOURING PARK
PERRANPORTH
FOR MORE INFORMATION CALL FOR A FREE COLOUR BROCHURE NOW!
AA • Perran Springs Touring Park • RAC
Bodmin Road • Goonhavern • Truro • Cornwall • TR4 9QG • Tel: (01872) 540568

CORNWALL

PORTREATH
Tehidy Holiday Park, Harris Mill, Redruth, Cornwall, TR16 4JQ.
Tel: Redruth 216489 Std: 01209
Nearest Town/Resort Portreath.
Directions Take Redruth Porthtowan exit from A30. Take Porthtowan North Country exit from double roundabout, turn left at first crossroads. Cross next two crossroads Tehidy Holiday Park 200 yards on left pass Cornish Arms Public House.
Acreage 1 **Open** Easter to October
Access Good   **Site** Level
Sites Available ▲ ⌘ ⇌ **Total** 18
Low Season Band B
High Season Band B
Facilities ⌘ ⇌
Nearby Facilities
⇌ Redruth.
Near beach, scenic views, ideal touring.

REDRUTH
Tresaddern Holiday Park, St. Day, Redruth, Cornwall, TR16 5JR.
Tel: 820459 Std: 01209
Nearest Town/Resort Redruth
Directions From A30 2 miles east of Redruth take A3047 Scorrier, in 400yds B3298 Falmouth, site 1½ miles on right.
Acreage ½ **Open** Easter to October
Access Good   **Site** Lev/Slope
Sites Available ▲ ⌘ ⇌ **Total** 25
Low Season Band A
High Season Band B
Facilities
Nearby Facilities
⇌ Redruth
Quiet rural site, central for touring south Cornwall.

RUAN MINOR
Chy-Carne Chalet, Caravan & Camping Park, Kuggar, Kennack Sands, Ruan Minor, Helston, Cornwall, TR12 7LX.
Tel: 290541 Std: 01326
Nearest Town/Resort Helston
Directions From Helston follow the A3083 for approx. 2 miles, at mini roundabout turn left onto the B3293 signposted St Keverne. Approx. 1 mile past Goonhilly Earth Satellite Station turn right, onto T-Junction turn left, site is on the left.
Open February to December
Access Good   **Site** Level
Sites Available ▲ ⌘ ⇌ **Total** 80
Low Season Band B
High Season Band B
Facilities
Nearby Facilities
⇌ Penzance
¼ mile from the beach, ideal touring.

RUAN MINOR
The Friendly Camp, Tregullas Farm, Penhale, Ruan Minor, Helston, Cornwall, TR12 7LJ.
Tel: 240387 Std: 01326
Nearest Town/Resort Mullion
Directions 7 miles south of Helston on left hand side of A3083, just before junction of B3296 to Mullion which is 1 mile.
Acreage 1¼ **Open** April to November
Access Good   **Site** Level
Sites Available ▲ ⌘ ⇌ **Total** 18
Facilities
Nearby Facilities
⇌ Redruth
Nice views, ideal touring, nice moorland walks.

SALTASH
Dolbeare Caravan & Camping Park, Landrake, Saltash, Cornwall, PL12 5AF.
Tel: 851332 Std: 01752
Nearest Town/Resort Saltash.
Directions 4 miles west of Saltash, turn off A38 at Landrake immediately after footbridge into Pound Hill, signposted.
Acreage 9 **Open** All Year
Access Good   **Site** Lev/Slope
Sites Available ▲ ⌘ ⇌ **Total** 60.
Facilities
Nearby Facilities
⇌ Saltash.
Quality touring park in magnificent countryside. Free, plentiful hot water. Level hard standings and large grass areas. Please telephone for a brochure.

SALTASH
Stoketon Touring Park, Stoketon Cross, Trematon, Saltash, Cornwall, PL12 4RZ.
Tel: 841447 Std: 01752
Nearest Town/Resort Saltash
Directions A38, once over Tamar Bridge, 2 miles west (towards Liskeard). Follow signs for Crooked Inn.
Open April to October
Access Good   **Site** Lev/Slope
Sites Available ▲ ⌘ ⇌ **Total** 60
Low Season Band B
High Season Band B
Facilities
Nearby Facilities
⇌ Saltash.
First site into Cornwall on the A38. Quiet, friendly, uncommercialised site with grassy terraces. Ideal base for touring. Country Inn adjacent. Some electric hook-ups.

ST. AGNES
Beacon Cottage Farm Camping Park, Beacon Drive, St. Agnes, Cornwall.
Tel: 552347 Std: 01872.
Nearest Town/Resort St. Agnes.
Directions From A30, take B3277 to St. Agnes, take road to the Beacon. Follow signs to site.
Acreage 2 **Open** April to September
Access Good   **Site** Level
Sites Available ▲ ⌘ ⇌ **Total** 50
High Season Band C
Facilities
Nearby Facilities
⇌ Truro.
On working farm, surrounded by National Trust Land. Sandy beach 1 mile, beautiful sea views.

ST. AUSTELL
Croft Farm Touring Park, Luxulyan, Bodmin, Cornwall, PL30 5EQ.
Tel: 850228 Std: 01726
Fax: **850498** Std: **01726**
Nearest Town/Resort St. Austell
Directions From A390 (Liskeard to St Austell) turn right past the level crossing in St Blazey (signposted Luxulyan). In 1½ mile turn right at T-Junction, continue to next T-Junction and turn right. The park is on the left within ½ mile. N.B. DO NOT take any other routes signposted Luxulyan/Lux Valley.
Acreage 4 **Open** End March to End October
Access Good   **Site** Level
Sites Available ▲ ⌘ ⇌ **Total** 53
Low Season Band B
High Season Band C
Facilities

Nearby Facilities
⇌ Luxulyan
Close to Luxulyan Valley, good walking and ideal for touring.

ST. AUSTELL
River Valley Holiday Park, London Apprentice, St Austell, Cornwall, PL26 7AP.
Tel: 73533 Std: 01726
Nearest Town/Resort St Austell
Directions Take the B3273 from St Austell to Mevagissey, 1 mile to London Apprentice, site is on the left hand side.
Acreage 4 **Open** April to October
Access Good   **Site** Level
Sites Available ▲ ⌘ ⇌ **Total** 20
Low Season Band B
High Season Band C
Facilities
Nearby Facilities
⇌ St Austell
Alongside a river with woodland walk and a cycle trail.

ST. AUSTELL
Sun Valley Holiday Park, Pentewan Road, St. Austell, Cornwall.
Tel: Mevagissey 843266 Std: 01726.
Nearest Town/Resort Mevagissey
Directions Take B3273 from St. Austell, site 1 mile past 'London Apprentice', on right.
Acreage 20 **Open** April to October
Access Good   **Site** Level
Sites Available ▲ ⌘ ⇌ **Total** 22
Low Season Band B
High Season Band C
Facilities
Nearby Facilities
⇌ St. Austell.
Site situated in woodland and pasture surrounding. 1 mile from sea. Ideal touring centre. Tennis and indoor swimming pool on site.

ST. AUSTELL
Trencreek Farm Holiday Park, Hewaswater, St. Austell, Cornwall.
Tel: St. Austell 882540 Std: 01726
Nearest Town/Resort St. Austell.
Directions From St. Austell take A390 towards Truro, after 4 miles fork left onto B3287 (St. Mawes) entrance 1 mile on left.
Acreage 10 **Open** Easter to October
Access Good   **Site** Lev/slope
Sites Available ▲ ⌘ ⇌ **Total** 140
Low Season Band A
High Season Band C
Facilities
Nearby Facilities
⇌ St. Austell.
A family run park with real farm atmosphere. Ideal for families with young children. Coarse fishing lakes. Tennis court, pitch & putt.

ST. AUSTELL
Treveor Farm Caravan & Camping Park, Gorran, St. Austell, Cornwall.
Tel: 842387 Std: 01726
Nearest Town/Resort Gorran Haven.
Directions Take the B2373 from St Austell. After Pentewan park at top of hill turn right to Gorran. Approx 4 miles on turn right at signboard.
Acreage 4 **Open** April to October
Access Good   **Site** Level
Sites Available ▲ ⌘ ⇌ **Total** 50
Low Season Band B
High Season Band C

CADE'S WEST COUNTRY CAMPING, TOURING & MOTOR CARAVAN SITE GUIDE 1997   27

CORNWALL

CORNWALL
ST IVES BAY
HOLIDAY PARK
CHALETS CARAVANS AND CAMPING
with private access to a huge sandy beach. With a large indoor pool and 2 clubs on the Park. Phone us NOW on the toll free number below for your FREE colour brochure

right on the beach!

Call our 24hr BROCHURE LINE on 0800 317713

Facilities / ⚡ 🆙 🍴 ∩ ☉ ⌐ ◢ ◯ ♈
℥ ✪ 🏠 ⌷
Nearby Facilities ⌐ ✎ ⊥ ✹ ♪
☩ St Austell
Near to beach and coastal path.

ST. AUSTELL
Trewhiddle Holiday Estate, Trewhiddle, St. Austell, Cornwall, PL26 7AD.
Tel: 67011 Std: 01726
Nearest Town/Resort St. Austell.
Directions From St Austell roundabout on the By-Pass, take the B3273 road towards Mevagissey, the site entrance is ½ mile from the roundabout on the right.
Acreage 16 **Open** March to January
Access Good **Site** Lev/Slope
Sites Available ⛺ 🚐 🚍 **Total** 105
Facilities / 🆙 🍴 ∩ ☉ ⌐ ◢ ◯ ♈
℥ ◯ ⛹ ✗ ♀ ♈ ↯ ⌷
Nearby Facilities ⌐ ✎ ⊥ ✹ U ♪ ♪
☩ St. Austell.
Set in 16 acres of beautiful grounds. Excellent facilities for family holidays. Heated pool with water flume. Ideal touring centre.

ST. BURYAN
Treverven Touring Caravan & Camping Site, Treverven Farm, St. Buryan, Cornwall, TR19 6DL.
Tel: 810221 Std: 01736.
Nearest Town/Resort Penzance
Directions B3315 midway between Penzance and Lands End.
Acreage 6 **Open** Easter to October
Access Good **Site** Level
Sites Available ⛺ 🚐 🚍 **Total** 115
Low Season Band B
High Season Band C
Facilities / 🆙 🍴 ∩ ☉ ⌐ ◢ ◯ ♈
№ ✪ 🏠 ⌷
Nearby Facilities ✎ ⊥ ✹ ♪ ♪
☩ Penzance.
Near coast, sea views.

ST. IVES
Carbis Bay Holiday Village, Laity Lane, Carbis Bay, St. Ives, Cornwall, TR26 3HW.
Tel: 797580 Fax: 797580 Std: 01736
Nearest Town/Resort St. Ives
Directions 1¼ miles south west of Hayle on the A30, turn north west onto the A3074 (St. Ives). When approaching Carbis Bay turn left at the crossroads by Cost Cutters Shop, follow the road to the next crossroads and go straight across. We are the next turning on the right.
Acreage 36 **Open** Witsun to October
Access Good **Site** Sloping
Sites Available ⛺ 🚐 🚍 **Total** 450

Facilities ♿ / 🆙 🍴 ∩ ☉ ⌐ ◢ ◯ ♈
℥ ℥ ◯ ⛹ ✗ ♀ 🍴 ♈ ↯ ⌷
Nearby Facilities ⌐ ✎ ⊥ ✹ U ♪ ♪
☩ Carbis Bay
Scenic views, near the beach.

ST. IVES
Penderleath Caravan & Camping Park, Towednack, St. Ives, Cornwall, TR26 3AF.
Tel: 798403 Std: 01736
Nearest Town/Resort St. Ives
Directions B3311 from St. Ives, after Halsetown first right to Towednack.
Acreage 8 **Open** Easter to October
Access Good **Site** Lev/Slope
Sites Available ⛺ 🚐 🚍 **Total** 75
Low Season Band B
High Season Band C
Facilities ♿ / 🆙 🍴 ∩ ☉ ⌐ ◢ ◯
℥ ◯ ⛹ ✗ ♀ 🍴 🏠 ⌷
Nearby Facilities ⌐ ✎ ⊥ ✹ U ♪ ♪
☩ St. Ives
Set in classified area of outstanding natural beauty with unrivalled views. Peaceful family run site.

ST. IVES
Polmanter Tourist Park, Halsetown, St. Ives, Cornwall, TR26 3LX.
Tel: 795640 Std: 01736
Fax: **795640** Std: **01736**
Nearest Town/Resort St. Ives.
Directions Take the A3074 to St. Ives from the A30. First left at the mini-roundabout taking Holiday Route to St. Ives (Halsetown). Turn right at the Halsetown Inn, then first left.
Acreage 13 **Open** Easter to October
Access Good **Site** Level
Sites Available ⛺ 🚐 🚍 **Total** 240
Low Season Band B
High Season Band C
Facilities / ⚡ 🆙 🍴 ∩ ☉ ⌐ ◢ ◯ ♈
℥ ℥ ◯ ⛹ ✗ ♀ 🍴 ♈ ↯ ⌷
Nearby Facilities ⌐ ✎ ⊥ ✹ U ♪ ♪
☩ St. Ives.
Just 1½ miles from St. Ives and beaches. Central for touring the whole of West Cornwall. Tennis on site. TV for individual pitches.

ST. IVES
St. Ives Bay Holiday Park, Upton Towans, Hayle, Cornwall TR27 5BH.
Tel: Hayle 752274 Std: 01736
Fax: **754523** Std: **01736**
Nearest Town/Resort Hayle.
Directions A30 from Camborne to Hayle, at roundabout take Hayle turn-off and then turn right onto B3301, 600yds on left enter park.
Acreage 12 **Open** May to September

Access Good **Site** Lev/Slope
Sites Available ⛺ 🚐 🚍 **Total** 200
Low Season Band B
High Season Band C
Facilities 🆙 ∩ ☉ ⌐ ◢ ◯ ♈
℥ ℥ ◯ ⛹ ✗ ♀ 🍴 ♈ ↯ ⌷
Nearby Facilities ⌐ ✎ ⊥ ✹ U ♪
☩ Hayle.
Park adjoining own sandy beach, onto St. Ives Bay. Children very welcome. Pets welcome. Seaviews. Dial-a-Brochure 24 hours, Mr R. White. (See full page colour advertisement).

ST. IVES
Trevalgan Family Camping Park, St. Ives, Cornwall, TR26 3BJ.
Tel: 796433 Std: 01736
Nearest Town/Resort St. Ives
Directions Follow the holiday route round St. Ives. From the B3306 follow brown camping park signs.
Acreage 5 **Open** May to September
Access Good **Site** Level
Sites Available ⛺ 🚐 🚍 **Total** 120
Low Season Band B
High Season Band C
Facilities / 🆙 🍴 ∩ ☉ ⌐ ◢ ◯ ♈
℥ ℥ ◯ ⛹ ✗ ♀ 🍴 ♈ ↯ ⌷
Nearby Facilities ⌐ ✎ ⊥ ✹ U ♪ ♪
☩ St. Ives
Rural park with own stretch of Cornish coast. Superb views and walking. Some facilities for the disabled.

ST. JUST
Bosavern Garden Caravan Site, Bosavern House, St. Just, Penzance, Cornwall.
Tel: 788301 Std: 01736
Nearest Town/Resort St. Just/Penzance.
Directions Take the A3071 from Penzance towards St. Just. Approximately 550yds before St. Just turn left onto the B3306 signposted Lands End and airport. Bosavern Garden Caravan Park is 500yds from the turn off, behind Bosavern House.
Acreage 2¼ **Open** March to October
Access Good **Site** Level
Sites Available ⛺ 🚐 🚍 **Total** 12
Facilities / ⚡ 🆙 🍴 ∩ ☉ ⌐ ◢ ◯ ♈
℥ ✪ ⌷
Nearby Facilities ⌐ ✎ U ♪
☩ Penzance
Sea and moorland views, walled garden site surrounded by trees and flowers. Clay pigeon shooting nearby.

---

28   *CADE'S WEST COUNTRY CAMPING, TOURING & MOTOR CARAVAN SITE GUIDE 1997*

CORNWALL

ST. JUST
Kelynack Caravan & Camping Park, Kelynack, St. Just, Nr. Penzance, Cornwall.
Tel: 787633 Std: 01736
Nearest Town/Resort St. Just in Penwith.
Directions From Penzance take A3071 St. Just road, then after 6 miles turn left onto the B3306 Lands End coast road, ½ mile to site sign.
Acreage 2 **Open** April to October
Access Good   **Site** Level
Sites Available 🛖 ⛺ 🚐 **Total** 20
Low Season Band B
High Season Band B
Facilities 🚻 ♿ 🚿 🍳 📞 ⊙ ♻ 🛒 ℗ ♿
💲 ℹ️ ☎ 🏪 🐕 🎣 ⚠️ 🅿
Nearby Facilities ┌ ✓ ⊥ ≫ ﹢
🚉 Penzance.
¾ mile beach, alongside stream in valley setting. Ideal for touring. On coast road. E.T.B. graded very good. Sheltered site.

ST. JUST
Levant House, Levant House, Levant Road, Pendeen, Penzance, Cornwall, TR19 7SX.
Tel: 788795 Std: 01736
Nearest Town/Resort St. Just-in-Penwith.
Directions From St. Just-in-Penwith take the B3306 towards St. Ives. At Trewellard turn left. Site is in two fields 200yds on the left.
Acreage 2½ **Open** April to October
Access Good   **Site** Lev/Slope
Sites Available 🛖 ⛺ 🚐 **Total** 43
Low Season Band A
High Season Band B
Facilities ♿ 🚿 🍳 📞 🛒 ℗ 🎣 ♿ 🅿
Nearby Facilities ┌ ✓ ℛ ﹢
🚉 Penzance.
Approx. 8 minutes wlak to the Coastal Path. Rock climbing at Bosegran.

ST. JUST
Roselands Caravan and Camping Park, Dowran, St. Just, Penzance, Cornwall, TR19 7RS.
Tel: Penzance 788571 Std: 01736
Nearest Town/Resort Penzance.
Directions Take A3071 from Penzance. Turn left at crossroads ½ mile east of St. Just. Signposted with camping sign and Sancreed 2¾ miles.
Acreage 2 **Open** April to October
Access Good   **Site** Level
Sites Available 🛖 ⛺ 🚐 **Total** 20
Low Season Band A
High Season Band C
Facilities 🚻 ♿ 🚿 🍳 📞 🛒 ℗ ♿ 🅿
💲 ℹ️ ☎ 🏪 ✕ 🐕 🎣 🏠 ⚠️ 🅿
Nearby Facilities ┌ ✓ ⊥ ≫ U ﹢ ℛ ﹢
🚉 Penzance.
Sea views, close to beaches, scenic walks. Dogs allowed if kept on lead. Static caravans for hire also.

ST. JUST
Trevaylor Caravan and Camping Park, Botallack, St Just, Cornwall.
Tel: 787016 Std: 01736
Nearest Town/Resort Penzance
Directions Situated on the B3306 Lands End to St Ives road, approx 1 mile to the north of St Just.
Acreage 5 **Open** Mid March to October
Access Good   **Site** Level
Sites Available 🛖 ⛺ 🚐 **Total** 85
Low Season Band A
High Season Band B
Facilities 🚻 ♿ 🚿 🍳 📞 ⊙ 🛒 ℗ ♿
💲 ℹ️ ☎ 🏪 🎣 🅿
Nearby Facilities ┌ ✓ ⊥ ≫ U ﹢ ℛ

🚉 Penzance
Easy access to the golden sands, white surf from the Atlantic Ocean, rugged cliffs and coastal paths. Off License and take-away on site.

ST. MAWES
Trethem Mill Touring Park, St. Just-in-Roseland, Truro, Cornwall.
Tel: 580504 Std: 01872
Fax: 580968 Std: 01872
Nearest Town/Resort St. Mawes.
Directions St. Austell to St. Mawes A3078.
Acreage 4 **Open** April to October
Access Good   **Site** Lev/Slope
Sites Available 🛖 ⛺ 🚐 **Total** 84
Low Season Band B
High Season Band C
Facilities 🚻 ♿ 🚿 🍳 📞 ⊙ 🛒 ℗ ♿
💲 ☎ 🏪 ☎ 🐕 🅿
Nearby Facilities ┌ ✓ ⊥ ≫ U ﹢ ℛ
🚉 Truro.
St. Mawes.

ST. MERRYN
Tregavone Farm Touring Park, St. Merryn, Padstow, Cornwall, PL28 8JZ.
Tel: 520148 Std: 01841
Nearest Town/Resort Padstow
Directions Turn right off A39 (Wadebridge-St. Columb) onto A389 (Padstow) come to T junction turn right in 1 mile turn left, entrance on left after 1 mile.
Acreage 4 **Open** March to October
Access Good   **Site** Level
Sites Available 🛖 ⛺ 🚐 **Total** 40
Low Season Band B
High Season Band B
Facilities ♿ ✕ 🚿 🍳 📞 ⊙ 🛒 ℗ ♿ 🅿
Nearby Facilities ┌ ✓ ⊥ ≫ U ﹢ ℛ
🚉 Newquay
Quiet family run site situated near sandy surfing beaches, country views, well maintained and grassy.

ST. MERRYN
Trethias Farm Caravan Park, St. Merryn, Padstow, Cornwall.
Tel: Padstow 520323 Std: 01841
Nearest Town/Resort Padstow
Directions From Wadebridge follow signs to St. Merryn, go past Farmers Arms, third turning right (our signs from here).
Acreage 5 **Open** April to September
Access Good   **Site** Level
Sites Available 🛖 ⛺ 🚐 **Total** 62
Low Season Band B
High Season Band C
Facilities ♿ 🚿 📞 ⊙ 🛒 ℗ ☎ 🅿
Nearby Facilities ┌ ✓ ⊥ ≫ U ﹢
🚉 Bodmin Parkway
Near beach, scenic views.

ST. MERRYN
Trevean Farm Caravan & Camping Park, St. Merryn, Padstow, Cornwall, PL28 8PR.
Tel: 520772 Std: 01841
Nearest Town/Resort Padstow
Directions From St. Merryn village take the B3276 Newquay road for 1 mile. Turn left for Rumford, site ¼ mile on the right.
Acreage 2 **Open** April to October
Access Good   **Site** Level
Sites Available 🛖 ⛺ 🚐 **Total** 36
Low Season Band A
High Season Band A
Facilities ♿ 🚿 🍳 📞 🛒 ℗ ♿
💲 ☎ 🏪 🅿
Nearby Facilities ┌ ✓ ⊥ ≫ U ﹢ ℛ
🚉 Newquay
Situated near several sandy, surfing beaches.

ST. MERRYN
Treyarnon Bay Caravan Park, Treyarnon Bay, Padstow, Cornwall, PL28 8JR.
Tel: 520681 Std: 01841
Nearest Town/Resort Padstow.
Directions Follow road for Treyarnon from B3276 Newquay to Padstow road. Follow lane and into car park at the bottom of the village. (Holiday park adjoins car park).
Acreage 4 **Open** April to September
Site Level
Sites Available 🛖 ⛺ 🚐 **Total** 60
Low Season Band A
High Season Band B
Facilities ♿ 📞 ⊙ 🛒 ℗ ♿
💲 ℹ️ ☎ 🏪 🅿
Nearby Facilities ┌ ✓ ⊥ ≫ U
🚉 Newquay
Overlooking bay. Ideal for touring, surfing, golf, swimming or just lazing by the sea.

ST. MINVER
Dinham Farm Caravan & Camping Park, St. Minver, Wadebridge, Cornwall, PL27 6RH.
Tel: 812878 Std: 01208
Nearest Town/Resort Wadebridge.
Directions Take B3314, on approaching Polzeath/Rock from Camelford fork right, after 2 miles take left turn at sign for above site 400yds on right
Acreage 2½ **Open** April to October
Access Good   **Site** Lev/Slope
Sites Available 🛖 ⛺ 🚐 **Total** 40
Low Season Band B
High Season Band B
Facilities 🚻 ♿ 🚿 🍳 📞 ⊙ 🛒 ℗ ♿
💲 ☎ 🏪 🐕 ⚠️ 🅿
Nearby Facilities ┌ ✓ ⊥ ≫ U ﹢ ℛ ﹢
🚉 Bodmin Parkway.
Overlooking River Camel. New super pitches, hook ups and heated swimming pool.

ST. MINVER
St. Minver Holiday Village, St. Minver, Nr. Wadebridge, Cornwall, PL27 6RR.
Tel: 862305 Std: 01208
Nearest Town/Resort Wadebridge
Directions Take the A39 from Camelford to Wadebridge, then take the B3314. Turn right at the mini-roundabout heading for Port Isaac. After 3¼ miles turn left at the road signposted to Rock. The park is 250yds along on the right hand side.
Acreage 6 **Open** 8 April to 7 October
Access Good   **Site** Sloping
Sites Available 🛖 ⛺ 🚐 **Total** 120
Facilities & ✕ ♿ 🚿 📞 ⊙ 🛒 ℗ ♿
💲 ℹ️ ☎ 🏪 ✕ 🐕 🎣 ⚠️ 🅿
Nearby Facilities ┌ ✓ ⊥
🚉 Bodmin Parkway
Set amidst 40 acres of wooded countryside, in the grounds of a lovely old Cornish Manor House.

TINTAGEL
Bossiney Farm Caravan Site, Tintagel, Cornwall, PL34 OAY.
Tel: 770481 Std: 01840
Nearest Town/Resort Tintagel
Directions ¾ miles from centre of Tintagel on main Boscastle road.
Acreage 2 **Open** April to October
Access Good   **Site** Lev/Slope
Sites Available 🛖 ⛺ 🚐 **Total** 20
Low Season Band A
High Season Band B
Facilities 🚻 ♿ 🚿 🍳 📞 ⊙ 🛒 ♻ 💲 ℹ️
Nearby Facilities ┌ ✓ ⊥ ≫ U
🚉 Bodmin Parkway
Ideal touring centre, near beach, inland views.

CADE'S WEST COUNTRY CAMPING, TOURING & MOTOR CARAVAN SITE GUIDE 1997

CORNWALL

Silverbow Park IS SIMPLY EXCELLENT

Silverbow Park set in beautiful landscaped parkland
- PERFECT PEACE ● WITH NO CLUBS OR BARS... JUST IMMACULATE FACILITIES!
- 14 LARGE SUPERIOR LEISURE HOMES AND LARGE INDIVIDUAL FULLY SERVICED TOURING PITCHES
- HEATED POOL ● All weather TENNIS COURTS
- Short mat BOWLS

1992 AA & CALOR GAS AWARDS

FREE Colour Brochure
Tel: (01872) 572347

Silverbow Park
GOONHAVERN · TRURO · CORNWALL TR4 9NX
Near Perranporth

TINTAGEL
The Headland Caravan & Camping Park, Atlantic Road, Tintagel, Cornwall, PL34 0DE.
Tel: 770239 Std: 0184.
Fax: 770239 Std: 01840
Nearest Town/Resort Tintagel.
Directions Follow camping/caravan signs from B3263 through village to Headland.
Acreage 4 **Open** Easter to October
Access Good **Site** Lev/Slope
Sites Available ▲ ⛺ 🚐 **Total** 60
Low Season Band B
High Season Band C
Facilities ƒ 🕮 ♨ ſ ☉ ⌐ 🞂 ◨ ☎
🆂🅿 ☉ ⛴ 🎱 🖺
Nearby Facilities ſ ✓ ⏉ ⤴ U ℛ
🚉 Bodmin Parkway
Three beaches walking distance. Scenic views. Ideal touring centre.

TINTAGEL
Trewethett Farm Tourist Park, Trethevy, Tintagel, Cornwall, PL34 0BQ.
Tel: 770533 Std: 01840
Fax: 770309 Std: 01840
Nearest Town/Resort Tintagel
Directions Midway between Boscastle and Tintagel, signposted off the B3263.
Acreage 10 **Open** April to October
Access Good **Site** Level
Sites Available ▲ ⛺ 🚐 **Total** 160
Low Season Band B
High Season Band C
Facilities ƒ 🖽 ♨ ƒ 🕮 ♨ ſ ☉ ⌐ 🞂 ◨ ☎
🆂🅿 ☉ 🖤 🖺
Nearby Facilities ſ ✓ ⏉ ⤴ U ⤵
🚉 Bodmin Parkway
Clifftop park with stunning views overlooking Bossiney Cove. Rock Valley, a well known beauty spot, is part of Trewethett Farm.

TORPOINT
Whitsand Bay Holiday Park, Millbrook, Torpoint, Cornwall, PL10 1JZ.
Tel: 822597 Std: 01752
Fax: 823444 Std: 01752
Nearest Town/Resort Torpoint.
Directions From Plymouth take the Torpoint Ferry (10 minutes). From Torpoint take the main road out, 3 miles to Anthony bear left, 2 miles turn left at T-Junction, 1 mile past Tregantle Fort turn right onto coast road. After 2½ miles turn left into the park.
Acreage 27 **Open** April to October
Access Good **Site** Lev/Slope
Sites Available ▲ ⛺ 🚐 **Total** 280
Low Season Band B
High Season Band C
Facilities ƒ 🖽 ♨ ƒ 🕮 ♨ ſ ☉ ⌐ 🞂 ◨ ☎
🆂🅿 ☉ ⛴ 🖤 🎱 🖺 🖨 🖺

Nearby Facilities ſ ✓ ⏉ U
🚉 Plymouth.
Situated in an historic fort with spectacular views from every pitch. 10 minutes from the beach. 6 miles from Plymouth.

TREVERVA
Menallack Farm, Menallack Farm Treverva, Penryn, Cornwall.
Tel: Falmouth 340333 Std: 01326
Nearest Town/Resort Falmouth/Helston
Directions Follow the A39 over the double roundabouts and go straight on towards Helston (A394). Go straight across the first roundabout and take the second exit from the second roundabout (no signpost). In Mabe straight over crossroad. In 2 miles at crossroads turn right to Gweek. The Treverva ¾ mile towards Gweek. Site is on left.
Acreage 1½ **Open** Good Friday to October
Access Good **Site** Lev/slope
Sites Available ▲ ⛺ 🚐 **Total** 30
Low Season Band B
High Season Band B
Facilities 🖽 ♨ ſ ☉ ⌐ 🆂🅿 ⛴ 🖺 🖺
Nearby Facilities ſ ✓ ⏉ ⤴ U ⤵
🚉 Falmouth.
Peaceful, isolated, with beautiful views. Easy access to north and south coasts.

TRURO
Carnon Downs Caravan & Camping Park, Carnon Downs, Truro, Cornwall, TR3 6JJ.
Tel: 862283 Std: 01872.
Fax: 862800 Std: 01872
Nearest Town/Resort Truro.
Directions On the A39 Falmouth road, 3 miles West of Truro.
Acreage 9 **Open** April to October
Access Good **Site** Level
Sites Available ▲ ⛺ 🚐 **Total** 150
Low Season Band B
High Season Band B
Facilities 🅱 δ ƒ 🖽 ♨ ſ ☉ ⌐ 🞂 ◨ ☎
🆂🅿 ☉ ⛴ 🎱 🖨 🖺
Nearby Facilities ſ ✓ ⏉ U ⤵ ℛ
🚉 Truro
Ideally central for touring. Excellent location for sailing and water sports.

TRURO
Chacewater Camping & Caravan Park, Coxhill, Chacewater, Truro, Cornwall.
Tel: St. Day 820762 Std: 01209
Nearest Town/Resort Truro.
Directions From A30 take the A3047 to Scorrier. Turn left at Crossroads Hotel onto the B3298. 1½ miles left to Chacewater ½ mile sign directs you to the park.
Acreage 6 **Open** May to End September
Access Good **Site** Level

TRURO
Cosawes, Perranworthal, Truro, Cornwall, TR3 7QS.
Tel: 863724 Std: 01872
Fax: 870268 Std: 01872
Nearest Town/Resort Falmouth
Directions Midway between Truro and Falmouth on the A39.
Acreage 100 **Open** All Year
Access Good **Site** Level
Sites Available ▲ ⛺ 🚐 **Total** 50
Facilities ƒ 🖽 ♨ ſ ☉ ⌐ 🞂 ◨ ☎
🅿 ☉ ⛴ 🖺
Nearby Facilities ſ ✓ ⏉ ⤴ U ⤵ ℛ
🚉 Perranwell
Situated in a 100 acre wooded valley, an area of outstanding natural beauty.

TRURO
Leverton Place, Greenbottom, Nr. Truro, Cornwall, TR4 8QW.
Tel: Std:
Nearest Town/Resort Truro.
Directions 3 miles west of Truro. Take the A390 to Truro, right at the first roundabout signposted Chacewater. Right at the mini roundabout and Leverton Place is 100yds on the right.
Acreage 10 **Open** All Year
Access Good **Site** Level
Sites Available ▲ ⛺ 🚐 **Total** 110
Low Season Band B
High Season Band C
Facilities 🅱 δ ƒ 🖽 ♨ ſ ☉ ⌐ 🞂 ◨ ☎
🆂🅿 ☉ ⛴ ✗ 🖤 🎱 🖨 🖺 ❋
Nearby Facilities ſ ✓ ⏉ U ℛ ℛ
🚉 Truro.
Ideal touring and exploring centre for Cornwall.

TRURO
Liskey Touring Park, Greenbottom, Truro, Cornwall, TR4 8QN.
Tel: 560274 Std: 01872
Fax: 560274 Std: 01872
Nearest Town/Resort Truro.
Directions 3½ miles west of Truro, off A390 between Threemilestone and Chacewater.
Acreage 8 **Open** April to September
Access Good **Site** Lev/slope
Sites Available ▲ ⛺ 🚐 **Total** 68
Low Season Band B

---

30   *CADE'S WEST COUNTRY CAMPING, TOURING & MOTOR CARAVAN SITE GUIDE 1997*

CORNWALL

High Season Band C
Facilities ƒ ⬚ ♣ ⌐ ☉ ⌐ ◧ ◆
♋ ○ ♣ ⊞ ⧖ ❋ ⊡
Nearby Facilities ⌐ ✦ ⊥ ➘ ∪ ⊅ ⋌
♯ Truro.
Small family site, central for exploring Cornwall. Take away meals, hardstandings, all-service pitches, adventure play barn, family bathroom and dishwashing sinks. 10 minutes to the sea.

TRURO
Ringwell Holiday Park, Bissoe Road, Carnon Downs, Truro, Cornwall, TR3 6LQ.
Tel: 862194 Std: 01872
Fax: **864343** Std: **01872**
Nearest Town/Resort Truro
Directions From Truro take the A39 to Falmouth. After approx. 2½ miles turn right at large roundabout to Carnon Downs. Take the second right, Bissoe Road, and we are ¾ mile on the right hand side.
Acreage 12 **Open** April to October
Access Good   **Site** Lev/Slope
Sites Available ⚐ ⌂ ⚑ **Total** 37
Low Season Band B
High Season Band C
Facilities ƒ ⬚ ♣ ⌐ ☉ ⌐ ◧ ◆
♋ ⓘ ○ ♣ ⊠ ✦ ⧖ ⊡
Nearby Facilities ⌐ ⊥ ➘ ∪ ⊅
♯ Truro
Set in 12 acres of a picturesque valley with open views from most of the pitches. Ideally situated for exploring both North and South coasts. All facilities but no crowds.

TRURO
Summer Valley Touring Park, Shortlanesend, Truro, Cornwall.
Tel: Truro 77878 Std: 01872.
Nearest Town/Resort Truro.

Directions 2 miles out of Truro on Perranporth road (B3284). Sign on left just past Shortlanesend.
Acreage ½ **Open** April to October
Access Good   **Site** Level
Sites Available ⚐ ⌂ ⚑ **Total** 60
Low Season Band B
High Season Band C
Facilities ⊟ ƒ ⬚ ♣ ⌐ ☉ ⌐ ◧ ◆
♋ ○ ⊞ ⧖ ⊡
Nearby Facilities ⌐ ✦ ⊥ ➘ ∪ ⊅
♯ Truro.
Ideal centre for touring Cornwall. British Holiday Parks   grading 4 ticks.

TRURO
Trevarth Holiday Park, Blackwater, Truro, Cornwall, TR4 8HR.
Tel: 560266 Std: 01872
Nearest Town/Resort Truro
Directions A30 to Chiverton roundabout, 300yds from Blackwater exit.
Acreage 2 **Open** April to Mid October
Access Good   **Site** Level
Sites Available ⚐ ⌂ ⚑ **Total** 30
Low Season Band B
High Season Band B
Facilities ƒ ⬚ ♣ ⌐ ☉ ⌐ ◧ ◆
⌂ ○ ♣ ⊠ ⧖ ❋ ⊡
Nearby Facilities ⌐ ✦ ∪ ⊅
♯ Truro.
Rural park in an excellent location for touring North and South coast resorts.

WADEBRIDGE
The Laurels, Whitecross, Cornwall, PL27 7JQ.
Tel: 813341 Std: 01208
Nearest Town/Resort Wadebridge
Directions On A39/A389 Wadebridge/ Padstow junction.

Acreage 2¼ **Open** Easter to October
Access Good   **Site** Level
Sites Available ⚐ ⌂ ⚑ **Total** 30
Low Season Band B
High Season Band B
Facilities ⊟ ƒ ⬚ ♣ ⌐ ☉ ⌐ ◧ ◆
♋ ♣ ⧖ ❋ ⊡
Nearby Facilities ⌐ ✦ ⊥ ➘ ∪ ⊅ ⋌
♯ Bodmin Parkway
Designated an area of outstanding beauty. Overlooking River Camel, Atlantic Ocean and Bodmin Moor. Set in glorious surroundings.

WADEBRIDGE
Trewince Farm Holiday Park, St. Issey, Wadebridge, Cornwall.
Tel: 812830 Std: 01208
Nearest Town/Resort   Wadebridge/ Padstow.
Directions Take the A39 from Wadebridge then the A389 to Padstow. We are signposted 1 mile on the left.
Open Easter to October
Access Good   **Site** Level
Sites Available ⚐ ⌂ ⚑ **Total** 120
Low Season Band B
High Season Band C
Facilities ƒ ⬚ ♣ ⌐ ☉ ⌐ ◧ ◆
♋ ⓘ ○ ♣ ⊠ ⧖ ⊅ ⊡
Nearby Facilities ⌐ ✦ ∪ ⊅ ⋌
♯ Bodmin
Scenic views, close to many sandy beaches and the Camel Trail. Ideal for cycling and walking.

CADE'S

Wadebridge,
Cornwall PL27 6EG
Telephone: (01208) 812323 RAC

Nearest to the Camel Trail. Ideal touring centre, close to superb beaches. Fully tiled toilet & shower blocks. Baby Room, Laundrette, Electric Hookups, Heated Outdoor Pool. Watershute Splash Pool, Shop, Crazy Golf, Pets Corner, Play Area, Games Room, Licensed Club House, Bar Meals, Take-Away, Entertainment in main season. Luxury caravans for hire, Club Rallies Welcome. Municipal indoor pool & sports complex 3 min-walk, 6 golf courses within 20 mins car ride.
BROCHURES ON REQUEST

CORNWALL
PLACES OF INTEREST

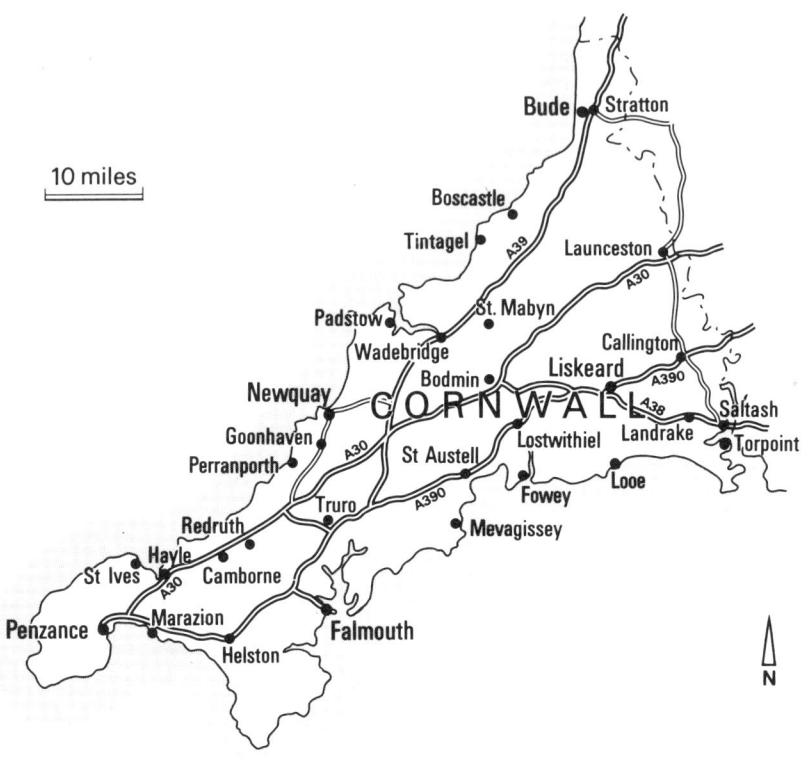

CORNWALL

BODMIN
The county town of Cornwall, Bodmin is sited on the steep edge of Bodmin Moor. Surrounded by an area of outstanding natural beauty, Bodmin has an interesting regimental museum and Cornwalls largest old church. The district is rich in Roman and prehistoric remains, and Bodmin Beacon bears an Obelisk to General Sir Walter Raleigh Gilbert.

BODMIN
BODMIN & WENFORD RAILWAY : General Station, Lostwithiel Road, Bodmin, Cornwall, PL31 1AQ. Tel : 01208 73666. Fax : 01208 77963.
Nearest Railway Station : Bodmin Parkway. Location : Quarter of a mile south of Bodmin town centre on the B3288. Open : Easter to the end of October. Daily June to September, weekends only in December. Please telephone for exact dates and times. **Special Attractions:** Preserved steam railway (diesel used on Saturdays), operating two branch lines to Bodmin Parkway (BR) 3.5 miles and to Boscarne Junction 3 miles, which connects with Camel Trail. Good area for walking and cycling opportunities. Shop and Buffet at General Station. Special events and galas throughout the year.

BODMIN
MILITARY MUSEUM : The Keep, Bodmin, Cornwall, PL31 1EG. Tel & Fax : 01208 72810.
Nearest Railway Station : Bodmin Parkway. Location : Half a mile south east of the town centre. Open : 9am-5pm Monday to Friday. Also Sundays during July and August. **Special Attractions:** History of the Duke of Cornwall's Light Infantry (DCLI). Fine display of medals, uniforms and small arms.

BODMIN
PENCARROW : Washway, Bodmin, Cornwall. Tel : St Mabyn 01208 84369.
Nearest Railway Station : Bodmin Parkway. Location : Signposted off the A389 Bodmin-Wadebridge Road and the B3266 Bodmin-Camelford Road. Open : Easter Saturday to 15th October Sunday to Thursday 1.30pm-5pm. 1st June to 10th September and Bank Holiday Mondays 11am-5pm. **Special Attractions:** Historic Georgian House with an exceptionally fine collection of fine paintings, furniture and china. Still owned and lived in by the family. Extensive grounds which include an ancient British encampment, Victorian rock garden, lake, Italian garden and ice house. Noted specimen collection of conifers and rhododendrons. Dogs are welcome in the grounds. Tea rooms, craft centre, self pick soft fruit.

32 *CADE'S WEST COUNTRY CAMPING, TOURING & MOTOR CARAVAN SITE GUIDE 1997*

CORNWALL

BOSCASTLE
A picturesque village, Boscastle has a small harbour guarded by cliffs on either side, giving the neighbouring coastal scenery a rugged aspect.

The rocky beach has odd patches of sand and allows access for bathing. Saint Symphorian Church is Norman with a tower dating from 1750. Welltown Manor dates from circa 1640.

BOSCASTLE
BOSCASTLE POTTERY : The Old Bakery, Bascastle, Cornwall, PL35 0HE. Tel : 01840 250291.
Nearest Railway Station : Bodmin Parkway. Location : Opposite the main car park, near the picturesque harbour. Open : Summer 9am till dusk, Winter 9am-5.30pm. **Special Attractions:** Studio pottery. Come and watch the pots being made and the trees grow on them as if by magic. "The World's only Mochaware maker".

BOSCASTLE
THE OLD FORGE : Boscastle Harbour, Boscastle, Cornwall. Open : April to end of October every day 11am-6pm. **Special Attractions:** A National Trust Information Centre and shop housed in the old blacksmiths forge. Boscastle harbour.

BUDE
Bude is a popular resort with fine beaches that face the prevailing wind. These conditions make the area ideal for surfing and enthusiasts come from all over the country. Ridges of downland separate the town from the coastline. One of two principal beaches, Summerlease Beach has a large swimming pool which is refilled at every tide and is ideal for bathers who wish to avoid the long rollers of the open sea. Rock scenery around Bude is particularly notable. Compass Point and Efford Beacon provide excellent viewpoints and walks along the cliff are also of interest.

BUDE
BUDE-STRATTON MUSEUM : The Wharf, Bude, Cornwall. Tel & Fax : 01288 353576.
Nearest Railway Station : Exeter. Location : At the wharf by the castle, Bude. Open : From Easter to the end of September 11am-5pm. Other times or visits by parties for the same mine at be arranged by appointment by the Clerk of the Council Bude-Stratton Town Council. **Special Attractions:** Development of the town is shown mostly in photographs. Interesting and updated canal and port display, shipping and railway photographs and artifacts related to development of town, life saving and shipwrecks. Working model of incline plane and an improved military section. Splash leisure pool. Ample parking. Cafe adjacent. Facilities for the disabled.

CAMBORNE
CORNISH ENGINES : Near Camborne, Cornwall. Tel : 01209 216657. Fax : 01209 612142.
Location : Two engines at Pool, 2 miles East of Camborne one on either side of A3047. The East Pool Whim (winding engine) stands beside the road, the pumping engine for the same mine at Taylors Shaft quarter of a mile to the North East. Open : 1st April to the 1st November every day 11am-5.30pm or sunset if earlier (last admission 1/2 an hour before closing). **Special Attractions:** Impressive relics of the Tin Mining industry, these great beam engines (one with a cylinder 7.5 feet in diameter) were used both for pumping water from 200 feet deep and for winding men and tin ore. The engines exemplify the use of high pressure steam patented by the Cornish Engineer Richard Trevithick in 1802. Owned by the National Trust (members free) and operated by the Trevithick Trust.

CAMELFORD
This small town was once, according to legend, the site of King Arthurs Camelot.
Slaughter Bridge crosses a stream and is said to have been the scene of Arthurs last battle. The towns market hall dates from 1790.

CAMELFORD
BRITISH CYCLING MUSEUM : The Old Station, Camelford, Cornwall, PL32 9TZ. Tel : 01840 212811.
Nearest Railway Station : Bodmin Parkway. Location : 1 mile north of Camelford on the B3266 Boscastle road. Open : All Year, 10am-5pm. **Special Attractions:** The Nation's foremost museum of Cycling History. Over 400 examples of various cycles with Old Cycle Workshop, library of books and window displays of lighting and ceramics. A full history of cycling from 1818 to present day, housed in an old railway station. Lots to see!

CAMELFORD
NORTH CORNWALL MUSEUM, GALLERY & TOURIST INFORMATION CENTRE : The Clease, Camelford, Cornwall. Tel: 01840 212954.
Nearest Railway Station : Bodmin Parkway, 16 miles. Location : Just off the A39 in Camelford on B3266. Open : April 1st to September 30th Daily except Sunday, 10am-5pm. **Special Attractions:** Opened in 1974, this privately owned museum is set in a building that was originally used for making coaches and wagons. The museum covers many aspects of life in North Cornwall from 50 to 100 years ago. These include farming, the dairy, cider making and wagons. A special feature is the reconstruction of a moorland cottage at the turn of the century. There are sections on the tools of the plumber, blacksmith, saddler, cobbler, tailor, printer, doctor and granite and slate quarrymen. On the domestic side there is a wide range of exhibits from lace bonnets to early vacuum cleaners and a collection of Cornish and Devonshire pottery. The gallery has changing exhibitions throughout the season of crafts and paintings.

FALMOUTH
CORNWALL MARITIME MUSEUM : 2 Bell's Court, Market Street, Falmouth, Cornwall, TR11 5BX. Tel : 01326 316881.
Nearest Railway Station : Falmouth. Location : In Falmouth town centre up a short lane (20yds) opposite Marks & Spencer. Open : Every day in Summer, 10am-4pm. End of October to the end of May, Monday to Saturday 10am-3pm. **Special Attractions:** Housed in the Historic Bells Court which was the office of the Packet Ship Service until the mid 19th Century, exhibits include the History of the Falmouth Packet (International Mail of UK for 150 years), shipbuilding, fishing and smuggling. Many fine models of Historic ships, craftsman's tools, navigation instruments and a full size reconstruction of workshops and a ships cabin. Much interest for all ages.

FALMOUTH
PRINCESS PAVILION & GARDENS : 41 Melvill Road, Falmouth, Cornwall, TR11 4AR. Tel : 01326 311277. Fax : 01326 315382.
Nearest Railway Station : Falmouth Dell. Location : Adjacent to Falmouth's sea front. Open : 9am-11pm. **Special Attractions:** 400 seat theatre and multi-purpose hall with a full Summer of entertainment, family programme. Our beautiful gardens are well known for their floral displays and regular concerts are presented from the ornate Bandstand. Licensed bar and cafeteria open all day May to September.

FALMOUTH
TREBAH GARDEN : Mawnan Smith, Falmouth, Cornwall, TR11 5JZ. Tel : 01326 250448. Fax : 01326 250781.
Nearest Railway Station : Falmouth. Location : Follow the A39 towards Falmouth, at Treliever Cross roundabout follow the brown and white tourism signs. Open : Every day of the Year, 10.30am-5pm. **Special Attractions:** Discover the magical old Cornish garden set on the banks of the Helford River. Glades of huge subtropical palms and tree ferns overarching a cascading stream travelling the length of this exotic valley to a private cove below. Coffee shop, gift shop, plant sales and childrens activities.

CADE'S WEST COUNTRY CAMPING, TOURING & MOTOR CARAVAN SITE GUIDE 1997

CORNWALL

GUNNISLAKE
TAMAR VALLEY DONKEY PARK : St. Anns Chapel, Gunnislake, Cornwall, PL18 9HW. Tel : 01822 834072. Nearest Railway Station : Gunnislake. Location : On the A390 Callington to Tavistock road, in the village of St. Anns Chapel. Open : Daily, Easter to the end of October. Weekends, November to March. Closed January. **Special Attractions:** Donkey and tame cuddly animal park. Ride the donkeys, feed and play with lambs, goats and rabbits. Acres of space to explore, adventure and toddlers playgrounds. Cafe, picnic garden and gift shop. Free parking.

HAYLE
A port and market town on the estuary of the Hayle River in St Ives Bay. The beach offers fine sands and dunes.

HELSTON
An ancient Stannary Town where locally mined Tin used to be weighed and taxed. The Cornish floral dance takes place on May 8th every year.

A plaque on a house in Wendron Street marks the birth place of Bob Fitzsimmons - The only Englishman to have held the World Heavyweight Boxing Championship. Coinagehall Street is delightful and the 18th century houses can be seen in Menage Street.

HELSTON
FLAMBARDS VILLAGE THEME PARK : Helston, Cornwall. Open : Most days Easter to the end of October 10am-5pm. Extended opening last week of July and whole of August until 7pm. **Special Attractions:** West Country's premier, all-weather attraction. Flambards Victorian Village, Britain in the Blitz and many special exhibitions. Super family rides including the Hornet rollercoaster and Canyon River log flume. Giant childrens play area, childrens rides and live entertainment. Award winning gardens.

HELSTON
HELSTON FOLK MUSEUM : Market Place, Helston, Cornwall, TR13 8TH. Tel : 01326 564027. Nearest Railway Station : Redruth. Location : In the centre of Helston, directly behind the Guildhall. Open : Monday to Saturday, 10.30am-1pm then 2pm-4.30pm. Wednesday, 10.30am-12pm only. FREE admission. **Special Attractions:** Emphasis on the former crafts and industries which flourished in and around Helston during the 19th and early 20th Centuries. Housed in the former Market House built in 1837.

HELSTON
HELSTON SPORTS CENTRE : Church Hill, Helston, Cornwall. Tel : 01326 563320. Nearest Railway Station : Redruth or Camborne. Location : On Helston Comprehensive School site. Open : Daily, ring for details. **Special Attractions:** Swimming pool, two squash courts, sunbed, vending area, sports hall. Fitness room, tennis courts, outdoor floodlit sports areas. Also Coronation Park and Boating Lake - Tel : 01326 572144. Lakeside cafe, boats, tennis, putting, childrens adventure area.

INDIAN QUEENS
GNOME WORLD OF CORNWALL : Indian Queens, Near St Columb, Cornwall, TR9 6HN. Tel : 01726 860812. Location : On the old A30. Open : All Year, 9am-7pm. **Special Attractions:** One of Cornwall's most unusual tourist attractions. Now one of the leading manufacturers of hand painted and finished concrete garden ornaments in the country. Come and meet over 150 different garden gnomes... they all have a character of their own! Nature trail to an old disused tramway cutting and tunnel. Childrens activity play area, picnic area and refreshments. Visit our Farm Shop selling real Cornish pasties, cream and other fresh produce. Gnome Shop selling gnomes and a range of Cornish crafts. Enjoyable for all the family.

ISLES OF SCILLY
ISLES OF SCILLY MUSEUM : Church Street, St. Mary's, Isles of Scilly, Cornwall, TR21 0JT. Tel : 01720 422337. Nearest Railway Station : Penzance. Location : In the centre of Hugh Town, the islands' capital. Open : Easter to October, 10am-12pm then 1.30pm-4.30pm. Also Whitsun to September, 7.30pm-9pm. **Special Attractions:** Collections of Archaeology, natural and social history and shipwrecks, all related to the islands.

LAUNCESTON
LAKESIDE GALLERY : Lezant, Launceston, Cornwall, PL15 9NW. Tel & Fax : 01579 370760. Nearest Railway Station : Plymouth. Location : Approx. 4.5 miles from Launceston, 5 miles from Callington on the A388. There is a small lake by the entrance. Open : Monday to Saturday, 10am-5pm. **Special Attractions:** Showing the work of Internationally known illustrators, Linda and Roger Garland. Including over 40 paintings from J.R.R. Tolkiens "Lord of the Rings" and "The Hobbit". Originals, limited edition prints, cards and jewellery are on sale from the gallery.

LAUNCESTON
LAUNCESTON STEAM RAILWAY : Newport, Launceston, Cornwall, PL15 8DA. Tel : 01566 775665. Nearest Railway Station : Plymouth. Location : Near the industrial estate at Newport in Launceston. Open : June to September, Sunday to Friday, 10.30am-4.30pm. April to May and October, Tuesday and Sunday only. **Special Attractions:** Narrow gauge steam railway running 2.75 miles into pleasant countryside. Tickets cover unlimited rides plus a visit to the museum and workshops. Souvenir and book shops. Buffet on site.

LISKEARD
MERLIN GLASS OF LISKEARD : Barn Street Station Road, Liskeard, Cornwall. Tel & Fax : 01579 342399. Nearest Railway Station : Liskeard. Location : 2 minutes from the town centre on the B3254. Open : 10am-5.30pm Monday to Friday, 10am-1.30pm Saturday. **Special Attractions:** Hand made glass by Liam Carey. You may watch the Glassmaker at work and see a display of many exclusive designs in the showroom.

LISKEARD
STERTS MOORLAND THEATRE : Sterts, Upton Cross, Liskeard, Cornwall, PL14 5AZ. Tel : 01579 362382/362962. Nearest Railway Station : Liskeard. Location : On the B3254 Liskeard to Launceston road, in the village of Upton Cross. Open : All Year. **Special Attractions:** Moorland open-air theatre. Professional theatre, music and dance events from June to September. Gallery, craft shop and cafe all year round.

LOOE
The twin fishing towns of East and West Looe are joined by a modern bridge spanning the Looe River. Natural amenities include a sandy beach, sea fishing and river angling. West Looe church displays a detached belltower. East Looe features quaint streets and a pillory preserved outside the 16th century Guild Hall. Looe has an interesting museum and monkey sanctuary. Looe Island lies off shore and the area has developed into a well known shark fishing area. The name is of Celtic origin and means a pool or inlet of water.

LOOE
THE MONKEY SANCTUARY : Looe, Cornwall, PL13 1NZ. Tel & Fax : 01503 262532. Nearest Railway Station : Looe. Location : 4 miles from Looe off B3253. Open : May to September, Sundays to Thursdays, 10.30am-5pm. Also Easter two weeks, including Good Friday. **Special Attractions:** First protected breeding colony of Amazon Woolly Monkeys in the world. Mother monkeys and their babies are invited to forage in the gardens with visitors.

CORNWALL

LOOE
OLD GUILDHALL MUSEUM : Higher Market Street, East Looe, Cornwall.
Nearest Railway Station : Looe. Location : Situated in the centre of the town in the main street leading to the sea front. Open : Easter Week then Whitsun to the end of September, 11.30am-4.30pm. Closed Saturdays. **Special Attractions:** Lovely 16th Century Court building with original Magistrates Bench and two cells intact. Collection consists of local domestic and Historical interest including fishing, smuggling, mining and ship models.

MEVAGISSEY
THE LOST GARDENS OF HELIGAN : Pentewan, St Austell, Cornwall, PL26 6EN. Tel : 01726 844157. Fax : 01726 843023.
Nearest Railway Station : St Austell. Location : From St Austell take the B3273 and follow brown tourism signs. Open : Daily 10am-6pm. Last tickets available 4.30pm. **Special Attractions:** Europe's largest garden restoration project - 57 acres of working Victorian gardens including:- Kitchen Garden, 5 walled gardens, Italian and Grotto Gardens, exotic fruit houses and 22 acres of sub-tropical "Jungle Garden". Tea rooms, shop and usual facilities. Free parking.

MEVAGISSEY
WORLD OF MODEL RAILWAYS : Meadow Street, Mevagissey, Cornwall. Tel : 01726 842457.
Nearest Railway Station : St Austell. Location : In the middle of the town. Open : Summer season, from 11am. **Special Attractions:** Outstanding "Snow" Scene and China Clay Exhibit. Also many miniature scenes of every day life. Model Shop.

NEWQUAY
A well known holiday resort, Newquay has a harbour, excellent sands, surfing, bathing and golf are among the local amenities. Fine cliff scenery can be enjoyed beyond Watergate Bay. It is the perfect centre for holiday makers who like to tour during the day and enjoy entertainment in the evening.

Newquay abounds in delightful walks and open spaces and has a special attraction to anglers because of the variety of fishing available. Fly fishing by the rocks, or by boat and shark fishing for those who prefer the really big stuff.

NEWQUAY
DAIRYLAND FARM WORLD : Summercourt, Newquay, Cornwall, TR8 5AA. Tel : 01872 510246. Fax : 01872 510349.
Nearest Railway Station : Newquay. Location : On the A3058 St Austell to Newquay road, 4 miles from Newquay. Open : Early April to late October and two weeks prior to Christmas. 10.30am-5pm (12pm-5pm Christmas). **Special Attractions:** Britain's premier farm attraction - quality entertainment for the whole family. Merry-go-round Milking Parlour, Heritage Centre, Nature Trail and playground. Meet friendly animals and pets, enjoy the rally-karts, assault course and trampolines. Daily events include pony rides, bottle feeding and "Pat-A-Pet". Cafe and shop, homemade Ice Cream and Cornish Clotted Cream.

NEWQUAY
THE SEA LIFE CENTRE : Towan Promenade, Newquay, Cornwall, TR7 1DU. Tel : 01637 878134. Fax : 01637 872578.
Nearest Railway Station : Newquay. Location : On the sea front (Towan Promenade) at Towan beach in the centre of Newquay. Open : Every day except Christmas Day, 10am-5pm, later in Summer holidays. **Special Attractions:** Come face to face with hundreds of exciting marine creatures, innovative displays and a spectacular underwater tunnel. New for Summer '96 only - "Danger in the Depths" - Piranhas, lionfish and more!

NEWQUAY
NEWQUAY ZOO : Trenance Park, Newquay, Cornwall, TR7 2LZ. Tel : 01637 873342. Fax : 01637 815318.
Nearest Railway Station : Newquay. Open : Easter to October, 9.30am-6pm. November to Easter, 10am-5pm. **Special Attractions:** Newquay Zoo for conservation, education and fun.

The zoo is set in delightful lakeside gardens and islands are home to many of our animals. Large open enclosures ensure that our animals live in natural surroundings. Keeper talks. Cafe, picnic areas and gift shop.

NEWQUAY
TRERICE : Near Newquay, Cornwall. Fax : 01637 879300.
Location : 3 miles south east of Newquay via the A3058 (turn right) Kestel Mill. Open : Daily 28th March to 2nd November, except Tuesday and Saturday. Every day from 28the July to the 7th September. 11am-5.30pm, last admission 5pm. Closes 5pm in October. **Special Attractions:** A small manor house, rebuilt in 1571, containing fine plaster ceilings and fireplaces, oak and walnut furniture and clocks. Lawn mower museum. Tea room in the Barn Shop.

PADSTOW
Situated on the Camel Estuary and includes an ancient harbour. Natural amenities include excellent sands and sea bathing. A curious hobby horse dance is held annually on May Day. An interesting bird garden is situated in Fentonluna Lane. The mainly decorated church contains Prideaux monuments and Prideaux Place an Elizabethan Mansion has one of the oldest deer parks to be found in Britain. Quaint old streets slope down to the harbour. Pepper Hole, Butter Hole and the narrow rock cleft of Tregudda Gorge can be seen on the coast.

PAR
MID CORNWALL GALLERIES : St Blazey Gate, Par, Cornwall, PL24 2EG. Tel : 01726 812131.
Nearest Railway Station : Par. Location : 3 miles east of St Austell on the A390 at St Blazey Gate. Open : Monday to Saturday, 10am-5pm. **Special Attractions:** We present eight or nine exhibitions a year of fine paintings, ceramics, glass, silks, woodwork, jewellery, sculpture, leather, prints, etchings and collages as well as countless other things. Some of the country's finest work is to be found here. Ample parking.

PAR
TREGREHAN GARDEN & COTTAGES : Tregrehan House, Par, Cornwall, PL24 2SJ. Tel : 01726 812438. Fax : 01726 814389.
Nearest Railway Station : Par or St. Austell. Location : On the A390 2 miles west of St. Austell. Open : Mid March to the end of June, 10.30am-5pm. **Special Attractions:** Large woodland garden created since the early 19th Century, concentrating on species from warm temperate regions. Fine glasshouse range in a walled garden. Nursery also open by appointment. Teas available. Self catering cottages.

PENDEEN
GEEVOR TIN MINE : Pendeen, Penzance, Cornwall, TR19 7EW. Tel : 01736 788662. Fax : 01736 786059.
Nearest Railway Station : Penzance. Location : 6 miles from Penzance on the A3071 or the B3306 to St. Just. Open : March to October, Sunday to Friday, 10.30am-5pm. November to February, Museum and Shop only. **Special Attractions:** Surface and Underground Tours of a Tin Mine which closed in 1990. The Surface Tours show how Tin was processed from ore to tin concentrate. Shop and cafe.

PENZANCE
A coastal Harbour Town with a chequered past - invaded by Spaniards in 1595, disturbed by Cromwell's Armies, visited by the Barbary Pirates and even bombed by German Tip and Run raiders in the last war.

Penzance never the less offers the holiday maker an abundance of pleasure with a tranquil and wonderful countryside.

The Market House dates from 1836, a Natural History Museum can be seen in Penlee Park, sub-tropical plants are grown in the Morrab Gardens, steamer and helicopter service ply between Penzance and the Isles of Scilly.

CADE'S WEST COUNTRY CAMPING, TOURING & MOTOR CARAVAN SITE GUIDE 1997   35

CORNWALL

Penzance has still retained its distinctive character as a fishing village and one of its chief interests is the busy fish market on the quay.

PENZANCE
THE ACORN THEATRE : Parade Street, Penzance, Cornwall, TR18 4BU. Tel & Fax : 01736 65520.
Nearest Railway Station : Penzance. Location : Close to the town centre. **Special Attractions:** Summer World Music Season theatre and exhibitions.

PENZANCE
LAMORNA POTTERY : Lamorna, Penzance, Cornwall, TR19 6NY. Tel : 01736 810330.
Nearest Railway Station : Penzance. Location : On B3315 3.5 miles South West of Penzance. Open : All Year, Summer seven days a week. **Special Attractions:** Gift Shop, Restaurant, Tea Gardens. Roast Sunday Lunches, Cream Teas etc. Bed and Breakfast.

PENZANCE
THE MINACK THEATRE & EXHIBITION CENTRE : Porthcurno, Penzance, Cornwall. Tel : 01736 810181. Fax : 01736 810779.
Nearest Railway Station : Penzance. Location : On the cliffs at Porthcurno, 3 miles from Lands End. Open : Exhibition Centre daily - Easter to end of October. Theatre - Summer season of plays and musicals, late May to mid September. **Special Attractions:** For programme send S.A.E.

PENZANCE
NEWLYN ART GALLERY : New Road, Newlyn, Penzance, Cornwall, TR18 5PZ. Tel : 01736 63715. Fax : 01736 331578.
Nearest Railway Station : Penzance. Open : Monday to Saturday 10am - 5pm. Closed during exhibition change overs, please telephone. **Special Attractions:** Newlyn Art Gallery plays an important role in the South West as a leading venue for contemporary art. The programme reflects current UK and International art practice and includes regular shows from locally-based artists. As an educational charity the gallery aims to promote and encourage a greater understanding of contemporary art. Gallery shop and coffee point.

PENZANCE
PENLEE HOUSE ART GALLERY & MUSEUM PENZANCE : Morrab Road, Penzance, Cornwall, TR18 4HE. Tel : 01736 63625.
Nearest Railway Station : Penzance. Location : In Penlee Park, off Morrab Road, between the town centre and promenade. Parking available at "Penlee" car park. Open : Monday to Friday 10.30am-4.30pm. Saturday 10.30am-12.30pm. Open bank Holidays. **Special Attractions:** Victorian house set in a beautiful public park housing important displays of paintings and decorative art by the Newlyn School; local history and archaeology (including computer interactive displays and a changing programme of exhibitions. Cafe, shop and full disabled access.

PENZANCE
TRINITY HOUSE NATIONAL LIGHTHOUSE CENTRE : Wharf Road, Penzance, Cornwall, TR18 4BN. Tel : 01736 60077.
Location : Beside Penzance harbour. Open : One week before Easter to October 31st, 11am-5pm daily including Sundays. **Special Attractions:** A unique collection of lighthouse artefacts including optics of many types from the largest downwards. Replica rock tower living quarters, complete with original curved furniture and a video theatre showing a brief history of the Eddystone Light.

PORTHCURNO
MUSEUM OF SUBMARINE TELEGRAPHY : Porthcurno, Nr Penzance, Cornwall. Tel & Fax : 01209 612142.
Location : Lands End road (A30), turn left to St. Buryan, follow signs to Porthcurno. Park at Cove. Open : Every Friday April to the end of October. Every Wednesday July to the end of September. Tours begin every hour on the hour at Cable Hut at the top of Porthcurno beach, or the entrance to public car park if raining. First tour starts 11am, last tour 3pm. Tour lasts about 75 minutes. Special parties at any time by prior appointment. **Special Attractions:** Cornwall's secret wartime communications centre in the underground "tunnels". Porthcurno was the largest international cable station in the world with 14 undersea cables fanning out from the beach to all parts of the Empire and Beyond. The tunnels, built to protect the system in World War II, house a unique museum of historic equipment, some of which date from the 1870's. You will see blast-proof doors, the underground power station, early telegraph systems, vintage wireless and the "regenerator" system that led to todays digital and computer technology and much more.

PORTREATH
CORNISH GOLDSMITHS : Tolgus Mill, Portreath, Cornwall, TR16 4HN. Tel : 01209 218198. Fax : 01209 219786.
Nearest Railway Station : Redruth. Open : All Year. Monday to Saturday, 9.30am-5.30pm. Sunday, 10.30am-4.30pm. **Special Attractions:** The largest selection of Gold jewellery in the West Country - Plus lots to see and do on your visit. See 1,000,000 in 5 notes, 1m Gold Bullion on display, or why not pan for Gold and see how the Goldrush began, plus lots more!!

REDRUTH
Redruth is a virile progressive town with an atmosphere compounded of industry, tradition and love of living, for Redruth always has a lively feeling about it.

William Murdock the inventor lived in this important mining town and had the first gas-lit house in the country. The area has associations with John Wesley the Methodist, and George Fox the founder of the Society of Friends. St Eunys Church dates from 1768 and a local museum of mineral specimens is of interest.

Redruth has hotels, restaurants and many varied sporting and entertainment opportunities.

REDRUTH
CARN BREA LEISURE CENTRE : Station Road, Pool, Redruth, Cornwall, TR15 3QS. Tel : Camborne 01209 714766. Fax : 01209 716225.
Nearest Railway Station : Redruth or Camborne. Location : Midway between Redruth and Camborne on A30 turn left at mini roundabout at Pool (when heading West). Open : Monday to Friday 9am-10.30pm. Saturday and Sunday 9am-5.30pm all year round. **Special Attractions:** Swimming pools, squash courts and an 8 court sports hall. Modern health and fitness suite, including "Fast-Tan" sunbeds and sauna. Free parking, cafeteria and bar. 76 metre water slide and Space Bowl. All weather athletics track and weights room.

REDRUTH
SHIRE HORSE FARM & CARRIAGE MUSEUM : Lower Cryllis Farm, Treskillard, Redruth, Cornwall. Tel : Camborne 01209 713606.
Nearest Railway Station : Camborne or Redruth. Location : Between Camborne and Redruth, 1.5 miles from Leisure Centre, 4 miles from Portreath. To find us aim for Four Lanes, Redruth. Open : 10am-6pm Easter until September. Closed Saturdays. October, Sundays and Tuesdays only. **Special Attractions:** All three heavy English breeds. Working blacksmith and wheelwright shop. Heavy English horse wagon rides. Farm walk, blacksmiths shop and farmhouse cream teas.

ST AUSTELL
St Austell provides a succession of golden beaches, quiet fishing villages, quaint harbours with all the amenities of a fair sized modern town.

China clay is the towns principal industry and was first discovered by Cookworthy in 1775. For those interested in the clay workings, there is an excellent museum at Cathew on the St Austell to Bodmin Road, with a restored clay works and has slides of the Cornish clay industry.

36 *CADE'S WEST COUNTRY CAMPING, TOURING & MOTOR CARAVAN SITE GUIDE 1997*

CORNWALL

The 13th century church carries a fine perpendicular tower, the market house of 1791, the Menagew Stone in Fore Street and the Menacuddle Holly Well are also of interest.

ST AUSTELL
AUTOMOBILIA (CORNWALL'S MOTOR MUSEUM) : The Old Mill, St Stephen, St Austell, Cornwall, PL26 7RX. Tel & Fax : 01726 823092.
Nearest Railway Station : St Austell. Location : On the A3058 on the west edge of St Stephen Village. Open : Easter, April, May and 1st October to late October, 10am-4pm, closed Saturday early and late season. June to September, 10am-6pm. Last admission 5pm. **Special Attractions:** Collection of over 50 vehicles covering period 1904 to the 1960's displayed on three floors. Exhibition of Associated Automobilia, Permanent Autojumble, audio visual display and a cafe serving light meals. Small shop selling associated models, postcards, books, etc..

ST AUSTELL
POLKYTH LEISURE CENTRE : Carlyon Road, St Austell, Cornwall. Tel : 01726 61585.
Nearest Railway Station : St Austell. Location : On the Eastern side of St Austell half a mile from railway station. Open : 9am-10pm Monday to Friday, 9am-5pm Weekends. **Special Attractions:** Swimming Pools, sports hall, squash courts, sauna, UVA sunbed, Greens Restaurant and bar, fitness area and hydrotherapy pool. Pool hoist available for disabled swimmers.

ST AUSTELL
WHEAL MARTYN CHINA CLAY HERITAGE CENTRE : Carthew, St Austell, Cornwall, PL26 8XG. Tel & Fax : 01726 850362.
Nearest Railway Station : St Austell. Location : 2 miles North of St Austell on the B3274 to Bugle. Open : Easter to October, 10am-6pm daily. **Special Attractions:** Wheal Martyn is the historic centre of one of Cornwalls most important industries. The dramatic story of the recovery of China Clay is told by an Audio Visual Show and two trails. The Nature Trail includes a visit to a spectacular working pit and the Historic Trail includes the Largest Water Wheel in Cornwall. Coffe shop and gift shop.

ST IVES
A well know resort with a harbour which is especially popular with artists. No small town in Britain has been so often painted and photographed. It is an art centre with a world wide reputation, which has grown not only from wonders of its ever changing sea and its magnificent coastline but because of artists attracted there by the special qualities of light.

It is a town rich in ancient customs, with a legendary Saint, an old fishing port, sub-tropical gardens and full amenities for the tourist.

The 15th century church carries a tower rising to almost 120 ft, and a lantern cross can be seen in the churchyard. Old houses and quaint alleys add to the interest of the town. A number of prehistoric remains exist in the neighbourhood.

ST IVES
BARBARA HEPWORTH MUSEUM & SCULPTURE GARDEN : Barnoon Hill, St Ives, Cornwall. Tel : 01736 796226. Fax : 01736 794480.
Nearest Railway Station : St Ives. Location : In old part of town, off Fore Street, near Parish Church and the harbour. Open : All year except Christmas Day, Boxing Day and Good Friday. April to September, Monday to Saturday 11am-7pm, Sunday 11am-5pm. October to March, Tuesday to Sunday 11am-5pm. **Special Attractions:** Museum is the former private house and garden of the late Dame Barbara Hepworth. 40 sculptures from 1928 to 1974 displayed both indoors and in the adjoining garden. Working studio showing tools. Photograph and writing archive.

ST IVES
PENWITH GALLERIES : Back Road West, St Ives, Cornwall, TR26 1NL. Tel : 01736 795579.
Nearest Railway Station : St Ives. Location : Near the town centre and harbour. Open : Tuesday to Saturday, 10am-1pm then 2.30pm-5pm. **Special Attractions:** Art gallery showing paintings, sculpture and ceramics. Bookshop with prints, postcards and greetings cards.

ST IVES
TATE GALLERY ST IVES : Porthmeor Beach, St Ives, Cornwall, TR26 1TG. Tel : 01736 796226. Fax : 01736 794480.
Nearest Railway Station : St Ives. Location : Situated by Porthmeor Beach. Open : April to September, Monday to Saturday 11am-7pm, Sunday 11am-5pm, Bank Holidays 11am-5pm. October to March, Tuesday to Sunday 11am-5pm. **Special Attractions:** Tate Gallery St Ives offers a unique introduction to modern art, where over 200 works can be seen in the surroundings and atmosphere which inspired them. Changing displays from the Tate Gallery's collections are complemented by a series of exhibitions and artists projects which explore the diversity of contemporary practise.

TORPOINT
MOUNT EDGCUMBE HOUSE & PARK : Cremyll, Torpoint, Cornwall, PL10 1HZ. Tel : 01752 822236.
Nearest Railway Station : Plymouth. Location : The gateway to Cornwall, on the Tamar and Plymouth Sound immediately west of Plymouth. Use the half hourly pedestrian Cremyll Ferry from Plymouth (Stonehouse) or the Torpoint vehicle ferry. **Special Attractions:** Beautiful 18th Century Park with colourful formal gardens, the Tudor house is filled with the Mount Edgcumbe family's furniture and paintings. Stunning gardens which house the National Camellia Collection, lovely trees, with follies seats and grottoes. A sublime landscape with wild fallow deer, surrounded by the sea makes this one of the most spectacular attractions in Cornwall. Restaurant and shops.

TRURO
Truro is Cornwalls only city and has an atmosphere of assurance if somewhat dignified. It was one of the first towns in Cornwall to receive a Municipal Charter in 1135. The modern Cathedral began in 1879 by J.C.Pearson and was the first Cathedral to be built in England since Wren rebuilt St Pauls. Today, Truro is the seat of Cornwall County Council.

Truro offers the holiday maker all the comforts of urban life, such as cinemas, shops, cafes, hotels, libraries, art galleries and museums.

A steamer service plys between Truro and Falmouth and the Wheal Jane Goldfields, a tin mine which came into operation in 1971 - the first to be opened in Europe for over fifty years.

TRURO
CALLESTOCK CIDER FARM : Penhallow, Truro, Cornwall, TR4 9LW. Fax : 01872 573056.
Nearest Railway Station : Truro. Location : Signposted off the A3075 Newquay-Redruth Road at Penhallow. Open : Easter to end of September, Monday to Saturday 9am-5pm. July and August 9am-8pm. Sundays 9am-6pm. **Special Attractions:** See how real farm cider, country wines, jams and preserves are made. Learn about cider making today, its history and associated trades of Coopers and Blacksmiths in our museum. Friendly farm animals and tractor and trailer rides through the orchards.

TRURO
ROYAL CORNWALL MUSEUM : River Street, Truro, Cornwall. Tel : 01872 72205.
Nearest Railway Station : Truro. Location : Close to the town centre. Open : January to December, Monday to Saturday, 10am-5pm. Closed Bank Holidays. **Special Attractions:** Eye-catching modern displays of paintings, china, silver, minerals, local history and archaeology. New extension houses changing exhibitions and a super new cafe with outdoor seating. Excellent gift shop. Full facilities for the disabled.

TRURO
ST MAWES CASTLE : St Mawes, Near Truro, Cornwall. Tel : 01326 270526.
Nearest Railway Station : Truro. Location : On the western point of the beautiful village of St Mawes. Open : Good Friday to 31st October, 10am-6pm daily. 1st November to Maundy Thursday, 10am-4pm except Monday and Tuesday. **Special Attractions:** A coastal defence fort showing Tudor military architecture at its finest in a charming setting and with a good collection of old cannons.

DEVON

DEVON

ASHBURTON
Ashburton Caravan Park, Waterleat, Ashburton, Devon, TQ13 7HU.
Tel: 652552 Std: 01364
Nearest Town/Resort Ashburton/Newton Abbot.
Directions Off A38, Ashburton Centre North Street bear right before bridge signposted Waterleat 1½ miles.
Acreage 2 **Open** Easter to September
Access Reasonable **Site** Level
Sites Available A ⊞ **Total** 35
Low Season Band B
High Season Band C
Facilities ⌂ ƒ ⊞ ♨ ſ ⊙ ⌐ ☐ ☎
⚲ ○ ☎ ☐
Nearby Facilities ſ ✓ ∪ ⁊
⇌ Newton Abbot.
In beautiful wooded valley, River Ashburn flowing through. Within Dartmoor National Park.

ASHBURTON
Landscove Camping Site, Landscove, Ashburton, Newton Abbot, Devon.
Tel: 762225 Std: 01803
Nearest Town/Resort Ashburton
Directions From A38 at Ashburton take Slipway (Peartree). Follow signs to Landscove for 2¼ miles, then left to Woolston Green.
Acreage ¼ **Open** Easter to End of Sept
Site Level
Sites Available A ⊞ **Total** 6
Low Season Band A
High Season Band A
Facilities ⚿ ⊞ ⚲ ℓ ☎ ☐
Nearby Facilities ✓ ∪ ᴩ
Quiet country site by village green. Near Dartmoor and within easy reach of the sea.

ASHBURTON
Parkers Farm Holidays, Higher Mead Farm, Ashburton, Devon, TQ13 7LJ.
Tel: 652598 Std: 01364
Fax: 654004 Std: 01364
Nearest Town/Resort Ashburton
Directions Take the A38 to Plymouth, when you see the sign 26 miles Plymouth take second left at Alston Cross marked Woodland - Denbury. The site is behind the bungalow.
Acreage 10 **Open** April to October
Access Good **Site** Level Terrace
Sites Available A ⊞ **Total** 60
Facilities ⚿ ⌂ ƒ ⊞ ♨ ſ ⊙ ⌐ ☐ ☎
⚲ ♬ ℓ ○ ☎ ♀ ♠ ⊓ ☐
Nearby Facilities ſ ✓ ⊥ ⟲ ∪ ⁊ ᴩ ⁊
⇌ Newton Abbot
A real working farm environment with goats, sheep, pigs, cows, ducks and rabbits set amidst beautiful countryside.

AXMINSTER
Andrewshayes Caravan Park, Dalwood, Axminster, Devon.
Tel: 831225 Std: 01404
Fax: **831225** Std: **01404**
Nearest Town/Resort Seaton.
Directions A35 Axminster 3 miles. Honiton 6 miles. Take 2nd. turning signpost Dalwood and Stockland. Site entrance 100yds. off A35.
Acreage 10 **Open** Easter/1 April to October
Access Good **Site** Sloping
Sites Available A ⊞ ⊟ **Total** 90
Low Season Band C
High Season Band C
Facilities ⌂ ƒ ⊞ ♨ ſ ⊙ ⌐ ☐ ☎
⚲ ○ ☎ ☓ ⊓ ♠ ⊓ ⊰ ☐
Nearby Facilities ſ ✓ ⊥ ⟲ ∪ ᴩ
⇌ Axminster.
Peaceful, clean park on a working farm, in beautiful countryside. Ideal for family holiday. Easy reach of resorts. New toilet building with family rooms and disabled room.

BARNSTAPLE
Brightlycott Farm Camping & Caravanning Site, Brightlycott Farm, Barnstaple, Devon, EX31 4JJ.
Tel: 850330 Std: 01271
Nearest Town/Resort Barnstaple.
Directions Leave Barnstaple on the A39 to Lynton and after 2 miles take a right turning.
Acreage 4 **Open** May to October
Access Good **Site** Level
Sites Available A ⊞ ⊟
Low Season Band B
High Season Band B
Facilities ☐ ⊞ ♨ ſ ⊙ ☎ ℓ
Nearby Facilities ſ ✓ ∪
⇌ Barnstaple.
Working dairy farm with panoramic views. Between beaches and Exmoor, ideal base for touring.

BERRYNARBOR
Watermouth Cove Holiday Park, Berrynarbor, Nr. Ilfracombe, North Devon, EX34 9SJ.
Tel: 862504 Std: 01271
Nearest Town/Resort Ilfracombe/Combe Martin.
Directions Leave the M5 at junction 27 and join the North Devon link road. Leave the link road at Aller Cross roundabout and follow signs for Combe Martin. Go through Combe Martin and Watermouth is 2 miles on.
Acreage 27 **Open** Easter to End October
Access Good **Site** Level
Sites Available A ⊞ ⊟ **Total** 90

Facilities ƒ ⊞ ♨ ſ ⊙ ⌐ ☐ ☎
⚲ ℓ ○ ☎ ☓ ⊓ ♠ ⊓ ⊰ ☐
Nearby Facilities ſ ✓ ⊥ ⟲ ∪ ⁊ ᴩ ⁊
⇌ Barnstaple.
Picturesque views and private sandy beach. Headland walks. Adjacent to small craft harbour.

BIDEFORD
Steart Farm Touring Park, Horns Cross, Bideford, Devon.
Tel: 431836 Std: 01237
Nearest Town/Resort Bideford
Directions From Bideford follow the A39 west (signed Bude). Pass through Fairy Cross and Horns Cross, 2 miles after Horns Cross site will be on the right. 8 miles from Bideford.
Acreage 10¼ **Open** Easter to October
Access Good **Site** Lev/Slope
Sites Available A ⊞ ⊟ **Total** 60
Low Season Band B
High Season Band B
Facilities ƒ ⊞ ♨ ſ ⊙ ⌐ ☐ ☎
ℓ ○ ☎ ⊓ ☐
Nearby Facilities
⇌ Barnstaple
Set in 17 acres overlooking Bideford Bay, 1 mile from the sea. 2¼ acre dog exercise area and daytime dog kennelling. 2 acre childrens play area.

BRATTON FLEMING
Greenacres Farm Touring Caravan Park, Bratton Fleming, Barnstaple, North Devon, EX31 4SG.
Tel: 763334 Std: 01598
Nearest Town/Resort Barnstaple.
Directions From North Devon link road (A361), turn right at Northaller roundabout (by Little Chef). Take the A399 to Blackmoor Gate, approx 10 miles. Park signed (300yds from the A399).
Acreage 4 **Open** April to October
Access Good **Site** Level
Sites Available ⊞ ⊟ **Total** 30
Low Season Band A
High Season Band B
Facilities ☐ ⌂ ƒ ⚿ ⊞ ♨ ſ ⊙ ⌐ ☐ ☎
ℓ ○ ☎ ⊓ ※ ☐
Nearby Facilities ✓ ∪
⇌ Barnstaple
Moors and coast 5 miles, towns 10 miles. Peaceful, secluded park with scenic views. Ideal for touring, walking and cycling.

BRAUNTON
Lobb Fields Caravan & Camping Park, Saunton Road, Braunton, Devon, EX33 1EB.
Tel: 812090 Std: 01271
Fax: **812090** Std: **01271**
Nearest Town/Resort Braunton

PARKERS FARM HOLIDAYS

HIGHER MEAD FARM, ASHBURTON, DEVON TQ13 7LJ.

Resident Proprietors: Roger & Rhona Parker Tel: **(01364) 652598**

A real working farm environment with goats, sheep, pigs, cows, ducks, rabbits and wild fowl. All our visitors are made especially welcome on the Farm.
• Level touring caravan & camping site • Electric hook-ups •
• Showers • Modern toilet block • Laundry • Shop on site •
Also available Holiday Cottages and Holiday Caravans.

HOW TO FIND US: Take the A38 to Plymouth, when you see the sign '26 miles Plymouth' - take the second left at Alston *marked woodland - Denbury. The Touring Site is behind the bungalow and the cottages, and caravans are further up the road. Please call at Reception.

---

38 *CADE'S WEST COUNTRY CAMPING, TOURING & MOTOR CARAVAN SITE GUIDE 1997*

HILLHEAD
HOLIDAY CAMP
BRIXHAM DEVON

This superb family run campsite is set in 20 acres of camping and playing fields with panoramic views of Mansands Bay, the English Channel and the South Devon countryside. Facing south, the playing fields overlook the whole of Torbay.

FREE
Live Entertainment
Children's Clubroom
Teenagers Disco Room
Heated Swimming Pool
Children's Pool
Hot Water

PLUS
Licensed Bar
Cafeteria
Self Service Shop
Launderette
Television Room
Amusement Arcade
Children's Playground
Electric Hook-ups

For full colour brochure, write or telephone
Hillhead Holidays (CA), Brixham, Devon. TQ5 0HH
Tel: (01803) 853204 / 842336
See editorial entry.

DEVON

Directions A361 to Braunton, turn left onto B3231. The park is 1 mile on the right.
Acreage 14 **Open** 28th March to 31st October
Access Good **Site** Level
Sites Available ▲ ⌘ ⌘ **Total** 180
Facilities ⌘ ⌘ ⌘ ⌘ ⌘ ⌘
⌘ ⌘ ⌘ ⌘ ⌘
Nearby Facilities ⌘ ⌘ ⌘ ⌘ ⌘ ⌘ ⌘
⌘ Barnstaple
Facing south with panoramic views. Quiet site with Saunton beach and golf course 1¼ miles away. Dogs on leads.

BRIXHAM

Centry Touring, Mudberry House, Centry Road, Brixham, Devon, TQ5 9EY.
Tel: 853215 Std: 01803
Nearest Town/Resort Brixham
Directions Approach on the A3022 and bear right at the first set of traffic lights. Follow signs for Berry Head Country Park past the rugby club on your left. Park entrance is on the left just past Centry Road in ½ mile.
Acreage 1¼ **Open** Easter to October
Access Good **Site** Level
Sites Available ▲ ⌘ ⌘ **Total** 30
Low Season Band B
High Season Band B
Facilities ⌘ ⌘ ⌘ ⌘ ⌘ ⌘ ⌘
Nearby Facilities ⌘ ⌘ ⌘ ⌘ ⌘ ⌘
⌘ Paignton
Scenic views. Ideal for cliff walking, touring and all water sports.

BRIXHAM

Galmpton Touring Park, Greenway Road, Galmpton, Brixham, Devon, TQ5 0EP.
Tel: 842066 Std: 01803
Nearest Town/Resort Brixham
Directions Signposted right off the A379 Brixham road ¼ mile past the end of the A380 Torbay ring road.
Acreage 10 **Open** Easter to September
Access Good **Site** Lev/Slope
Sites Available ▲ ⌘ ⌘ **Total** 120
Facilities ⌘ ⌘ ⌘ ⌘ ⌘ ⌘ ⌘
⌘ ⌘ ⌘ ⌘ ⌘
Nearby Facilities ⌘ ⌘ ⌘ ⌘
⌘ Paignton
Stunning River Dart views, in a central Torbay location.

BRIXHAM

Hillhead Camp, Brixham, Devon, TQ5 0HH.
Tel: Off842336 Site853204 Std: 01803
Nearest Town/Resort Brixham.
Directions Follow A380 towards Brixham. Turn on to A379 (Dartmouth) at Prouts Garage (avoiding Brixham town centre). After B.P. Garage Take left fork (Kingswear Lower Ferry) camp 300 yds
Acreage 22½ **Open** Easter to October
Site Lev/Slope
Sites Available ▲ ⌘ ⌘ **Total** 330
Facilities ⌘ ⌘ ⌘ ⌘ ⌘ ⌘ ⌘
⌘ ⌘ ⌘ ⌘ ⌘ ⌘ ⌘
Nearby Facilities ⌘ ⌘ ⌘ ⌘ ⌘ ⌘ ⌘
⌘ Paignton.
Near beaches and river overlooking sea. Panoramic views of sea and country.

BRIXHAM

Upton Manor Farm Camping Site, St. Mary's Road, Brixham, Devon, TQ5 9QH.
Tel: 882384 Std: 01803
Fax: 882384 Std: 01803
Nearest Town/Resort Brixham.
Directions At traffic lights on the outskirts of Brixham follow Upton Manor Farm signposting to camp.

Acreage 10 **Open** End of May to 2nd Week Sept
Site Level
Sites Available ▲ ⌘ **Total** 250
Low Season Band B
High Season Band C
Facilities ⌘ ⌘ ⌘ ⌘ ⌘ ⌘ ⌘
⌘ ⌘ ⌘ ⌘ ⌘ ⌘
Nearby Facilities ⌘ ⌘ ⌘ ⌘ ⌘ ⌘
⌘ Paignton.
Amid countryside, close to town and beach.

BUCKFAST

Churchill Farm, Buckfastleigh, Devon, TQ11 0EZ.
Tel: 642844 Std: 01364
Nearest Town/Resort Buckfastleigh/Buckfast.
Directions Exit A38 at Dartbridge, follow signs for Buckfast Abbey, proceed up hill to crossroads. Turn left into no-through road towards church. Farm entrance is opposite the church 1½ miles from the A38.
Acreage 2 **Open** All Year
Access Good **Site** Level
Sites Available ▲ ⌘ ⌘ **Total** 25
Low Season Band B
High Season Band B
Facilities ⌘ ⌘ ⌘ ⌘ ⌘ ⌘
Nearby Facilities ⌘ ⌘ ⌘ ⌘ ⌘ ⌘
⌘ Totnes.
Stunning views of Dartmoor and Buckfast Abbey, the latter being within easy walking distance as are the Steam Railway, Butterfly Farm, Otter Sanctuary and local inns. Seaside resort 10 miles.

BUCKFASTLEIGH

Beara Farm Camping Site, Colston Road, Buckfastleigh, Devon.
Tel: Buckfastleigh 642234 Std: 01364.
Nearest Town/Resort Buckfastleigh.
Directions Coming from Exeter take first left after passing South Devon Steam Railway and Butterfly Centre at Buckfastleigh, signpost marked Beara, fork right at next turning then 1 mile to site, signposted on roadside and junctions.
Acreage 3¼ **Open** All Year
Access Good **Site** Level
Sites Available ▲ ⌘ ⌘ **Total** 45
Low Season Band A
High Season Band A
Facilities ⌘ ⌘ ⌘ ⌘ ⌘ ⌘
Nearby Facilities ⌘ ⌘
⌘ Totnes.
Quiet, select, sheltered site adjoining River Dart. Within easy reach of sea and moors and 1½ miles southeast of Buckfastleigh.

CHUDLEIGH

Finlake Holiday Park, Chudleigh, Nr. Newton Abbot, Devon, TQ13 0EJ.
Tel: 853833 Std: 01626
Fax: 854031 Std: 01626
Nearest Town/Resort Newton Abbot/Teignmouth
Directions Take the A38 towards Plymouth, exit at Chudleigh Knighton slip road. Turn right and Finlake is ½ mile on the right.
Acreage 130 **Open** All Year
Access Good **Site** Level
Sites Available ▲ ⌘ ⌘ **Total** 450
Low Season Band B
High Season Band C
Facilities ⌘ ⌘ ⌘ ⌘ ⌘ ⌘ ⌘
⌘ ⌘ ⌘ ⌘ ⌘ ⌘ ⌘
Nearby Facilities ⌘ ⌘ ⌘ ⌘ ⌘
⌘ Newton Abbot
Situated in a wooded park, some pitches overlooking a lake.

CHUDLEIGH

Holmans Wood Tourist Park, Harcombe Cross, Chudleigh, Devon, TQ13 0DZ.
Tel: 853785 Std: 01626
Nearest Town/Resort Chudleigh.
Directions From Exeter take the A38 Towards Plymouth. Go past the racecourse and after 1 mile take the B3344 for Chudleigh. We are on the left at the end of the sliproad.
Acreage 11 **Open** March to December
Access Good **Site** Level
Sites Available ▲ ⌘ ⌘ **Total** 144
Low Season Band B
High Season Band B
Facilities ⌘ ⌘ ⌘ ⌘ ⌘ ⌘ ⌘
⌘ ⌘ ⌘ ⌘
Nearby Facilities ⌘ ⌘ ⌘ ⌘ ⌘ ⌘ ⌘
⌘ Newton Abbot.
Ideal touring for Dartmoor, Haldon Forest, Exeter and Torbay.

CLOVELLY

Dyke Green Farm, Clovelly, Bideford, Devon, EX39 5RU.
Tel: 431279 Std: 01237
Nearest Town/Resort Clovelly.
Directions On roundabout at Clovelly Cross.
Acreage 3½ **Open** March to October
Access Good **Site** Level
Sites Available ▲ ⌘ ⌘
Facilities ⌘ ⌘ ⌘ ⌘ ⌘ ⌘
⌘ ⌘ ⌘ ⌘ ⌘
Nearby Facilities ⌘ ⌘ ⌘ ⌘ ⌘
⌘ Barnstaple.
Clovelly village and beach. Sheltered bays, ideal walks etc.

COMBE MARTIN

Newberry Farm, Combe Martin, North Devon, EX34 0AT.
Tel: 882333/882334 Std: 01271
Nearest Town/Resort Combe Martin/Ilfracombe.
Directions Leave the M5 at junction 27 and take the A361 to Aller Cross Roundabout. A399 to Combe Martin.
Acreage 6 **Open** Easter to October
Access Good **Site** Level
Sites Available ▲ ⌘ ⌘ **Total** 100
Low Season Band B
High Season Band B
Facilities ⌘ ⌘ ⌘ ⌘ ⌘ ⌘ ⌘ ⌘
Nearby Facilities ⌘ ⌘ ⌘ ⌘
⌘ Barnstaple.
On the edge of Exmoor National Park. 5 minute walk to the beach and shops.

COMBE MARTIN

Stowford Farm Meadows, Combe Martin, Devon, EX34 0PW.
Tel: 882476 Std: 01271
Fax: **883053** Std: **01271**
Nearest Town/Resort Combe Martin.
Directions Situated on the A3123 Combe Martin/Woollacombe Road at Berry Down.
Acreage 140 **Open** Easter to October
Access Good **Site** Lev/Slope
Sites Available ▲ ⌘ ⌘ **Total** 570
Low Season Band A
High Season Band C
Facilities ⌘ ⌘ ⌘ ⌘ ⌘ ⌘ ⌘
⌘ ⌘ ⌘ ⌘ ⌘ ⌘ ⌘
Nearby Facilities ⌘ ⌘ ⌘
⌘ Barnstaple.
Set in 450 acres of beautiful countryside. Ideal touring site at the heart of North Devon. Renowned for our extensive range of facilities at excellent value.

40 CADE'S WEST COUNTRY CAMPING, TOURING & MOTOR CARAVAN SITE GUIDE 1997

FINLAKE HOLIDAY PARK FOR
TOURING CARAVANS & CAMPING

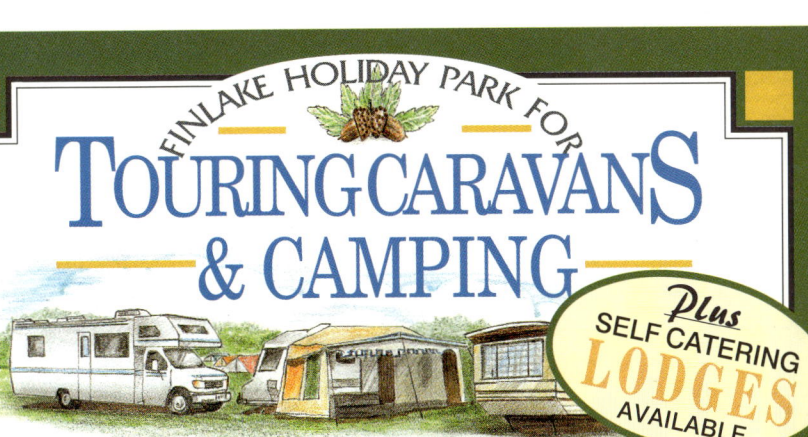

Plus SELF CATERING LODGES AVAILABLE

If you're looking for a quality Caravan or Camping Park, full of activities, situated in Glorious Devon, then FINLAKE is the ideal choice for you. Fabulous pitches with acres of space to suit everyone. Whether you have a Caravan, Tent or Motorhome, we have the perfect location suitable for both rallies and any special event.

FINLAKE offers everything in leisure and sporting activities for everyone. With superb Lodges and Cottages for hire, open all year round, including Christmas and New Year, that's what makes **FINLAKE** unique.
Contact us now by ringing **(01626) 853833** or fax **(01626) 854031** for further information and a brochure.

TELEPHONE (01626) 853833

Finlake
HOLIDAY PARK
CHUDLEIGH · DEVON

Book now to avoid disappointment.

Finlake Holiday Park
Chudleigh, Devon TQ13 0EJ. Telephone (01626) 853833 Fax (01626) 854031

DEVON

CREDITON

Yeatheridge Farm Caravan Park, East Worlington, Crediton, Devon, EX17 4TN.
Tel: Tiverton 860330 Std: 01884
Fax: **860330** Std: **01884**
Nearest Town/Resort Witheridge.
Directions Leave M5 at junction 27 take A361 to 1st roundabout A396 to mini-roundabout and follow A396 for approx 400yds turn right 200 yds turn left onto B3137 (Old A373) to Witheridge approx 10 miles. Turn left onto B3042 site 3¾ miles on left. Do not enter East Worlington, unsuitable for caravans. From Exeter take A377 to Barnstaple, turn right at Eggesford Station onto B3042, through Chawliegh Village the park is about 4 miles on right.
Acreage 9 **Open** Easter to October
Access Good **Site** Lev/Slope
Sites Available ▲ ♣ ☎ **Total** 85
Low Season Band B
High Season Band C
Facilities ∮ ▥ ♨ ₧ ⊙ ⊣ ⎌ ◘ ☎
♒ ⍰ ♥ ♠ ♣ ♥ ♠ ♬ ⊱ ⊛ ▣
Nearby Facilities ↾ ✔ ∪ ℛ
≢ Eggesford.
Indoor heated swimming pools, coarse fishing lakes all free on site. Scenic view from landscape park, working farm with animals. Fishing and horse riding on site.

CROYDE BAY

Bay View Farm Holidays, Bay View Farm, Croyde, Devon, EX33 1PN.
Tel: 890501 Std: 01271
Nearest Town/Resort Croyde
Directions At Braunton on A361 turn west on main road B3231 towards Croyde Village
Acreage 10 **Open** Easter to September
Site Level
Sites Available ▲ ♣ ☎

CROYDE BAY

Low Season Band B
High Season Band C
Facilities ⎎ ∮ ▥ ♨ ₧ ⊙ ◘ ☎
♒ ⍰ ♥ ♠ ♬ ▣
Nearby Facilities ↾ ✔ ⊥ ≾ ∪ ℛ ℛ ✤
≢ Barnstaple.
Near beach, 5 mins walking. Scenic views, ideal touring, booking advisable peak season. S.A.E. for information.

CROYDE BAY

Putsborough Sands Caravan Park, Orchard House, Putsborough, Georgeham, North Devon, EX33 1LB.
Tel: 890230 Std: 01271 Fax: 890980 Std: 01271
Nearest Town/Resort Ilfracombe/Barnstaple.
Directions Directions given upon booking.
Open April to October
Access Poor **Site** Sloping
Sites Available ♣ **Total** 21
Low Season Band C
High Season Band C
Facilities ∮ ♨ ▥ ♨ ₧ ⊙ ⊣ ⎌ ☎
♒ ⍰ ♥ ⊛ ▣
Nearby Facilities ↾ ✔ ⊥ ≾ ∪ ℛ ℛ ✤
≢ Barnstaple.
Adjacent to Gold Award Winning beach, top beach in North Devon. Unique position. Booking is essential, please contact Park Management.

CULLOMPTON

Forest Glade Holiday Park, Cullompton, Devon, EX15 2DT.
Tel: 841381 Std: 01404 Fax: 841593 Std: 01404
Nearest Town/Resort Cullompton.
Directions A373 Cullompton/Honiton, turn for Sheldon at Keepers Cottage Inn, 2½ miles east of Cullompton. Touring caravans via Dunkeswell Road only.

Acreage 10 **Open** Mid March to End October
Access See Directions **Site** Level
Sites Available ▲ ♣ ☎ **Total** 80
Facilities ⎇ ⎎ ∮ ▥ ♨ ₧ ⊙ ⊣ ⎌ ◘ ☎
♒ ⍰ ♥ ♠ ♣ ♥ ♠ ♬ ⊱ ⊛ ▣
Nearby Facilities ↾ ✔ ∪ ℛ
≢ Honiton/Tiverton Parkway
Central for southwest twixt coast and moors. Large flat sheltered camping pitches. Caravans for hire. Free heated indoor swimming pool and Paddling pool, riding, gliding and Tennis.

DARTMOUTH

Leonards Cove, Stoke Fleming, Dartmouth, Devon, TQ6 0NR.
Tel: 770206 Std: 01803
Fax: **770206** Std: **01803**
Nearest Town/Resort Dartmouth
Directions On A379 2 miles Dartmouth Within village of Stoke Fleming.
Acreage 1 **Open** March to October
Access Good **Site** Lev/Slope
Sites Available ▲ ♣ ☎ **Total** 50
Low Season Band A
High Season Band A
Facilities ⎇ ∮ ▥ ♨ ₧ ⊙ ⎌
⍰ ♒ ⍰ ♥ ♠ ✕ ⋈ ▣
Nearby Facilities ↾ ✔ ⊥ ≾ ∪ ℛ ℛ
≢ Totnes
On clifftop spectacular views, ½ mile famous Blackpool Sands.

DARTMOUTH

Little Cotton Caravan Park, Darmouth, South Devon.
Tel: 832558 Std: 01803
Nearest Town/Resort Dartmouth
Directions Leave the A38 ta Buckfastleigh, A384 to Totnes, from Totnes to Halwell on the A381. At Halwell take the A3122

STOWFORD FARM MEADOWS
Touring Caravan and Camping Park
COMBE MARTIN : ILFRACOMBE : DEVON : EX34 0PW : TEL: 01271 882476

AA
BEST U.K. SITES
CARAVAN LIFE 1995 STOWFORD FARM MEADOWS 6th PLACE
CAMPING AND CARAVANNING GUIDE ATTRACTIVE ENVIRONMENT 1994-5
GRADED HOLIDAY PARKS ✓✓✓✓ BRITISH
PRACTICAL CARAVAN PARKS REGIONAL WINNER

Situated on a farm in Beautiful Devon Countryside, only a short distance from the coast with it's superb choice of 5 local beaches; and on the fringe of Exmoor National Park.

Great Facilities · 3 Bars · Shop · Take-Away & Carvery · Indoor Swimming Pool · Pitch & Putt · Snooker · Games Room · Crazy Golf · Nature Walks · Horse Riding · Undercover Mini Zoo · Large Play Area · Kiddies Kars ·
Phone for a FREE Colour Brochure

---

42   CADE'S WEST COUNTRY CAMPING, TOURING & MOTOR CARAVAN SITE GUIDE 1997

DEVON

YEATHERIDGE FARM AA ►
(Touring) Caravan Park
E. WORLINGTON, CREDITON, DEVON EX17 4TN
Telephone Tiverton 860 330 STD (01884)
RAC. AA ►►► OFF THE A377 AND B3137 (OLD A373)
WHY ARE WE DIFFERENT? We are a small Central Park with panoramic views on a genuine working farm with plenty of animals to see and some to touch! We also offer peace and space with freedom to roam the farm its woodland walks, coarse fishing lake, indoor heated swimming with 200ft waterflume ride, TV lounge, children's play area, hot and cold showers, wash cubicles - ALL FREE. A welcome for dogs. Other amenities include horse riding from the park, electric hook-up points, campers dish washing, laundry room, shop with frozen foods, fresh dairy products, ice pack service * Summer parking in our storage area to save towing * Ideally situated for touring coast, Exmoor and Dartmoor. Golf and Tennis locally.
ALSO: 2 CARAVANS TO LET - PROPRIETORS/OWNERS-GEOFFREY & ELIZABETH HOSEGOOD
W.C.T.B. Member   WRITE, PHONE OR FAX FOR FREE COLOUR BROCHURE   RAC

Dartmouth road, park is on the right at entrance to town.
Acreage 7½ **Open** 15 March to October
Access Good   **Site** Lev/Slope
Sites Available ▲ ⊕ ⊟ **Total** 95
Facilities &c. ...
Ƨ 匣 ⊙ ☎ 🄻
Nearby Facilities Γ ✓ ⊥ ↘ ⁊ ♬
⇌ Totnes
Scenic views, ideal touring. Park and ride service in the next field. Luxurious new toilet and shower facilities.

DARTMOUTH
Woodland Leisure Park, Blackawton, Totnes, Devon, TQ9 7DQ.
Tel: 712598 Std: 01803
Fax: 712680 Std: 01803
Nearest Town/Resort Dartmouth
Directions 4 miles from Dartmouth on main road A3122 (formally B3207).
Acreage 8 **Open** 15th March to 15th Nov
Access Good   **Site** Level
Sites Available ▲ ⊕ ⊟ **Total** 80
Low Season Band B
High Season Band C
Facilities &c. ...
Ƨ 匣 ⊙ ☎ 🄻
Nearby Facilities Γ ✓ ⊥ U
⇌ Totnes
Free entrance to extensive leisure park attached, 75 acres of entertainment. Animal farm and twelve play zones. Paddling pool. 34,000sq ft of indoor play.

DAWLISH
Cofton Country Holiday Park, Devon
Swan Holidays, Starcross, Nr Dawlish, Devon, EX6 8RP.
Tel: 890141 Std: 01626
Nearest Town/Resort Dawlish Warren.
Directions On A379 Exeter - Dawlish road ½ mile after fishing village at Cockwood.
Acreage 16 **Open** Easter to October
Access Good   **Site** Level
Sites Available ▲ ⊕ ⊟ **Total** 450
Low Season Band A
High Season Band B
Facilities &c. ...
Ƨ 匣 ⊙ ☎ 🄻
Nearby Facilities Γ ✓ ⊥ ↘ ⁊ ♬
⇌ Dawlish.
In beautiful rural countryside close to sandy Dawlish Warren beach Clean and tidy family run park. Superb complex and swimming pool, Swan pub with family lounge and snack bar. Ideal centre to discover Devon. Excellent Quality grading and ETB Rose Award Holiday Park. See our advert on back cover.

DAWLISH
Golden Sands Holiday Park, Week Lane, Dawlish, South Devon, EX7 0LZ.
Tel: 863099 Std: 01626
Nearest Town/Resort Dawlish.
Directions From M5 junction 30 take the A379 Dawlish, through Starcross. After 2 miles Week Lane is the second left past filling station.
Acreage 2¼ **Open** Easter to October
Access Good   **Site** Level
Sites Available ⊕ ⊟ **Total** 60
Low Season Band B
High Season Band C
Facilities &c. ...
Ƨ 匣 ⊙ ☎ 🄻
Nearby Facilities Γ ✓ ⊥ ↘ U ⁊ ♬
⇌ Dawlish
Family run for family fun! Small touring park, ½ mile from Dawlish Warren beach with free nightly, family entertainment in the licensed club. Unique indoor/outdoor swimming pool.

COFTON COUNTRY HOLIDAY PARK
NR. DAWLISH • SOUTH DEVON
Family-owned park in beautiful countryside. Touring & Camping. Heated swimming pool complex. 'Swan' Pub & Family lounges. Coarse fishing lakes. Excellent facilities and amenities.
(See advertisement on back cover.)

DEVON *Swan* HOLIDAYS   *The firm family favourite*   **01626 890111**

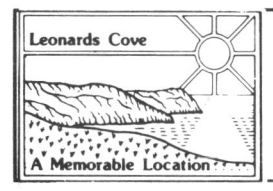

Leonards Cove

Cliff top caravanning and camping in peaceful setting designated an area of outstanding natural beauty. Magnificent unrestricted sea views. Situated within the heart of delightful coastal village, walking distance of famous Blackpool sands. Two miles River Dart and Dartmouth.
Tel. or Fax: Stoke Fleming (01803) 770206 or write to:
Enid Longrigg
Leonard's Cove, Stoke Fleming, Dartmouth, South Devon TQ6 0NR.
A Memorable Location

Try the taste of Peppermint Park

The Caravanners' Holiday Treat

FREE Family Entertainment

NEW STYLE Club & Bar

Just under ½ mile from Dawlish Warren's famous stretch of golden sands, you'll find Peppermint Park Touring and Camping Park. Nestled away from the road in pleasant sheltered grassland. Individually marked pitches on level terraces for touring caravans and tents – offering the best of greenery, scenery and seaside holiday fun. Telephone now for our FREE brochure.

Peppermint Park · Warren Road
Dawlish Warren · South Devon EX7 0PQ

- Heated swimming pool and water chute
- Children's play area
- Well-stocked shop
- Launderette
- Free hot water and showers
- Electric hook-ups
- Modern toilet facilities
- Holiday homes at Peppermint Paddocks

☎ **01626 863436** *or* **01626 862211**

Ask for extension 3

DEVON

DAWLISH
Lady's Mile Touring Caravan & Camping Park, Dawlish, Devon, EX7 0LX.
Tel: Dawlish 863411 Std: 01626.
Nearest Town/Resort Dawlish.
Directions On A379 road 1 mile Exeter side of Dawlish.
Acreage 16 **Open** March to October
Access Good **Site** Level
Sites Available A ♛ ⚐ **Total** 486
Low Season Band A
High Season Band B
Facilities ...
Nearby Facilities ...
⚐ Dawlish.
Family run popular park in green Devon countryside. Ideal touring centre. Short walk to Dawlish Warren beach. 100 foot water slide. Excellent Quality Grading - see our colour advertisement. New 9 hole golf course, bar and indoor swimming pool on site.

DAWLISH
Leadstone Camping, Warren Road, Dawlish, Devon, EX7 0NG.
Tel: 864411/872239 Std: 01626
Fax: **873833** Std: **01626**
Nearest Town/Resort Dawlish.
Directions Leave the M5 at junction 30 and take signposted road A379 to Dawlish. As you approach Dawlish, turn left on brow of hill, signposted Dawlish Warren. Our site is ½ mile on right.
Acreage 7 **Open** 20th June to 6th September
Access Good **Site** Lev/Slope
Sites Available A ♛ ⚐ **Total** 160
Facilities ...
Nearby Facilities ...

⚐ Dawlish Warren.
Rolling grassland in a natural secluded bowl within ½ mile of sandy 2 mile Dawlish Warren Beach and nature reserve. Ideally situated for discovering Devon. E.T.B. Graded "Very Good".

DAWLISH WARREN
Peppermint Park, Warren Road, Dawlish Warren, Devon, EX7 0PQ.
Tel: 863436/86221 Std: 01626
Nearest Town/Resort Dawlish
Directions Leave M5 at Exeter and follow A379 signposted to Dawlish then Dawlish Warren.
Acreage 16 **Open** Easter to September
Access Good **Site** Lev/Slope
Sites Available A ♛ ⚐ **Total** 300
Low Season Band A
High Season Band B
Facilities ...
Nearby Facilities ...
⚐ Dawlish Warren.
Closest touring park to Dawlish Warren beach (600 metres). Family run for families and couples. Graded ETB Excellent and AA 4 Pennants.

DOLTON
Dolton Caravan Park, The Square, Dolton, Winkleigh, Devon, EX19 8QF.
Tel: 804536 Std: 01805
Nearest Town/Resort Great Torrington
Directions From the B3220 turn at the Beacon Garage signposted Dolton. Go into the village and turn right at the Union Inn, the site is at the rear of Royal Oak Inn.
Acreage 2¼ **Open** Mid March to October
Access Good **Site** Level
Sites Available A ♛ ⚐ **Total** 25
Low Season Band B

High Season Band B
Facilities ...
Nearby Facilities ...
Scenic views. Ideal for touring Exmoor and Dartmoor. Walking on the Tarka Trail.

EXETER
Haldon Lodge Caravan & Camping Park, Kennford, Nr. Exeter, Devon, EX6 7YG.
Tel: 832312 Std: 01392
Nearest Town/Resort Exeter
Directions 4¼ miles South of Exeter, ½ mile from the end of M5 turn off A38 at Kennford Services. Follow signs for Haldon Lodge turning left through Kennford Village past the Post Office. Proceed to Motorway bridge turning left to Dunchideock, 1 mile to site.
Open All Year
Access Good **Site** Lev/Slope
Sites Available A ♛ ⚐
Low Season Band A
High Season Band B
Facilities ...
Nearby Facilities ...
⚐ Exeter
Peaceful family site with beautiful forest scenery, nature walks, fishing lakes, riding holidays and barbeques. Excellent touring centre. Sea and Exeter 15 minutes.

EXETER
Kennford International Caravan Park, Exeter, Devon, EX6 7YN.
Tel: 833046 Std: 01392
Nearest Town/Resort Exeter.
Directions ½ mile from end of M5 on A38. 4 miles south of Exeter.
Acreage 8 **Open** All Year
Access Good **Site** Level
Sites Available A ♛ ⚐ **Total** 120

GOLDEN Sands
Family Run for Family Fun

DAWLISH SOUTH DEVON
Only ½ mile from sandy Dawlish Warren Beach.

- Entertainment Centre, Licensed Club and Bar
- FREE entertainment for all the family – kids welcome
- Heated Indoor/Outdoor Pool
- Choice of Holiday Caravans, Chalets and Apartments
- Touring Park for Caravans and Motorhomes

Golden Sands Holiday Park, Dawlish, Devon EX7 0LZ
01626 863099

'OUTSTANDING LEISURE FACILITIES'

DEVON

A Great little Site
7 Acres of rolling grassland in a natural secluded bowl Est'd 1974

LISTED SITE

Friendly, uncommercialised and quiet is how Ian and Jean Bulpin describe their site now in its 24th year. Situated within 1/2 mile of Dawlish Warren's golden sands and dunes, it remains one of the few smaller coastal sites not to have fallen into the hands of building developers - so don't miss this little gem which will prove an ideal base from which to 'Day-Tour' Devon. Plenty of level pitches for tents and motorcaravans. One night 'Stop Overs' welcomed.

★ Electric Hook-Ups ★ Toilets ★ Showers ★ Children's Adventure Playground ★ Launderette ★

Write or phone for our full colour brochure
WARREN ROAD, DAWLISH, SOUTH DEVON, EX7 0NG
Telephone Site Office (Late June/early Sept): 01626 864411 or at other times 01626 872239 Fax. 01626 873833

Leadstone Camping
Always Improving Never Changing

RAC Selected Site **Hedley Wood Caravan & Camping Park** **AA ▶**
Bridgerule, Holsworthy, Devon EX22 7ED Tel & Fax 01288 381404

16 acre woodland family run site with outstanding views, where you can enjoy a totally relaxing holiday with a ' laid back' atmosphere, sheltered & open camping areas. Just 10 minutes drive from the beaches, golf coarses, riding stables & shops. **On site Facilities include**: Children's adventure areas, Bar's, Clubroom's, Shop, Laundry, Meals & all amenities. Free Hot showers & water. Nice dogs/pets are welcome. Daily kennelling facility Dog walks/Nature trail. Clay pigeon shoot. Static caravans for hire, caravan storage available. Open All Year.

HALDON LODGE FARM
CARAVAN & CAMPING SITE
KENNFORD, Nr. EXETER
20 minutes from sea, Dawlish, Teignmouth and Torbay

Enjoy a family farm holiday set in glorious rural Devon, this private Caravan Camping Park offers beautiful forest scenery, peace, seclusion and personal service. Many activities are offered: 2 coarse fishing lakes, forest riding/trekking for children and experienced riders, woodland walks, weekly barbecue, Country & Western evening plus Hayride to a friendly country inn with Sounds of the Sixties. Excellent facilities: hook-ups, showers, toilets, launderette, hairdryers, adventure play area, picnic tables and farm shop. The site offers children the delights of farm animals, also freedom and safety for all the family. Pets accepted. Personal welcome given by David & Betty Salter.

Open all year. For Brochure Tel: 832312 STD 01392. *4½ miles South of Exeter off A38 at Kennford Services. Follow signs Haldon Lodge from Anchor Inn, turning left down through village 1¼ miles to site.*

SPECIAL FAMILY SITE FEE

OS Ref. SX782897

CLIFFORD BRIDGE Park

SEE ENTRY UNDER "MORETONHAMPSTEAD"

A small family run picturesque country estate within the Dartmoor National Park, surrounded by woodland and bordered by the River Teign. An area of outstanding natural beauty - the Teign Gorge is noted for its superb view points and magnificent woodland trails. **Pitches for tents (40) and touring caravans (24). Three holiday caravans for hire.** HEATED SWIMMING POOL. Small shop by farmhouse. Fly - fishing. Golf at nearby Moretonhamstead.

AA 3 Pennant   **RAC Appointed**

Write or phone for colour brochure: Nr. Drewsteignton, Devon EX6 6QE Tel: (01647) 24226

KENNFORD INTERNATIONAL CARAVAN PARK
EXETER DEVON EX6 7YN Tel: (01392) 833046

Jan and Paul Harper welcome you to their 4 Pennant park which provides an exceptionally comfortable base from which to explore Exeter, Dartmoor and the South Devon resorts of Exmouth, Dawlish and Torquay. The information Room is well stocked and our staff are always happy to help visitors plan their days. For parents with young children, we have provided pitches overlooking the grassy Adventure Playground whilst our other visitors can enjoy the privacy of individually hedged pitches. The pine panelled facilities with free hot showers are kept immaculately clean and are placed centrally in both sections of the Park - no long treks through wet grass for our customers! After a day touring or at the beach, you can return to a quiet drink on the patio, in the Bar or in the Family Lounge, play a game of Pool or enjoy a meal from our Food Bar/Take-a-way. If you prefer to cook, we have a well stocked Shop with an Off Licence. Each evening in the main season we have a log fire in the covered stone fireplace-a focal point on the park and a nice place to sit around at the end of the day! We shall be delighted to send you our full colour brochure.

INTERNATIONAL CARAVAN PARK

at the centre of the Big K

Advance bookings welcome   AA Four Pennant Rating

---

46   *CADE'S WEST COUNTRY CAMPING, TOURING & MOTOR CARAVAN SITE GUIDE 1997*

LADY'S MILE

With the NEW 'Jewel of the Mile' Indoor Pool & Bar

Whatever the Weather!

- Licensed Shop
- Electric Hook-ups
- Adventure Fort & Play Area
- Families & Rallies welcome
- Restaurant & Takeaway
- 9-hole Golf Course
- Games room/Pool room
- Luxury Self-Catering Flats

EXCEPTIONAL VALUE!

- *TWO* Swimming Pools
- *TWO* Waterslides
- "The Mile" family bar
- *TWO* Launderettes
- Free hot water & showers

AA AWARD FOR EXCELLENCE, SPORTS AND RECREATIONAL FACILITIES 1996

Send for our FREE colour brochure:
Mrs W. C. Jeffery Lady's Mile Touring & Camping Park, Freepost Dawlish, South Devon EX7 9YZ

TEL: (01626) 863411   FAX: (01626) 888689

DEVON

Low Season Band C
High Season Band C
Facilities ⊞ ƒ ⓒ ♿ ⌐ ⊙ ┘ ▲ ⊡ ☎
✠ ☉ ● ✕ ♥ ♠ ⊞ ✹ ⊡
Nearby Facilities Γ ✓ ⊥ ↘ ∪ ⊅ ℛ
⌻ Exeter.
Excellent touring centre in beautiful rural setting with easy access to main roads. Individually hedged sites. Children's adventure playground. Family lounge and bar with takeaway and the very popular log fire cabin. Holiday bungalows and caravans to rent.

EXMOUTH
Castle Brake, Castle Lane, Woodbury, Near Exeter, Devon, EX5 1HA.
Tel: 232431 Std: 01395
Nearest Town/Resort Exmouth
Directions M5 junction 30 take the A3052 to Halfway Inn. Turn right onto the B3180, after 2 miles turn right to Woodbury. The park is 500yds on the right.
Acreage 10 Open March to October
Access Good   Site Level
Sites Available ⛺ ⊞ ⊟ Total 42
Low Season Band A
High Season Band C
Facilities ⊞ ƒ ⓒ ♿ ⌐ ⊙ ┘ ▲ ⊡ ☎
☉ ● ✕ ♥ ♠ ⊞ ⊡
Nearby Facilities Γ ✓ ⊥ ↘ ∪ ℛ
⌻ Exmouth
Beautiful views of the River Exe. Exmouth beach 4 miles. Good touring centre for East Devon and beyond.

EXMOUTH
Devon Cliffs Holiday Centre, Sandy Bay, Exmouth, Devon, EX8 5BT.
Tel: 223000 Std: 01395
Fax: 223111 Std: 01395

Nearest Town/Resort Exmouth
Directions Turn off the M5 at exit 30 and take the A376 for Exmouth. At Exmouth follow the signs to Sandy Bay.
Acreage 10 Open Easter to November
Access Good   Site Lev/Slope
Sites Available ⛺ ⊞ ⊟ Total 195
Facilities ♿ ƒ ⓒ ⌐ ⊙ ┘ ▲ ⊡ ☎
☉ ● ✕ ♥ ⊞ ♠ ⊞ ✹ ⊞ ⊡
Nearby Facilities Γ ✓ ⊥ ∪
⌻ Exmouth
Overlooking the beautiful Sandy Bay, with access to a private beach.

EXMOUTH
Webbers Farm Caravan Park, Castle Lane, Woodbury, Exeter, Devon.
Tel: 232276 Std: 01395
Fax: 233389 Std: 01395
Nearest Town/Resort Exmouth
Directions Leave the M5 junction 30 (Exeter Services) and follow the A376 Exmouth road. At the second roundabout take the B3179 (Budleigh Salterton/Woodbury). From the village centre follow the International signs.
Acreage 8 Open Easter to September
Access Good   Site Lev/Slope
Sites Available ⛺ ⊞ ⊟ Total 100
Low Season Band B
High Season Band C
Facilities ♿ ƒ ⓒ ♿ ⌐ ⊙ ┘ ▲ ⊡ ☎
☉ ⓘ ☉ ● ⊞ ⊡
Nearby Facilities Γ ✓ ⊥ ↘ ∪ ℛ
⌻ Exmouth
Outstanding view over the River Exe towards Dartmoor. 4 miles from the sea, quiet popular site. Van storage available.

HAWKCHURCH
Hunters Moon Touring Park, Hawkchurch, Axminster, Devon, EX13 5UL.
Tel: 678402 Std: 01297
Nearest Town/Resort Lyme Regis
Directions From Axminster take A35 towards Dorchester for 3 miles. At main crossroads take left B3165 towards Crewkerne. Follow for 2¼ miles turn left to Hunters Moon.
Acreage 8 Open 15th Mar to 31st Oct
Access Good   Site Level
Sites Available ⛺ ⊞ ⊟ Total 179
Low Season Band B
High Season Band C
Facilities ƒ ⓒ ♿ ⌐ ⊙ ┘ ▲ ⊡ ☎
☉ ● ✕ ♥ ⊞ ♠ ⊞ ✹ ⊡
Nearby Facilities Γ ✓ ⊥ ∪ ⊅ ℛ
⌻ Axminster.
All weather bowling greens, super views over Axe Valley.

HOLSWORTHY
Hedley Wood Caravan & Camping Park, Bridgerule, Near Bude, Holsworthy, Devon, EX22 7ED.
Tel: 381404 Std: 01288
Nearest Town/Resort Bude
Directions Travel west on A3072 from Holsworthy for 5¼ miles, turn left on B3254 for 2¼ miles turn right, site entrance 500 yards on right (signposted).
Acreage 8 Open All Year
Access Good   Site Lev/Slope
Sites Available ⛺ ⊞ ⊟ Total 120
Low Season Band B
High Season Band C
Facilities ⊞ ♿ ƒ ⓒ ♿ ⌐ ⊙ ┘ ▲ ⊡ ☎
☉ ● ✕ ♥ ⊞ ♠ ⊞ ⊡
Nearby Facilities Γ ✓ ↘ ∪ ℛ ϟ
16 acre woodland site. Pets welcome. Daily

MULLACOTT X
CARAVAN PARK
Touring sites & Camping

Pub & Restaurant
Foodstore, Launderette, Showers, Childrens Play Area.

A family owned Park situated between Ilfracombe and Woolacombe with views over the coast to the sea.

For Brochure write to: Dept. C,
Mullacott Cross Caravan Park,
Ilfracombe, Devon, EX34 8NB
or phone (01271) 862212 or 862200

Dogs allowed under strict control.
We also offer top quality caravan accommodation.

---

48   *CADE'S WEST COUNTRY CAMPING, TOURING & MOTOR CARAVAN SITE GUIDE 1997*

DEVON

kennelling facility and dog walk. Static and touring vans for hire and caravan storage available. Clay pigeon shooting. Nature trail.

HOLSWORTHY
Newbuildings, Brandis Corner, Holsworthy, Devon, EX22 7YQ
Tel: 221305 Std: 01409
Nearest Town/Resort Holsworthy/Bude
Directions Where the A3079 from Okehampton meets the A3072 Hatherliegh to Holsworthy Road. Newbuildings is at this Cross i.e Dunsland Cross.
Open All Year
Access Good **Site** Level
Sites Available A ⊕ ⊕
Low Season Band A
High Season Band A
Facilities ƒ ⌂ ⌐ ☎ SƎ I£ ⊞ ⍓ ⊞
Nearby Facilities ⌐ ✓ ⊥ ⊁ U ⌐ ⁊ ⌃
⇌ Exeter
Small family farm camping holiday within easy reach of beaches, Dartmoor, Exmoor etc.

HOLSWORTHY
Noteworthy, Bude Main Road, Holsworthy, Devon.
Tel: Holsworthy 253731 Std: 01409
Nearest Town/Resort Holsworthy/Bude.
Directions 2½ miles west of Holsworthy on A3072.
Acreage 5 **Open** All year
Access Good **Site** Level
Sites Available A ⊕ ⊕
Low Season Band A
High Season Band A
Facilities ƒ ⌂ ⌐ ☎ ⊞
Nearby Facilities ⌐ ✓ ⊁ U ⌐
⇌ Exeter.
Views, 6 miles Cornish coast. Rural site.

ILFRACOMBE
Big Meadow Touring Caravan & Camping Park, Watermouth, Ilfracombe, Devon. EX34 9SJ
Tel: 862282 Std: 01271
Nearest Town/Resort Ilfracombe
Directions Situated on the A399 coastal road approximately 2 miles from Ilfracombe, opposite Watermouth Castle Tourist Attraction.
Acreage 9 **Open** Easter to 31 October
Access Good **Site** Level
Sites Available A ⊕ ⊕ **Total** 125
Facilities ƒ ⌂ ⌐ ☎ ⌐ ⊙ ⌑ ⊞ ⊞
SƎ I£ ⊚ ⌂ ⌂ ⊞ ⊗ ⊞
Nearby Facilities ⌐ ✓ ⊥ ⊁ U ⌐ ⁊ ⌃
⇌ Barnstaple
Near Watermouth Harbour, sheltered family site with stream running through.

ILFRACOMBE
Hele Valley Holiday Park, Hele Bay, Ilfracombe, North Devon, EX34 9RD.
Tel: 862460 Std: 01271
Nearest Town/Resort Ilfracombe.
Directions Take A399 to Ilfracombe turn at signpost Hele village, to bottom of lane, take righthand turning into Holiday Park.
Acreage 4 **Open** Easter to End October
Access Good **Site** Level
Sites Available A ⊕ ⊕ **Total** 50
Facilities ⊞ ƒ ⌂ ⌐ ☎ ⌐ ⊙ ⌑ ⊞ ⊞
SƎ ⊚ ⌂ ⊞ ⊞
Nearby Facilities ⌐ ✓ ⊥ ⊁ U ⌐
⇌ Barnstaple.
Only camping park in Ilfracombe. Beach only a few minutes walk. Tranquil, secluded valley. Alongside stream, scenic views.

ILFRACOMBE
Little Meadow Camp Site, Watermouth, Ilfracombe, Devon. EX34 9SJ
Tel: 862222 Std: 01271
Nearest Town/Resort Ilfracombe
Directions On A399 between Ilfracombe and Combe Martin.
Acreage 5 **Open** Whitsun to September
Access Good **Site** Terraced
Sites Available A ⊕ ⊕ **Total** 50
Facilities ƒ ⌂ ⊞ ⌐ ☎ ⊞
⊞ I£ ⊞ ⊞ ⊞
Nearby Facilities ⌐ ✓ ⊥ ⊁ U ⌐
⇌ Barnstaple
Quiet and peaceful and the best view in Devon.

ILFRACOMBE
Mill Park Touring Site, Berrynarbor, Nr. Ilfracombe. Devon, EX34 9SH.
Tel: 882647 Std: 01271
Nearest Town/Resort Ilfracombe.
Directions Situated on the A399 coast road between Combe Martin and Ilfracombe near Watermouth Castle. Take the turning opposite the Sawmills Inn signposted to Berrynarbor.
Acreage 30 **Open** 15th March to 15th Nov
Access Good **Site** Level
Sites Available A ⊕ ⊕ **Total** 165
Low Season Band B
High Season Band C
Facilities ƒ ⌂ ⌐ ☎ ⌐ ⊙ ⌑ ⊞ ⊞
SƎ ⊚ ⊞ ⌂ ⊞ ⊞ ⊞
Nearby Facilities ⌐ ✓ ⊥ ⊁ U ⌐ ⁊ ⌃
⇌ Barnstaple
Well sheltered site with woodland walks. Coarse fishing lake. Well stocked shop, take away food, off licence, laundry, etc..

ILFRACOMBE
Mullacott Cross Caravan Park, Mullacott Cross, Ilfracombe, Devon, EX34 8NB.
Tel: 862212/862200 Std: 01271
Fax: 862979 Std: 01271
Nearest Town/Resort Ilfracombe
Directions On A361 1½ miles south of Ilfracombe.
Acreage 5 **Open** Easter to Mid Oct
Access Good **Site** Lev/Slope
Sites Available A ⊕ ⊕ **Total** 110
Low Season Band B
High Season Band C
Facilities ⊞ ƒ ⌂ ⌐ ☎ ⌐ ⊙ ⌑ ⊞ ⊞
SƎ ⊚ ⊞ ✕ ⊞ ⊞
Nearby Facilities ⌐ ✓ ⊥ U ⌐
⇌ Barnstaple
Excellent centre for touring north Devon.

ILFRACOMBE
Napps Caravan Site, Napps, Old Coast Road, Berrynarbor, Ilfracombe, North Devon.
Tel: 882557 Std: 01271
Fax: 882557 Std: 01271
Nearest Town/Resort Ilfracombe.
Directions On A399, 1¼ miles west of Combe Martin, turn right onto Old Coast Road (signposted). Site 400yds along Old Coast Road.
Acreage 11 **Open** March to November
Access Good **Site** Level
Sites Available A ⊕ ⊕ **Total** 250
Low Season Band A
High Season Band B
Facilities ƒ ⌂ ⊞ ⌐ ☎ ⌐ ⊙ ⌑ ⊞ ⊞
SƎ ⊚ ⊞ ✕ ⊞ ⊞ ⊞ ⊞
Nearby Facilities ⌐ ✓ ⊥ ⊁ U
⇌ Barnstaple.
Probably the most beautiful coastal setting you will see. Beach 200yds. Popular family site with woodland and coastal walks.

tennis on site. Summer parking and Winter storage available.

ILFRACOMBE
Sandaway Beach Holiday Park, John Fowler Holidays, Combe Martin, Ilfracombe, Devon.
Tel: 883155 Std: 01271
Nearest Town/Resort Ilfracombe
Directions ½ mile from Combe Martin towards Ilfracombe.
Open March to October
Access Good **Site** Level
Sites Available A ⊕ ⊕ **Total** 25
Low Season Band B
High Season Band C
Facilities ⊞ ƒ ⌂ ⌐ ☎ ⌐ ⊙ ⌑ ⊞ ⊞
SƎ ⊚ ⊞ ✕ ⊞ ⊞ ⊞ ⊞
Nearby Facilities ⌐ ✓ ⊥ ⊁ U ⌐ ⁊ ⌃
⇌ Barnstaple
Breathtaking sea views and our own private beach.

IVYBRIDGE
Cheston Caravan & Camping Park, Folly Cross, Wrangaton Road, South Brent, Devon, TQ10 9HF.
Tel: 72586 Std: 01364
Nearest Town/Resort Ivybridge.
Directions From Exeter, after by-passing South Brent, turn left at Wrangaton Cross slip road then right A38. From Plymouth take South Brent (Woodpecker) turn, at end of slip road turn right, go under A38 and rejoin A38 and follow directions from Exeter.
Acreage 1¼ **Open** 15th March to 15th Jan
Access Good **Site** Level
Sites Available A ⊕ ⊕ **Total** 23
Low Season Band B
High Season Band B
Facilities ⊞ ƒ ⌂ ⌐ ☎ ⌐ ⊙ ⌑ ⊞ ⊞
SƎ I£ ⊚ ⌂ ⌂ ⊞
Nearby Facilities ⌐ ✓ ⊥ ⊁ U ⌐ ⁊
Set in beautiful Dartmoor. Perfect for touring, walking and bird watching. Nearest beach 9 miles. Pets welcome. Easy access from A38.

IVYBRIDGE
Whiteoaks Caravan & Camp Site, Davids Lane, Filham, Ivybridge, Devon, PL21 0DW.
Tel: 892340 Std: 01752
Nearest Town/Resort Ivybridge
Directions Turn off the A38 (Exeter to Plymouth road) at signpost for Ermington and Modbury onto the B3213 (Ivybridge). In about 2 miles turn left at Daveys X. Site is on the right in 100yds.
Acreage 1 **Open** 15th March to 15th November
Access Good **Site** Level
Sites Available A ⊕ ⊕ **Total** 24
Low Season Band B
High Season Band B
Facilities ⊞ ƒ ⌂ ⌐ ☎ ⌐ ⊙ ⌑ ⊞ I£
Nearby Facilities ⌐ ✓ ⊥ U ⌐
⇌ Ivybridge
On the edge of Dartmoor, at the start/finish of "Two Moors Way". Ideal for walkers.

KINGSBRIDGE
Island Lodge, Stumpy Post Cross, Kingsbridge, Devon, TQ7 4BL.
Tel: Kingsbridge 852956 Std: 01548
Nearest Town/Resort Kingsbridge.
Directions Travelling from Totnes to Kingsbridge on A381 turn right onto A381 at Stumpy Post Cross then turn left into lane leading to site entrance. Approx 200yds from Stumpy Post Cross.
Acreage 3 **Open** Easter to October

CADE'S WEST COUNTRY CAMPING, TOURING & MOTOR CARAVAN SITE GUIDE 1997   **49**

DEVON

Access Good **Site** Level
Sites Available ▲ ⚲ ⚙ **Total** 35
Facilities ⚿ ƒ ▥ ♨ ┌ ☉ ⌐ ◨ ☎
▧ ♨ ☐ ▣
Nearby Facilities ┌ ✔ ⊥ ⤴ ∪ ⇒ ♪
⇌ Totnes.
Sea glimpses, very central for all beaches and villages in the South Hams area. Suitable for families with young children. Small friendly site with new purpose built facilities. Proprietor - Mrs Kay Parker.

KINGSBRIDGE
Karrageen Caravan and Camping Site, Bolberry, Malborough, Kingsbridge, Devon, TQ7 3EN.
Tel: 561230 Std: 01548
Fax: 560192 Std: **01548**
Nearest Town/Resort Salcombe
Directions Take the A381 Kingsbridge to Salcombe road, turn sharp right into Malborough Village. In 0.6 miles turn right (signposted Bolberry), after 0.9 miles the site is on the right and reception is at the house on the left.
Acreage 7½ **Open** Easter to 1st Oct
Access Good **Site** Lev/slope
Sites Available ▲ ⚲ ⚙ **Total** 75
Low Season Band B
High Season Band C
Facilities ƒ ▥ ♨ ┌ ☉ ⌐ ◨ ☎
▧ ▧ ☐ ▣
Nearby Facilities ┌ ✔ ⊥ ⤴ ∪ ⇒ ♪
⇌ Totnes/Plymouth
Nearest and best park to Hope Cove, beaches 1 mile away. Situated in beautiful, scenic countryside and surrounded by superb National Trust coastline. Parents and baby room. Superb cliff top walking. A site with a view.

KINGSBRIDGE
Mounts Farm Touring Park, The Mounts, Nr. East Allington, Kingsbridge, South Devon, TQ9 7QJ.
Tel: 521591 Std: 01548
Nearest Town/Resort Kingsbridge.
Directions On the A381 Totnes/Kingsbridge. 3 miles north of Kingsbridge. Entrance from A381 - DO NOT go to East Allington Village.
Acreage 5 **Open** April to October
Access Good **Site** Level
Sites Available ▲ ⚲ ⚙ **Total** 27
Low Season Band B
High Season Band B
Facilities ▤ ƒ ▥ ♨ ┌ ☉ ⌐ ◨ ☎
▧ ▣ ☐
Nearby Facilities ┌ ✔ ⤴ ∪ ♪
⇌ Totnes.
In an area of outstanding natural beauty. Ideal for touring all South Devon.

KINGSBRIDGE
Parkland, Sorley Green Cross, Kingsbridge, Devon, TQ7 4AF.
Tel: 852723 Std: 01548.
Nearest Town/Resort Kingsbridge.
Directions From A381 turn onto B3194 continue to Sorley Green Cross go straight ahead site 100yds on left.
Acreage 3 **Open** All Year
Access Good **Site** Level
Sites Available ▲ ⚲ ⚙
Low Season Band B
High Season Band B
Facilities ƒ ▥ ♨ ┌ ☉ ⌐ ◨ ☎
▧ ☐ ♨ ▣ ▣
Nearby Facilities ┌ ✔ ⊥ ⤴ ∪ ⇒ ♪
Central for beaches and touring (river 1 mile). Well sheltered. One pitch with hard standing, hook-up water point and T.V. point (Super Pitch).

MODBURY
Pennymoor Caravan Park, Modbury, Devon.
Tel: 830269/830542 Std: 01548
Nearest Town/Resort Kingsbridge/Salcombe.
Directions Approx 30 miles West of Exeter, leave A38 at Wrangaton Cross. Turn left, then straight across at next crossroads and continue for approx 4 miles. Pass petrol garage on left, then take second left, site is 1 mile on the right.
Acreage 6 **Open** 15 March to 15 November
Access Good **Site** Level
Sites Available ▲ ⚲ ⚙ **Total** 155
Facilities ƒ ⚿ ▥ ♨ ┌ ☉ ⌐ ◨ ☎
▧ ☐ ♨ ▣ ※ ▣
Nearby Facilities ┌ ✔ ⊥ ⤴ ∪ ♪
⇌ Plymouth.
Peaceful rural site. Ideal touring base. Central to towns, moors, beaches. Bigbury-on-Sea only 5 miles. Holiday caravans to let. New superb toilet/shower block. Free colour brochure.

MORETONHAMPSTEAD
Clifford Bridge Park, Nr. Drewsteignton, Exeter, Devon, EX6 6QE.
Tel: 24226 Std: 01647
Nearest Town/Resort Moretonhampstead.
Directions Leave A30 Dual carriage way to Cheriton Bishop, left at Old Thatch 2 miles to crossroads turn right, 1 mile to Clifford.
Acreage 8 **Open** Easter to September.
Access Good **Site** Level
Sites Available ▲ ⚲ ⚙ **Total** 65
Low Season Band B
High Season Band C
Facilities ƒ ▥ ♨ ┌ ☉ ⌐ ◨ ☎
▧ ☐ ♨ ▣ ⤴ ※ ▣
Nearby Facilities ┌ ✔ ∪

⇌ Exeter.
The upper Teign valley and Gorge is noted for it's outstanding natural beauty, superb viewpoints and magnificent woodland tracks, it's location in Dartmoor National Park makes it a unique touring centre for walking fishing, riding and golf.

MORTEHOE
Easewell Farm Holiday Park, Mortehoe, Nr. Woolacombe, North Devon, EX34 7EH.
Tel: 870225 Std: 01271
Nearest Town/Resort Woolacombe.
Directions
Acreage 17 **Open** Easter to September
Access Good **Site** Lev/Slope
Sites Available ▲ ⚲ ⚙ **Total** 200
Low Season Band B
High Season Band C
Facilities ƒ ▥ ♨ ┌ ☉ ⌐ ◨ ☎
▧ ▧ ☐ ♨ ⤴ ▣ ▣ ☐ ▣
Nearby Facilities ┌ ✔ ∪ ♪
⇌ Barnstaple.
Near beach with scenic views. Golf on site.

MORTEHOE
Warcombe Farm Camping Park, Mortehoe, Near Woolacombe, North Devon, EX34 7EJ.
Tel: 870690 Std: **01271**.
Fax: **871070** Std: **01271**
Nearest Town/Resort Barnstaple.
Directions Turn left off the A361, Barnstaple to Ilfracombe road at Mullacott Cross roundabout signposted Woolacombe. After 2 miles turn right towards Mortehoe. Site is first on the right in less than a mile.
Acreage 19 **Open** 15th Mar to 31st October
Access Good **Site** Level
Sites Available ▲ ⚲ ⚙ **Total** 145
Low Season Band B
High Season Band B
Facilities ƒ ▥ ♨ ┌ ☉ ⌐ ◨ ☎
▧ ☐ ♨ ▣ ▣
Nearby Facilities ┌ ✔ ⊥ ⤴ ∪ ♪
⇌ Barnstaple
1¼ miles to Woolacombe beach. Panoramic sea views. Well drained level land, family run. Fishing on site.

NEWTON ABBOT
Compass Caravans Touring Park, Higher Brocks Plantation, Teigngrace, Newton Abbot, Devon.
Tel: 832792 Std: 01626
Nearest Town/Resort Newton Abbot.
Directions Alongside the A38 (westbound) at junction with Teigngrace turn off.
Acreage 3 **Open** 15 March to 15 January
Access Good **Site** Level
Sites Available ⚲ ⚙ **Total** 36

Pennymoor Camping & Caravan Site

A.A. 3
Pennant Site

Modbury, South Devon PL21 0SB
Proprietors:
R.A. & M.D. Blackler

Tel: Modbury: (01548)
830269 & 830542

Immaculately maintained, well - drained peaceful, rural site, with panoramic views.
Central to beaches, moors and towns. Luxury caravans for hire, with all services, colour TV.
Ideal for touring caravans and tents. New super, luxury toilet/shower block - fully tiled
walls and floors. Laundry room, Dishwashing room, separate room for disabled.
Free hot water in handbasins, and showers.
Shop. Gas. Public telephone. Children's equipped playground.
Write or phone for free colour brochure

---

50   *CADE'S WEST COUNTRY CAMPING, TOURING & MOTOR CARAVAN SITE GUIDE 1997*

DEVON

Moor View Touring Park

Peaceful rural setting, superb views, in the heart of Souh Hams countryside yet quick and easy access to Moors, Beaches, Plymouth, Torbay and South Devon attractions. Individual large level pitches some hard standing. Member countryside discovery. Spotless modern facilities, free forceful hot showers. Takeaway, bread baked daily, games room, TV room, All dogs welcome, Exercise area.

AA

GRADED EXCELLENT

For Free brochure phone

01548 821485

Near California Cross · Modbury · South Devon · PL21 0SG

Facilities ! ▥ ▲ ┌ ⊙ ⌐ ♥ ⑫ ◉ ▤ ▯
Nearby Facilities ┌ ✎ ⊥ ↘ ∪ ♃ ♇ ≭
⇌ Newton Abbot
Ideal touring, only 3 miles from Dartmoor.

NEWTON ABBOT
Dornafield, Two Mile Oak, Newton Abbott, Devon, TQ12 6DD.
Tel: 812732 Std: 01803
Nearest Town/Resort Newton Abbot.
Directions Take the A381 (Newton Abbott to Totnes), in 2 miles at Two Mile Oak Inn turn right. In ½ mile turn first left, site is 200 yards on the right.
Acreage 30 **Open** 20th March to October
Access Good **Site** Level
Sites Available ▲ ♛ ♛ **Total** 135
Low Season Band B
High Season Band C
Facilities ∆ ! ▥ ▣ ▲ ┌ ⊙ ⌐ ▬ ◻ ♥
▧ ◎ ◉ ▥ ▲ ▯ ▯
Nearby Facilities ┌ ✎ ⊥ ↘ ∪ ♇ ≭
⇌ Newton Abbot.
Beautiful 14th Century farmhouse location with superb facilities to suit discerning caravanners and campers.

NEWTON ABBOT
Lemonford Caravan Park, Bickington, Newton Abbot, Devon, TQ12 6JR.
Tel: 821242 Std: 01626
Nearest Town/Resort Ashburton
Directions From Exeter along A38 take A382 turnoff, on roundabout take 3rd exit and follow site signs to Bickington. From Plymouth take A383 turnoff, follow road for ¼ mile and turn left into site.
Acreage 7 **Open** Easter to October
Access Good **Site** Level
Sites Available ▲ ♛ ♛ **Total** 90
Low Season Band B
High Season Band C
Facilities ! ▥ ▲ ┌ ⊙ ⌐ ▬ ◻ ♥
▧ ◎ ◉ ▯ ▯
Nearby Facilities ┌ ✎ ⊥ ↘ ∪ ♇ ≭
⇌ Newton Abbot
In a beautiful setting and scrupulously clean. Close to Torbay and the Dartmoor National Park.

NEWTON ABBOT
Stover International Caravan Park, Lower Staple Hill, Newton Abbot, Devon, TQ12 6JD.
Tel: 821446 Std: 01626
Nearest Town/Resort Newton Abbot.
Directions A38 to junction of A382, turn towards Newton Abbot and in 600 yards turn right at island signed Trago Mills. Site on left before you reach Trago Mills entrance.
Acreage 18 **Open** Easter to Oct

Access Good **Site** Lev/Slope
Sites Available ▲ ♛ ♛ **Total** 200
Facilities ∆ ! ╱ ▥ ▲ ┌ ⊙ ⌐ ▬ ◻ ♥
▧ ▮ ◎ ◉ ▲ ✗ ♀ ▥ ♠ ∧ ≳ ▯
Nearby Facilities ┌ ✎ ∪ ♇ ≭
On edge of Dartmoor National Park, 8 miles from many beaches, ideal touring base. 18 hole golf course immediately adjoining. Some hard standings. Course fishing adjoining. A.A., R.A.C., A.D.A.C. and A.N.W.B. recommended. FREE indoor heated swimming pool. Luxury 6 berth log cabins for Hire.

NEWTON ABBOT
Ware Barton Caravan Site, Ware Barton, Kingsteignton, Newton Abbot, Devon TQ12 3QQ.
Tel: Newton Abbot 54025 Std:
Nearest Town/Resort Teignmouth
Directions On A381 Teignmouth to Newton Abbot road.
Acreage 2 **Open** Easter to October
Access Good **Site** Lev/Slope
Sites Available ▲ ♛ ♛ **Total** 50
Low Season Band A
High Season Band A
Facilities ▥ ▲ ┌ ⊙ ⌐ ▬ ◉ ▯
Nearby Facilities ✎ ⊥ ↘ ∪ ♃ ♇
⇌ Newton Abbot
Very central, near sea and moors.

OKEHAMPTON
'Yertiz' Caravan and Camping Site, Exeter Road, Okehampton, Devon, EX20 1QF.
Tel: 52281 Std: 01837
Nearest Town/Resort Okehampton.
Directions From Exeter on A30 take the B3260 signed Okehampton, site on left 50 yards past 'Moorcroft', look for sign on bank.
Acreage ½ **Open** All Year
Access Good **Site** Level
Sites Available ▲ ♛ ♛ **Total** 30
Low Season Band A
High Season Band A
Facilities ∆ ! ▥ ▲ ┌ ⊙ ⌐ ▬ ◻ ♥
▧ ◎ ◉ ▥ ▯
Nearby Facilities ┌ ✎ ∪ ♇ ≭
On the edge of Dartmoor, 30 miles from North and South coasts. Ideal touring centre, good for walking on Dartmoor.

OKEHAMPTON
Bridestowe Caravan Park, Bridestowe, Nr. Okehampton, Devon.
Tel: 861261 Std: 01837
Nearest Town/Resort Bude
Directions Leave M5 for A30 to Okehampton 3 miles west of Okehampton

turn off A30 to Bridestowe village, follow camping signs to site.
Open March to December
Access Good **Site** Level
Sites Available ▲ ♛ ♛ **Total** 53
Low Season Band B
High Season Band B
Facilities ▥ ! ▥ ▲ ┌ ⊙ ⌐ ▬ ◻ ♥
▧ ▮ ◎ ◉ ◉ ▯
Nearby Facilities ┌ ✎ ∪
Dartmoor National Park 2 miles, ideal for walking, horse riding and fishing and touring Devon and Cornwall. Within easy reach of coastal resorts.

OKEHAMPTON
Bundu Camping & Caravan Park, Sourton Down, Okehampton, Devon, EX20 4HT.
Tel: 861611 Std: 01837
Nearest Town/Resort Okehampton.
Directions Slip road off the A30 dual carriageway to the A386 Tavistock/Sourton. Turn left then left again after 100yds, site is at the top of the road on the right.
Acreage 4 **Open** March to November
Access Good **Site** Level
Sites Available ▲ ♛ ♛ **Total** 38
Low Season Band B
High Season Band B
Facilities ! ▥ ▲ ┌ ⊙ ⌐ ◻ ♥ ⑫ ◉ ☸ ▯
Nearby Facilities ┌ ✎ ∪
⇌ Okehampton
Situated on Dartmoor, ideal for walking. Centrally based for touring Devon and Cornwall.

OKEHAMPTON
Culverhayes Camping Park, Sampford Courtenay, Nr Okehampton, Devon, EX20 2TG.
Tel: 82431 Std: 01837
Nearest Town/Resort Okehampton.
Directions From M5 junction 31 take the A30, at first roundabout turn left and follow yellow holiday route signs. Sampford Courtenay on A3072, in Sampford Courtenay go over mini roundabout, campsite is 300yds on the right, steep hill.
Acreage 3¼ **Open** Mid March to End October
Access Good **Site** Lev/Slope
Sites Available ▲ ♛ ♛ **Total** 25
Low Season Band B
High Season Band B
Facilities ▣ ! ▥ ▲ ┌ ⊙ ⌐ ▬ ♥
⑫ ◉ ◎ ▯
Nearby Facilities ┌ ✎ ∪ ♇
⇌ Exeter
Ideal site to explore Devon and North Cornwall. Views of Dartmoor. Cycle routes and walks. Fishing on site.

CADE'S WEST COUNTRY CAMPING, TOURING & MOTOR CARAVAN SITE GUIDE 1997   51

DEVON

OKEHAMPTON
Dartmoor View Caravan Park, Whiddon Down, Okehampton, Devon, EX20 2QL.
Tel: 231545 Std: 01647
Fax: **231654** Std: **01647**
Nearest Town/Resort Okehampton.
Directions Take the A30 from Exeter (17 miles), turn left at Whiddon Down roundabout, park is ½ mile on the right.
Acreage 5 **Open** March to 9th November
Access Good   **Site** Level
Sites Available 🛖 🚐 🚙 **Total** 75
Low Season Band B
High Season Band C
Facilities ƒ 🎱 ♿ ⌂ ⌇ ⌒ 🏪 ▭ ☕
⚛ ⚿ ⊙ 🛒 ✗ 🍴 🎮 🎣 ⟲ ✳ 🅿
Nearby Facilities ┌ ⁄ ∪ ℛ ✈
✈ Exeter.
Excellent facilities, close to Dartmoor National Park. Letterboxing centre. Ideal for touring.

OKEHAMPTON
Moorcroft Leisure Park, Exeter Road, Okehampton, Devon, EX20 1QF.
Tel: 55116 Std: 01837
Fax: **55116** Std: **01837**
Nearest Town/Resort Okehampton
Directions ½ mile from Okehampton, A30 (Exeter to Cornwall) ½ mile.
Open All Year
Access Good   **Site** Level
Sites Available 🛖 🚐 🚙 **Total** 35
Low Season Band B
High Season Band B
Facilities ▣ ♿ ƒ ✳ 🎱 ♿ ⌂ ⌇ ⌒ 🏪 ▭ ☕
⚿ ⊙ ⟲ 🅿
Nearby Facilities ⁄ ∪ ✈
✈ Exeter
Scenic views, ideal for touring.

PAIGNTON
Beverley Park Holiday Centre, Goodrington Road, Paignton, Devon.
Tel: Churston 843887 Std: 01803
Fax: **845427** Std: **01803**
Nearest Town/Resort Paignton.
Directions 2 miles south of Paignton (ring road) A3022. Turn left into Goodrington Road.
Acreage 9½ **Open** Easter to October
Access Good   **Site** Level
Sites Available 🛖 🚐 🚙 **Total** 194
Low Season Band B
High Season Band C
Facilities ▣ ƒ 🎱 ♿ ⌂ ⌇ ⌒ 🏪 ▭ ☕
⚛ ⚿ ⊙ 🛒 ✗ 🍴 🎣 ⟲ ✳ 🅿
Nearby Facilities ┌ ⁄ ⊥ ✳ ∪ ✈
✈ Paignton.
Views across Torbay. Indoor heated swimming pool, tennis court. Sauna.

PAIGNTON
Byslades Camping and Touring Park, Totnes Road, Paignton, Devon, TQ4 7PY.
Tel: 555072 Std: 01803.
Nearest Town/Resort Paignton.
Directions 2¼ miles west of Paignton on the A385
Acreage 23 **Open** April to October
Access Good   **Site** Level
Sites Available 🛖 🚐 🚙 **Total** 150
Low Season Band B
High Season Band C
Facilities ▣ ♿ ƒ ✳ 🎱 ♿ ⌂ ⌇ ⌒ 🏪 ▭ ☕
⚛ ⊙ 🛒 ✗ 🍴 🎣 ⟲ ✳ 🅿
Nearby Facilities ┌ ⁄ ⊥ ✳ ∪ ✳
✈ Paignton
The site is overlooking a beautiful valley and is centrally situated to visit all parts of Devon. Tennis on site.

PAIGNTON
Grange Court Holiday Centre, Grange Road, Goodrington, Paignton, Devon, TQ4 7JP.
Tel: 558010 Std: 01803
Nearest Town/Resort Paignton
Directions From junc 31 of M5, travel south for approx 20 miles on A380 to junction with A385. Continue south on A380 (Paignton Ring Road) for 1 mile, turn left into Goodrington Road by Esso Filling Station. After ¾ mile turn left into Grange Road and follow signs to park.
Acreage 20 **Open** Mid-Feb to Mid-Jan
Access Good   **Site** Sloping
Sites Available 🚐 🚙 **Total** 157
Low Season Band C
High Season Band C
Facilities ƒ 🎱 ♿ ⌂ ⌇ ⌒ 🏪 ▭ ☕
⚛ ⊙ 🛒 ✗ 🍴 🎮 🎣 ⟲ ✳ 🅿 ✳
Nearby Facilities ┌ ⁄ ⊥ ✳ ∪ ✳
✈ Paignton
Panoramic views over Torbay, close to Goodrington beach. New indoor pool complex opened in 1996.

PAIGNTON
Higher Well Farm Holiday Park, Stoke Gabriel, Totnes, Devon, TQ9 6RN.
Tel: 782289 Std: 01803
Nearest Town/Resort Paignton.
Directions From Paignton take A385 towards Totnes, turn off left at Parkers Arms Hotel. Go 1½ miles then turn left again, site is 200 yards down road.
Acreage 8 **Open** Easter to October
Access Good   **Site** Lev/Slope
Sites Available 🛖 🚐 🚙
Low Season Band B
High Season Band B
Facilities ƒ ⚔ 🎱 ♿ ⌂ ⌇ ⌒ ⚛ 🏪 ▭ ☕ ⚿ ⊙ 🅿 🅿

AA Listed as one of Britain's Best Parks set in 23 acres of beautiful Devon countryside but close to safe sandy beaches.
Tranquility, Fun, Peace, Entertainment, Good Food, Good Company - which ever makes your holiday

ANWB EUROPEAN CAMPSITE OF THE YEAR 1994

COME TO BYSLADES

FOR MORE INFORMATION AND FREE COLOUR BROCHURE
PHONE 01803 - 555072
BYSLADES CAMPING & TOURING PARK,
TOTNES ROAD, PAIGNTON, DEVON TQ4 7PY

PAIGNTON HOLIDAY PARK

A beautifully landscaped Touring and Camping Park and a wide range of luxury Caravan Holiday Homes.

Set in an area of outstanding natural beauty and close to the beaches & attractions of the English Riviera. There is a full range of facilities for you to enjoy including a licensed club with entertainment & dancing, pool & snooker club. Large heated swimming pool & toddlers pool, shop, cafe, children's activity & play area, laundry & shower facilities. Seasonal pitches available, rallies welcome.

For free brochure:
Tel: 01803 550504 (24hr answer 01803 521684)

or write to Paignton Holiday Park, Dept. CC, Totnes Rd, Paignton, S.Devon TQ4 7PY   DOGS NOT ACCEPTED

DEVON

PAIGNTON DEVON
Widend Park

A beautiful award winning family run Touring Park for caravans, motor homes & tents. A friendly atmosphere, superb views of sea & countryside. We offer excellent value with no hidden extras.

- ★ Swimming Pool
- ★ Shop/Takeaway
- ★ Seasonal storage
- ★ Adventure playground
- ★ Family room
- ★ Couples & families only
- ★ Games room
- ★ Country style bar
- ★ No dogs mid July & August

WIDEND TOURING PARK, BERRY POMEROY RD, MARLDON, PAIGNTON, DEVON, TQ3 1RT TELEPHONE: 01803 550916

CARAVAN AND CAMPING CLUB LISTED
GRADED EXCELLENT
AA Listed as One of Britain's Best Campsite
AA Award for Excellence
RAC APPOINTED ANWB HOLLAND

Nearby Facilities ┌ ✓ ⊥ ↘ U
≢ Paignton.
Within 4 miles Torbay beaches, 1 mile village Stoke Gabriel and River Dart.

PAIGNTON
Marine Park Holiday Centre, Grange Road, Paignton, Devon.
Tel: Churston 843887 Std: 01803
Fax: **845427** Std: **01803**
Nearest Town/Resort Paignton.
Directions 2 miles south of Paignton off A379.
Acreage 4 **Open** May to September
Access Good   **Site** Lev/Slope
Sites Available ⚐ ⊟ **Total** 30
Low Season Band B
High Season Band C
Facilities ⊟ ⨍ ⊞ ♨ ┌ ⊙ ⌐ ⌂ ⊠ ☏
♀ ⌂ ⊛ ⋀ ⋈ ⊟
Nearby Facilities ┌ ✓ ⊥ ↘ U ♂ ♀
≢ Paignton.

PAIGNTON
Paignton Holiday Park, Totnes Road, Paignton, Devon, TQ4 7PW.
Tel: 550504 Std: 01803
Nearest Town/Resort Paignton.
Directions 1½ miles west of Paignton on the A385.
Acreage 20 **Open** March to October
Access Good   **Site** Lev/Slope
Sites Available ▲ ⚐ ⊟ **Total** 250
Low Season Band B
High Season Band C
Facilities ⨍ ⊞ ♨ ┌ ⊙ ⌐ ⌂ ⊠ ☏
♀ ⌂ ⊛ ⋀ ⋈ ⊟ ❋ ⋈ ⊟
Nearby Facilities ┌ ✓ ⊥ ↘ U ♂ ♀
≢ Paignton.
Ideal touring site near beaches with outstanding views.

PAIGNTON
Ramslade Touring Park, Stoke Road, Stoke Gabriel, Paignton, Devon.
Tel: 782575 Std: 01803
Fax: **782828** Std: **01803**
Nearest Town/Resort Paignton.
Directions From Paignton take A385, turn left at Parkers Arms, site 1½ miles on right.
Acreage 9 **Open** 15 March to October
Access Good   **Site** Lev/Slope
Sites Available ▲ ⚐ ⊟ **Total** 135
Facilities ⊟ ⨍ ⊞ ♨ ┌ ⊙ ⌐ ⌂ ⊠ ☏
♀ ⌂ ⊛ ⊟ ⋀ ⊟
Nearby Facilities ┌ ✓ ⊥ ↘ U ♂ ♀
≢ Paignton.
Quiet site. Top Tourist Board Grade - 5 ticks. No dogs high season. Babies bathroom, Logland Play areas and paddling pool with waterfall.

PAIGNTON
Whitehill Farm Holiday Park, Stoke Road, Paignton, Devon, TQ4 7PF.
Tel: 782338 Std: 01803
Fax: **782722** Std: **01803**
Nearest Town/Resort Paignton
Directions Turn off the A385 at Parkers Arms Public House ½ mile from Paignton Zoo. Park is 1 mile along road to Stoke Gabriel.
Acreage 30 **Open** Mid May to End September
                           Site Lev/Slope
Sites Available ▲ ⚐ ⊟ **Total** 400
Low Season Band B
High Season Band C
Facilities ⊟ ⨍ ⊞ ♨ ┌ ⊙ ⌐ ⌂ ⊠ ☏
♀ ⌂ ⊛ ⋈ ♀ ⋀ ⋈ ⊟
Nearby Facilities ┌ ✓ ⊥ ↘ U ♂ ♀
≢ Paignton
Beautifully situated in rolling Devon countryside yet within easy reach of the sea (2½ miles), Torquay and the Dartmoor National Park. Licensed bar.

PAIGNTON
Widend Camping Park, Berry Pomeroy Road, Marldon, Paignton, Devon, TQ3 1RT.
Tel: 550116 Std: 01803.
Nearest Town/Resort Paignton/Torquay.
Directions Turn into Five Lanes Road towards Berry Pomeroy off the main Torquay ring road (A380) and duel carriageway at Marldon. Singmore Hotel is on the corner.
Acreage 20 **Open** April to October
Access Good   **Site** Level
Sites Available ▲ ⚐ ⊟ **Total** 185
Low Season Band B
High Season Band C
Facilities ♿ ⨍ ⊞ ♨ ┌ ⊙ ⌐ ⌂ ⊠ ☏
♀ ⌂ ⊛ ⋀ ⋈ ❋ ⊟
Nearby Facilities ┌ ✓ ⊥ ↘ U ♂ ♀ ⚐
≢ Torquay
A most central site for most of the sea and country amenities in South Devon. S.A.E. for brochure and site fees. Quiet, family run park graded 5 Ticks "Excellent". Dogs not allowed in peak season.

PLYMOUTH
Riverside Caravan Park, Longbridge Road, Marsh Mills, Plymouth, Devon, PL6 8LD.
Tel: 344122 Std: 01752
Fax: **344122** Std: **01752**
Nearest Town/Resort Plymouth.
Directions 3 miles from Plymouth city centre, follow the A374.
Acreage 10½ **Open** All Year
Access Good   **Site** Level
Sites Available ▲ ⚐ ⊟ **Total** 290

Low Season Band B
High Season Band C
Facilities ⊟ ⨍ ⊞ ♨ ┌ ⊙ ⌐ ⌂ ⊠ ☏
♀ ⌂ ⊛ ⋁ ⊞ ⋀ ⋈ ⊟
Nearby Facilities ┌ ✓ ⊥ ↘ U ♂
≢ Plymouth.
Woodland site alongside a river.

PRINCETOWN
The Plume of Feathers Inn, The Square, Princetown, Tavistock, Devon, PL20 6QG.
Tel: 890240 Std: 01822
Fax: **890780** Std: **01822**
Nearest Town/Resort Tavistock
Directions In the Square of Princetown, which is situated in Dartmoor.
Acreage 3 **Open** All Year
                           Site Sloping
Sites Available ▲ ⚐ ⊟ **Total** 75
Low Season Band B
High Season Band B
Facilities ♿ ⊞ ♨ ┌ ⊙ ♀ ⌂ ⊛ ⋁ ⊟
Nearby Facilities ┌ ✓ ⊥ ↘ U ♂ ♀
≢ Plymouth
In the heart of Dartmoor.

SALCOMBE
Alston Farm Camping & Caravan Site, Nr. Salcombe, Kingsbridge, Devon TQ7 3BJ.
Tel: 561260 Std: 01548
Fax: **561260** Std: **01548**
Nearest Town/Resort Salcombe.
Directions Signposted on left of A381 between Kingsbridge and Salcombe towards Salcombe.
Acreage 15 **Open** Easter to October
Access Good   **Site** Level
Sites Available ▲ ⚐ ⊟ **Total** 200
Low Season Band B
High Season Band C
Facilities ⨍ ⊞ ♨ ┌ ⊙ ⌐ ⌂ ⊠ ☏
♀ ⌂ ⊛ ⊟
Nearby Facilities ┌ ✓ ⊥ ↘ U ♂ ♀ ⚐
≢ Totnes.
Secluded, sheltered site. Dish washing facilities.

SALCOMBE
Bolberry House Farm Camping & Caravanning Park, Bolberry, Malborough, Nr Kingsbridge, Devon, TQ7 3DY.
Tel: 561251/560926 Std: 01548
Nearest Town/Resort Salcombe.
Directions Take the A381 from Kingsbridge to Malborough. Turn right through the village, follow signs to Bolberry ¾ mile.
Acreage 6 **Open** March to October
Access Good   **Site** Level

---

54   CADE'S WEST COUNTRY CAMPING, TOURING & MOTOR CARAVAN SITE GUIDE 1997

PAIGNTON : SOUTH DEVON
WHITEHILL
PITCHES WITH 16 AMP ELECTRIC HOOK UPS FOR TOURING CARAVANS, TENTS AND MOTORHOMES

This lovely park is beautifully situated amidst rolling green Devonshire countryside, yet within easy reach of the sea, Torquay and the Dartmoor National Park.

LUXURY HOLIDAY CARAVANS FOR HIRE WITH OWN SHOWER, TOILET AND COLOUR T.V.

Self-service shop - Childrens playground - Colour T.V. - Launderette - Free showers - Games room - Bus stop at entrance - 3 Payphones - Free hot water - Families and couples only - No dogs - Licensed bar - Heated swimming pool - Family room - Cafe - Adventure playground - Woodland trails - The Granary Disco. How to find us : Turn off Paignton-Totnes road (A385) at "Parkers Arms", ½ mile from Paignton Zoo. Signpost to Stoke Gabriel. Camping park 1 mile.

Send for 1997 prices and colour brochure.
Whitehill Farm Holiday Park
STOKE ROAD, PAIGNTON, SOUTH DEVON TQ4 7PF
Telephone: (01803) 782338   Fax: (01803) 782722

DEVON

Sites Available ▲ ⬜ ⬜ Total 70
Low Season Band B
High Season Band B
Facilities ⌐ ▥ ♣ ┌ ⊙ ┘ ⌐ ◙ ♥
▥ ▨ ◘ ♣ ⌂ ▣
Nearby Facilities ┌ ✓ ⊥ ⤴ ∪ ⌐ ♫
➡ Totnes.
A friendly and peaceful, family run park on a coastal farm. Mostly level. Wonderful sea views and stunning cliff top walks. Safe, sandy beaches 1 mile at the quaint old fishing village of Hope Cove. Salcombe's scenic and pretty estuary, a boating paradise - 2½ miles. B.G.H.P. 3 Ticks and A.A. 2 Pennant site.

SALCOMBE

Sun Park, Soar, Malborough, Nr. Kingsbridge, Devon, TQ7 3DS.
Tel: 561378 Std: 01548
Nearest Town/Resort Salcombe.
Directions A381 fron Kingsbridge to Malborough, turn right through village, follow sign Soar Mill Cove for 1¼ miles, site on right.
Acreage 3¼ **Open** Easter to End October
   Site Level
Sites Available ▲ ⬜ ⬜ **Total** 70
Low Season Band A
High Season Band C
Facilities ⌐ ▥ ♣ ┌ ⊙ ┘ ⌐ ◙ ♥
▥ ▨ ◘ ♣ ⌂ ▣
Nearby Facilities ┌ ✓ ⊥ ⤴ ∪ ♫
➡ Totnes.
Within walking distance of Soar Mill Cove, in an area of outstanding natural beauty, Ideal centre for touring.

SEATON

Leacroft Touring Park, Colyton Hill, Colyton, Devon.
Tel: 552823 Std: 01297
Fax: **552823** Std: 01297
Nearest Town/Resort Seaton/Beer.
Directions A3052 Sidmouth to Lyme Regis road, 2 miles west of Seaton. Turn left at Stafford Cross international caravan sign, site is 1 mile on the right.
Acreage 10 **Open** March to October
Access Good   **Site** Lev/Slope
Sites Available ▲ ⬜ ⬜ **Total** 138
Facilities ⌐ ▥ ♣ ┌ ⊙ ┘ ⌐ ◙ ♥
▥ ◘ ♣ ⌂ ▣
Nearby Facilities ┌ ✓ ⊥ ⤴ ∪
➡ Axminster
Quiet, peaceful site in open countryside. Picturesque villages to explore and woodland walks nearby.

SEATON

Manor Farm Caravan Site, Seaton Down Hill, Seaton, Devon.
Tel: 21524 Std: 01297
Nearest Town/Resort Seaton
Directions From Lyme Regis A3052, left at Tower Cross, ½ mile entrance on left.
Acreage 22 **Open** April to 15th Nov
Access Good   **Site** Lev/Slope
Sites Available ▲ ⬜ ⬜ **Total** 274
Low Season Band B
High Season Band B
Facilities ⌐ ▥ ♣ ┌ ⊙ ┘ ⌐ ◙ ♥ ▣
Nearby Facilities ┌ ✓ ⊥ ⤴ ∪
➡ Axminster
Glorious scenic views of valley and Lyme Bay. Farm animals, rare breeds. A quiet site only 1 mile from beach. Ideal touring centre for glorious East Devon.

SIDMOUTH

Oakdown Touring & Holiday Home Park, Weston, Sidmouth, Devon, EX10 0PH.
Tel: 680387 Std: 01297
Fax: **513731** Std: **01395**
Nearest Town/Resort Sidmouth.
Directions 1½ miles east of Sidford on A3052, take the second Weston turning at the Oakdown sign. Site 50 yards on left. Also signposted with international Caravan/Camping signs.
Acreage 13 **Open** April to October
Access Good   **Site** Level
Sites Available ▲ ⬜ ⬜ **Total** 120
Low Season Band B
High Season Band C
Facilities ▣ ♣ ⌐ ▥ ♣ ┌ ⊙ ┘ ⌐ ◙ ♥
▥ ▨ ◘ ♣ ⌂ ✽ ▣
Nearby Facilities ┌ ✓ ⊥ ⤴ ∪ ⌐ ♫
➡ Honiton.
Sidmouths Award Winning park set in glorious East Devon Heritage coast, near beautiful Weston Valley owned by National Trust, lovely cliff walks. Caravan storage. Fully serviced pitches for touring units. Field trail to nearby world famous Donkey Sanctuary. Caravan holiday homes to let.

SIDMOUTH

Salcombe Regis Camping and Caravan Park, Salcombe Regis, Sidmouth, Devon, EX10 0JH.
Tel: 514303 Std: 01395
Fax: **514303** Std: **01395**
Nearest Town/Resort Sidmouth
Directions 1½ miles east of Sidmouth, signposted off the A3052 Exeter to Lyme Regis coast road. ½ mile down the lane on the left hand side.
Acreage 16 **Open** Easter to October
Access Good   **Site** Level
Sites Available ▲ ⬜ ⬜ **Total** 100
Low Season Band B
High Season Band C
Facilities ▣ ♣ ⌐ ▥ ♣ ┌ ⊙ ┘ ⌐ ◙ ♥
▥ ◘ ♣ ⌂ ▣
Nearby Facilities ┌ ✓ ⊥ ⤴ ∪ ⌐ ♫
➡ Exeter
Situated in an area of outstanding natural beauty, within walking distance of the sea and famous Donkey Sanctuary. Hardstandings with own water supply available for motor caravans and tourers. Heated amenity block. Quiet, "Excellent" graded park.

SLAPTON

Newlands Farm Camping & Caravan Site, Newlands Farm, Slapton, Nr. Dartmouth, Devon.
Tel: 580366 Std: 01548
Nearest Town/Resort Dartmouth
Directions From Totnes take the A381 towards Kingsbridge, after Halwell Village take the fourth left signposted Slapton. Go 4 miles to Buckland Cross, proceed for ¼ mile, site is on the left hand side.
Acreage 10 **Open** 23 May to September
Access Good   **Site** Level
Sites Available ▲ ⬜ ⬜ **Total** 45
Low Season Band A
High Season Band B
Facilities ⌐ ▥ ♣ ┌ ┘ ♥
▥ ▨ ◘ ♣ ⌂ ▣
Nearby Facilities ┌ ✓ ⊥ ⤴ ∪ ⌐ ♫
We have a friendly, uncommercialised, quiet site overlooking beautiful countryside and sea. Within 1 mile of glorious beaches, cliff walks and a nature reserve. Woodlands Leisure Centre is close by with fun for all the family.

SOUTH BRENT

Webland Farm Holiday Park, Avonwick, Nr. South Brent, Devon. TQ10 9EX
Tel: 73273 Std: 01364
Nearest Town/Resort Totnes.
Directions Leave the A38 at Marley Head A385 exit. Follow Webland signs from the roundabout and along lane for about 1¼ miles.
Acreage 5 **Open** 15th March to 15th November
Access Good   **Site** Lev/Gentle Slope
Sites Available ▲ ⬜ ⬜ **Total** 35
Low Season Band B
High Season Band B
Facilities ⌐ ♣ ┌ ⊙ ⌐ ◙ ♥
▣ ◘ ♣ ⌂ ▣
Nearby Facilities ┌ ∪
➡ Totnes.
Overlooked by Dartmoor Hills, very quiet country park, well placed for touring the coast and Dartmoor and the many tourist attractions in the area.

SOUTH MOLTON

Molland Camping & Caravan Park, Blackcock Inn, Molland, South Molton, North Devon.
Tel: 550297 Std: 01769
Nearest Town/Resort Barnstaple.
Directions Proceed along the A361 from either Tiverton or South Molton and Molland is signposted. Camping signs lead directly to the site.
Acreage 9¼ **Open** 15 March to 15 November
Access Good   **Site** Level
Sites Available ▲ ⬜ ⬜ **Total** 65
Low Season Band B
High Season Band C
Facilities ⌐ ▥ ♣ ┌ ⊙ ┘ ⌐ ◙ ♥
▥ ▨ ♣ ✕ ♀ ▣ ♣ ⌂ ▣
Nearby Facilities ┌ ✓ ∪
➡ Barnstaple/Tiverton.
Edge of Exmoor National Park. Ideal for touring, hiking, riding, etc..

SOUTH MOLTON

Romansleigh Holiday Park, Odam Hill, South Molton, North Devon, EX36 4NB.
Tel: 550259 Std: 01769
Nearest Town/Resort Barnstaple.
Directions Take the B3137 South Molton to Witheridge road. Site is signposted right approximately 4 miles from South Molton and 2 miles past Alswear.
Acreage 2 **Open** 15 March to 31 October
Access Good   **Site** Level
Sites Available ▲ ⬜ ⬜ **Total** 20
Low Season Band B
High Season Band B
Facilities ⌐ ▥ ♣ ┌ ⊙ ┘ ⌐ ◙ ♣ ♥ ▣ ♣ ▣
Nearby Facilities ┌ ✓ ∪
➡ Umberleigh
Secluded, wooded valley with magnificent all-round views. In the grounds of 14 acres. Ideal touring location.

TAVISTOCK

Dartmoor Country Holidays, Magpie Leisure Park, Bedford Bridge, Horrabridge, Yelverton, Devon, PL20 7RY.
Tel: 852651 Std: 01822
Nearest Town/Resort Tavistock
Directions 2¼ miles south east of Tavistock off the A386 Plymouth road.
Acreage 8 **Open** 15th March to 15th January
Access Good   **Site** Level
Sites Available ▲ ⬜ ⬜ **Total** 90

DEVON

Low Season Band A
High Season Band B
Facilities ! ⌂ ♿ ♣ ⌐ ☉ ⌐ ▬ ☐ ☎
⛽ ○ ♨ ⛵ ☂
Nearby Facilities ⌐ ✈ ∪
⚑ Plymouth
Wooded level site, situated along banks of River Walkham in Dartmoor National Park. Luxury Pine Lodges sleeping 2-7 also available.

TAVISTOCK
Harford Bridge Holiday Park, Peter Tavy, Tavistock, Devon.
Tel: 810349 Std: 01822
Nearest Town/Resort Tavistock
Directions A386 Okehampton road 2 miles north of Tavistock.
Acreage 16½ **Open** March to November
Access Good **Site** Level
Sites Available ▲ ⛺ ☗ **Total** 120
Facilities ! ⌂ ♣ ⌐ ☉ ⌐ ▬ ☐ ☎
⛽ ○ ♨ 📺 ♣ ☐
Nearby Facilities ⌐ ✈ ∪ ♞ ✈
⚑ Plymouth
Scenic views, riverside pitches, fishing and tennis, ideal touring Dartmoor National Park. W.C.T.B. Rose Award 5 Ticks.

TAVISTOCK
Higher Longford Farm, Moorshop, Tavistock, Devon.
Tel: 613360 Std: 01822
Nearest Town/Resort Tavistock.
Directions Tavistock/Princetown road, 2 miles from Tavistock on the B3357.
Acreage 4 **Open** All Year
Access Good **Site** Level
Sites Available ▲ ⛺ ☗ **Total** 52
Low Season Band B
High Season Band C
Facilities ! ⌂ ♣ ⌐ ☉ ⌐ ▬ ☐ ☎
⛽ ○ ♨ ☒ ⛵ ☐ ☎
Nearby Facilities ⌐ ✈ ∪ ✈
⚑ Plymouth.
Situated in the Dartmoor National Park, central for touring Devon and Cornwall.

TAVISTOCK
Woodovis Holiday Park, Tavistock, Devon, PL19 8NY.
Tel: 832968 Std: 01822
Nearest Town/Resort Tavistock.
Directions Take A390 Liskeard road from Tavistock. Site signposted right in 3 miles.
Acreage 14 **Open** March to December
Access Good **Site** Lev/Slope
Sites Available ▲ ⛺ ☗ **Total** 72
Low Season Band B
High Season Band C
Facilities ⌂ ! ⌂ ♣ ⌐ ☉ ⌐ ▬ ☐ ☎
⛽ ○ ♨ ♣ ☐ ✳ ☐
Nearby Facilities ⌐ ✈ ⊥ ✈ ∪ ♞ ♣ ✈
⚑ Plymouth
Scenic views, close to Tamar river. Ideal place for exploring Devon and Cornwall. R.A.C. Three Stars, A.A. Three Stars, A.N.W.B. Approved, E.T.B. Graded Four Ticks and A.A. Award for Environmental Excellance. Heated indoor swimming pool.

TEIGNMOUTH
Bishopsbrook Camping Park, Newton Road, Bishopsteignton, Teignmouth, Devon.
Tel: 775501 Std: 01626
Nearest Town/Resort Teignmouth
Directions On A381 Newton Abbot to Teignmouth Road.
Acreage 2¼ **Open** Easter to October

Access Good **Site** Lev/Slope
Sites Available ▲ ⛺ **Total** 77
Low Season Band A
High Season Band A
Facilities ⌂ ♣ ⌐ ☎ ⛽ ○ ♣ ☐
Nearby Facilities ⌐ ✈ ⊥ ✈ ∪ ♞ ♣ ✈
⚑ Newton Abbot
Within walking distance of River Estuary and river beach. Area of outstanding natural beauty. Fishing and board sailing nearby.

TEIGNMOUTH
Coast View Holiday Park, Torquay Road, Teignmouth, Shaldon, South Devon, TQ14 0BG.
Tel: 872392 Std: 01626
Nearest Town/Resort Teignmouth.
Directions Follow A38 from Exeter, take left fork A380 to Torquay. Proceed along the A380 for about 6 miles taking the A381 towards Shaldon. Turn right at traffic lights, cross Shaldon bridge and follow main road. Camp is on the right hand side.
Acreage 17
Access Good **Site** Level
Sites Available ▲ ⛺ ☗ **Total** 100
Low Season Band A
High Season Band C
Facilities ! ⌂ ♣ ⌐ ☉ ⌐ ▬ ☐ ☎
⛽ ⛽ ○ ♣ ☒ ⛵ ☐ ♣ ♨ ✷ ☐
Nearby Facilities ⌐ ✈ ⊥ ✈ ∪ ♞ ♣ ✈
⚑ Teignmouth
Scenic views across the sea to the South Devon coastline, Devon coast. Ideal for touring.

TEIGNMOUTH
Wear Farm Caravan Site, E. S. Coaker & Co., Newton Road, Bishopsteignton, Nr. Teignmouth, Devon, TQ14 9PT.
Tel: 775249 Std: 01626
Nearest Town/Resort Teignmouth.
Directions Off the A380 take the A381 towards Teignmouth, Wear Farm can be found ¼ a mile on the right from the dual carriageway.
Acreage 15 **Open** Easter to October
Access Good **Site** Lev/Slope
Sites Available ▲ ⛺ ☗ **Total** 147
Low Season Band B
High Season Band C
Facilities ! ⌂ ♣ ⌐ ☉ ⌐ ▬ ☐ ☎
⛽ ○ ♣ ☐ ☐
Nearby Facilities ⌐ ✈ ⊥ ✈ ∪ ♞ ♣
⚑ Newton Abbot
Alongside a river, scenic views and ideal touring.

TIVERTON
West Middlewick Farm, Nomansland, Nr. Tiverton, Devon, EX16 8NP.
Tel: 860286 Std: 01884
Nearest Town/Resort Tiverton.
Directions Take the old A373 (now the B3137) W.N.W.from Tiverton, farm is beside road one mile beyond Nomansland, on right (9 miles from Tiverton).
Acreage 3 **Open** All Year
Access Good **Site** Level
Sites Available ▲ ⛺ ☗ **Total** 15
Low Season Band A
High Season Band A
Facilities ⌂ ♣ ⌐ ☉ ☎ ⛽ ⛽ ☐
Nearby Facilities ⌐ ✈ ✈ ∪
⚑ Tiverton Parkway
Panoramic view towards Exmoor, quiet surroundings, children welcome. Genuine farm with the same family management since 1933.

TIVERTON
Zeacombe House Caravan Park, Zeacombe House, East Anstey, Tiverton, Devon, EX16 9JU.
Tel: 341279 Std: 01398
Fax: **341279** Std: **01398**
Nearest Town/Resort Tiverton/South Molton
Directions Junction 27 of the M5 take the A361 Barnstaple to South Molton road. Travel for 16 miles in a straight direction. Turn right signed Knowstone and travel road for 2¼ miles. Gates are on the left.
Acreage 4¼ **Open** 11 March to October
Access Good **Site** Level
Sites Available ▲ ⛺ ☗ **Total** 70
Low Season Band B
High Season Band C
Facilities ⌂ ! ⌂ ♣ ⌐ ☉ ⌐ ▬ ☐ ☎
⛽ ○ ♣ ✷ ☐
Nearby Facilities ⌐ ✈ ∪
⚑ Tiverton
Scenic views across Exmoor, ideal for touring. Flat, landscaped park with flowers, trees and shrubs.

TORQUAY
Manor Farm Camp Site, Manor Farm, Daccombe, Nr Torquay, Devon.
Tel: 328294 Std: 01803
Nearest Town/Resort Torquay.
Directions From Newton Abbot take the A380 for Torquay. Go through roundabout at Kerswell Gardens to next set of traffic lights, turn left into Kingskerswell Road, follow camp signs.
Acreage 4 **Open** 20 May to 20 September
Site Lev/Slope
Sites Available ▲ ⛺ ☗ **Total** 75
Facilities ⌂ ♣ ⌐ ☉ ⌐ ▬ ☐ ☎ ⛽ ☐
Nearby Facilities ⌐ ✈ ⊥ ✈ ∪ ♞ ♣ ✈
⚑ Torquay
Near the beach, scenic views, ideal touring.

TORQUAY
Widdicombe Farm Tourist Park, The Ring Road, Marldon, Torbay, Devon, TQ3 1ST.
Tel: 558325 Std: 01803
Fax: **558325** Std: **01803**
Nearest Town/Resort Torquay
Directions At the large roundabout at Newton Abbot, follow signs to Torquay at the next roundabout turn right into Hamlyn Way, straight on at third roundabout, look to right see Widdicombe Farm, continue onto next roundabout, turn back following directions back to Torquay. Widdicombe Farm is ¼ mile on left.
Acreage 10 **Open** Easter to Mid October
Access Good **Site** Level
Sites Available ▲ ⛺ ☗ **Total** 200
Facilities ⌂ ! ⌂ ♣ ⌐ ☉ ⌐ ▬ ☐ ☎
⛽ ○ ♣ ✷ ⛵ ☐ ☐
Nearby Facilities ⌐ ✈ ⊥ ✈ ∪ ♞ ♣
⚑ Torquay
Easy access, no narrow country lanes to negotiate. Quiet, family run site, known for our hospitality and cleanliness. Lovely setting with scenic views, the nearest site to Torquay. Heated baby bathroom. Bargain Breaks available (send for details). 50 all weather sites. Three 6 berth holiday caravans for hire, all electric with shower/ toilet, TV etc.. BGHP 5 Ticks Excellent.

TORRINGTON
Greenways Valley, Torrington, Devon, EX38 7EW.
Tel: 622153 Std: 01805 Fax: 622320 Std: 01805
Nearest Town/Resort Torrington/Westward Ho!
Directions Site is just one mile from

CADE'S WEST COUNTRY CAMPING, TOURING & MOTOR CARAVAN SITE GUIDE 1997 57

DEVON

Torrington town centre. Take B3227 (to South Molton) turn right into Borough Road then 3rd left to site entrance.
Acreage 8 **Open** Mid March to October
Access Good **Site** Level
Sites Available A ⊕ ⊟ **Total** 10
Low Season Band A
High Season Band C
Facilities ▣ ⫽ ⒰ ♣ ⌒ ⊙ ⌐ ▄ ▣ ☂
♨ ◊ ▨ ♧ ☂
Nearby Facilities ➤ ⁄ ⊥ ↘ ∪ ∩ ℛ ✻
☀ Barnstaple
Peaceful well tended site with a southerly aspect overlooking a beautiful wooded valley, ideal base for touring North Devon. E.T.B. Graded Four Ticks. Tennis on park.

TORRINGTON
Smytham Manor Holidays, Smytham Manor, Little Torrington, Devon, EX38 8PU.
Tel: 622110 Std: 01805
Nearest Town/Resort Westward Ho!
Directions 2 miles south Torrington on A386 to Okehampton.
Acreage 25 **Open** Mid March to October
Access Good **Site** Level
Sites Available A ⊕ ⊟ **Total** 30
Low Season Band B
High Season Band C
Facilities ⫽ ⒰ ♣ ⌒ ⊙ ⌐ ▄ ▣ ☂
♨ ◊ ▨ ♧ ☂
Nearby Facilities ➤ ⁄ ⊥ ↘ ∪ ∩ ℛ ✻
☀ Barnstaple
Attractive landscaped grounds, close to moors and beach with direct access to the Tarka Trail. Good base for exploring Devon.

TOTNES
Edeswell Farm Country Caravan Park, Edeswell Farm, Rattery, South Brent, Devon, TQ10 9LN.
Tel: 72177 Std: 01364

Nearest Town/Resort Totnes
Directions Fron Exeter follow the A38 approx 22 miles ignore Rattery signs leave at Marley Head Junction signposted Paignton, Totnes A358. Site ½ mile on right.
Acreage 6 **Open** March to October
Access Good **Site** Terraced
Sites Available A ⊕ ⊟ **Total** 46
Low Season Band B
High Season Band C
Facilities ⫽ ⒰ ♣ ⌒ ⊙ ⌐ ▣ ☂
♨ ▧ ◊ ♧ ✕ ▨ ♠ ∩ ≾ ⊛ ▣
Nearby Facilities ➤ ⁄ ⊥ ↘ ∪ ∩ ℛ ✻
☀ Totnes
Dartmoor, country site for quiet family holidays but with all facilities. Indoor heated swimming pool.

UMBERLEIGH
Umberleigh Camping & Caravanning Club, Over Weir, Umberleigh, Devon, EX37 9DU.
Tel: 560009 Std: 01769
Nearest Town/Resort Barnstaple.
Directions Situated in the Taw Valley, ¼ mile from Umberleigh on the B3227.
Open 3rd November to October
Access Good **Site** Lev/Slope
Sites Available A ⊕ ⊟ **Total** 60
Facilities ⫽ ⒰ ♣ ⌒ ⌐ ▣ ☂
▣ ▨ ♠ ∩ ▣
Nearby Facilities ⁄ ℛ
☀ Umberleigh.
Ideal for exploring North Devon; good sandy beaches, excellent walking; three nearby towns offering traditional craft shops, museums, sports etc., as well as Rosemoor Gardens.

WINKLEIGH
Wagon Wheels Holiday Village, Winkleigh, Devon, EX19 8DP.
Tel: 83456 Std: 01837
Nearest Town/Resort Okehampton.
Directions On B3220 Crediton to Torrington Road, 1 mile north of the village of Winkleigh.
Acreage 1 **Open** 15th March to October
Access Good **Site** Level
Sites Available A ⊕ ⊟ **Total** 20
Facilities ⒰ ♣ ⌒ ⊙ ⌐ ▣ ☂
♨ ▧ ◊ ▨ ♧ ♠ ∩ ▣
Nearby Facilities ➤ ⁄ ∪
☀ Eggesford.
Scenic views of Dartmoor.

WOOLACOMBE
Europa Holiday Village, Station Road, Woolacombe, Devon.
Tel: 870159 Std: 01271
Nearest Town/Resort Woolacombe
Directions Less than a mile from and above Woolacombe on the right hand side of the main road leading into the resort.
Acreage 11 **Open** Easter to October
Access Good **Site** Lev/slope
Sites Available A ⊕ ⊟ **Total** 100
Facilities ▣ ⫽ ⒰ ♣ ⌒ ⊙ ⌐ ▣ ☂
♨ ▯ ◊ ♧ ▨ ♠ ∩ ≾ ⊛ ▣
Nearby Facilities ➤ ⁄ ⊥ ↘ ∪ ∩ ℛ ✻
☀ Barnstaple
Panoramic views of surrounding countryside and Woolacombe Bay. Quietly situated informal site where well behaved animals (and children!) are welcome.

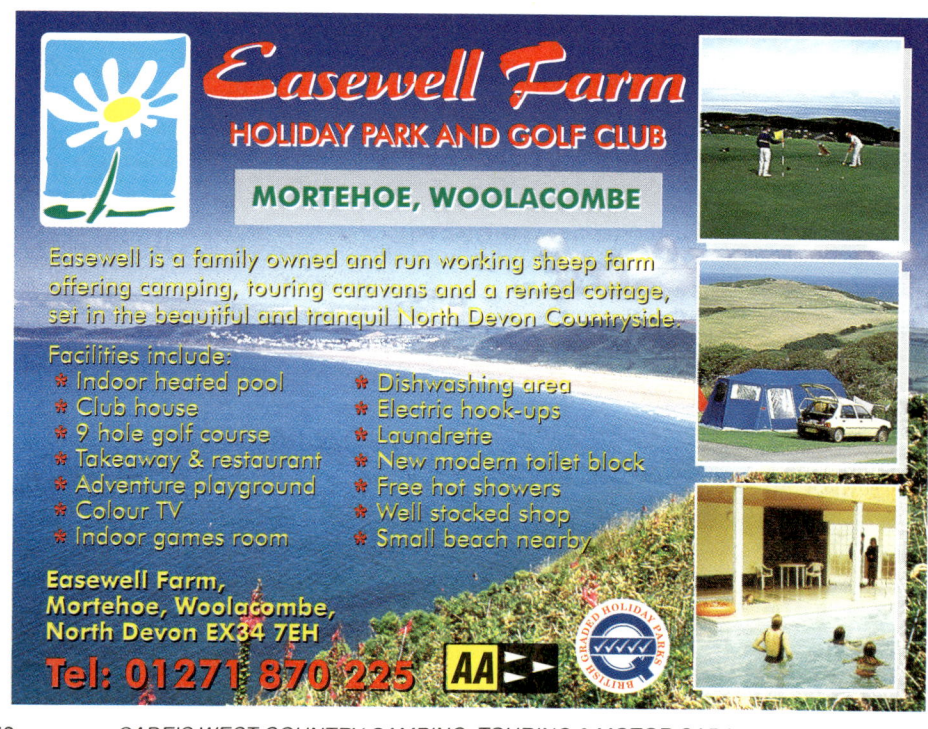

Easewell Farm
HOLIDAY PARK AND GOLF CLUB
MORTEHOE, WOOLACOMBE

Easewell is a family owned and run working sheep farm offering camping, touring caravans and a rented cottage, set in the beautiful and tranquil North Devon Countryside.

Facilities include:
- Indoor heated pool
- Club house
- 9 hole golf course
- Takeaway & restaurant
- Adventure playground
- Colour TV
- Indoor games room
- Dishwashing area
- Electric hook-ups
- Laundrette
- New modern toilet block
- Free hot showers
- Well stocked shop
- Small beach nearby

Easewell Farm, Mortehoe, Woolacombe, North Devon EX34 7EH
Tel: 01271 870 225

DEVON

WOOLACOMBE
Little Roadway Farm Camping Park, Woolacombe, Devon, EX34 7HL.
Tel: 870313 Std: 01271
Nearest Town/Resort Woolacombe
Directions Barnstaple to Mullacott Cross on the A361, then the B3343 towards Woolacombe. Then take the B3231 towards Georgeham and Croyde. About 4 miles on the left.
Acreage 22 **Open** March to October
Site Level
Sites Available ▲ ⏏ ☗ **Total** 200
Low Season Band A
High Season Band B
Facilities ⌂ ♨ ┏ ☉ ╝ ☎ ☒ ▣ ⊡
Nearby Facilities ┏ ✓ ⊥ ✢ U ♬ ✈
╬ Barnstaple

WOOLACOMBE
Morte Point Caravans, 23 Brooks Road, Wylde Green, Sutton Coldfield, B72 1HP.
Tel: 354 1551 Std: 0121
Fax: **354 1551** Std: **0121**
Nearest Town/Resort Woolacombe
Directions From Barnstaple/Ilfracombe take the A361 to the junction with the B3343 at Mullacott Cross roundabout, signposted Woolacombe/Mortehoe. Turn right in Mortehoe by the post office, site is 300yds on the left.
Acreage 75 **Open** April to October
Access Good   **Site** Level
Sites Available ▲ ⏏ ☗
Facilities ⌂ ♨ ┏ ☉ ╝ ☎ ▣
⊡ ▣ ☉ ☗ ⊞ ⛱ ▣
Nearby Facilities ┏ ✓ ⊥ ✢ U ♬ ✈
╬ Barnstaple

Closest site to the sea with magnificent views.

WOOLACOMBE
Twitchen Park, Mortehoe, Woolacombe, North Devon, EX34 7ES.
Tel: 870476 Std: 01271
Nearest Town/Resort Woolacombe.
Directions From Barnstaple/Ilfracombe road (A361) to junction with B3343 at Mullacott Cross, first left signposted Woolacombe for 1¾ miles, then right signposted Mortehoe. Park is 1¼ miles on left.
Acreage 20 **Open** April to October
Access Good   **Site** Sloping
Sites Available ▲ ⏏ ☗ **Total** 131
Low Season Band B
High Season Band C
Facilities ƒ ⌂ ♨ ┏ ☉ ╝ ▣ ☎
⊡ ▣ ☉ ☗ ⊞ ⛱ ▣ ✳ ❋ ▣
Nearby Facilities ┏ ✓ ⊥ ✢ U ♬
╬ Barnstaple.

Rural, scenic setting, close to Woolacombe's glorious sandy beach and spectacular coastal walks.

WOOLACOMBE
Woolacombe Bay Holiday Village, Sandy Lane, Woolacombe, Devon, EX34 7AH.
Tel: 870221 Std: 01271
Fax: **871042** Std: **01271**
Nearest Town/Resort Woolacombe/Ilfracombe
Directions A361 from Barnstaple, left at roundabout (Mullacott Cross). After 3 miles take right turn to Mortehoe, site is ¼ mile on the left.

Acreage 11 **Open** May to October
Site Sloping
Sites Available ▲ **Total** 200
Low Season Band B
High Season Band C
Facilities ⌂ ♨ ┏ ☉ ╝ ▣ ☎
⊡ ▣ ☉ ☗ ⊞ ⛱ ▣ ✳ ❋
Nearby Facilities ┏ ✓ ⊥ ✢ U ♬ ✈
╬ Barnstaple

Situated in an unspoilt area of West Country amidst glorious National Trust Hills and breathtaking views of Woolacombe Bay. ¾ mile from beach.

WOOLACOMBE
Woolacombe Sands Holiday Park, Beach Road, Woolacombe, North Devon, EX34 7AF.
Tel: 870569 Std: 01271
Fax: **870606** Std: **01271**
Nearest Town/Resort Woolacombe
Directions Take the A361 from Barnstaple to Mullacott Cross, then the B3343 to Woolacombe. Park is on the left on the last bend before the village of Woolacombe.
Acreage 20 **Open** Easter to September
Access Good   **Site** Lev/Slope
Sites Available ▲ ⏏ ☗ **Total** 300
Low Season Band B
High Season Band C
Facilities ▣ ƒ ⌂ ♨ ┏ ☉ ╝ ▣ ☎
⊡ ▣ ☉ ☗ ⊞ ⛱ ▣ ✳ ▣
Nearby Facilities ┏ ✓ ⊥ U ♬ ✈
╬ Barnstaple

Nearest site to Woolacombe's 3 mile beach. Set in beautiful countryside with scenic views overlooking the sea.

CADE'S WEST COUNTRY CAMPING, TOURING & MOTOR CARAVAN SITE GUIDE 1997

DEVON
PLACES OF INTEREST

DEVON

APPLEDORE
THE NORTH DEVON MARITIME MUSEUM : Odun House, Odun Road, Appledore, North Devon. Tel : Bideford 01237 474852.
Nearest Railway Station : Barnstaple. Open : Easter to end of October, every afternoon, from 2pm-5pm, also Monday-Friday mornings from Spring bank holiday to 30th September, 11am-1pm. At other times of the year by appointment for schools and other parties. **Special Attractions:** Models, dioramas, pictures. All aspects of North Devons maritime heritage. Video show. Free parking in the public car park opposite.

ASHBURTON
ASHBURTON MUSEUM : 1 West Street, Ashburton, Devon.
Nearest Railway Station : Newton Abbot. Location : Town centre near the car park. Open : May to September, Tuesday, Thursday, Friday and Saturday, 2.30pm-5pm. **Special Attractions:** Local history, American Indian display.

ASHBURTON
THE RIVER DART COUNTRY PARK : Holne Park, Ashburton, Devon, TQ13 7NP. Tel : 01364 652511.
Nearest Railway Station : Newton Abbot. Location : Situated 1 mile from Ashburton on the Two Bridges Road, off A38 Exeter-Plymouth Road. Open : April to September. **Special Attractions:** Childrens adventure playgrounds, swimming pool, Kon-Tiki bathing lake and pony riding.

BARNSTAPLE
Barnstaple is a popular seaside resort combined with an industrial and commercial centre complete with a thriving market, situated on the North bank of the River Tavy, it spans the river with an ancient bridge circa 1350 of about 500 feet in length. Originally constructed for pedestrian and pack horse traffic.

Interesting features of the town are The Square with its Albert Memorial clock tower and Queen Anne's Walk a colonnaded passage over which stands a statue of Queen Anne. Below the statue is the "Tome Stone" originally used by merchants upon which to seal bargains.

The church of St Peter is early 14th century and has a number of beautiful features.

In September the Barnstaple Great Fair takes place, it is spread over three days and is opened by civic dignitaries, although now a pleasure fair, many of the ancient customs are revived and the festival attracts thousands of extra visitors from Barnstaple hinterland.

Barnstaple also has an interesting group of well preserved 17th century almshouses which are well worth looking at.

BARNSTAPLE
ARLINGTON COURT - NATIONAL TRUST : Arlington Court, Arlington, Barnstaple, Devon, EX31 4LP. Tel : 01271 850296. Fax : 01271 850711.
Nearest Railway Station : Barnstaple. Location : 8 miles north-east of Barnstaple on the A39. Open : 28th March to the end of October, Sunday to Friday, 11am-5.30pm, last entry 5pm. **Special Attractions:** Mansion full of collectors items, large collection of carriages, many walks through parks and woods.

BARNSTAPLE
THE BUTTERFLY HOUSE : Ashford Gardens, Ashford, Barnstaple, North Devon, EX31 4BW. Tel : 01271 42880. Fax : 01271 23972.
Nearest Railway Station : Barnstaple. Location : On the A361 midway between Barnstaple and Braunton. Open : Easter to the end of October. **Special Attractions:** A tropical butterfly house set in beautiful surroundings, with a 2 acre show garden, large lake and also a tea room serving morning coffee, lunches and cream teas. Overlooking the beautiful Taw Estuary.

BARNSTAPLE
MISS PIGGYLAND : North Devon Farm Park, Landkey, Barnstaple, Devon. Tel : 01271 830255.
Nearest Railway Station : Barnstaple. Location : Off the A361 at Landkey junction. Open : Easter to 30th September, 10am-5pm daily. **Special Attractions:** Miss Piggyland, Rabbit World, Sike Deer to feed, cattle, poultry and pheasants. Pick your own fruit in season. Play area, indoor Jungle World the fun centre for the under 12's. Picnic area.

BARNSTAPLE
NEWPORT POTTERY : 72 Newport Road, Barnstaple, North Devon. Tel : 01271 72103.
Location : From South Molton take new A361, turn left after Tesco, then right at traffic lights. From Bideford, take new A39, turn left at sign for Newport, then left at traffic lights. From Barnstaple, take new A361, turn right at SWEB, then right at traffic lights. Open : All year, Monday-Friday 10am-6pm. Saturday 10am-1pm. **Special Attractions:** Denis Fowler, craft potter, specialising in house name and number plates, commemorative bowls, plates, dishes, tankards and other items including lamp bases and shades, candles and candle holders. Free parking in adjacent Congrams Close.

BARNSTAPLE
QUEEN'S THEATRE : Boutport Street, Barnstaple, Devon, EX31 1SY. Tel : 01271 324242. Fax : 01271 326412.
Nearest Railway Station : Barnstaple. Location : In the centre of town. Parking is available in Queen Street (free after 6pm). Open All Year, Monday to Saturday, 10am-4.30pm. Performance Evenings 5.30pm till late. **Special Attractions:** The Queen's Theatre is a 700 seater theatre that attracts over 100,000 visitors each year. Its all-year round programme includes many famous names and World class theatre companies with an impressive variety of drama, comedy, ballet, music, opera and childrens shows (which include the ever-popular Christmas Pantomime).

BARNSTAPLE
ST JOHN'S GARDEN CENTRE & JUNGLE LAND : St John's Lane, Newport, Barnstaple, North Devon. Tel : 01271 43884. Fax : 01271 77072.
Nearest Railway Station : Barnstaple. Location : By car via St John's Lane or over footbridge from Tesco Superstore, Whiddon Valley, Barnstaple. Open : All year Monday to Saturday 9am-5.30pm, Sunday 10.30am-4.30pm. **Special Attractions:** Large well stocked garden centre with attractive cafeteria. Jungleland - Chipmunks, Terrapins, birds and fish in exotic setting of Giant Cacti, Tropical Jungle Plants and Waterfalls. All under cover. Free entry.

BEER
PECORAMA : Beer, Seaton, Devon, EX12 3NA.
Nearest Railway Station : Axminster. Open : Indoor exhibition all year. Outdoor activities Easter to early October. Sundays from Spring Bank Holiday to early September. **Special Attractions:** Extensive childrens activity areas complete throughout with safety surfacing. Childrens entertainers on many dates in peak season. "PECORAMA" is situated high on the hill side at the back of the delightful fishing village of Beer, just West of Seaton and is well signposted from the A3052.

The highlight must be the light railway with its fascinating coal-fired steam locomotives which take you for nearly a mile long ride through the flowers, exciting cuttings and a 183 feet long tunnel leading to 'Wildway Park' and 'Mount Delight' to see the wonderful vista down the valley and over the village.

60   *CADE'S WEST COUNTRY CAMPING, TOURING & MOTOR CARAVAN SITE GUIDE 1997*

DEVON

BIDEFORD
THE BIG SHEEP : Abbotsham, Bideford, North Devon. Tel : 01237 472366.
Nearest Railway Station : Barnstaple. Location : On the A39 North Devon link road, 2 mins west of the New Bideford Bridge. Open : 10am-6pm daily. **Special Attractions:** A working farm turned wacky tourist attraction combining sheep racing (odds on for Red Ram), duck trialling, sheep milking, sheep dog trialling, woolcrafts centre, bottle fed lambs, sheep shearing, home cooked food and the great value SHEEPY SHOP. Great fun, hands-on, all under cover.

BIDEFORD
HARTLAND ABBEY : Hartland, Bideford, devon, EX39 6DT. Tel : 01237 441264.
Nearest Railway Station : Barnstaple. Location : Between Hartland and Hartland Quay. Open : Bank Holiday Sundays and Mondays, Easter to September. Wednesday, May to September. Thursday and Sunday, June to September. **Special Attractions:** Historic House and grounds, family home from the 16th Century, Abbey founded Circa 1157. Woodland and coastal walks. Documents dating from 1160, photographic exhibition, pictures, furniture and porcelain. Teas are available provided by Hartland Church for church funds.

BOVEY TRACEY
BECKY FALLS : Manaton, Near Bovey Tracey, Devon, TQ13 9UG. Tel : 01647 221259.
Nearest Railway Station : Newton Abbot. Location : Situated on the B3344 Bovey Tracey to Manaton road. 4 miles from Bovey Tracey and 7 miles from the A38. Open : 17th March to 4th November, every day, 10am-6pm or dusk if earlier. **Special Attractions:** Becky Falls is the natural day out set within over 50 acres of woodlands. 70' waterfall tumbling over huge granite boulders, nature trails and river walks, all set in the heart of magnificent Dartmoor. Enter our nature trail competitions. Licensed Woodland Restaurant and Tea Room, Ice Cream Parlour and a super Gift and Craft Shop.

BOVEY TRACEY
BOVEY HANDLOOM WAEVERS : 1 Station Road, Bovey Tracey, Newton Abbot, Devon, TQ13 9AL. Tel : 01626 833424.
Nearest Railway Station : Newton Abbot. Location : 2 miles off the A38 opposite the large free 'Lower Car Park'. Open : Shop - Normal opening hours, closed 1pm-2pm, half day Wednesday. Workshop - Easter to October, 10am-12.45pm then 2pm-5pm, half day Wednesday. **Special Attractions:** Visit our workshop and watch our Tweeds being woven. Individually designed exclusive materials for skirts, coats, hats and caps, ties, scarves and knee rugs. Our shop also stocks travelling rugs and a large selection of knitwear in Shetland and lambswool. Order a skirt in the Tweed of your choice.

BOVEY TRACEY
CARDEW DESIGN TEA POTTERY : Newton Road, Bovey Tracey, Devon, TQ13 9DX. Tel : 01626 834441.
Nearest Railway Station : Newton Abbot. Location : Off the A38 at Drum Bridges roundabout, follow signs to Bovey Tracey (A382), 1 mile down the road on the left. Open : Shop & Restaurant - 7 days a week, 9.30am-5.30pm. Pottery Tour - Monday to Friday, 9.30am-4pm. **Special Attractions:** Cardew Design is a successful, dynamic Devon based company producing a wide range of unique, collectable teapots. Our imaginative designs and zany marketing techniques have resulted in international sales and recognition. Here, at Bovey Tracey, we have our factory shop selling at 50% discount our famous teapots and an excellent restaurant, plenty of free parking.

BRADWORTHY
THE GNOME RESERVE & WILD FLOWER GARDEN : West Putford, Near Bradworthy, Devon, EX22 7XE. Tel & Fax : 01409 241435.
Location : 10 miles South of Bideford. Open : 21st March to 31st October 10am-6pm daily. **Special Attractions:** The worlds largest population of Gnomes inhabiting a 2 acre beach wood. Also the 'Pixies Wildflower Garden', 2 acres with about 250 labelled species of wild flowers, herbs, grasses and ferns etc. 'The Pixie Kiln' see pottery pixies being made. Shops selling Gnomes and Pixies. Gnome hats loaned free of charge so the Gnomes think you are one of them - and to have fun with your cameras!. 1000 plus Gnomes and Pixies to meet. For children and the young at heart. 37 times on television.

BRATTON FLEMING
EXMOOR ZOOLOGICAL PARK : Bratton Fleming, Barnstaple, North Devon. Tel & Fax : 01598 763352.
Nearest Railway Station : Barnstaple. Location : On A399 (B3226) midway between Blackmoor Gate and Bratton Fleming. Open : April to October 10am-6pm. November to March 10am-4pm. Closed Christmas Day. **Special Attractions:** Unique zoo, offering a relaxed and informal atmosphere with many of the birds and animals at liberty within the grounds. Facilities for the disabled.

BRIXHAM
This picturesque small resort is built in a valley and terraced enclosing cliffs, it is one of the few 'watering holes' which still has a thriving fishing fleet. Between the year 1799 and early in this century, the harbour was extensively improved and with the construction of a 3000 feet long breakwater the sheltered harbours were increased to approximately 140 acres.

The town offers limitless scope for the many residents and visiting artists and is a favourite focus for both gifted and amateur photographers.

Among the principal points of interest is the quay where fishermen repair boats and nets, tackle ships, and the modern fish market where auctioneers exercise their skill. In the harbour, the replica of Sir Francis Drakes ship 'The Golden Hind' attracts people of all ages.

The Brixham Cavern is interesting for evidence of our early ancestors and their life styles with some excellent examples of stalactites and stalagmites. Hardy walkers will enjoy the journey to Berry Head, whilst the lighthouse, coastguard station and fort are also worthy of attention.

BRIXHAM
BRIXHAM MUSEUM : Bolton Cross, Brixham, Devon. Tel : 01803 856267.
Nearest Railway Station : Paignton. Location : Opposite Brixham main Post Office, next to the Town Hall. Open : Easter to end of October 10am-5pm. Moderate charges.

BRIXHAM
WELLHOUSE POTTERY LIMITED : Milton Street, Brixham, Devon. Tel : 01803 858033.
Nearest Railway Station : Paignton. Location : Short walk from St Mary's Square. Open : Monday to Friday 8.30am-4pm. Closed Saturdays, Sundays and Bank Holidays. **Special Attractions:** Watch potters at work.

BUCKFAST
BUCKFAST BUTTERFLY FARM & DARTMOOR OTTER SANCTUARY : Buckfast, Devon, TQ11 0DZ. Tel : 01364 642916.
Location : Just off A38 Exeter-Plymouth trunk road at Dart Bridge junction. Open : Daily Good Friday to the end of October. **Special Attractions:** Inclusive admission. The Butterfly Farm - A tropical landscaped garden with ponds, waterfalls and bridges providing the perfect habitat for the exotic butterflies that live and breed here as they would in the wild. There is also a special hatching room where butterflies can be seen being 'born'. The Otter Sanctuary has purpose built large landscaped enclosures housing four pairs of otters which can be seen at play from elevated observation platforms and swimming under water through the special under water viewing tunnel.

DEVON

BUCKFASTLEIGH
BUCKFAST ABBEY : Buckfastleigh, Devon, TQ11 0EE. Tel : 01364 642519. Fax : 01364 643891.
Nearest Railway Station : Totnes. Location : 0.5 miles from the A38 Exeter to Plymouth road, at Dart Bridge (A384) turn off. Follow brown signs to the car park. Open : All Year, daily 5.30am-7pm. Amenities - Easter to October 9am-5.30pm, November to Easter 10am-4pm. **Special Attractions:** The Benedictine monks of Buckfast welcome visitors to their Abbey, which they rebuilt themselves on its medieval foundations. The Abbey is famous today for its pioneering work in beekeeping, its tonic wine and its spectacular modern stained glass. Few visitors leaved untouched by the peace and serenity of Buckfast.

BUDLEIGH SALTERTON
FAIRLYNCH ARTS CENTRE & MUSEUM : 27 Fore Street, Budleigh Salterton, Devon. Tel : 01395 442666.
Nearest Railway Station : Exmouth. Location : Adjacent to sea front. Open : Easter to Mid October Daily 2pm-4.30pm. July and August also 11am-1pm except Sundays. **Special Attractions:** Period Costume, lace making, local history and environment, special Summer exhibition.

BUDLEIGH SALTERTON
GOTCHALAND AT BICTON PARK : East Budleigh, Budleigh Salterton, Devon, EX9 7DP. Tel : 01395 568465. Fax : 01395 568889.
Nearest Railway Station : Exmouth. Location : 2 miles north of Budleigh Salterton on the B3178. Open : 7 days a week. March to October, 10am-6pm. November to February, 10am till dusk. **Special Attractions:** 60 acres of glorious gardens and parkland. Display greenhouses, Tropical House, Palm House, Phibbers Pharm, Childrens Fun World and play area, the Phibbers Family Tree, Indoor Activity Centre for the under teens and Bicton Woodland Railway Ride. Gift shop and plant shop, self service restaurant and bar. Good disabled facilities, mother and baby changing room. Dogs allowed on leads.

CHITTLEHAMPTON
THE COBBATON COMBAT COLLECTION : Chittlehampton, Umberleigh, North Devon. Tel : 01769 540740.
Nearest Railway Station : Umberleigh. Location : 5.5 miles South East of Barnstaple signed from A361, A377 and B3227. Open : April 1st to October 31st 7 days a week 10am-6pm. Winter - Please telephone for hours. **Special Attractions:** Over 50 vehicles including tanks, and thousands of smaller items, mostly from 1939-45. One mans hobby which got out of hand. Play vehicles including Sherman Tank. Militaria shop.

CHUDLEIGH
CANONTEIGN FALLS : Chudleigh, Near Exeter, Devon, EX6 7NT. Tel : 01647 252434. Fax : 01647 252617.
Nearest Railway Station : Newton Abbot. Location : 3 miles off the A38 at Chudleigh. Open : 10th March to 10th November, Daily 10am-5pm. Winter, Sundays and school holidays, 11am-4pm. Last admission 1 hour before closing. **Special Attractions:** Englands highest waterfall located in an area of outstanding natural beauty.

CLOVELLY
CLOVELLY VILLAGE : Clovelly, Near Bideford, Devon, EX39 5SY. Tel : 01237 431781.
Nearest Railway Station : Barnstaple. Location : 11 miles west of Bideford, on the A39. Open : All day, every day (except Christmas Day. Summer 9am-5pm, Winter 10am-4pm. **Special Attractions:** C.18th fishing village built on a 400ft cliff with donkeys and sledges the only means of transport down the cobbled street to the C.14th harbour. Audio-visual programme in the visitor centre and a guided tour of a fishermans cottage. Access to the Kingsley Exhibition and parking included in the entry charge.

CLOVELLY
THE MILKY WAY : Downland Farm, Clovelly, Bideford, Devon, EX39 5RY. Tel : 01237 431255. Fax : 01237 431735.
Nearest Railway Station : Barnstaple. Location : On main A39, 2 miles Bideford side of Clovelly. Open : 1st April to 31st October daily, 10.30am-6pm. **Special Attractions:** One of the South Wests leading attractions offers you a day in the country thats simply out of this world. Attractions include Time Warp - The South Wests largest indoor adventure zone with Death Slide and much more; The North Devon Bird of Prey Centre (daily flying displays); laser target shooting; archery centre; golf driving nets; Lynbarn Fun'd' Raiser Railway; North Devon Sheepdog Centre (daily displays); Countryside Collection and Bottle Feeding Showtime.

COMBE MARTIN
THE COMBE MARTIN MOTORCYCLE COLLECTION : Cross Street, Combe Martin, North Devon. Tel : 01271 882346.
Nearest Railway Station : Barnstaple. Location : Behind the beach adjacent to the main car park in Cross Street, Combe Martin. Open : 17th May to 31st October also Easter, every day 10am-5pm. **Special Attractions:** The collection contains over 50 British Motorcycles displayed against a background of old petrol pumps, signs and garage memorabilia. Motoring nostalgia in an old world atmosphere.

CULLOMPTON
COLDHARBOUR MILL WORKING WOOL MUSEUM : Uffculme, Cullompton, Devon, EX15 3EE. Tel & Fax : 01884 841459.
Nearest Railway Station : Tiverton Parkway. Location : 2 miles from the M5 junction 27 off the B3181. Follow signs to Willand and then to Uffculme. Buses from Exeter, Cullompton and Tiverton. Open : Easter to October, 7 days a week, 10.30am-5pm. Winter, Monday to Friday, 10.30am-5pm. Last tour 4pm. **Special Attractions:** Working 18th Century woollen mill, original working machinery spinning Worsted and woollen yarn. Fully restored 1910 Vintage steam engine working on "Steam-Up" days. Guided tours of the mill and The New World Tapestry. Mill Shop and Waterside Restaurant.

DARTMOUTH
DART PLEASURE CRAFT LTD. : 5 Lower Street, Dartmouth, Devon, TQ6 9AJ. Tel : 01803 834488. Fax : 01803 835248.
Nearest Railway Station : Totnes. Location : River Dart, from Dartmouth to Totnes. Open : Every day, April to October. Other months by arrangement. **Special Attractions:** Circular cruises for 1 hour and 1.5 hours. Daily cruises to Totnes (see timetable). Commentary is given on all trips to point out places of interest including Dartmouth and Kingswear castles, Bayards Cove, Warfleet Creek, Britannia Royal Naval College, villages of Dittisham and Galmpton and the estate of late Dame Agatha Christie.

DARTMOUTH
WOODLANDS LEISURE PARK : Blackawton, Totnes, Devon, TQ9 7DQ. Tel & Fax : 01803 712598.
Nearest Railway Station : Totnes. Location : From the A38 at Buckfastleigh turn left to Totnes. A381 to Kinsbridge, at Halwel turn left to Dartmouth, the A3122 (B3207). Park is on the right in 2.5 miles. Open : 15th March to 15th November. **Special Attractions:** Extensive leisure park including Watercoaster, Toboggan Run, 12 Venture Zones, animals and a 34,000 square foot indoor play area.

DAWLISH
DAWLISH MUSEUM SOCIETY : The Knowle, Barton Terrace Dawlish, Devon, EX7 9QH.
Nearest Railway Station : Dawlish. Location : At the top of the towns main car park. Open : May to October, 10.30am-5pm Sundays, 2pm-5pm. **Special Attractions:** Three floors of exhibits. Victorian kitchen, shop, parlour and bathroom. Tools and artefacts of local trades and industries such as farming, milling, fishing, blacksmiths and lace making. Military room, railway room, Victorian toys, dolls and games. China, pottery, prints, pictures of old Dawlish and geology.

DEVON

DREWSTEIGNTON
CASTLE DROGO : Drewsteignton, Exeter, Devon, EX6 6PB. Tel : 01647 433306. Fax : 01647 433186.
Nearest Railway Station : Exeter. Location : 4 miles South of A30 Exeter to Okehampton road via Crockernwell. Coaches must travel via Sandy Park on the A382. Open : April to October. Castle and Restaurant daily except Fridays (open Good Friday). Shop, Tearoom and Garden daily. **Special Attractions:** Extraordinary Castle by Sir Edwin Luttens. Elegant dining and drawing rooms and fascinating kitchen and scullery. Terraced formal garden with colourful herbaceous and shrub borders and rose beds. Croquet Lawn. Panoramic views over Dartmoor and delightful walks along the gorse and down to the River Teign.

EXETER
Formerly the Roman city of Isca Dumnoriorum, this River Exe University City includes a decorated cathedral which preserves two remarkable Norman transceptal towers. Other old churches in the area include St Mary's Steps which displays a curious old 16th century clock.

The Guild Hall dates from 1330, Wynard's Hospital was founded in 1436 and the restored Saint Nicholas Priory is an interesting building of Tudor date. Parts of Norman Rougement Castle and sections of city walls have survived. Mol's coffee house dated from the 16th century and fine panelling is preserved in the 15th century Tuckers Hall. Numerous Georgian and Regency houses and terraces exist in the city.

The Maritime Museum on Town Quay is reputed to be the finest in England and the Albert Memorial Museum and Art Gallery is also of interest.

EXETER
CREALY : Sidmouth Road, Clyst St. Mary, Exeter, Devon, EX5 1DR. Tel : 01395 233200. Fax : 01395 233211.
Nearest Railway Station : Exeter Central. Location : On the A3052 Exeter to Sidmouth road, 4 miles from junction 30 on the M5. Open : Normally 10.30am-6pm, Summer Holidays 10am-6.30pm and Winter 10.30am-5pm. **Special Attractions:** NEW Children's Kingdom and THE BIG SECRET attractions opening in 1997 at this favourite adventure and animal park. Also Bumper Boats, Go-Karts, Prairie Train, Animal Land, World of Pets, Farm Nursery, huge Adventure Zone - the biggest indoor playground and much more! Crealy - Easy to Find, Hard to Leave!

EXETER
EXETER MARITIME MUSEUM : The Haven, Exeter, Devon, EX2 8DT. Tel : 01392 58075.
Nearest Railway Station : Exeter St. Davids. Location : The Haven, Exeter. Open : 1st October to 31st March, 10am-4pm. 1st April to 30th September, 10am-5pm. **Special Attractions:** The best World-Wide collection of working boats from every continent. Junks, Dhow, Proas and many other beautiful, exotic and extraordinary boats displayed afloat and in lovely old listed warehouses.

EXMOUTH
A LA RONDE : Summer Lane, Exmouth, Devon, EX8 5BD. Tel : 01395 265514.
Nearest Railway Station : Exmouth. Location : 2 miles north of Exmouth on the A376. Open : 28th March to 2nd November, 11am-5pm. Closed Friday and Saturday. **Special Attractions:** A unique sixteen sided house completed about 1796. Many 18th Century contents and collections brought back by two spinster cousins. Fascinating interior decoration includes a feather frieze and shell encrusted gallery viewed by closed circuit television.

EXMOUTH PAVILION :
The Esplanade, Exmouth, Devon. Tel & Fax : 01395 263986.
Nearest Railway Station : Exmouth Town. Location : Seafront, Exmouth. Open : 9am-11.30pm Monday to Saturday. 9am-10.30pm Sunday. **Special Attractions:** Regular dances, special attractions, family and Summer shows throughout the Summer season. Licensed bar and restaurant.

EXMOUTH
WORLD OF COUNTRY LIFE : Sandy Bay, Exmouth, Devon, EX8 5BU. Tel : 01395 274533.
Nearest Railway Station : Exmouth. Open : Good Friday to October, daily 10am-6pm. **Special Attractions:** Adventure playground, deer parks, Falconry displays, craft demonstrations, vintage vehicles, working machines. Senior and Junior Play Parks. Pets Centre and Animal Nursery.

EXMOUTH
THE WORLDS LARGEST OO MODEL RAILWAY COMPLEX :
Sea Front, Exmouth, Devon, EX8 2AY. Tel : 01395 278383.
Nearest Railway Station : Exmouth. Location : Exmouth Sea Front by Queens car and coach park. Open : Easter to 22nd July, 10.30am-5.30pm. 23rd July to 6th September 10.30am-9.30pm. 7th September to 1st November 10.30am-5.30pm. **Special Attractions:** Up to 25 trains running simultaneously through countryside and towns over 7500 feet of track indoors also extension outdoors around 100ft Koi-Carp and Goldfish pool, in use weather permitting.

HONITON
ALLHALLOWS MUSEUM : High Street, Honiton, Devon. Tel : 01404 44966.
Nearest Railway Station : Honiton. Open : Monday before Easter to the 30th September, 10am-5pm weekdays only. 1st October to 28th October, 10am-4pm weekdays only. **Special Attractions:** Superb display of Honiton Lace. Lace making demonstrations June to August. Also local history exhibits.

ILFRACOMBE
An immensely popular coastal resort, Ilfracombe lies deep set into surrounding hills and has a busy harbour and well sheltered beaches. There are magnificent walks and panoramic views of the town and cliffs. The houses along the ancient quay are of a unique arrangement and make for interesting study. Steamer services operate regularly to Lynmouth, Clovelly, Minehead and Bristol as well as Channel Cruises to Lundy Island and the Mumbles. Places worth visiting are Lantern Hill named for the lighthouse which stands at its summit. Above Rapporee Cove rises Hillsborough Hill, headland approximately 500 feet high, which gives extensive views of the town and inland countryside.

The Copstave Rock is another important promontory over 150 feet high with sheer North and West sides, and easy slopes from the town side. From the enormous rock, Lundy Island can be seen with the coast of South Wales on the distant Horizon.

Other interesting walks, beauty spots and picnic areas are the Torre Walks with continuously changing channel views, and Cairn Top which rises over 500 feet. cairn Top is remarkable for Austrian and Scots pine trees and borders of Rhododendron and Laurel. The views from the top are breathtaking.

ILFRACOMBE
MULLACOTT MINIATURE PONIES & SHIRE HORSE CENTRE
: Mullacott Farm, Ilfracombe, North Devon, EX34 8NA. Tel & Fax : 01271 866877.
Nearest Railway Station : Barnstaple. Location : On the A361 Barnstaple to Ilfracombe road 1 mile from Ilfracombe. Open : Easter to the end of October, 10am-4pm. Please telephone for Saturday opening. **Special Attractions:** Large collection of miniature ponies and shire horses, large Pets Corner, Falconry Centre and Red Deer Park. Off road riding centre giving safe and scenic rides with horses to suit all capabilities, qualifid staff. Many other animals to see. Pet shop and garden centre.

ILFRACOMBE
WATERMOUTH CASTLE : Nr. Ilfracombe, North Devon, EX34 9SL. Tel : 01271 863879. Fax : 01271 865864.
Nearest Railway Station : Barnstaple. Location : Between Ilfracombe and Combe Martin on the A399 Coast road. Open : April to October - Limited times early and late season - always closed Saturdays. **Special Attractions:** The castle and grounds provide over 50 different attractions ranging from Victorian displays, a village of gnomes to crazy pit-pat, also our indoor fountain theatre. Cafe, gift shops, etc.

CADE'S WEST COUNTRY CAMPING, TOURING & MOTOR CARAVAN SITE GUIDE 1997   63

DEVON

ISLE OF LUNDY
LUNDY ISLAND : Lundy, Bristol Channel, Via Bideford, Devon. Tel : 01237 431831.
Nearest Railway Station : Barnstaple. Location : Passenger ship M.S. Oldenburg sails from Ilfracombe and Bideford. Open : All year round. **Special Attractions:** Unique offshore island with excellent facilities.

KINGSBRIDGE
STANCOMBE TRADITIONAL FARMHOUSE CYDER : Stancombe, Sherford, Kingsbridge, South Devon, TQ7 2BE. Tel : 01548 531634. Fax : 01548 531012.
Nearest Railway Station : Totnes. Location : In the South Hams, between Kingsbridge and Dartmouth. Follow the "Cyder Press" signs. Open : Every day during the season, 9am-5pm. **Special Attractions:** Traditional farmhouse cyder, fermented in oak casks, made from pure Devon apple juice. Free admission, free samples and free parking.

LYNMOUTH
EXMOOR BRASS RUBBING & HOBBYCRAFT CENTRE : Watersmeet Road, Lynmouth, Devon, EX35 6EP. Tel : 01598 52529. Fax : 01598 752529.
Nearest Railway Station : Barnstaple or Minehead. Location : Situated beside East Lyn River and next to the Watersmeet Road car park in picturesque Lynmouth village. Open : Easter to end of October 10.30am-5pm. February school half term. 7 days a week in school holidays, Monday to Friday at other times. **Special Attractions:** Free Entry. Popular family run attraction with exciting collection of over 200 facsimiles of brasses and special rubbing plates. Selection includes Knights, Ladies, Clergy, Royalty, Skeletons, Oriental Dancers, Childrens Stories and animals. Help given. Prices from £1.35.

MODBURY
WOODTURNERS (SOUTH DEVON) CRAFT CENTRE, MRS ANN TRIPPAS & MR JOHN TRIPPAS EST. 1959 : New Road, Modbury, South Devon, PL21 0QH. Tel : 01548 830405.
Nearest Railway Station : Plymouth. Location : 12 miles from Plymouth, 5 miles from Kingsbridge on the A379. Open : From February to December 10.30am-6pm (every day). Sundays and January by appointment, telephone Plymouth 892832 STD 01752. **Special Attractions:** Woodturning and carving demonstrations which you can watch, also furniture being made. Customers own designs. We stock locally made crafts and have them for sale, together with our own work. We look forward to seeing you.

NEWTON ABBOT
Newton Abbot is an important railway junction and agriculture centre. Cider-apple orchards are cultivated to the South of the Teign Estuary town.

Only the tower of the old church of St Leonard remains. Jacobean Forde House visited by Charles I in 1625 and William of Orange in 1688 and picturesque Bradley Manor with a fine hall and chapel are worth visiting.

NEWTON ABBOT
GORSE BLOSSOM MINIATURE RAILWAY & WOODLAND PARK : Bickington, Newton Abbot, Devon, TQ12 6JD. Tel : 01626 821361.
Location : Off the old A38 between Drumbridges roundabout (A38/A382) and Bickington (A38/A383). Open : Easter to the last Sunday in October. **Special Attractions:** Set amidst 35 acres of woodland, the park provides a unique blend of woodland leisure and activity including a challenging assault course and giant slide. Two great family attractions, the three quarter mile steam miniature railway, with unlimited rides, and the Swiss Outdoor Model Railway in its mountain setting. Also a train you can drive.

OKEHAMPTON
THE NATIONAL TRUST : The Stables, Lydford Gorge, Okehampton, Devon, EX20 4BH. Tel : 01822 820320.

Nearest Railway Station : Exeter. Location : At the West end of Lydford village, halfway between Okehampton and Tavistock off the A386. Open : April 1st to October 31st daily, 10am-5.30pm. **Special Attractions:** A deep ravine scooped out by the River Lyd. 90' Whitelady Waterfall and a riverside walk to the exciting whirlpool of the Devils Cauldron. Walks of between one to two hours, stout footwear required.

OTTERTON
OTTERTON MILL CENTRE & WORKING MUSEUM : Fore Street, Otterton, Near Budleigh Salterton, Devon. Tel : 01395 568521.
Nearest Railway Station : Exmouth. Location : In the village of Otterton, near the coastal resorts of Exmouth and Sidmouth. Open : Summer 10.30am-5.30pm daily. Winter 11.30am-4.30pm daily. **Special Attractions:** Art and craft exhibitions during the Summer, work shops, craft shop and working water mill producing wholemeal flour. Restaurant.

OTTERY ST MARY
CADHAY : Ottery St Mary, Devon. Tel : 01404 812432.
Nearest Railway Station : Feniton. Location : 1 mile Ottery St Mary, 6 miles Sidmouth, 11 miles Exeter. Open : Spring Bank Holiday May 25th and 26th, Tuesday to Thursday in July and August. Late Summer Bank Holiday, Sunday and Monday August 24th and 25th. 2pm-6pm (last admission 5.30pm).

PAIGNTON
PAIGNTON & DARTMOUTH STEAM RAILWAY : Queens Park Station, Torbay Road, Paignton, Devon, TQ4 6AF. Tel : 01803 555872.
Nearest Railway Station : Paignton (Next Door). Location : Centre of Paignton town. Open : Sunday, Tuesday and Thursday, April, May and October. Daily June, July, August and September. Santa Specials during December. **Special Attractions:** The holiday line with Steam Trains running for 7 miles in Great Western Tradition along the spectacular Torbay coast, through wooded slopes bordering the Dart Estuary to Kingswear. The scenery is superb with seascapes right across Lyme Bay to Portland Bill, across the River Dart is Dartmouth.

PLYMOUTH
The city of Plymouth has always had a long association with The Royal Navy and is a principal port, base and training area. Along with Portsmouth and Southampton in Hampshire, it was one of the most heavily bombed cities in the Second World War, and much of the pre-war city was destroyed.

The city was re-built under the guidance of Lord Astor and his principal associates and much of the planning for reconstruction was conceived while the city was still under attack. Many of the ancient and aesthetic buildings have been carefully reconstructed and there are still small areas of the original Plymouth to discover. Plymouth is now a leading commercial centre as well as a major port. Among the many interesting places to visit are the Eddystone Lighthouse and Harbour Breakwater.

Finally, Buckland Abbey close to Plymouth established in 1278 by Cistercian Monks and of the rare survivors of Henry VIII's rape of the monasteries is compulsory visiting. The fine Abbey also houses a remarkable exhibition of Sir Francis Drake's possessions.

PLYMOUTH
CROWNHILL FORT : Crownhill Fort Road, Plymouth, Devon PL6 5BX. Tel & Fax : 01752 787374.
Nearest Railway Station : Plymouth. Location : 3 miles north of Plymouth city centre, off the A386. Open : March to November, 7 days a week, 10am-5pm. **Special Attractions:** A 16 acre Victorian fortification with ramparts, tunnels and secret stairways to explore. Exhibition rooms, tea room, free car/coach parking. It is the largest and best preserved of the Palmerston Fortifications.

PLYMOUTH
THE NATIONAL SHIRE HORSE CENTRE : Yealmpton, Plymouth, Devon, PL8 2EL. Tel : 01752 880268. Fax : 01752 881014.

64   *CADE'S WEST COUNTRY CAMPING, TOURING & MOTOR CARAVAN SITE GUIDE 1997*

DEVON

Nearest Railway Station : Plymouth. Location : On A379 Plymouth-Kingsbridge road. Open : All year round. Every day, 10am-5pm. **Special Attractions:** See the Shire horses and new foals. Parade of horses 11.30am, 2.30pm and 4.15pm. Craft centre, childrens adventure playground, pets area, licensed restaurant and bar, cart rides, film show, country woodland walk, picnic areas and shops. Free Fall Slide and Butterfly centre. Falconry centre with flying displays 1pm and 3.30pm.

PLYMOUTH
PLYMOUTH AQUARIUM : Citadel Hill, Plymouth, Devon, PL1 2PB. Tel : 01752 633333. Fax : 01752 633102.
Nearest Railway Station : Plymouth. Open : March to October, daily 10am-5pm. Winter, weekends, school holidays and other times by arrangement. **Special Attractions:** See the animals in naturalistic settings showing the diverse habitats of the South West. So much for all the family to see and enjoy, come rain or shine.

PLYMOUTH
PLYMOUTH DOME : The Hoe, Plymouth, Devon, PL1 2NZ. Tel : 01752 600608 (Recorded Information). Fax : 01752 256361.
Nearest Railway Station : Plymouth. Location : Overlooking Plymouth Sound on Plymouth Hoe. Open : Every day (except Christmas Day) from 9am. Last admission 6pm (Summer), 5pm (Winter). **Special Attractions:** This Award-winning, purpose-built complex tells the story of this exciting city. Two theatres with Audio-Visual shows, great hands on viewing gallery with radar, zoom television etc. Shop and cafe.

PLYMOUTH
PLYMOUTH DRY GIN DISTILLERY : Blackfriars Distillery, 60 Southside Street, Plymouth, Devon, PL1 2LQ. Tel : 01752 665292. Fax : 01752 220062.
Nearest Railway Station : Plymouth. Location : Barbican, Plymouth. Open : Easter to the end of September, Guided Tours 10.30am-4.45pm. **Special Attractions:** A 200 year old distillery, which is the ONLY remaining gin distillery on its original site, still producing exactly the same fine quality gin.

PLYMOUTH
SALTRAM (NATIONAL TRUST) : Plympton, Plymouth, Devon, PL7 3UH. Tel : 01752 336546.
Nearest Railway Station : Plymouth. Location : 2 miles west of Plympton between the A38 and the A379. Open : April to October, Sunday to Thursday (including House), 12.30pm-5.30pm. Garden & Grounds, 11am-5.30pm. **Special Attractions:** Rooms designed by Robert Adam, fine period furniture and pictures including portraits by Sir Joshua Reynolds. Great kitchen, stables with exhibition and orangery.

PLYMOUTH
SMEATON'S TOWER : The Hoe, Plymouth, Devon, PL1 2NZ. Tel : 01752 600608 (Recorded Information). Fax : 01752 256361.
Location : Overlooking Plymouth Sound on Plymouth Hoe. Open : Easter to Mid September, 10.30am-4.30pm. Last Admission 4pm. **Special Attractions:** The former Eddystone Lighthouse, rebuilt on Plymouth Hoe.

SALCOMBE
OVERBECK'S MUSEUM (NATIONAL TRUST) : Sharpitor, Salcombe, Devon. Tel : 01548 842893.
Nearest Railway Station : Totnes. Location : 1 mile south west of Salcombe. Open : 24th March to October, Sunday to Friday 11am-5pm, except July and August. September and October, Sunday to Thursday 11am-4pm. Garden all year 10am-8pm (or dusk). **Special Attractions:** Secret room and quiz for children. Guilbenkien Award winners. Sub tropical gardens.

SHALDON
SHALDON WILDLIFE TRUST : Ness Drive, Shaldon, Devon, TQ14 0HP. Tel : 01626 872234.
Nearest Railway Station : Teignmouth. Location : Off A379 Torquay-Teignmouth road. Bus 185 alight at Ness Drive or Woodleigh Park. Opposite car park on the Ness. Open : All year 10am-6.30pm, Easter until end of September. 11am-4pm, October until Easter. **Special Attractions:** Breeding centre for rare and endangered animals including tree shrews, monkeys, parrots, owls, lemurs and snakes.

SIDMOUTH
THE DONKEY SANCTUARY : Sidmouth, Devon, EX10 0NU. Tel : 01395 578222. Fax : 01395 579266.
Nearest Railway Station : Honiton. Location : Situated on the A3052 between Sidford and the turning for Branscombe (look for the brown tourism signs). Open : Daily 9am until dusk. **Special Attractions:** The Donkey Sanctuary is the largest registered donkey and mule charity in the UK. Over 6800 donkeys have found peace, safety and care for life and can roam on our 1400 acres of land. No donkey is ever sold and all are guaranteed expert loving care for the rest of their natural lives.

SIDMOUTH
MOTORING MEMORIES : The Old Fire Station, 107 High Street, Sidmouth, Devon, EX10 8EF. Tel : 01297 552341.
Nearest Railway Station : Honiton. Location : In the High Street of Sidmouth. Open : Easter to the end of October, daily 10am-5pm. **Special Attractions:** A museum of motoring memorabilia and artefacts including cars and motorcycles.

SIDMOUTH
NORMAN LOCKYER OBSERVATORY : Salcombe Hill, Sidmouth, devon, EX10 0NY. Tel : 01395 568591.
Nearest Railway Station : Honiton. Open : Every Wednesday and Sunday afternoon, July and August. Evenings in Winter. (Please telephone or ask at the Tourist Information Centre). **Special Attractions:** Planetarium, telescopes, radio and weather station.

SIDMOUTH
SAND HISTORIC HOUSE : Sand, Sidbury, Sidmouth, Devon, EX10 0QN. Tel : 01395 597230.
Nearest Railway Station : Honiton. Location : 0.25 miles off the A375, signs 0.75 miles north of Sidbury. Open : 30th and 31st March. 4th, 5th, 25th and 26th May. 7th to the 10th then 24th and 25th August. 2pm-5.30pm, last tour at 4.45pm. **Special Attractions:** A lived in historic house owned by the Huyshe family since 1560, largely rebuilt in 1594, in an unspoilt valley. Screens, passage, Heraldry and family documents. Also Sand Lodge, roof structure of late 15th century Hall House.

SOUTH MOLTON
INTERNATIONAL ANIMAL RESCUE : Animal Tracks, Ash Mill, South Molton, Devon, EX36 4QW. Tel : 01769 550277. Fax : 01769 550917.
Nearest Railway Station ; Tiverton Parkway. Location : Just outside the village towards Tiverton, approx. 6 miles from South Molton. Open : 10am-6pm. **Special Attractions:** A 60 acre Animal Rescue Centre with a rare plant nursery. The centre offers the opportunity to meet our rescued animals and purchase a wide variety of plants that are often unavailable elsewhere.

SOUTH MOLTON
QUINCE HONEY FARM : North Road, South Molton, Devon. Tel : 01769 572401.
Nearest Railway Station : Barnstaple. Open : Easter to the end of October, 9am-6pm. Shop open all year. **Special Attractions:** An entertaining education for young and old alike at Britain's largest Honey Farm, incorporating the Worlds best exhibition of living Honeybees (behind glass). Unique opening hives expose the busy world of the Honeybee. Posters, photographs and video shows complement the live action. Shop for honey and beeswax products.

SOUTH MOLTON
SOUTH MOLTON MUSEUM : The Town Hall, South Molton, Devon. Tel : 01769 572951.
Nearest Railway Station : Barnstaple. Location : Guildhall, in the square. Open : Mondays, Tuesdays and Thursdays from 10.30am-1pm and 2pm-4pm. Wednesdays and Saturdays, 10.30am-12.30pm. Closed Friday and Sunday. Closed

CADE'S WEST COUNTRY CAMPING, TOURING & MOTOR CARAVAN SITE GUIDE 1997   65

DEVON

December, January and February, public holidays. Admission Free. **Special Attractions:** Old fire engines, pewter, local history displays and monthly exhibitions.

TAVISTOCK
Situated on the Western fringe of Dartmoor National Park near the River Tavy, Tavistock is a good touring centre for the beautiful surrounding countryside. Sir Francis Drake was born at Crowndale, but the house is no longer standing. A wild gorge known as Tavy Cleave can be seen on Dartmoor. Several foundry buildings stand in the town, and the areas around Tavistock Canal preserves a few Georgian cottages and stores.

TAVISTOCK
MORWELLHAM QUAY : Off A390, Near Tavistock, West Devon, PL19 8JL. Tel & Fax : 01822 833808.
Nearest Railway Station : Gunnislake. Open : Daily, all year (except Christmas). Mine train ride and grounds only in Winter. **Special Attractions:** Award winning visitor centre at historic rover port. Train ride into old mine workings. Horsedrawn carriage ride, costumes to try on, cottages, workshops, waymarked trails, all in a beautiful valley.

TIVERTON
The most notable feature of Tiverton is its renowned public school - Blundell's School founded in 1604. The school retains many of its original buildings. R.D. Blackmore of Lorna Doone fame was a pupil here.

Many old buildings and houses have continued to retain their character around the town. The town has two almshouses dating back to the 16th Century. St George's church originates from 1614 and Chilcot School founded in 1611.

The countryside surrounding Tiverton is very lush and quite beautiful, there are many lakes and fish farms in the area which caters for the keen pursuit of fishermen.

TIVERTON
DEVONSHIRE'S CENTRE : Bickleigh Mill, Bickleigh, Near Tiverton, Devon, EX16 8RG. Tel : 01884 855419.
Nearest Railway Station : Tiverton Junction. Location : Exe Valley. Open : April to September inclusive, 10am-5pm daily. January to March inclusive, 10am-5pm Saturday and Sunday only. **Special Attractions:** Devons most famous working watermill. Its own pottery and craft studios supporting an extensive range of good quality gifts, garments, leather work, confectionery and food for sale. Complimented still further by the restaurant, well known for Devonshire Cream Teas. A fishing centre is adjacent to the mill which is open within the main season.

TIVERTON
GRAND WESTERN HORSEBOAT CO. : The Wharf, Canal Hill, Tiverton, Devon, EX16 4HX. Tel : 01884 253345. Fax : 01884 255984.
Nearest Railway Station : Tiverton Parkway. Open : 1st April (or Easter) to early October. Public trips operate to a published timetable which is available from Tourist Information Centres and other outlets. Private hire available outside these times. **Special Attractions:** Within this beautiful Davon Country park, experience a bygone journey on a traditionally painted Horsedrawn Barge as the rushes nod their approving heads, birds sing and shadows dance attendance while a heavy horse gently pulls you along this peaceful canal. Canal Shop, Floating Restaurant, boat hire, walks, picnic area and car park.

TIVERTON
KNIGHTSHAYES COURT : Bolham, Tiverton, Devon, EX16 7RQ. Tel : 01884 254665.
Location : 2 miles North of Tiverton, off Tiverton-Bampton road A396. Open : 1st April to 31st October 1996. House Open 11am-5.30pm (closed Fridays). Garden Open 11am-5.30pm. **Special Attractions:** A richly decorated Victorian mansion and one of the finest gardens in Devon.

TIVERTON
TIVERTON CASTLE : Tiverton, Devon, EX16 6RP. Tel : 01884 253200. Fax : 01884 254200.
Nearest Railway Station : Tiverton Parkway. Location : Centre of Tiverton, next to St Peter's Church. Open : 2.30pm-5.30pm, Easter Sunday to end of June and September: Sundays and Thursdays only. August Sundays to Thursdays. Also open Bank Holiday Mondays (except Christmas and New Year). **Special Attractions:** Historic Fortress of Henry I built in 1106. Medieval Gatehouse and Tower housing interesting collection of English Civil War arms and armour; notable Campbell Clock Collection; romantic ruins, Solar and curtain walls, fine furniture and pictures. Free car park inside. Coach parties by prior appointment only.

TIVERTON
TIVERTON CRAFT CENTRE : 1 Bridge Street, Tiverton, Devon, EX16 5LY. Tel : 01884 258430.
Nearest Railway Station : Tiverton Parkway. Location : In the centre of Tiverton. Open : Monday to Saturday, 9am-5.30pm. Closed Sunday. **Special Attractions:** Handmade crafts with over 170 craftsmens work on display. We are reputed to be the largest locally handmade Craft Centre in the South West.

TIVERTON
TIVERTON MUSEUM : St Andrew Street, Tiverton, Devon, EX16 6PH. Tel : 01884 256295.
Nearest Railway Station : Tiverton Parkway. Location : In centre of town. St Andrew Street runs off main shopping street (Fore Street). Locate Town Hall and follow signs. Open : Monday to Saturday, 10.30am-4.30pm. Closed Sundays, and from December 24th to January 31st inclusive. **Special Attractions:** A comprehensive local museum of unusual scope embodying "Tivvy Bumper" GWR 042 Tank Engine, lace machine gallery, Waggon gallery, agricultural implements and many other interesting exhibits.

TORQUAY
A well known resort, yachting harbour and Spa, Torquay has an excellent beach of sand pebbles and shingle, and the warm climate allows the cultivation of sub-tropical vegetation in the public gardens.

There are many picturesque cliff walks in the area and the cliffs of Torquay often attract rock climbers nationwide. Splendid views are also available from the Ilsham Marine Drive.

In August, Torquay Regatta for sailing craft is an annual, popular event, attracting numerous entries and spectators. Apart from the harbour and extensive leisure facilities of Torquay, Torre Abbey and Art Gallery and St Michael's Chapel are well worth a visit and you will certainly find Anstey's Cave and Babbacombe Beach to be very attractive.

TORQUAY
BABBACOMBE POTTERY : Babbacombe Road, Torquay, Devon, TQ1 3SY. Tel : 01803 323322. Fax : 01803 315444.
Nearest Railway Station : Torquay. Location : Situated on the main Babbacombe Road approx 1 mile from harbour side. Number 32 bus route. Open : Works - Monday to Friday 9am-5pm. Shop and Tea Gardens - 7 days a week. Open Bank Holidays. **Special Attractions:** See how the pottery is made. "Have-A-Go" at throwing a pot or chose from a wide selection of pottery to paint yourself. Seating for 40 in our new art room. Fun for all the family. Visit the shop and beautiful Tea Gardens. Parking for cars and coaches. Entry is FREE.

TORQUAY
BYGONES LIFESIZE VICTORIAN STREET : Fore Street, St Marychurch, Torquay, Devon. Tel : 01803 326108.
Nearest Railway Station : Torquay. Location : 200yds from the Model Village at Babbacombe. Open : All year. July and August 10am-10pm. April, May, June, September and October 10am-5pm. November to March 10am-2pm. Last admission 1 hour before closing. Extended opening during school holidays.

66   *CADE'S WEST COUNTRY CAMPING, TOURING & MOTOR CARAVAN SITE GUIDE 1997*

DEVON

Special Attractions: Wander back in time and see a real olde worlde street including a forge, pub and period rooms. Enormous illuminated fantasy land and model railways, real steam engine and much more. Coffee Shop. New World War I walk through trench. Something for all the family. Allow 1 hour for your visit.

TORQUAY
COMPTON CASTLE : Marldon, Near Torquay, Devon. Tel : 01803 872112.
Location : 4 miles West of Torquay, 1 mile North of Marldon. From the Newton Abbot-Totnes road (A381) turn left at Ipplepen crossroads and West of Torbay ring road via Marldon. Open : April to the end of October, Monday Wednesday and Thursday, 10am-12.15pm and 2pm-5pm, last admission half hour before closing, when the courtyard, restored great hall, kitchen, chapel, solar and rose garden are shown. Special Attractions: A fortified Manor house built at three periods - 1320, 1440 and 1520 - by the family of Gilbert (Sir Humphrey Gilbert, coloniser of Newfoundland and half-brother to Sir Walter Raleigh) and still the family's home.

TORQUAY
KENTS CAVERN SHOWCAVES : 91 Ilsham Road, Wellswood, Torquay, Devon, TQ1 2JF. Tel : 01803 215136. Fax : 01803 211034.
Nearest Railway Station : Torquay. Location : Just off Ilsham Road, 1 mile from Torquay Harbour. Open : November to March, 10am-5pm. April to September, 10am-6pm. Evening opening until 10.30pm July and August - Special 'Ghost' Tours. Special Attractions: Torquay's Caves & Exhibition! A guided tour creates an atmosphere of mystery and discovery as you wander through this ancient prehistoric dwelling, with spectacular natural formations. A NEW exhibition re-creates the scenes of our first explorers and excavators!

TORQUAY
RIVIERA CENTRE : Chestnut Avenue, Torquay, Devon, TQ2 5LZ. Tel : 01803 299992. Fax : 01803 212827.
Nearest Railway Station : Torquay. Location : Opposite Torre Abbey Sands, Torquay's seafront. Open : Every day from 9am. Pool closes at various times, please telephone for details. Special Attractions: Tropical leisure pool with waves, flume, paddling pool, yellow submarine and giant Robo-Ant inflatable. Health and fitness suite with a gym, sauna, steam room, sunbeds and aerobics studio. Exciting entertainments schedule of shows, cinema, dances and Summer Shows. Also a coffee shop, restaurant, bars, American Diner and childrens activities.

TORQUAY
TORQUAY MUSEUM: 529 Babbacombe Road, Torquay, Devon. Tel: 01803 293975. Fax : 01803 294186.
Open: 10am-4.45pm Mondays to Fridays throughout the year, Saturdays 10am-4.45pm and Sundays 1.30pm-4.45pm from Easter to October. Closed Good Friday, Christmas and New Year. Small admission charge. Special Attractions: An impressive Natural History Gallery, important finds from Kents Cavern and other local caves, archaeology of South Devon, overseas ethnography, Devon folk life, local pottery, Victoriana and an Agatha Christie Exhibition.

TORRINGTON
ROSEMOOR GARDEN : RHS Rosemoor Garden, Great Torrington, Devon, EX38 8PH. Tel : 01805 624307. Fax : 01805 624717.
Nearest Railway Station : Umberleigh. Location : 1 mile south of Great Torrington on the B3220 to Exeter. Open : All Year. October to March, 10am-5pm. April to September, 10am-6pm. Special Attractions: Famous 40 acre National Garden in a stunning Devon valley setting. Ranging from Lady Anne's mature planting and arboretum around Rosemoor House, past Shream Garden and rock gorge to the lake and magnificent new gardens of wide variety. 2000 Roses. Fruit and vegetable garden. Award Winning Visitors Centre. Licensed restaurant, shop, plants and picnic area.

TOTNES
DEVONSHIRE COLLECTION OF PERIOD COSTUME : Bogan House, High Street, Totnes, South Devon, TQ9 6DS.
Location : In the centre of the town opposite the Civic Hall, under the Butter Walk. Open : Spring Bank Holiday to October 1st, Monday to Friday inclusive 11am-5pm. Special Attractions: A new exhibition of costumes from the Collection each summer. Exhibition for 1997 "At the Court of St James - A Celebration of the Golden Jubilee of Queen Victoria".

TOTNES
LOTUS POTTERY : Stoke Gabriel, Near Totnes, Devon, TQ9 6SL. Tel : 01803 782303.
Nearest Railway Station : Totnes/Paignton. Location : 4 miles from Totnes and Paignton on the Torbay side of the River Dart. Open : Monday to Friday, 9am-5.30pm (closed 1pm-2pm). Special Attractions: Wide range of wood-fired stoneware and porcelain.

TOTNES
TOTNES ELIZABETHAN MUSEUM : 70 Fore Street, Totnes, Devon, TQ9 5RU. Tel : 01803 863821.
Nearest Railway Station : Totnes. Location : In the centre of town, just before the East Gate Archway. Open : Monday to Friday, 10.30am-5pm. Saturday 2pm-5pm. Special Attractions: A family museum in a rich Tudor merchant's house. Interest for all, our world famous exhibition about Charles Babbage and his computers. Delightful setting with a herb garden.

YELVERTON
BUCKLAND ABBEY (NATIONAL TRUST) : Buckland Abbey, Yelverton, Devon, PL20 6EY. Tel : 01822 853607. Fax : 01822 855448.
Nearest Railway Station : Plymouth. Location : 11 miles north of Plymouth, 6 miles south of Tavistock. Signposted from the A386 at Yelverton. Open : April to October, daily except Thursday, 10.30am-5.30pm. November to March, Saturday and Sunday only, 2pm-5pm. Last admission 45 minutes before closing. Special Attractions: Former medieval Cistercian monastery, then home of Sir Francis Drake and Sir Richard Grenville. Furnished rooms; DRAKE/ARMADA museum; ancient buildings; estate walks; independent craft workshops. Shop and restaurant/tea room. Special events and children's holiday activity programme.

YELVERTON
YELVERTON PAPERWEIGHT CENTRE : 4 Buckland Terrace, Leg O' Mutton, Yelverton, Devon, PL20 6AD. Tel & Fax : 01822 854250.
Nearest Railway Station : Plymouth. Location : West Devon, north of Plymouth, south of Tavistock on the A386. Open : Two weeks before Easter to the end of October, 10am-5pm Monday to Saturday. Sundays, 18th May to 14th September, 10am-5pm. All Winter Wednesday 1pm-5pm, Saturday 10am-5pm. 1st to the 24th December, 10am-5pm. Special Attractions: This unusual centre is the home of The Broughton Collection - a glittering display of Glass Paperweights, all shapes, sizes and age. Modern paperweights for sale, prices range from a few pounds to over 800 pounds for the serious collector. Original oil and watercolour paintings including Dartmoor scenes by local artists.

PLEASE MENTION CADE'S WHEN REPLYING TO ADVERTISERS

DORSET

DORSET

BERE REGIS
Rowlands Wait Touring Park, Rye Hill, Bere Regis, Dorset, BH20 7HH.
Tel: 471958 Std: 01929
Nearest Town/Resort Wareham
Directions At Bere Regis take road signposted to Wool/Bovington, about ¾ mile at top of Rye Hill turn right. Site 300yds.
Acreage 8 **Open** March to January
Access Good **Site** Lev/Slope
Sites Available A ⊕ ⊜ **Total** 71
Low Season Band B
High Season Band C
Facilities ▨ ⌂ ƒ ⎍ ⚿ ⎈ ∩ ⊖ ⎙ ⎚ ⌨
⚐ ◎ ⊜ ⚘ ⎱ ✲ ⊟
Nearby Facilities ⌁ ⁄ ⌠ ⌡ U ⨀ ℘
⋑ Wool
Situated in area of outstanding natural beauty. Within easy reach of coast, direct access from site into heath and woodland. Ideal walking, touring and the quiet family holiday. Rallies welcome.

BLANDFORD
The Inside Park, Blandford, Dorset, DT11 OHG.
Tel: 453719 Std: 01258
Fax: **454026** Std: **01258**
Nearest Town/Resort Blandford Forum
Directions 1¼ miles south west of Blandford on the road to Winterborne Stickland. Signposted from junction of A350 and A354 on Blandford bypass.
Acreage 13 **Open** Easter to October
Access Good **Site** Lev/Slope
Sites Available A ⊕ ⊜ **Total** 100
Low Season Band B
High Season Band C
Facilities ▨ ⌂ ƒ ⎍ ⚿ ⎈ ∩ ⊙ ⎙ ⎚ ⌨
⚐ ◎ ⊜ ⚘ ⎱ ✲ ⊟
Nearby Facilities ⌁ ⁄ U ℘
Rural environment, ideal for touring, extensive wildlife.

BRIDPORT
Binghams Farm Touring Caravan Park, Binghams Farm, Melplash, Bridport, Dorset, DT6 3TT.
Tel: 488234 Std: 01308
Nearest Town/Resort West Bay/Bridport.
Directions Turn off A35 in Bridport at the roundabout onto A3066, signposted Beaminster. In 1¼ miles turn left into Farm Road.
Acreage 3 **Open** All Year
Access Good **Site** Level
Sites Available A ⊕ ⊜ **Total** 60
Low Season Band C
High Season Band A
Facilities ▨ ⌂ ƒ ⎍ ⚿ ⎈ ∩ ⊙ ⎚ ⌨
⚐ ◎ ⊜ ⚘ ⎱ ✲ ⊟
Nearby Facilities ⌁ ⁄ ⌠ ⌡ U ⨀ ℘
⋑ Dorchester
An Award Winning Park set in an area of outstanding natural beauty yet only 3 miles from the coast. An ideal base to explore Dorset. All modern heated facilities.

BRIDPORT
Coastal Caravans, Annings Lane, Burton Bradstock, Dorset.
Tel: 897361 Std: 01308
Nearest Town/Resort Bridport.
Directions 3 miles east of Bridport off main Weymouth road, Burton Bradstock Anchor Hotel turn left and the second right.
Acreage 5 **Open** Easter to October
Access Good **Site** Level
Sites Available A ⊕ ⊜ **Total** 75

Facilities ƒ ⎍ ⚿ ⎈ ∩ ⊙ ⎙ ⎚ ⌨
Nearby Facilities ⌁ ⁄ U
⋑ Dorchester.
1 mile beach, river frontage, scenic views, ideal centre for touring Dorset, Devon and Hampshire.

BRIDPORT
Freshwater Beach Holiday Park, Burton Bradstock, Bridport, Dorset.
Tel: 897317 Std: 01308
Nearest Town/Resort Bridport.
Directions From Bridport take B3157 towards Weymouth site 2 miles on right.
Acreage 40 **Open** Easter to October
Access Good **Site** Level
Sites Available A ⊕ ⊜ **Total** 500
Facilities ƒ ⎍ ⚿ ⎈ ∩ ⊙ ⎙ ⎚ ⌨
⚐ ⎘ ◎ ⊜ ⚘ × ⎱ ✲ ⊟
Nearby Facilities ⌁ ⁄ ⌠ ⌡ U
⋑ Dorchester
On beach, cliff walks, golf course adjoining site.

BRIDPORT
Highlands End Farm Holiday Park, Eype, Bridport, Dorset, DT6 6AR.
Tel: Bridport 422139 Std: 01308;
Nearest Town/Resort Bridport.
Directions On approach to Bridport from east (Dorchester) on A35 turn left at roundabout, follow Bridport By-pass. Second roundabout take third exit signposted A35 West 1 mile turn left to Eype and follow signposts.
Acreage 8 **Open** March to October
Access Good **Site** Level
Sites Available A ⊕ ⊜ **Total** 195
Low Season Band B
High Season Band C
Facilities ƒ ⎍ ⚿ ⎈ ∩ ⊙ ⎙ ⎚ ⌨
⚐ ⎘ ◎ ⊜ ⚘ × ⎱ ✲ ⊟
Nearby Facilities ⌁ ⁄ ℘
⋑ Axminsterr.
Exceptional views across Lyme Bay, 500 metres from the beach, indoor heated swimming pool. Tennis on site. Hard standing with all weather awning area. British Graded Park - Excellent.

BRIDPORT
Uploders Farm, Uploders, Bridport, Dorset, DT6 4NZ.
Tel: 423380 Std: 01308
Nearest Town/Resort Bridport
Directions A35 3 miles east of Bridport. Just off main road.
Acreage 2 **Open** April to October
Access Good **Site** Level
Sites Available A ⊕ ⊜ **Total** 25
Low Season Band B
High Season Band A
Facilities ⎈ ⊙ ⊟
Nearby Facilities ⌁ ⁄ ⚘ U
⋑ Dorchester
Beach 4 miles, ideal touring area. Lovely countryside.

BRIDPORT
West Bay Holiday Park, West Bay, Bridport, Dorset, DT6 4HB.
Tel: 422424 Std: 01308
Nearest Town/Resort Weymouth
Directions A35 from Dorchester. West Bay is towards the harbour.
Open Easter to End Oct
Access Good **Site** Level
Sites Available A ⊕ ⊜ **Total** 150
Facilities ⌂ ƒ ⎍ ⚿ ⎈ ∩ ⊙ ⎙ ⎚ ⌨
⚐ ⎘ ◎ ⊜ ⚘ × ⎱ ✲ ⊟
Nearby Facilities ⌁ ⁄ ⌠ ⌡

⋑ Weymouth.
Riverside, next to the harbour. Indoor swimming pool.

CHARMOUTH
Manor Farm Holiday Centre, Manor Farm, Charmouth, Bridport, Dorset, DT6 6QL.
Tel: 560226 Std: 01297
Fax: **560429** Std: **01297**
Nearest Town/Resort Charmouth.
Directions Come off the Charmouth bypass at east end Manor Farm is ¾ mile on right, in Charmouth.
Acreage 30 **Open** All year
Access Good **Site** Lev/Slope
Sites Available A ⊕ ⊜ **Total** 345
Low Season Band B
High Season Band C
Facilities ▨ ⌂ ƒ ⎍ ⚿ ⎈ ∩ ⊙ ⎙ ⎚ ⌨
⚐ ⎘ ◎ ⊜ ⚘ × ⎱ ✲ ⊟
Nearby Facilities ⌁ ⁄ ⌠ ⌡ U ⨀ ℘
⋑ Axminster.
Ten minutes level walk to beach, alongside river. In area of outstanding natural beauty. Ideal touring.

CHARMOUTH
Monkton Wylde Farm Caravan Park, Charmouth, Dorset, DT6 6DB.
Tel: 34525 Std: 01297
Fax: **33594** Std: **01297**
Nearest Town/Resort Charmouth
Directions A35 west from Charmouth. At Greenway Head take the B3165 to Marshwood site ½ mile down lane on left.
Acreage 6 **Open** Easter to October
Access Good **Site** Level
Sites Available A ⊕ ⊜ **Total** 60
Low Season Band B
High Season Band C
Facilities ⌂ ƒ ⎍ ⚿ ⎈ ∩ ⊙ ⎙ ⎚ ⌨
⎘ ◎ ⊜ ⚘ ✲ ⊟
Nearby Facilities ⌁ ⁄ ⌠ ⌡ U ⨀ ℘
⋑ Axminster
3 miles from sea. Surrounded by woods and fields, on working farm. Quiet park.

CHARMOUTH
Newlands Caravan Park, Charmouth, Dorset, DT6 6RB.
Tel: 560259 Std: 01297
Fax: **560797** Std: **01297**
Nearest Town/Resort
Directions From the eastern end of Charmouth by-pass (A35), turn toward Charmouth Village. Site is 100 metres on the left.
Acreage 23 **Open** 16 March to October
Access Good **Site** Lev/Slope
Sites Available A ⊕ ⊜ **Total** 200
Low Season Band C
High Season Band C
Facilities ⌂ ƒ ⎍ ⚿ ⎈ ∩ ⊙ ⎙ ⎚ ⌨
⚐ ⎘ ◎ ⊜ ⚘ × ⎱ ✲ ⊟
Nearby Facilities ⌁ ⁄ ⌠ ⌡ U ⨀ ℘
⋑ Axminster
Famous fossil beach. Ideal for Lyme Regis, Hardy Country, etc..

CHARMOUTH
Wood Farm Caravan & Camping Park, Axminster Road, Charmouth, Bridport, Dorset DT6 6BT.
Tel: 560697 Std: 01297.
Fax: **560697** Std: **01297**.
Nearest Town/Resort Charmouth.
Directions On A35, ½ mile west Charmouth.
Acreage 12
Access Good **Site** Terraced
Sites Available A ⊕ ⊜ **Total** 216

68 *CADE'S WEST CUONTRY CAMPING, TOURING & MOTOR CARAVAN SITE GUIDE 1997*

DORSET

MANOR FARM HOLIDAY CENTRE
Charmouth   Dorset   DT6 6QL
Tel: (01297) 560226

Large open site for touring caravans, motor caravans and tents. Also caravans and houses to hire.

Facilities include: New Shower Block for 1996/7 with disabled facilities, Baby Room, Launderette and Dish Washing Area. Swimming Pool and Children Pool, Bar with Family Room. At Charmouth 10 minute level walk to the beach.

Colour Brochure from Mr G. Loosmore or Tel: 01297 560226

Low Season Band B
High Season Band C
Facilities ! ▨ ♨ ⌒ ⌣ ▲ ◻ ☂
▨ ◯ ◉ ♞ ⌂ ⊕ ✳ ▤
Nearby Facilities ⌐ ⁄ ⊥ ⌦ ∪ ♪ ♫
✤ Axminster.
Beach ¾ mile. Country setting. Tennis on site. Indoor heated swimming pool.

CHIDEOCK
Golden Cap Holiday Park, Seatown, Chideock, Nr. Bridport, Dorset.
Tel: 422139 Std: 01308
Nearest Town/Resort Bridport
Directions On approach to Bridport from east (Dorchester) follow A35 signs around Bridport by-pass. After 2 miles west of Bridport turn left for Seatown, at Chideock park is signposted.
Acreage 10 **Open** March to October
Access Good   **Site** Level
Sites Available ▲ ⬚ ⚌ **Total** 120
Low Season Band B
High Season Band C
Facilities ♿ ! ▨ ♨ ⌒ ⌣ ▲ ◻ ☂
▨ ◯ ◉ ⌂ ▤
Nearby Facilities ⌐ ⁄ ♫
✤ Axminster.
100 metres from beach, overlooked by the famous Golden Cap cliff top. Indoor swimming pool available 5 minutes travelling time. Hard standings with all weather awning extra. British Graded Park - Excellent. Take-away food available. Unique location on the Heritage Coastline.

CHRISTCHURCH
Grove Farm Meadow Holiday Park, Stour Way, Christchurch, Dorset, BH23 2PQ.
Tel: 483597 Std: 01202
Fax: **483878** Std: **01202**
Nearest Town/Resort Christchurch.
Directions From Christchurch take the A35 west for 1¼ miles. Turn right at the roundabout near Crooked Bean Restaurant into The Grove. Stour Way is second on the left. Park is at extreme end of Stour Way (signposted).
Acreage 3 **Open** March to October
Access Good   **Site** Level
Sites Available ⬚ ⚌ **Total** 48
Low Season Band B
High Season Band C
Facilities ♿ ! ▨ ♨ ⌒ ⌣ ▲ ◻ ☂
▨ ◯ ◉ ⌂ ⊕ ✳ ▤
Nearby Facilities ⌐ ⁄ ⊥ ⌦ ∪ ♪ ♫
✤ Christchurch.
On banks of River Stour. Ideal touring base for Bournemouth, New Forest, Dorset coast and heritage. Tourist Board and Rose Award graded excellent.

CHRISTCHURCH
Hoburne Park, Hoburne Lane, Christchurch, Dorset, BH23 4HU.
Tel: 273379 Std: 01425
Nearest Town/Resort Christchurch.
Directions From junction of A35 with A337 at Christchurch, take first exit left onto A337 towards Lymington and then left off next roundabout. Park entrance is 100yds on right.
Acreage 17 **Open** March to October
Access Good   **Site** Level
Sites Available ⬚ ⚌ **Total** 285
Low Season Band C
High Season Band C
Facilities ! ▨ ♨ ⌒ ⌣ ▲ ◻ ☂
▨ ◯ ◉ ♞ ⌦ ▨ ♨ ⌂ ⊕ ✳ ▤
Nearby Facilities ⌐ ⁄ ⊥ ⌦ ∪ ♪ ♫
✤ Christchurch
Approx 8 miles from Bournemouth, close to sandy beaches, the New Forest, the Solent and the Isle of Wight. Caravan Holiday Park of the Year 1994, England for Excellence Awards (ETB).

CHRISTCHURCH
Port View Caravan Park, Matchams Lane, Christchurch, Dorset, BH23 6AW.
Tel: 474214 Std: 01202
Nearest Town/Resort Bournemouth
Directions Take the A338 Ringwood to Bournemouth road, exit Christchurch turn right, mini roundabout right, next left into Matchams Lane. Port View is exactly 1 mile on the right hand side.
Acreage 5 **Open** March to October
Access Good   **Site** Lev/Slope
Sites Available ▲ ⬚ ⚌ **Total** 75
Low Season Band B
High Season Band C
Facilities ♿ ! ▨ ♨ ⌒ ⌣ ▲ ◻ ☂
▨ ◯ ◉ ♞ ⌂ ▤
Nearby Facilities ⌐ ⁄ ⊥ ⌦ ∪ ♪ ♫
✤ Christchurch.
New Forest, Bournemouth and beautiful beaches.

CORFE CASTLE
The Woodland Camping Park, Glebe Farm, Bucknowle, Wareham, Dorset, BH20 5NS.
Tel: 480280 Std: 01929
Nearest Town/Resort Swanage/Wareham
Directions Take Church Knowle and Kimmeridge road off A351 at Corfe Castle ruins site ½ mile on right.
Acreage 6½ **Open** Easter to October
        Site Lev/Slope
Sites Available ▲ ⬚ ⚌ **Total** 65
Facilities ▨ ♨ ⌒ ⌣ ▲ ☂ ▨ ⊕ ◯ ◉ ▤

Nearby Facilities ⌐ ⁄ ⊥ ⌦ ∪ ♪ ♫
Direct access onto Purbeck Hills by public footpath. 3 beaches within 5 miles. A quiet family site. SAE for full information.

DORCHESTER
Clay Pigeon Caravan Park, Wardon Hill, Evershot, Dorchester, Dorset.
Tel: 83492 Std: 01935
Nearest Town/Resort Dorchester.
Directions On A37 midway between Yeovil and Dorchester.
Acreage 3¼ **Open** All Year
Access Good   **Site** Level
Sites Available ▲ ⬚ ⚌ **Total** 60
Low Season Band B
High Season Band C
Facilities ◻ ! ▨ ♨ ⌒ ⌣ ☂
▨ ◯ ◉ ▨ ▤
Nearby Facilities ⌐ ⁄
✤ Dorchester
Views over Dorset Downs. Ideal for touring. Lyme Bay and Weymouth close by. Separate 4¼ acre rally field. British Graded Holiday Park 4 Ticks.

DORCHESTER
Crossways Caravan Club Site, Crossways, Dorchester, Dorset, DT2 8BE.
Tel: 852032 Std: 01305
Nearest Town/Resort Dorchester/Weymouth
Directions From Dorchester take the A352 signposted Wareham, at the second roundabout follow signs for Crossways. Turn left at the B3390, enter the site through the Shell Garage on the right.
Acreage 11 **Open** 26th March to 27th October
Access Good   **Site** Level
Sites Available ⬚ ⚌ **Total** 150
Facilities ♿ ! ♨ ⌒ ⌣ ☂ ▨ ◯ ◉ ▨
Nearby Facilities ⌐ ⁄ ⊥ ⌦ ∪ ♪ ♫
✤ Morton
Thomas Hardy country, 9 miles from Weymouth. Adventure play area, showers and toilets.

DORCHESTER
Giants Head Caravan & Camping Park, Old Sherborne Road, Dorchester, Dorset.
Tel: 341242 Std: 01300
Nearest Town/Resort Dorchester
Directions From Dorchester avoiding by-pass, at top of town roundabout take Sherborne Road approx 500 yards fork right at Loaders Garage signposted.
Acreage 3 **Open** March to October
Access Good   **Site** Lev/Slope
Sites Available ▲ ⬚ ⚌ **Total** 50
Low Season Band B
High Season Band B

CADE'S WEST COUNTRY CAMPING, TOURING & MOTOR CARAVAN SITE GUIDE 1997

DORSET

Facilities ▨ ∮ ⌸ ⚓ ┌ ⊙ ⌐ ⌬ ▢ ☗
⚹ ◯ ⎕ ⊟
Nearby Facilities ┌ ✦ ⊥ ≿ ∪ ⇘ ♪
≢ Dorchester.
Ideal touring, wonderful views, good walking. Car is essential. Licensed.

DORCHESTER

Warmwell Country Touring Park, Warmwell, Nr. Dorchester, Dorset, DT2 8JE.
Tel: 852313 Std: 01305
Nearest Town/Resort Weymouth
Directions From A31 Dorchester to Poole road take the B3390 signposted Warmwell.
Acreage 15 **Open** March to January
Access Good **Site** Level
Sites Available ⚐ ⛃ ⛁ **Total** 190
Low Season Band A
High Season Band C
Facilities ▨ ⚘ ∮ ⌸ ⚓ ┌ ⊙ ⌐ ⌬ ▢ ☗
⚹ ⚟ ⎘ ◯ ⚑ ✦ ⎕ ♣ ⌂ ✱ ⊟
Nearby Facilities ┌ ✦ ⊥ ≿ ∪ ⇘ ♪
≢ Moreton
Opposite major leisure attractions. Rallies welcome.

FERNDOWN

St. Leonards Farm, Ringwood Road, West Moors, Ferndown, Dorset.
Tel: 872637 Std: 01202
Nearest Town/Resort Bournemouth.
Directions 5 miles west of Ringwood on the A31 opposite Gulf Garage.
Acreage 8 **Open** April to September
Access Good **Site** Level
Sites Available ⚐ ⛃ ⛁ **Total** 150
Low Season Band C
High Season Band C
Facilities ▨ ⚘ ∮ ⌸ ⚓ ┌ ⊙ ⌐ ⌬ ▢ ☗
⎘ ◯ ⚑ ⎕ ⊟
Nearby Facilities ┌ ✦ ⊥ ≿ ∪ ⇘ ♪
≢ Bournemouth.
Pleasant rural style park. Central for Bournemouth, Poole and the New Forest.

GILLINGHAM

Thorngrove Caravan & Camping Park, Common Mead Lane, Gillingham, Dorset, SP8 4RE.
Tel: 822242 Std: 01747
Fax: 825966 Std: 01747
Nearest Town/Resort Gillingham
Directions From the Gillingham relief road, take the B3081 signposted Wincanton. Take the second turning on the left signposted Kington Magna. Thorngrove is ¾ mile on the right.
Acreage 2½ **Open** All Year
Access Good **Site** Level
Sites Available ⚐ ⛃ ⛁ **Total** 40
Low Season Band B
High Season Band B
Facilities ▨ ⚘ ∮ ⌸ ⚓ ┌ ⊙ ⌐ ⌬ ▢ ☗
⚹ ⎕ ⚑ ⊟
Nearby Facilities ✦ ∪
≢ Gillingham
Peacefully situated with a delightful view of rural Dorset. Modern purpose built facilities in individual rooms. British Graded Holiday Park 5 Ticks.

LYME REGIS

Shrubbery Caravan Park, Rousdon, Lyme Regis, Dorset, DT7 3XW.
Tel: 442227 Std: 01297
Nearest Town/Resort Lyme Regis.
Directions 3 miles west of Lyme Regis on the A3052.
Acreage 10 **Open** March to November
Access Good **Site** Level
Sites Available ⚐ ⛃ ⛁ **Total** 120

Low Season Band B
High Season Band B
Facilities ▨ ∮ ⌸ ⚓ ┌ ⊙ ⌐ ⌬ ▢ ☗
⚹ ◯ ⚑ ⎕ ⊟
Nearby Facilities ┌ ✦ ⊥ ≿ ∪ ⇘ ♪
≢ Axminster.
Quiet, level, sheltered site.

LYME REGIS

Westhayes Caravan Park, Rousdon, Nr. Lyme Regis, Dorset, DT7 3RD.
Tel: Seaton 23456 Std: 01297
Fax: **625079** Std: **01297**
Nearest Town/Resort Lyme Regis/Seaton.
Directions Leave Axminster on A358 Seaton road, 3 miles turn left at Boshill Cross signposted Lyme Regis, site 1 mile on left.
Acreage 7½ **Open** All Year
Access Good **Site** Level
Sites Available ⚐ ⛃ ⛁ **Total** 150
Low Season Band B
High Season Band C
Facilities ▨ ∮ ⌸ ⚓ ┌ ⊙ ⌐ ⌬ ▢ ☗
⚹ ⎘ ◯ ⚑ ✦ ⊟
Nearby Facilities ┌ ✦ ⊥ ≿ ∪ ⇘ ♪
≢ Axminster.
Rallies welcome. Storage facilities. Static caravans for sale. Seasonal tourers.

OWERMOIGNE

Sandyholme Holiday Park, Moreton Road, Owermoigne, Nr. Dorchester, Dorset, DT2 8HZ.
Tel: 852677 Std: 01305
Nearest Town/Resort Dorchester/Weymouth
Directions Situated off the A352 Dorchester/Wareham Road - 1 mile through the pretty village of Owermoigne.
Acreage 6 **Open** Easter to October
Access Good **Site** Level
Sites Available ⚐ ⛃ ⛁ **Total** 65
Facilities ▨ ∮ ⚓ ┌ ⊙ ⌐ ⌬ ▢ ☗
⚹ ⎘ ◯ ⚑ ✦ ⚟ ⎕ ♣ ⌂ ✱ ⊟
Nearby Facilities ✦
≢ Moreton
Quiet family site in Hardy countryside, ideal touring spot with all facilities, situated between Lulworth Cove and Weymouth. Swimming pool nearby.

POOLE

Beacon Hill Touring Park, Blandford Road North, Poole, Dorset, BH16 6AB.
Tel: 631631 Std: 01202
Nearest Town/Resort Poole/Bournemouth
Directions Situated ¼ mile north from the junction of the A35 and A350 towards Blandford approx 3 miles north of Poole.
Acreage 30 **Open** Easter to September
Access Good **Site** Level
Sites Available ⚐ ⛃ ⛁ **Total** 170
Low Season Band B
High Season Band C
Facilities ⚘ ∮ ⌸ ⚓ ┌ ⊙ ⌐ ⌬ ▢ ☗
⚹ ⎕ ⚑ ⎘ ⚑ ✦ ⊟
Nearby Facilities ┌ ⊥ ≿ ∪ ⇘
≢ Poole
Partly wooded, lovely peaceful setting, scenic views. Proximity main routes. Ideal touring base for Bournemouth, New Forest and Dorset. Coarse fishing and tennis on site. Take away meals.

POOLE

Merley Court Touring Park, Merley, Wimborne, Nr Poole, Dorset, BH21 3AA.
Tel: 881488 Std: 01202
Nearest Town/Resort Poole.
Directions Direct access from Wimborne bypass south A31 junction A349 Poole road.

Acreage 11 **Open** March to Jan 7th
Access Good **Site** Level
Sites Available ⚐ ⛃ ⛁ **Total** 160
Low Season Band B
High Season Band C
Facilities ⚘ ∮ ⌸ ⚓ ┌ ⊙ ⌐ ⌬ ▢ ☗
⚹ ⎘ ◯ ⚑ ✦ ⎕ ⚟ ⌂ ☀ ⊟
Nearby Facilities ┌ ✦ ⊥ ≿ ∪ ⇘ ♪
≢ Poole.
Bournemouth 8 miles, Poole 4 miles, Purbeck and New Forest 7 miles. A.A. 3 pennant park, R.A.C. appointed, English Tourist Board Caravan Holiday Park of the Year 1991 (Grading 'Excellent'). 'Practical Caravan' Magazine's "Best Family Park" 1993 and 'Caravan Plus' Magazine's "Best Park" 1996.

POOLE

Organford Manor Caravans and Holidays, Organford, Poole, Dorset, BH16 6ES.
Tel: 622202 Std: 01202
Nearest Town/Resort Poole.
Directions Approaching from the Poole direction on the A35. At the Lytchett roundabout/junction of the A35/A351 continue on the A35 (signposted Dorchester) for ¼ mile. Take the first left, site first entrance on right.
Acreage 3 **Open** 15 March to October
Access Good **Site** Level
Sites Available ⚐ ⛃ ⛁ **Total** 80
Low Season Band B
High Season Band C
Facilities ▨ ∮ ⌸ ⚓ ┌ ⊙ ⌐ ⌬ ▢ ☗
⚹ ⎘ ◯ ⚑ ⎕ ⊟
Nearby Facilities ┌ ✦ ⊥ ≿ ∪ ⇘
≢ Poole/Wareham
Quiet, secluded site in wooded grounds of 11 acres. House within 10 miles of good beaches from Bournemouth to Swanage. Facilities for the disabled limited, few motorcycles accepted at Proprietors discretion.

POOLE

Pear Tree Caravan Park, Organford, Poole, Dorset, BH16 6LA.
Tel: 622434 Std: 01202
Nearest Town/Resort Poole
Directions Take A35 Poole/Dorchester road. Turn onto A351 to Wareham at Lytchett Minster. Turn right within 1 mile signposted Organford. Second site on left hand side ½ mile.
Acreage 7½ **Open** April to October
Access Good **Site** Level
Sites Available ⚐ ⛃ ⛁ **Total** 125
Low Season Band B
High Season Band C
Facilities ⚘ ∮ ⌸ ⚓ ┌ ⊙ ⌐ ⌬ ▢ ☗
⚹ ⎘ ◯ ⚑ ✱ ⊟
Nearby Facilities ┌ ✦ ⊥ ≿ ∪ ⇘
≢ Wareham/Poole
Quiet, family, country park, centrally situated for Bournemouth, Poole and Swanage. The New Forest, the Purbeck Hills and the lovely sandy beaches at Sandbanks and Studland Bay are all within easy reach.

POOLE

Rockley Park, Napier Road, Hamworthy, Poole, Dorset, BH15 4LZ.
Tel: 753753 Std: 0345
Nearest Town/Resort Poole
Directions From town centre go over lifting bridge and follow road to traffic lights. Turn left and follow signs for the park.
Open Easter to October
Access Good **Site** Sloping
Sites Available ⚐ ⛃ ⛁ **Total** 80

70   CADE'S WEST CUONTRY CAMPING, TOURING & MOTOR CARAVAN SITE GUIDE 1997

BEACON HILL TOURING PARK

POOLE DORSET

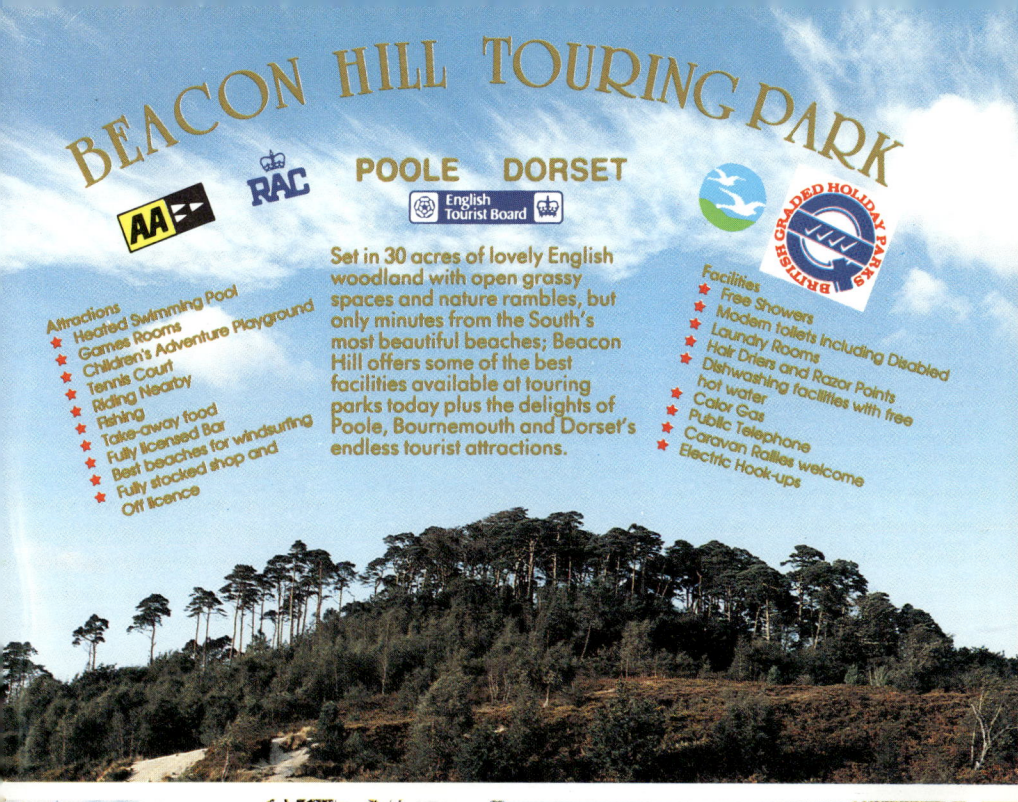

English Tourist Board

Set in 30 acres of lovely English woodland with open grassy spaces and nature rambles, but only minutes from the South's most beautiful beaches; Beacon Hill offers some of the best facilities available at touring parks today plus the delights of Poole, Bournemouth and Dorset's endless tourist attractions.

Attractions
- Heated Swimming Pool
- Games Rooms
- Children's Adventure Playground
- Tennis Court
- Riding Nearby
- Fishing
- Take-away food
- Fully licensed Bar
- Best beaches for windsurfing
- Fully stocked shop and Off licence

Facilities
- Free Showers
- Modern toilets including Disabled
- Laundry Rooms
- Hair Driers and Razor Points
- Dishwashing facilities with free hot water
- Calor Gas
- Public Telephone
- Caravan Rallies welcome
- Electric Hook-ups

Beacon Hill Touring Park, Blandford Road North, Poole, Dorset Tel: (01202) 631631

Directions: Situated ¼ mile north from the junction of the A35 and A350 towards Blandford, approximately 3 miles north of Poole

OVERNIGHT STOPS FOR POOLE-CHERBOURG, POOLE-ST. MALO, BRITTANY FERRIES, ONLY 3 MILES FROM FERRY TERMINAL

DORSET

Low Season Band A
High Season Band C
Facilities ↻ ƒ ⚿ ⛁ ☏ ⌂ ⊙⌐ ⊿ 🅿 ☎
⛽ ⊙ ⚑ ✕ ♀ ♠ ⚐ ⇄ ⊛ 🖃
Nearby Facilities ⌒ ✓ ⟂ ⤱ U ⇗ ♪
⚓ Poole
Direct access to the beach. Boat storage facilities.

POOLE

Sandford Holiday Park, Holton Heath, Poole, Dorset, BH16 6JZ.
Tel: 631600 Std: 01202
Fax: 445202 Std: **01392**
Nearest Town/Resort Poole
Directions Located on the A351 to Wareham which branches off the A35 5 miles west of Poole. Turn right at Holton Heath traffic lights by Texaco Petrol Station, park is on the left.
Acreage 60 **Open** Easter to October
Access Good **Site Level**
Sites Available ⛺ ⛽ ⚘ **Total** 525
Facilities ƒ ⛁ ☏ ⌂ ⊙⌐ ⊿ 🅿 ☎
⛽ ⊙ ⚑ ✕ ♀ ⚐ ⇄ 🖃 🖃
Nearby Facilities ⌒ ✓ ⟂ ⤱ U ⇗ ♪
⚓ Wareham.
Set in beautiful woodland, within easy driving distance of Poole, Swanage, Sandbanks, Lulworth Cove, the New Forest, Corfe Castle and many superb family attractions.

SHAFTESBURY

Blackmore Vale Filling Station, Sherborne Causeway, Shaftesbury, Dorset.
Tel: 852573 Std: 01747
Nearest Town/Resort Shaftsbury
Directions
Open All Year
Access Good **Site Level**
Sites Available ⛺ ⛽ ⚘ **Total** 50

Facilities ƒ ⛁ ⚿ ⌂ ⊙⌐ ☎ ⚑ ⌐ ⛁ ☎
Nearby Facilities ⌒
⚓ Gillingham
Scenic views, ideal touring.

ST. LEONARDS

Camping International, 229 Ringwood Road, St. Leonards, Nr. Ringwood, Dorset, BH24 2SD.
Tel: 872817 Std: 01202
Fax: 861292 Std: **01202**
Nearest Town/Resort Bournemouth
Directions 2¼ miles west of Ringwood on A31.
Acreage 8 **Open** March to October
Access Good **Site Level**
Sites Available ⛺ ⛽ ⚘ **Total** 205
Low Season Band B
High Season Band C
Facilities ⛁ ƒ ⛁ ⚿ ⌂ ⊙⌐ ⊿ 🅿 ☎
⛽ ⊙ ⚑ ✕ ♀ ⚐ ⇄ 🖃
Nearby Facilities ⌒ ✓ U ♪
⚓ Bournemouth.
New Forest, Bournemouth and coast, ideal touring.

ST. LEONARDS

Shamba Holiday Park, 230 Ringwood Road, St. Leonards, Ringwood, Dorset, BH24 2SB.
Tel: 873302 Std: 01202.
Nearest Town/Resort Ringwood
Directions Just off the A31 midway between Ringwood and Wimborne.
Acreage 7 **Open** March to October
Access Good **Site Level**
Sites Available ⛺ ⛽ ⚘ **Total** 150
Low Season Band B
High Season Band C
Facilities ƒ ⛁ ⚿ ⌂ ⊙⌐ ⊿ 🅿 ☎
⛽ ⊙ ⚑ ⚐ ♀ ⚐ ⇄ 🖃 ⊛
Nearby Facilities ⌒ ✓ ⟂ ⤱ U

⚓ Bournemouth.
Close to the New Forest and Bournemouth. Tourist Board Graded 4 Ticks and AA 3 Pennants.

SWANAGE

"Haycrafts" Caravan & Camping Park, Haycrafts Lane, Harmans Cross, Nr. Swanage, Dorset, BH19 3EB.
Tel: 480572 Std: 01929
Nearest Town/Resort Swanage
Directions From A351 (Corfe Castle/Swanage road) turn right opposite Harmans Cross Post Office/general store into Haycrafts Lane. Proceed beyond the village hall on the right and site is a further ¼ mile on the left.
Acreage 5 **Open** Easter to September
Access Good **Site** Lev/Slope
Sites Available ⛺ ⛽ ⚘ **Total** 50
Low Season Band B
High Season Band C
Facilities ƒ ⚿ ⛁ ☏ ⌂ ⊙⌐ ⊿ ☎
⛁ ⚑ 🖃
Nearby Facilities ⌒ ✓ ⟂ ⤱ U ⇗ ♪ ⇙
Small, quality park, immaculately kept, in an area of outstanding natural beauty. Families and couples only. Ideal for walking, cycling and bird watching. Convenient for Studland beaches. Steam Railway halt 5 minutes walk. ETB Graded 5 Ticks Excellent.

SWANAGE

Herston Yards Farm, Wash Pond Lane, Swanage, Dorset, BH19 3DJ.
Tel: 422932 Std: 01929
Nearest Town/Resort Swanage.
Directions
Acreage 8 **Open** April to October
Access Good **Site**
Sites Available ⛺ ⛽ ⚘ **Total** 80

Camping International

The New Forest with its quaint villages set in unspoilt open country and full of wild life. Bournemouth with its shops and entertainments. Dorset & Hants coast and country. 60+ places of interest to visit in good or bad weather.

STATISTICALLY THE BEST WEATHER IN THE U.K.

Enjoy all this whilst staying at one of the most popular parks in the area. Designed for the more discerning camper/caravanner who demands superior continental standards along with all of the facilities.

AA ►► RAC APPOINTED
CAMPING INTERNATIONAL HOLIDAY PARK
229 Ringwood Rd., St. Leonard's, Ringwood, Hants BH24 2SD
Telephone: (01202) 872817 / 872742 Fax: (01202) 861292
ANWB RECOMMENDED

Beautiful Spaces in Breathtaking Places

Sandford Holiday Park in Dorset...

"You're simply the best. Better than all the rest. We'll be back..."

L Membly

Set in sixty acres of beautiful woodland. Within easy reach of Bournemouth, Poole & Weymouth, superb sandy beaches and the glorious New Forest, make Sandford Holiday Park the perfect choice for touring Dorset.

WESTSTAR Holiday★Parks

For our Latest Brochure & Friendly Service

Call (01202) 631 600 Quote: MP

- New for 97 FREE Heated Indoor Pool
- FREE Heated Outdoor Pool
- FREE Nightly Entertainment
- Pubs & Clubs
- Restaurant & Takeaway, Supermarket & Launderette
- FREE Children's Clubs
- FREE Adventure Playground
- Super Hook-Ups, TV, Electricity & Water
- Discounts to Local Attractions
- Holiday Homes & Lodges also Available

DORSET

Facilities 🛆 🎒 ♿ ᶜ ☺ 🏨 ⓘ ⓞ 🅿
Nearby Facilities ⛴ 🚴 ⚓ 🎣 🏌 ♞ 🎿
⇻ Wareham.
Quiet, family site. Milk and eggs available.

SWANAGE
Swanage Caravan Park, Priests Road, Swanage, Dorset.
Tel: 422130 Std: 01929
Fax: 427952 Std: 01929
Nearest Town/Resort Swanage
Directions 1 mile from the town centre to the South of the town.
Open April to October
Access Good   **Site** Level
Sites Available ⛺ 🚐 **Total** 18
Low Season Band B
High Season Band C
Facilities ✓ 🎒 ♿ ᶜ ☺ ⓙ 🚻 ⓠ 🛒
⛺ ⓞ 🅿 🅱 ✗ ♀ ♿ 🍴 ⛏ 🎠 🅿
Nearby Facilities ⛴ 🚴 ⚓ 🎣 ♞ 🎿
⇻ Wareham
1 mile from the beach and main shopping centre. Panoramic views of Swanage Bay and the Purbeck Hills.

SWANAGE
Tom's Field Camping Site, Tom's Field Road, Langton Matravers, Nr. Swanage, Dorset.
Tel: Std:
Fax: 427110 Std: 01929
Nearest Town/Resort Swanage
Directions
Acreage 4 **Open** Easter to October
  Site Lev/Slope
Sites Available ⛺ 🚐 **Total** 100
Low Season Band B
High Season Band B
Facilities ♿ 🎒 ♿ ᶜ ☺ ⓔ ⛺ ⓘ ⓞ 🛒 🅿
Nearby Facilities ⚓ 🎿 ⓤ 🎣 🎿
⇻ Wareham
The camp has a variety of fields and is well positioned amidst the Purbeck Hills in an area of outstanding natural beauty. Swanage, Corfe Castle and Studland all within easy reach. Access to coastal walk close by.

SWANAGE
Ulwell Cottage Caravan Park, Ulwell, Swanage, Dorset, BH19 3DG.
Tel: 422823 Std: 01929
Nearest Town/Resort Swanage
Directions 1¼ miles from Swanage on Studland Road. Turn left by telephone box (left hand side) on side of road.
Open March to 7 January
Access Good   **Site** Lev/Slope
Sites Available ⛺ 🚐 **Total** 70

Low Season Band C
High Season Band C
Facilities ♿ ✓ 🎒 ♿ ᶜ ☺ ⓙ 🚻 ⓞ 🛒
⛺ ⓞ 🅿 ✗ ♀ ⛏ 🅿
Nearby Facilities ⛴ 🚴 ⚓ 🎣 🏌 ♞ 🎿
⇻ Wareham
Near sandy beaches, scenic walks and ideal for all water sports.

WAREHAM
Birchwood Tourist Park, North Trigon, Wareham, Dorset, BH20 7PA.
Tel: 554763 Std: 01929
Nearest Town/Resort Wareham
Directions From Bere Regis follow the A35 towards Poole. After approx 1 mile fork right to Wareham. Birchwood Park is the second park on the left after approx 3 miles.
Acreage 25 **Open** March to October
Access Good   **Site** Level
Sites Available ⛺ 🚐 **Total** 175
Low Season Band B
High Season Band C
Facilities ♿ ✓ 🎒 ♿ ᶜ ☺ ⓙ 🚻 ⓞ 🛒
⛺ ⓞ 🅿 ✗ ♀ 🍴 ⛏ 🎠 🅿
Nearby Facilities ⛴ 🚴 ⚓ ⓤ 🎣 ♞ 🎿
⇻ Wareham
Situated in Wareham Forest with direct access to forest walks. Ideal for touring the whole of Dorset.

WAREHAM
Lookout Holiday Park, Stoborough, Wareham, Dorset, BH20 5AZ.
Tel: 552546 Std: 01929
Fax: 552546 Std: 01929
Nearest Town/Resort Wareham
Directions 1½ miles from Wareham on the A351 to Swanage.
Acreage 15 **Open** February to November
Access Good   **Site** Level
Sites Available ⛺ 🚐 **Total** 150
Low Season Band B
High Season Band C
Facilities ✓ 🎒 ♿ ᶜ ☺ ⓙ 🛒
⛺ ⓞ 🅿 ✗ ♀ 🍴 🎠 🅿
Nearby Facilities ⛴ 🚴 🎿 ⓤ
⇻ Wareham.
Ideal location for touring the Purbeck Hills.

WAREHAM
Manor Farm Caravan Park, 1 Manor Farm Cottage, East Stoke, Wareham, Dorset, BH20 6AW.
Tel: Bindon Abbey 462870 Std: 01929.
Nearest Town/Resort Wareham/Lulworth Cove.
Directions From Wareham take the A352, turn left onto the B3070. At the first cross-

roads signposted East Stoke turn right. Next crossroads signposted Manor Farm turn right. Park is 300yds on the left.
Acreage 2½ **Open** Easter to September
Access Good   **Site** Level
Sites Available ⛺ 🚐 **Total** 40
Facilities ⓓ ♿ ✓ 🎒 ♿ ᶜ ☺ ⓙ 🛒
⛺ ⓞ 🅿 🅱 🅿
Nearby Facilities ⛴ 🚴 ⓤ 🎣
⇻ Wool/Wareham.
Flat, grass touring park on a working farm in a rural area of outstanding natural beauty, central for most of Dorset. Family run park with clean facilities. Resident Proprietors David & Gillian Topp. A.A. 3 Pennant, RAC Appointed and A.A. Environment Award 1989-1996 - Alan Roger Good Sites Guide. No groups or singles.

WAREHAM
Ridge Farm Camping & Caravan Park, Barnhill Road, Ridge, Wareham, Dorset, BH20 5BG.
Tel: 556444 Std: 01929
Nearest Town/Resort Wareham
Directions Approx. 1½ miles south of Wareham turn left in the village of Stoborough towards Ridge. Follow signs down Barnhill Road to Ridge Farm at the end of the lane.
Acreage 3½ **Open** March to October
Access Good   **Site** Level
Sites Available ⛺ 🚐 **Total** 60
Low Season Band B
High Season Band B
Facilities 🎒 ♿ ᶜ ☺ ⓙ 🛒
⛺ ⓞ 🅿 🅱 🅿
Nearby Facilities ⛴ 🚴 ⚓ ⓤ 🎣 ♞ 🎿
⇻ Wareham
Under new management. Peaceful, family run site adjacent to a working farm and RSPB Reserve. In an area of outstanding natural beauty and ideally situated for the Purbeck Hills, Poole Harbour and the coast. Boat launching nearby.

WAREHAM
Wareham Forest Tourist Park, North Trigon, Wareham, Dorset, BH20 7NZ.
Tel: 551393 Std: 01929
Nearest Town/Resort Wareham
Directions Located midway between Wareham and Bere Regis (off A35)
Open All Year
Access Good   **Site** Level
Sites Available ⛺ 🚐 **Total** 200
Facilities ⓓ ✓ 🎒 ♿ ᶜ ☺ ⓙ 🛒
⛺ ⓞ 🅿 ✗ ♀ 🍴 ⛏ 🎠 🅿
Nearby Facilities ⛴ 🚴 🎿 ⓤ ♞ 🎣
⇻ Wareham
Forest and wild life.

SWANAGE
HERSTON YARDS FARM
WASHPOND LANE, SWANAGE, DORSET BH19 3DJ
Telephone: Swanage (STD 01929) 422932
SMALL SELECT FARM SITE FOR TOURING CARAVANS AND TENTS

Quiet Family Site
Set amidst beautiful countryside and scenery
For Touring Caravans and Campers

Flush toilets and showers. Electric Razor Points. 1½ miles from Swanage and the sea. ½ mile from the A351 and shops with easy parking at Herston Cross. Milk and Eggs at Farmhouse. Pets welcome but on leads and exercised in field off site.

Open April to October   **Terms on application with S.A.E.**

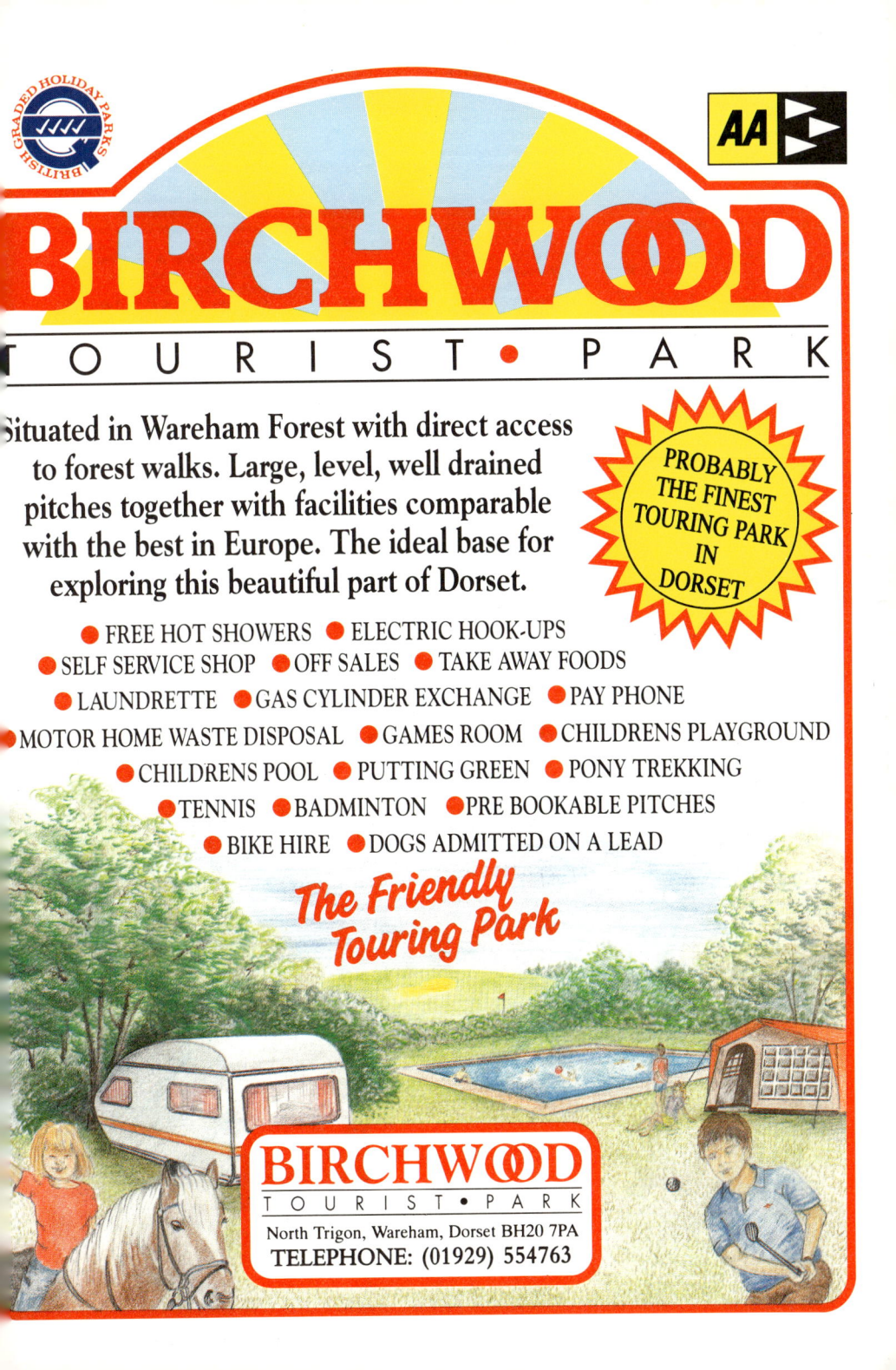

BIRCHWOOD
TOURIST · PARK

Situated in Wareham Forest with direct access to forest walks. Large, level, well drained pitches together with facilities comparable with the best in Europe. The ideal base for exploring this beautiful part of Dorset.

PROBABLY THE FINEST TOURING PARK IN DORSET

- FREE HOT SHOWERS
- ELECTRIC HOOK-UPS
- SELF SERVICE SHOP
- OFF SALES
- TAKE AWAY FOODS
- LAUNDRETTE
- GAS CYLINDER EXCHANGE
- PAY PHONE
- MOTOR HOME WASTE DISPOSAL
- GAMES ROOM
- CHILDRENS PLAYGROUND
- CHILDRENS POOL
- PUTTING GREEN
- PONY TREKKING
- TENNIS
- BADMINTON
- PRE BOOKABLE PITCHES
- BIKE HIRE
- DOGS ADMITTED ON A LEAD

The Friendly Touring Park

BIRCHWOOD
TOURIST · PARK
North Trigon, Wareham, Dorset BH20 7PA
TELEPHONE: (01929) 554763

DORSET

WEYMOUTH
Bagwell Farm Touring Park, Bagwell Farm, Chickerell, Weymouth, Dorset.
Tel: 782575 Std: 01305.
Nearest Town/Resort Weymouth.
Directions 4 miles from Weymouth, take the Bridport road, site entrance 500 yards past Victoria Inn on B3157.
Acreage 14 **Open** March to November
Access Good **Site** Lev/Slope
Sites Available ▲ ⊕ ⊟ **Total** 320
Low Season Band B
High Season Band C
Facilities ⊞ ∫ ▥ ♨ ⌠ ☺ ⌐ ▦ ⌂ ☎
℠ ⊘ ⊚ ♣ ⌂ ▣
Nearby Facilities ┌ ✓ ⊥ ⋇ ∪ ♖ ⊁
⚐ Weymouth.
Views of The Fleet and Chesil Beach.

WEYMOUTH
East Fleet Farm Touring Park, Fleet Lane, Chickerell, Weymouth, Dorset, DT3 4DW.
Tel: 785768 Std: 01305
Nearest Town/Resort Weymouth
Directions 3 miles west of Weymouth on the B3157, left at Chickerell T.A. Camp.
Acreage 20 **Open** 16 March to 15 January
Access Good **Site** Lev/Slope
Sites Available ▲ ⊕ ⊟ **Total** 210
Low Season Band A
High Season Band C
Facilities ♿ ∫ ♨ ▥ ♨ ⌠ ☺ ⌐ ▦
⌂ ☎ ℠ ⊘ ⊚ ▣
Nearby Facilities ┌ ✓ ⊥ ⋇ ∪ ♖
⚐ Weymouth
On edge of Fleet Water. Area of outstanding natural beauty.

WEYMOUTH
Littlesea Holiday Park, Lynch Lane, Weymouth, Dorset, DT4 9DT.
Tel: 774414 Std: 01305
Fax: 760338 Std: **01305**
Nearest Town/Resort Weymouth.
Directions From the outskirts of Weymouth turn right at the first and second roundabouts signposted Portland. At the third roundabout turn left signposted Chickerell, Portland. Go straight across the traffic lights and turn left into Lynch Lane. The Park is at the far end.
Acreage 11 **Open** 26 March to 29 October
Site Lev/Slope
Sites Available ▲ ⊕ ⊟ **Total** 265
Facilities ∫ ♨ ▥ ♨ ⌠ ☺ ⌐ ▦ ⌂ ☎
℠ ⊘ ⊚ ✕ ⚑ ♣ ⌂ ⁎ ▣
Nearby Facilities ┌ ✓ ⊥ ∪
⚐ Weymouth.
Pleasantly set on the sides of a small valley, overlooking The Fleet and Chesil Bank.

WEYMOUTH
Portesham Dairy Farm Camp Site, Bramdon Lane, Portesham, Weymouth, Dorset, DT3 4HG.
Tel: 871297 Std: 01305
Nearest Town/Resort Weymouth
Directions 7 miles from Weymouth on B3157 Coast road.
Acreage 3 **Open** 16th Mar to 31st October
Access Good **Site** Level
Sites Available ▲ ⊕ ⊟ **Total** 60
Facilities ♿ ∫ ▥ ♨ ⌠ ☺ ⌐ ▦ ☎
℠ ▯ ⊘ ⊚ ⌂ ▣
Nearby Facilities ✓ ♖
⚐ Weymouth
Ideal touring for Chesil area.

WEYMOUTH
Sea Barn Camping Park, Fleet, Weymouth, Dorset, DT3 4ED.
Tel: 782218 Std: 01305
Fax: 775396 Std: **01305**
Nearest Town/Resort Weymouth.
Directions From Weymouth take the B3157 towards Bridport. After 3 miles turn left at the only mini roundabout towards Fleet. After 1 mile turn left at the camping sign to Sea Barn.
Acreage 12 **Open** Easter to October
Access Good **Site** Level
Sites Available ▲ ⊕ ⊟ **Total** 250
Low Season Band B
High Season Band C
Facilities ∫ ▥ ♨ ⌠ ☺ ⌐ ▦ ⌂ ☎
℠ ⊘ ⊚ ✕ ⚑ ♣ ⌂ ▣
Nearby Facilities
⚐ Weymouth.
Quiet park with panoramic views over the sea and countryside. Links to South West Coastal Path and Fleet Nature Reserve.

WEYMOUTH
Seaview Holiday Park, Preston, Weymouth, Dorset, DT3 6DZ.
Tel: 833037 Std: 01305
Nearest Town/Resort Weymouth.
Directions Take the A353 from the centre of Weymouth, along the seawall to Preston. Seaview is ½ mile beyond the village, up the hill on the right.
Open Easter to October
Site Sloping
Sites Available ▲
Facilities ▥ ♨ ⌠ ┌ ⌐ ▦ ⌂ ☎
℠ ⊘ ⊚ ✕ ⚑ ♣ ⌂ ⋈ ▣
Nearby Facilities ┌ ⊥ ∪
⚐ Weymouth
Nestles on a hillside looking out over the charming Bowleaze Cove.

WAREHAM FOREST TOURIST PARK

Family site set in 40 acres of woodlands, open grassy spaces, direct access to forest walks.

★ Heated Swimming Pool (PEAK)
★ Children's Paddling Pool (PEAK)
★ Indoor Games Room
★ Children's Adventure Playground
★ Individual Cubicles in Toilet Block
★ Fully Serviced Pitches
★ Launderettes
★ Shop & Off-License (PEAK)
★ Snack Bar/TakeAway (PEAK)
★ Disabled Facilities
★ Long or Short Term Storage

OPEN ALL YEAR

For further details and free coloured brochure
**write or phone: Peter & Pam Savage
Wareham Forest Tourist Park
North Trigon Wareham Dorset BH20 7NZ
Tel: Wareham (01929) 551393**

DORSET

WEYMOUTH
Waterside Holiday Park Bowleaze Cove, Weymouth, Dorset, DT3 6PP
Tel: 833103 Std: 01305
Fax: 832830 Std: 01305
Nearest Town/Resort Weymouth
Directions From Weymouth take the Preston Road along the seafront approx. 1 mile, take the road signposted Bowleaze Cove to Waterside Holiday Park.
Open 1st April to 31st October
Access Good   **Site** Lev/Slope
Sites Available ▲ ⛺ 🚐 **Total** 120
Facilities 🅱 ♿ ƒ 🆎 ⚙ ⌐ 🍴 🛒 📞
🏪 🅿 ⛽ 🚻 🏠 🎯 🏳
Nearby Facilities ┌ ✓ ⚓ ⚡ ∪ ♪ ♫
🏊 Weymouth
Set in beautiful countryside close to the traditional seaside Town of Weymouth. Superb on-site facilities. Takeaway.

WEYMOUTH
West Fleet Holiday Farm, Fleet, Weymouth, Dorset, DT3 4ED.
Tel: 782218 Std: 01305
Fax: 775396 Std: 01305
Nearest Town/Resort Weymouth.
Directions From Weymouth take the B3157 Weymouth to Bridport road for 3 miles. Turn left at the only mini roundabout, after 1 mile turn right to West Fleet Farm.
Acreage 13 **Open** Easter to October
Site
Sites Available ▲ 🚐 **Total** 250
Low Season Band B
High Season Band C
Facilities ƒ 🆎 ♿ ⌐ 🍴 🛒 📞
🏪 🅿 🚻 🏠 🎯 🏳 🏊 ♪ ♫ 🏳

Nearby Facilities ∪ ♪
🏊 Weymouth.
Scenic Dorset countryside with views of the sea and coastline. Heated swimming pool. Mini-bus service direct from the park to Weymouth.

WEYMOUTH
Weymouth Bay Holiday Park, Preston, Weymouth, Dorset, DT3 6BQ.
Tel: 832271 Std: 01305
Fax: 825101 Std: 01305
Nearest Town/Resort Weymouth
Directions On the A353 Weymouth to Preston road, on the right about 10 minutes drive from Weymouth.
Open Easter to November
Access Good   **Site** Level
Sites Available ⛺ 🚐 **Total** 75
Facilities 🅱 ♿ ƒ 🆎 ♿ ⌐ 🍴 🛒 📞
🏪 🅿 ⛽ 🚻 🏠 🎯 🏳
Nearby Facilities ┌ ✓ ⚓ ⚡ ∪
🏊 Weymouth
Excellent indoor and outdoor swimming pools.

WIMBORNE
Charris Camping and Caravan Park, Candy's Lane, Corfe Mullen, Wimborne, Dorset, BH21 3EF.
Tel: 885970 Std: 01202
Nearest Town/Resort Wimborne
Directions A31 Wimborne bypass 1 mile west of Wimborne. Signs for entrance.
Acreage 3 **Open** March to October

DORSET
Access Good   **Site** Lev/Slope
Sites Available ▲ ⛺ 🚐 **Total** 45
Low Season Band B
High Season Band B
Facilities ƒ 🆎 ♿ ⌐ 🍴 🛒 📞
🏪 🅿 ⛽ 🚻 🏠
Nearby Facilities ┌ ✓ ⚓ ⚡ ∪ ♪ ♫
🏊 Poole.
English tourist board 4 Ticks, A.A. 3 Pennant, R.A.C. Approved, Caravan Club listed, Caravan and Camping Club listed. Good central site convienient for coast and New Forest. Poole 7½ miles, Bournemouth 8¼ miles. Good overnight stop for Cherbourg ferry. Cafe/restaurant close by.

WIMBORNE
Springfield Touring Park, Candys Lane, Corfe Mullen, Wimborne, Dorset.
Tel: 881719 Std: 01202
Nearest Town/Resort Wimborne
Directions 1¼ miles west of Wimborne just off main A31.
Acreage 3½ **Open** Mid March to October
Access Good   **Site** Lev/Slope
Sites Available ▲ ⛺ 🚐 **Total** 45
Low Season Band B
High Season Band C
Facilities 🅱 ♿ ƒ 🆎 ♿ ⌐ 🍴 🛒 📞
🏪 🅿 ⛽ 🚻 🏠
Nearby Facilities ┌ ✓ ⚓ ⚡ ∪ ♪ ♫
🏊 Poole
Family run park. Free showers and awnings, modern toilet block. Convenient for the coast and New Forest also ferry. English Tourist Board 5 Ticks. Members of B.H. and H.P.A.. Views over the Stour Valley. Hard standings and tarmac roads.

PLACES OF INTEREST

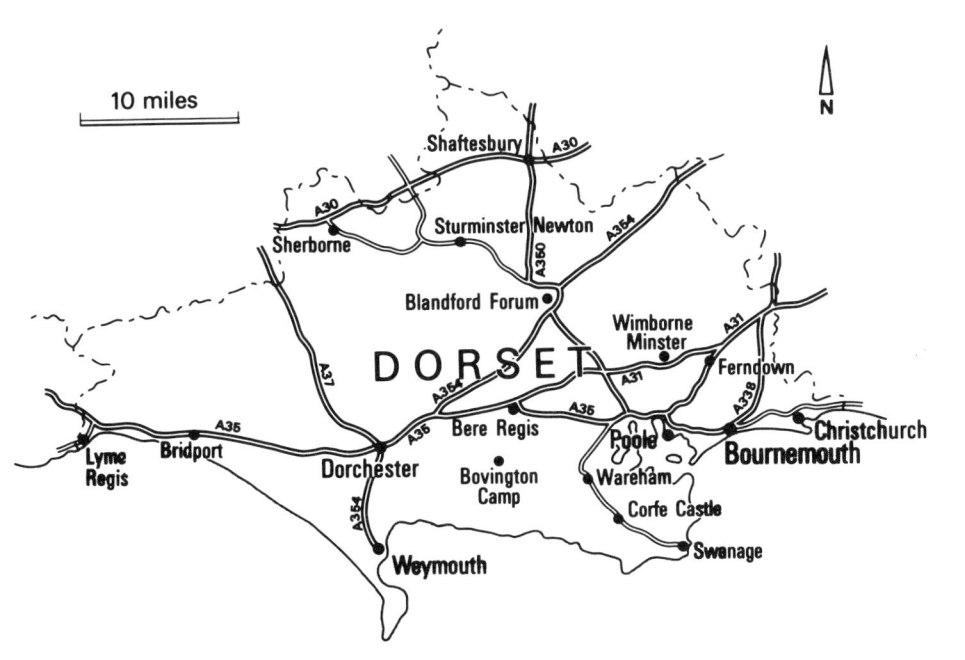

[Map of Dorset showing 10 mile scale, with locations including Shaftesbury, Sherborne, Sturminster Newton, Blandford Forum, Wimborne Minster, Ferndown, Lyme Regis, Bridport, Bere Regis, Dorchester, Poole, Christchurch, Bournemouth, Bovington Camp, Wareham, Corfe Castle, Weymouth, Swanage]

CADE'S WEST COUNTRY CAMPING, TOURING & MOTOR CARAVAN SITE GUIDE 1997   77

DORSET

DORSET

ABBOTSBURY
STRANGWAYS ENTERPRISES : West Yard Barn, West Street, Abbotsbury, Dorset, DT3 4JT. Tel : 01305 871130. Fax : 01305 871092.
Nearest Railway Station : Weymouth. Open : Swannery - March to October. Gardens - All year round. Tithe Barn - March to October. **Special Attractions:** The 600 year old Swannery is truly unique. Home for the only managed colony of swans in the world. The 20 acre sub-tropical gardens are the ultimate in lush, cultivated beauty. The Rural Bygones Museum, housed in the magnificent Tithe Barn, is an extensive collection which reconstructs the scenes of a Bygone Age.

BLANDFORD
CHETTLE HOUSE : Chettle, Blandford, Dorset. Tel : 01258 830209. Fax : 01258 830380.
Nearest Railway Station : Salisbury. Location : 6 miles North East of Blandford on A354. Open : 11am-5pm Good Friday to the end of September, closed Tuesdays and Saturdays. **Special Attractions:** Queen Anne House in English Baroque style by Thomas Archer. Attractive garden with many unusual plants.

BLANDFORD
RARE POULTRY, PIG & PLANT CENTRE : Long Ash Farm, Milton Abbas, Blandford, Dorset, DT11 0BX. Tel : 01258 880447.
Nearest Railway Station : Dorchester. Location : 3 miles off the Blandford to Dorchester road, between Milbourne St Andrew and Ansty. Open : Easter to the end of September, daily except Wednesday, 10am-6pm. Sundays only during October. **Special Attractions:** Come and see 100 breeds of poultry and 10 breeds of pig. Covered pets corner with animals to touch and best of all New Zealand Kune-Kune Pigs to pat, Kune-Kune's love people.

BLANDFORD CAMP
ROYAL SIGNALS MUSEUM : Blandford Camp, Dorset, DT11 8RH. Tel : 01258 482248.
Nearest Railway Station : Salisbury. Location : Located in School of Signals building in Blandford Camp. Camp is signposted off the Blandford-Wimborne road. Open : Monday to Friday 10am-5pm. Open at weekends and holidays during June to September (inclusive) from 10am-4pm. **Special Attractions:** Museum contains displays of Radios, telephones and Clandestine communication equipment. Motor cycles, used by Despatch Riders as well as Uniforms, Medals etc are on display.

BOURNEMOUTH
Bournemouth is a resort set among large gardens and pine clusters with a very mild climate. Nearly every form of entertainment and outdoor sport is available, and large events include tennis tournaments, county-cricket matches and league football.

The 100 foot cliffs that surround the bay are penetrated by deep ravines or chines and the beach offers good sand and safe bathing, two piers and lifts connect the beaches with street level.

The Russell-Cotes Art Gallery and Museum specializes in Victorian art and the Rothesay Museum exhibits many early Italian paintings. The Winter Gardens are the home of the world renowned Bournemouth Symphony Orchestra and the East Cliff Rock Garden is noted for its collection of geological specimens.

Robert Louis Stevenson's association with Bournemouth is commemorated by a memorial garden at his former home in Alum Chine Road.

Bournemouth is an excellent centre for touring in both the New Forest and the Wessex of Thomas Hardy. The latter described this town in his novel "Tess of the D'urbervilles".

BOURNEMOUTH
BOURNEMOUTH BEARS : Expocentre, Old Christchurch Lane, Bournemouth, Dorset, BH1 1NE. Tel : 01202 293544.
Open : 9.30am-5.30pm, 7 days per week, all year round. (Please phone for Winter hours). **Special Attractions:** Explore the wonderful world of the teddy and meet famous teddy-bear personalities at Dorset's only Teddy Bear Museum. The Bournemouth Bears are a joy for young and old alike. There are old bears, new bears, gigantic bears, tiny bears and costume bears, including limited editions and special creations.

BOURNEMOUTH
DINOSAUR SAFARI : Expocentre, Old Christchurch Lane, Bournemouth, Dorset, BH1 1NE. Tel : 01202 293544.
Open : 9.30am-5.30pm, 7 days per week, all year round. (Please phone for Winter hours). **Special Attractions:** A new and exciting type of museum experience. See actual size reconstructions of dinosaurs that almost seem alive, bones, fossils, skeletons, both real and rare casts from different parts of the world. Many hands-on and interactive displays make this a 'must' for all those with an interest in Dinosaurs. Exhibits come from around the world.

BOURNEMOUTH
MUMMIES OF THE PHARAOHS : Expocentre, Old Christchurch Lane, Bournemouth, Dorset, BH1 1NE. Tel : 01202 293544.
Open : 9.30am-5.30pm, 7 days per week, all year round. (Please phone for Winter hours). **Special Attractions:** This exhibition explores the ancient Egyptian way of death and their quest for immortality. From the first sand-dried mummies of over 5000 years ago to the amazing unwrapped Royal Mummies of some of the most famous Egyptian pharaohs and nobles, buried in once treasure filled tombs. The Royal Mummies, which include the unwrapped bodies of Seti I, Princess Nesitanebasher and Ramses the Great have been re-created using an amazing new British technique that makes it possible to produce accurate facsimiles of ancient bodies.

BOURNEMOUTH
THE SHELLEY ROOMS : C/O Russell-Cotes Art Gallery & Museum, East Cliff, Bournemouth, Dorset, BH1 3AA. Tel : 01202 303571.
Nearest Railway Station : Pokesdown. Location : Beechwood Avenue, Boscombe, Bournemouth. Open : Tuesday to Sunday, 2pm-5pm. Closed Mondays, Christmas Day, Boxing Day and Good Friday. **Special Attractions:** Small museum and reference library devoted to the poet Shelley and his circle of contemporaries.

BRIDPORT
BRIDPORT MUSEUM : South Street, Bridport, Dorset, DT6 3NR. Tel : 01308 422116. Fax : 01308 420659.
Nearest Railway Station : Dorchester and Crewkerne. Location : In the centre of the Town, near a car park and just down the street from the Town Hall. Open : Easter to October, Monday to Saturday 10am-5pm, Sunday 2pm-5pm. November to Easter, Wednesday and Saturday 10am-5pm, Sunday 2pm-5pm. **Special Attractions:** Local history information centre, displays include costume, fine art, rural life, natural history and local history. Small shop. Guided tours of the town by arrangement.

BRIDPORT
HARBOUR MUSEUM : The Salt House, West Bay, Bridport, Dorset, DT6 4SA. Tel : 01308 420997. Fax : 01308 420659.
Nearest Railway Station : Dorchester and Crewkerne. Location : Overlooking the harbour and near a car park. Open : April to October, Monday to Sunday, 10am-6pm (10am-8pm August). **Special Attractions:** Rope and net-making trade. Ship building, the history of West Bay, shop and tourist information point. Guided tours of West Bay by arrangement.

CHRISTCHURCH
RED HOUSE MUSEUM, ART GALLERY & GARDENS : Quay Road, Christchurch, Dorset. Tel : 01202 482860.

DORSET

Nearest Railway Station : Christchurch. Location : Next to Christchurch Priory. Open : Tuesday to Saturday, 10am-5pm. Sunday, 2pm-5pm. Last admission 4.30pm. **Special Attractions:** Costume Gallery telling the story of Victorian Fashionable Dress 1865-1915. Temporary exhibition gallery and Natural History Gallery. Attractive grounds featuring walled herb garden, collection of old roses and woodland walk. Exciting temporary exhibition programme including sculpture exhibitions in the garden. Workshops, events and childrens activities throughout the year. Archaeology Gallery "People, Place & Time". New galleries opening.

CORFE CASTLE
CORFE CASTLE (NATIONAL TRUST) : Tel : 01929 481294. Open : March to October, every day 10am-5.30pm, last admission 4.30pm during GMT. November to February, every day 12pm-3.30pm. Closed 25th/26th December. **Special Attractions:** One of the most dramatic ruins in England set on a hill above the only gap in the Purbeck Hills. Here King Edward I was murdered and the castle seized and finally slighted by Parliament forces in 1646.

DORCHESTER
The town of Dorchester is a pleasant bustling town on the River Frome called Durnovaria by the Romans and Casterbridge in Thomas Hardy's novels.

Many fascinating Roman remains including mosaics have been found in and around Dorchester. For instance, Maumbury Ring is the site of a Roman amphitheatre and seven miles length of the aqueduct supplying the Roman City with water can still be traced.

The town has had more than its share of natural disasters, having been ravaged by the Plague, and three times devastated by great fires between the years 1623 and 1725 with a lesser conflagration 50 years later. Very little of the medieval Dorchester survives with the St Peter's and Holy Trinity Churches being particularly affected. Holy Trinity was rebuilt for the 5th time in 1824 and St Peter's modernization completed some 30 years later. Visitors will find the interior of St Peter's Church interesting for the Copy of the Beeches Bible dated 1594, and a copy of Troubles of Jerusalem's Restoration, 1645 by John White.

The six Tolpuddle Martyrs were sentenced to transportation in the Old Crown Court of the Olde Shire Hall (1834) for demanding a wage increase. This building now forms a Tolpuddle Memorial. A Memorial to Thomas Hardy is his memorial room at the County Museum, which was opened in 1939 by the then poet Laureate - John Masefield. The room contains many memorabilia to Hardy but is chiefly of interest for the reconstruction of his study. Today, Dorchester is a busy town making beer and serving as the County's administrative headquarters, and has a very active and copious market. It is also a judicial centre for assizes and crown courts.

DORCHESTER
ATHELHAMPTON HOUSE & GARDENS : Athelhampton, Dorchester, Dorset, DT2 7LG. Tel : 01305 848363. Fax : 01305 848135.
Nearest Railway Station : Dorchester. Location : On the A35 5 miles east of Dorchester. Open : 23rd March to 26th October 1997, daily (except Saturday), 11am-5pm. **Special Attractions:** Athelhampton is one of the finest 15th Century houses in England, containing many magnificently furnished rooms including The Great Hall of 1485. The glorious Grade I gardens, dating from 1891, contain the world famous topiary pyramids, fountains, the River Piddle and collections of tulips, magnolias, roses, clematis and lilies in season. Restaurant serving lunches, cream teas and refreshments. Gift Shop and Free car park.

DORCHESTER
THE DINOSAUR MUSEUM : Icen Way, Dorchester, Dorset, DT1 1EW. Tel : 01305 269880. Fax : 01305 268885.
Open : Open all year, every day, 9.30pm-5.30pm. Please telephone for Winter hours. **Special Attractions:** The Dinosaur Museum situated in Dorchester, Dorset, is the only museum in Great Britain entirely devoted to dinosaurs and their world. It had twice been voted one of Britain's top ten hands on museums. The Dinosaur Museum has frequently been featured on national television. The incredible world of dinosaurs comes alive in a new and exciting way that visitors of all ages will love. Dinosaurs ruled the earth for over 140 million years making them one of the most successful groups of animal ever. They died out 65 million years ago, and for the past 150 years people have been fascinated by these monsters of prehistory.

The latest museological techniques are used to show and interpret the fascinating world of dinosaurs in exciting displays. Actual fossils, skeletons and life-size reconstructions combine with audio-visual, computerised and interactive displays to inform and entertain.

The Museum's fresh and exciting approach has made it extremely popular with visitors from all over the country and abroad. Displays are always changing meaning there is always something new to see. Why not choose a souvenir from the Museum's well stocked gift shop to round off your visit. A visit to the Museum is a total experience, fun for all the family. The Dinosaur Museum is truly Dorset's Monster Attraction.

DORCHESTER
DORSET COUNTY MUSEUM : High West Street, Dorchester, Dorset, DT1 1XA. Tel : Dorchester 01305 262735. Fax : 01305 257499.
Nearest Railway Station : Dorchester. Open : 10am-5pm Monday to Saturday inclusive. Sundays during July and August. **Special Attractions:** Award winning Museum of Dorset History and Life. Dinosaur's footprints, fabulous beasts, prehistoric settlements, Maiden Castle, Dorset rural life, Hardy's study.

DORCHESTER
ILSINGTON HOUSE : Puddletown, Dorchester, Dorset, DT2 8TQ. Tel : 01305 848454. Fax : 01305 848909.
Nearest Railway Station : Dorchester. Location : 4 miles due east from Dorchester on the A35. Open : 2pm-6pm (last tour 5pm) Wednesday and Thursday, 1st May to 25th September. Also Sundays and Bank Holiday Monday in August. Other days by appointment. **Special Attractions:** Built by the 7th Earl of Huntingdon in 1690. Childhood home of George III's illegitimate grandson. A family residence with fine period furniture, interesting art collection, formal gardens and paddocks and an unusual collection of irises and peonies.

DORCHESTER
KINGSTON MAURWARD GARDENS : Dorchester, Dorset, DT2 8PY. Tel : 01305 264738. Fax : 01305 250059.
Nearest Railway Station : Dorchester. Location : 2 miles east of Dorchester, signed from the by-pass. Open : Easter to the end of October, 7 days a week, 10am-5.30pm. **Special Attractions:** 35 acres of fine gardens and lawns, rolling parkland. Animal Park, Visitors centre, 5 acre lake and a nature trail. National collections of Penstemons and Salvias. Restaurant for coffee, light lunches and teas.

DORCHESTER
THE MILITARY MUSEUM OF DEVON & DORSET : The Keep, Dorchester, Dorset. Tel : Dorchester 01305 264066.
Nearest Railway Station : Dorchester. Location : Bridport Road. Open : Monday to Saturday, 9.30am-5pm. Closed: Saturday 1pm-2pm, and Sunday all day. **Special Attractions:** Newly renovated and stunning views from the battlements. Something for everyone, fashionable uniforms, deadly weapons, old photographs, colourful paintings and militaria of all kinds from our local Infantry, Yeomanry, Rifle Volunteers, Militia and Home Guard.

DORCHESTER
THE OLD CROWN COURT & CELLS : West Dorset District Council, Stratton House, High West Street, Dorchester, Dorset, DT1 1UZ. Tel : 01305 252241. Fax : 01305 257039.

DORSET

Nearest Railway Station : Dorchester. Location : In the town centre. Open : Court Room - 10am-12pm and 2pm-4pm (excluding Bank Holidays). Cells - Guided Tours end of July to early September. Tuesday to Friday 2.15pm-4.15pm, Wednesday 10.15am-12.15pm. **Special Attractions:** Famous for the trial of the Six Tolpuddle Martyrs. The Court Room remains as it was at the time in March 1834. The original Shire Hall, of which the court forms part, can be traced back as far as 1638. The Cells, both old and new, remain beneath the court.

DORCHESTER
TEDDY BEAR HOUSE : Antelope Walk, Dorchester, Dorset, DT1 1BE. Tel : 01305 263200.
Open : All Year, daily 9.30am-5pm. Please telephone for Winter hours. **Special Attractions:** A visit to Teddy Bear House is in fact a visit to the home of Mr Edward Bear and his large family of human-size teddy bears! Here in a quaint old house in Antelope Walk, in the picturesque town of Dorchester, these unique bears relax or busy themselves in the Old Dorset Teddy Bear Factory.

DORCHESTER
TUTANKHAMUN : 25 High West Street, Dorchester, Dorset. Tel : 01305 269571.
Open : 9.30am-5.30pm, 7 days a week, all year round. Please telephone for Winter hours. **Special Attractions:** Experience the excitement of the discovery of the world's greatest ancient treasure unearthed in Egypt in 1922. This fantastic exhibition recreates for the first time anywhere in the world, the ancient Egyptian King Tutankhamun's tomb filled with its priceless treasures and displays in facsimile golden treasures buried with the pharaoh almost 3500 years ago. Its the only exhibition on The Boy King outside Egypt. As you walk through the ante-chamber and burial chamber, audio programmes dramatize the events. All the senses are excited, even that of smell with the heavy but pleasant odours of fragrant woods, oils and ointments. It's an amazing experience.

EDMONDSHAM
EDMONDSHAM HOUSE & GARDENS : Edmondsham House, Edmondsham, Wimborne, Dorset, BH21 5RE. Tel : Cranborne 01725 517207.
Nearest Railway Station : Sailisbury/Bournemouth. Location : Between Verwood and Cranborne off B3081. Open : Easter Sunday and all Bank Holiday Mondays 2pm-5pm, also Wednesdays in April and October 2pm-5pm. Gardens only - Wednesdays and Sundays 2pm-5pm from May to September. Parties Welcome - Please telephone Cranborne 01725 517207. **Special Attractions:** The owner gives guided tours around the Tudor/Georgian manor house. Interesting furniture, lace and family exhibits. Fine Victorian stable block and dairy. 12th Century church nearby. Lovely walled gardens, cultivated organically, mature trees and Spring bulbs.

LYME REGIS
Lyme Regis is situated in the extreme South Western corner of coastal Dorset, and is beautifully set in a steep valley leading down to a wide bay. Though the beach is shingle, it offers beautiful aspects in the direction of Portland Island and round to Seaton in Devon. At low tide the beach is made up of sand upon which the water leaves many shallow pools, ideal for youngsters. The harbour is distinguished by its Quay or Cobb which is 600 feet long. Two of Lyme Regis's famous inhabitants are Captain Coran and Mary Anning. The former helped fund the State of Georgia in America and the Foundlings Hospital for Homeless and Unwanted London children - Mary Anning born in 1799 found fame for her careful and diligent extraction from the Lias Stone of Lyme Regis, the fossilized remains of an Ichthyosaurus, a 30 foot long fish/lizard previously unknown to science.

LYME REGIS
LYME REGIS MARINE AQUARIUM & COBB HISTORY : The Cobb, Lyme Regis, Dorset. (Correspondence: c/o Greystones, View Road, Lyme Regis). Home Tel : 01297 443678.
Nearest Railway Station : Axminster. Location : The Cobb (Harbour). Open : 10am-5pm, April to October. (Later in July and August). **Special Attractions:** Living Lyme Bay seafish and rockpool creatures, marine bygones and wreckage. Photo displays including Cobb history, filming "Persuasion" and "French Lieutenant's Woman". Adults 1.50p, OAPs 1.00, Children 5-16 70p, Under 5s FREE. Pre-booked groups: Guided Cobb Walks and Talks. Reduced entrance fees.

POOLE
Poole was originally the largest town in Dorset and is a thriving mixture of modern commerce, industry and pleasure facilities. The site of the old town has been settled and defended in succession by our ancestors from the Old and New Stone Ages, Bronze and Iron Ages, Roman and Saxon. The Danish King Canute landed here and since then men and ships have sailed forth to join the Siege of Calais and to meet the Spanish Armada.

The Harbour's main channel is dredged to receive ships up to 3500 tons. The coast line is broken with creeks and inlets and measures over ninety miles in length. It is unusual in that with Swanage and Southampton, it receives two tides in twelve hours, a feat of great importance to commercial shipping.

Many varieties of birds are attracted to Poole, including Mallards, Gulls, Herons and Cormorants. For artists and photographers there is an infinite number of subjects to capture.

Near the quay is a timbered inn dating from the 15th Century, and two groups of almshouses, the first 14th Century - built by the fraternity of St George, and the second 15th Century - gifted by a son of Poole who became wealthy from his trade as a leather merchant.

Among many interesting treasures to be found in and around Poole, the craftsmen at work in the workshops fashioning clay by hand and time-honoured practices into exquisite pottery. Also in the town's museum can be found Marconi's first aerial which conducted many of his experimental transmissions.

POOLE
THE AQUARIUM/SERPENTARIUM COMPLEX : The Quay, Poole, Dorset, BH15 1JH. Tel : 01202 686712.
Nearest Railway Station : Poole. Location : On the Quay front, Pooles natural harbour, next to tourism. Open : All year except Christmas Day. Summer 9am-9pm, Winter 10am-5pm. **Special Attractions:** Foremost educational and exciting establishment in the South. Huge array of fish, reptiles, amphibians, sharks, alligators, etc..

POOLE
COMPTON ACRES GARDENS : Canford Cliffs Road, Canford Cliffs, Poole, Dorset, BH13 7ES. Tel : 01202 700778. Fax : 01202 707537.
Nearest Railway Station : Poole/Bournemouth. Location : Mid-way between Poole and Bournemouth near sandbanks. Open : 1st March-31st October, 10.30am-last admission 5.45pm. **Special Attractions:** A range of separate, magnificent gardens. Reputed to be the finest privately owned gardens in Europe.

POOLE
SCAPLEN'S COURT MUSEUM : 4 High Street, Poole, Dorset Tel : 01202 683138. Fax : 01202 660896.
Nearest Railway Station : Poole. Location : High Street. Open : June to September. Monday to Saturday 10am-5pm, Sundays 2pm-5pm. **Special Attractions:** Part of Waterfront Museum. Incorporates a Victorian School Room, Chemist Shop and Kitchen area. Fine restored town house with walled garden and central courtyard.

POOLE
WATERFRONT : 4 High Street, Poole, Dorset. Tel : 01202 683138 Fax : 01202 660896.
Nearest Railway Station : Poole. Open : Daily, March to October **Special Attractions:** An exciting visitor complex set in the 15th

80   CADE'S WEST CUONTRY CAMPING, TOURING & MOTOR CARAVAN SITE GUIDE 1997

DORSET

century town cellars and adjacent to a 5 floored mill building set on Poole Quay. Displays and presentations based upon maritime themes incorporating The Studland Bay Wreck, an Iron Age boat found locally and 'Seatown Poole', with smugglers, pirates and local trades people. Displays are lively, educational and entertaining. Toilet facilities, gift shop and Oakley's Victorian Tea Room. Facilities for wheelchair users.

PORTLAND
PORTLAND MUSEUM : 217 Wakeham, Portland, Dorset. Tel : 01305 821804.
Nearest Railway Station : Weymouth. Location : At the bottom of Wakeham. Just above Church Ope Cove. Rufus Castle and Pennsylvania Castle. Open : Summer - 7 days a week. Winter - October to Easter, closed Wednesday and Thursday. 10.30am-5pm throughout. **Special Attractions:** Housed in two thatched cottages and a modern gallery. It is a community Museum reflecting many facets of the Islands natural and social History in its collections. Picnic in the garden or browse in the Shop for that special gift. Also regular, temporary exhibitions.

SHAFTESBURY
One an important ecclesiastical centre, Shaftesbury is chiefly memorable for the remains of its Abbey, which was founded by King Alfred for his daughter Elgiva, who became its first Abbess.

Shaftesbury is unique in the County of Dorset for the fact that it is the only hilltop town. It stands at 700 feet above the sea level and gives a splendid view over the Blakemore Vale and Glastonbury Tor, the town has four churches although once there were twelve.

Shaftesbury is the burial place of King Edward the Martyr, murdered by his stepmother at Corfe Castle, King Edmund's Queen, and in 1035 King Canute - he who tried to hold back the sea - was also buried here.

SHAFTESBURY
SHAFTESBURY ABBEY & MUSEUM : Park Walk, Shaftesbury, Dorset, SP7 8RJ. tel : 01747 852910.
Location : Junction of the A30 and A350, signed from Shaftesbury town centre. Open : April to October inclusive, 10am-5pm. **Special Attractions:** A peaceful setting, you will see the excavated remains of an important ancient monument - a Benedictine Abbey for women with links to the Royal House. During its lifetime this Abbey was one of the most important in the country. Set in a walled garden, the remains of the Abbey church can be viewed in an attractively laid out garden. A self-guided trail around the site highlights the many interesting features which can be viewed at leisure. The museum houses a fascinating collection of carved stonework and medieval floor tiles. In the garden there is also a reconstructed Anglo-Saxon herb bed.

SHERBORNE
SANDFORD ORCAS MANOR HOUSE : The Manor House, Sandford Orcas, Sherborne, Dorset, DT9 4SB. Tel : 01963 220206.
Nearest Railway Station : Sherborne. Location : 2.5 miles North of Sherborne off B3148 road. Entrance next to church. Open : May to September inclusive. Sundays 2pm-6pm. Mondays 10am-6pm. Also Easter Monday 10am-6pm. **Special Attractions:** Stone-built Tudor Manor House with gatehouse, spiral staircases, panelling, furniture, pictures, medieval stained glass. Terraced garden with topiary and herb garden. Personally conducted tours by owner.

SHERBORNE
SHERBORNE CASTLE : Sherborne, Dorset. Tel : Sherborne 01935 813182.
Nearest Railway Station : Sherborne. Location : Lakeside Park, 1 mile from centre of Sherborne. Open : Easter to the end of September. Grounds and Tea Room open : 12.30pm Thursdays, Saturdays, Sundays and Bank Holidays. House open : 1.30pm Thursdays, Saturdays, Sundays and Bank Holidays.

STURMINSTER NEWTON
STURMINSTER NEWTON MILL : c/o The Supervisor, 16 Old Boundary Road, Shaftesbury, Dorset, SP7 8ND. Tel : 01747 854355.
Nearest Railway Station : Gillingham. Location : 300yds from town bridge, just off the A357 Sherborne to Blandford road. Open : Easter to the end of September. Saturday, Sunday, Monday and Thursday, 11am-5pm. **Special Attractions:** A picturesque water mill in full working order, situated in the heart of "Hardy" Country. This is a very old building on an ancient site. (Adults 1.50, Children 50p. Guided Tours at no extra cost).

SWANAGE
PUTLAKE ADVENTURE FARM : Langton Matravers, Swanage, Dorset, BH19 3EU. Tel : 01929 422917.
Nearest Railway Station : Wareham. Location : Off the main A351 Wareham to Swanage road onto the B3069. Through the village. Open : 24th March to 26th October, daily 11am-6pm. November and December, weekends only. **Special Attractions:** Visitors are encouraged to explore and make contact with a variety of friendly animals in a relaxed atmosphere. You can bottle feed the lambs and goats and at 4pm have a go at hand milking. There are indoor and outdoor picnic and play areas, gift shop, tea room, farm trail to walk, pony rides and trailer rides. We have 8600sq ft under cover. Childrens birthday parties. Facilities for the disabled. Discount for group bookings. Free parking. Tearoom may be used by the general public not looking at the farm attractions.

WAREHAM
THE BLUE POOL : Furzebrook, Wareham, Dorset. Tel : 01929 551408.
Nearest Railway Station : Wareham. Location : Furzebrook, near Wareham. Signposted at the roundabout at the southern end of the Wareham Bypass (the A351). Open : Grounds - March to November. Tea House, Gift Shops and Museum - Easter to early October. **Special Attractions:** 25 acres of tranquil woods and heathland, designated a Site of Special Scientific Interest, surround this old claypit. Sandy paths climb to views of the Purbeck Hills, or lead down steps to the waters edge. Tea House with delicious cream teas, Gift Shops, Museum, Plant Centre. Some facilities for the disabled. Dogs on leads welcome. Childrens Play Area.

WAREHAM
A WORLD OF TOY'S : Arne House, Arne, Near Wareham, Dorset. Tel : 01929 552018.
Nearest Railway Station : Wareham. Location : Arne Village. Open : April to June and September, 1.30pm-5pm, closed Mondays and Saturdays. July and August, every day, 10.30am-5.30pm. Open every Bank Holiday Monday during the season. **Special Attractions:** Dorset first Toy and Musical Box Museum. Hundreds of Toys, a collection of antique and collectors Toys. Victorian Musical Boxes, automation etc. Also Bonzo's Tea Room serving Dorset clotted cream teas with its collection of picture postcards of Bonzo the dog from the 1920's.

WEYMOUTH
Weymouth has a beautiful bay extending in a crescent roughly five miles in extent and approximately two and a half miles from the beach to the line of the mouth of the bay. It has a fine sandy beach usually kept scrupulously clean, and shallow waters almost devoid of undertow or current.

The busy old harbour presents many opportunities for good pictures and photographs, and the town has a number of decent art galleries where good pictures can be looked at or bought for collection building.

Alongside Weymouth is the Isle of Portland with its large naval establishment. It is a home port of British and Nato ships and there are regular "Fleet Days" where all kinds of vessels from submarines to frigates can be inspected. The Navy also has a helicopter base on the Island and visitors can frequently see and hear the comings and goings of busy aircraft to ships anchored in Portland or manoeuvring in the expanse of Weymouth Bay.

CADE'S WEST COUNTRY CAMPING, TOURING & MOTOR CARAVAN SITE GUIDE 1997   81

From Weymouth run scheduled journeys to the Channel Islands and small boats showing passengers Weymouth Bay and neighbouring beauty spots.

Local places of interest well worth seeing include: Sandsfoot Castle on the cliff above Portland Harbour which was built by Henry VIII in 1539, Wyke Regis has a commanding height from which there are views of Portland, Ridgeway Hills, Golden Gap and Lyme Regis. Upwey village three miles North of Weymouth has an interesting wishing well of natural spring water, much favoured by George III.

WEYMOUTH
ABBOTSBURY OYSTER FARM & SEA FOOD BAR : Abbotsbury Oysters, Ferrybridge, Weymouth, Dorset, DT4 9YU. tel : 01305 788067. Fax . 01305 760661. Nearest Railway Station : Weymouth. Location : On the causeway between Weymouth and Portland. Open : Easter to the end of August, 7 days a week, 10am-6pm. **Special Attractions:** Explore a working oyster farm, learn about oysters and how they are grown. Relax whilst enjoying freshly prepared seafood in the tranquil setting of the beautiful Fleet Lagoon (Britain's oldest water reserve). Childrens play area and ample free parking.

WEYMOUTH
BENNETTS WATER GARDENS : Putton Lane, Chickerell, Weymouth, Dorset, DT3 4AF. Tel : 01305 785150. Nearest Railway Station : Weymouth. Location : 2 miles west of Weymouth, off the B3157 to Bridport. Open : April to October inc., 10am-5pm. April to August, Tuesday to Sunday. September, Tuesday to Saturday. October, Tuesday to Friday. Open Bank Holidays during season. **Special Attractions:** NCCPG National collection of over 100 varieties of water lilies, displayed within 6 acres of natural lakes, teeming with wildlife. Tropical House, Pond Shop and plant sales, tearoom and car park. Access to gardens and facilities for wheelchairs.

WEYMOUTH
BREWERS QUAY & THE TIMEWALK JOURNEY : Hope Square, Weymouth, Dorset, DT4 8TR. Tel : 01305 777622. Fax : 01305 761680. Nearest Railway Station : Weymouth. Location : Old Harbour. Open : Seven days a week, 9.30am-5.30pm. Late nights in school Summer holidays till 9.30pm. Closed 25th, 26th and 27th December and the last two weeks of January. **Special Attractions:** Converted Victorian Brewery now housing the Award Winning Timewalk Journey attraction, transporting the visitor through dramatic scenes spanning 6 Centuries of Weymouth's history. Under cover speciality shopping village with craft centre and workshops, Quay Brewery, cafe, restaurant and real ale bars. Plus a regularly changing programme of FREE exhibitions and events.

WEYMOUTH
DEEP SEA ADVENTURE FEATURING SHARKY'S : 9 Custom House Quay, Old Harbour, Weymouth, Dorset, DT4 8BG. Tel & Fax : 01305 760690. Nearest Railway Station : Weymouth. Location : On harbour side. Open : Every day, Summer 9.30am-10pm, Winter 9.30am-7pm. **Special Attractions:** Two separate attractions under one roof. This fascinating family attraction tells the story of underwater exploration and marine exploits including the Titanic disaster. SHARKY'S is Weymouth's newest attraction, an All-Weather Childrens Adventure Play Area with a separate area for toddlers. Including Sharky's Galley catering for families. Lift available, disabled toilets and baby changing facilities.

WEYMOUTH
DISCOVERY : Brewers Quay, Hope Square, Weymouth, Dorset, DT4 8TR. Tel : 01305 789007. Fax : 01305 778945. Nearest Railway Station : Weymouth. Location : Upstairs at Brewers Quay shopping village in the old harbour. Open : All Year, 10am-5.30pm. School Summer holidays, 9.30am-8pm. **Special Attractions:** Hands-on science centre suitable for all ages. Over 60 interactive exhibits including Weather Station, computers, Shadow Wall, Perplexing Puzzles, Mirror Magic and much, much more. Internet available.

WIMBORNE

DORSET HEAVY HORSE CENTRE : Edmondsham Road, Verwood, Dorset, BH21 5RJ. Tel : 01202 824040. Location : Near Verwood, Dorset, just over a mile from the crossroads at the centre of Verwood. Open : 10am-5pm, Good Friday to the 31st October, every day. **Special Attractions:** The Dorset Heavy Horse Centre attracts large numbers of tourists for whom the Gentle Giants have become a 'must'. BERTIE BASSETT a Shire standing 19.2 hands high (more than 6'4"). Heavy horses, plus miniature Shetland ponies. Foals born every spring. Picnic area, cafeteria, wagon rides, gift shop, facilities for the disabled. Ample free parking. Commentaries at 11.30am, 2pm and 4pm. A pleasant half-day out.

WIMBORNE
KINGSTON LACY : The National Trust, Wimborne, Dorset, BH21 4EA. Tel : 01202 883402. Nearest Railway Station : Poole. Location : On B3082 Blandford-Wimborne Road. Open : April to October inclusive. 11.30am-6pm Park. 12pm-4.30pm House. **Special Attractions:** 17th and 18th Century fine art collection in stately home.

WIMBORNE
KNOLL GARDENS : Hampreston, Near Wimborne, Dorset, BH21 7ND. Tel : 01202 873931. Fax : 01202 870842. Nearest Railway Station : Bournemouth. Location : Between Wimborne and Ferndown off B3073 at Hampreston. Exit Canford Bottom roundabout A31, signposted 1.5 miles. Open : April to October 31st, every day, 10am-5.30pm. (dusk if earlier). **Special Attractions:** A rare, unusual and exotic collection of plants started some 30 years ago from all over the world. Boasts well over 4,000 different named species. The Gardens are filled with beautiful Water Gardens, Ponds, Waterfalls, Streams, Rockeries, Herbaceous borders, Woodland Glens. Colourful, formal area and much, much more. Tea Rooms with Dorset Clotted Cream Teas, restaurant, Gift Shop, Plant sales, Book Shop, Gallery. No dogs or radios. Large free coach and car park.

WIMBORNE
MINSTER CHURCH OF ST. CUTHBERGA : High Street, Wimborne Minster, Dorset, BH21 1HT. Tel : 01202 884753. Nearest Railway Station : Poole/Bournemouth. Location : Centre of the town of Wimborne Minster. Open : All year round, 9.30am-5.30pm. **Special Attractions:** The Minster, founded in AD705 by Saint Cuthburga. Apart from the Norman architecture there is an astronomical clock, also a Quarterjack, a lifesize soldier, on the side of the West Tower. The chained library has hardly changed since it was founded in 1686. There is a shop in the Minster.

WIMBORNE
PRIEST'S HOUSE MUSEUM : 23-27 High Street, Wimborne Minster, Dorset, BH21 1HR. Tel : 01202 882533. Nearest Railway Station : Poole/Bournemouth. Location : In the centre of Wimborne opposite the Minster. Open : Monday to Saturday, April 1st to October 31st, 10.30am-5pm, plus Bank Holiday Sundays and Sundays June to September 2pm-5pm. **Special Attractions:** Award winning local history museum in a historic town house with 10 rooms of displays telling the story of Wimborne, its people and the surrounding areas. Reconstructed Ironmongers shop, tinsmiths forge and working Victorian kitchen all set in an exquisite walled garden, full of beautiful blooms. Tea room (Summer season only) and museum gift shop plus free childrens quizzes.

WIMBORNE
STAPEHILL ABBEY, CRAFTS & GARDENS : Wimborne Road West, Stapehill, Wimborne, Dorset, BH21 2EB. Tel : 01202 861686. Nearest Railway Station : Poole. Location : 0.5 miles east of Canford Bottom roundabout on the A31. Open : Easter to October, daily 10am-5pm. November to Easter, Wednesday to Sunday, 10am-4pm. Telephone for Christmas closing. **Special Attractions:** Discover for yourself the peace and tranquility hidden away for centuries at Stapehill. Set in 87 acres, Stapehill offers beautiful gardens, an outstanding museum, craft centre, farmyard, woodland walks plus much, much more. A treat for all ages and with everything but the gardens under cover is truly an all-weather at-

traction.

WIMBORNE
WIMBORNE MINSTER MODEL TOWN & GARDENS : 16 King Street, Wimborne, Dorset, BH21 1DY. Tel : 01202 881924. Nearest Railway Station : Poole. Location : Approximately 200yds west of the Minster. Open : Easter to the last weekend in September. Every day 10am-5pm. Charity Number - 298116. **Special Attractions**: One-tenth scale models of houses and shops of the town as it was in the early 1950's. You will be delighted by the beautiful landscaped gardens surrounding the model town. Visitors and Exhibition centres providing refreshments, souvenirs and plant sales. Facilities for the disabled. Public car park opposite.
HANTS

PLEASE MENTION
CADE'S
WHEN REPLYING TO
ADVERTISERS

HAMPSHIRE

ANDOVER
Wyke Down Touring Caravan & Camping Park, Picket Piece, Andover, Hampshire.
Tel: 352048 Std: 01264
Nearest Town/Resort Andover.
Directions International Camping Park Signs from A303 Trunk Road, follow signs to Wyke Down.
Acreage 7 **Open** All Year
Access Good   **Site** Level
Sites Available ▲ ⊞ ⊟ **Total** 150
Low Season Band C
High Season Band C
Facilities ƒ ▥ ♨ ☍ ⌒ ⌣ ⌐ ☎
♋ ⓘ ⦿ ⓑ ⋔ ⋏ ⋈ ✺ ◻
Nearby Facilities ⌐ ✓
≉ Andover.
Ideal touring area. Golf driving range. Country Pub.

ASHURST
Ashurst Camp Site, Lyndhurst Road, Ashurst, Hampshire, SO42 2AA.
Tel: 283771 Std: 01703
Fax: **283929** Std: **01703**
Nearest Town/Resort Lyndhurst.
Directions 5 miles southwest of Southampton on the A35, signposted.
Acreage 23 **Open** 21st March to 29th October
Access Good   **Site** Level
Sites Available ▲ ⊞ ⊟ **Total** 280
Low Season Band B
High Season Band C
Facilities & ▥ ♨ ⌒ ⌣ ⌐ ☎
♋ ⓘ ⦿ ⓑ ⦿
Nearby Facilities ⌐ ∪
≉ Ashurst
Lightwash area on site for walkers and cyclists. 10 minutes walk to the shops in Ashurst Village.

BRANSGORE
Holmsley Camp Site, Forest Road, Holmsley, Christchurch, Dorset, BH23 7EQ.
Tel: 283771 Std: 01703
Fax: **283929** Std: **01703**
Nearest Town/Resort Bransgore
Directions Turn west 8 miles southwest of Lyndhurst off the A35 and follow Holmsley Camp Site signs.
Acreage 89 **Open** 21st March to 29th September
Access Good   **Site** Level
Sites Available ▲ ⊞ ⊟ **Total** 700
Low Season Band B
High Season Band C
Facilities & ƒ ▥ ♨ ⌒ ⌣ ⌐ ☎
♋ ⓘ ⦿ ⓑ
Nearby Facilities ∪
≉ New Milton.
Coast within 5 miles. Shop and fast food takeaway on site.

BROCKENHURST
Hollands Wood Camp Site, Lyndhurst Road, Brockenhurst, Hampshire, SO42 7QH.
Tel: 283771 Std: 01703
Fax: **283929** Std: **01703**
Nearest Town/Resort Brockenhurst.
Directions ½ mile north of Brockenhurst on the A337, signposted.
Acreage 168 **Open** 21st March to 29th September
Access Good   **Site** Level
Sites Available ▲ ⊞ ⊟ **Total** 600
Low Season Band B
High Season Band C
Facilities & ▥ ♨ ⌒ ⌣ ⌐ ☎
♋ ⓘ ⦿ ⓑ
Nearby Facilities ⌐ ∪
≉ Brockenhurst.
Sheltered site in an oak woodland. Special tenting areas. Brockenhurst Village nearby.

BROCKENHURST
Roundhill Camp Site, Beaulieu Road, Brockenhurst, Hampshire, SO42 7QL.
Tel: 283771 Std: 01703
Fax: **283929** Std: **01703**
Nearest Town/Resort Brockenhurst.
Directions On the B3055, 2 miles south east of Brockenhurst off the A337, signposted.
Acreage 156 **Open** 21st March to 29th September
Access Good   **Site** Level
Sites Available ▲ ⊞ ⊟ **Total** 500
Low Season Band C
High Season Band C
Facilities & ▥ ♨ ⌒ ⌣ ♋ ⓘ ⦿ ⓑ
Nearby Facilities ⌐ ✓ ∪
≉ Brockenhurst.
Motorcyclists' area on campsite available, also rally site and lightweight camping on site.

CADNAM
Ocknell/Longbeech Campsite, Fritham, Nr. Lyndhurst, Hampshire, SO43 7NH.
Tel: 283771 Std: 01703
Fax: **283929** Std: **01703**
Nearest Town/Resort Lyndhurst.
Directions From the A31 at Cadnam take the B3079, then the B3078 via Brook and Fritham.
Acreage 48 **Open** 21st March to 29th September
Access Good   **Site** Level
Sites Available ▲ ⊞ ⊟ **Total** 480
Low-Season Band B
High Season Band C
Facilities & ⌀ ▥ ♨ ☎ ⦿ ⓑ ⦿
Nearby Facilities ⌐ ✓ ∪
Two contrasting sites. Permits from Ocknell. Toilets and hot showers at Ocknell.

FAREHAM
Dibles Park, Dibles Road, Warsash, Southampton, Hants, SO3 6SA.
Tel: Locksheath 575232 Std: 01489
Nearest Town/Resort Fareham
Directions Turn left off the A27 (Portsmouth to Southampton) opposite Lloyds Bank into Locks Road (sinposted Warsash). In about 1½ miles at the T-Junction turn right into Warsash Road, in about 300yds turn left into Fleet End Road. Take the first right and we are on the right.
Acreage ¾ **Open** Easter to October
Access Good   **Site** Level
Sites Available ▲ ⊞ ⊟ **Total** 14
Facilities ƒ ▥ ♨ ⌒ ⌣ ⌐ ☎ ⓘ ⦿ ⓑ ⦿
Nearby Facilities ✓ ∪
≉ Swanwick
Shingle beach 1½ miles.

FORDINGBRIDGE
New Forest Country Holidays, Sandy Balls Estate, Godshill, Fordingbridge, Hampshire, SP6 2JZ.
Tel: 653042 Std: 01425
Fax: **653067** Std: **01425**
Nearest Town/Resort Salisbury/Bournemouth.
Directions On B3078, 1½ miles from Fordingbridge. 8 miles from Cadnam. Easy access from the M27.
Acreage 120 **Open** All Year
Access Good   **Site** Level
Sites Available ▲ ⊞ ⊟ **Total** 340
Facilities & ƒ ▥ ♨ ⌒ ⌣ ⌐ ☎
♋ ⓘ ⦿ ⋉ ⓑ ⋔ ⋏ ⋈ ✺ ◻
Nearby Facilities ✓ ⌁ ∪ ⌁
≉ Salisbury.
Open all year round. Edge of New Forest. Superb woodland setting with high standard of amenities, many walks. Indoor heated pool and leisure complex. Winner of England for Excellence 1993. British Graded Holiday Parks 5 Ticks.

GOSPORT
Kingfisher Caravan Park, Brownown Road, Stokes Bay, Gosport, Hampshire, PO13 9BE.
Tel: 502076 Std: 01705
Fax: **583583** Std: **01705**
Nearest Town/Resort Gosport
Directions Exit 11 off the M27, take the A32 to Gosport. After approx. 3 miles at Fort Brockhurst follow caravan signs to Stokes Bay.
Acreage 14 **Open** February to November
Access Good   **Site** Level
Sites Available ▲ ⊞ ⊟ **Total** 100
Facilities ƒ ▥ ♨ ⌒ ⌣ ⌐ ☎ ⦿
♋ ⓘ ⦿ ⋉ ⓑ ⋔ ⋏ ⋈ ✺ ◻
Nearby Facilities ⌐ ✓ ⌁ ⌁
≉ Portsmouth Hard
Within easy reach of Portsmouth with ferries to the Continent and the Isle of Wight.

83

HAMPSHIRE

HAYLING ISLAND
Fishery Creek Caravan & Camping Park, Fishery Lane, Hayling Island, PO11 9NR.
Tel: 462164 Std: 01705
Nearest Town/Resort Hayling Island
Directions Turn off A27, cross bridge, follow signs turning left at first roundabout, left after town of Mengham, left into Fishery Lane. Park is at end of lane.
Acreage 8 **Open** March to October
Access Good   **Site** Level
Sites Available ▲ ⊕ ⊟ **Total** 165
Low Season Band B
High Season Band C
Facilities ⊞ & ƒ ⊠ ♨ ɾ ⊙ ⌐ ⬛ ☎
§ ⊙ ⊟ ⓣ ♠ ⚑ ⊟
Nearby Facilities ɾ ✔ ⊥ ⍤ U ⇗ ℛ
⇌ Havant.
Alongside a beautiful tidal creek, offering peace and tranquility. Own slipway, short path to beach. Fishing on site. Caravan storage available all year round.

HAYLING ISLAND
Fleet Park, Yew Tree Road, Hayling Island, Hampshire, PO11 0QF.
Tel: 463684 Std: 01705
Nearest Town/Resort Havant/Southsea.
Directions Follow A3023 from Havant. Approx. 2 miles on Island turn left into Copse Lane then first right into Yew Tree Road.
Acreage 3 **Open** March to October
Access Good   **Site** Level
Sites Available ▲ ⊕ ⊟ **Total** 75
Low Season Band B
High Season Band B
Facilities ⊞ ƒ ♨ ⊠ ɾ ⊙ ⌐ ☎
§ ⊙ ⊟ ⓢ ⚑ ⊠
Nearby Facilities ɾ ✔ ⊥ ⍤ U ⇗ ℛ
⇌ Havant.
Near Ferry Port. Portsmouth/Southsea, Isle of Wight. Easy touring for New Forest and Beaulieu. Quiet, family site.

HAYLING ISLAND
Lower Tye Camp Site, Copse Lane, Hayling Island, Hants, PO11 0QB.
Tel: 462479 Std: 01705
Nearest Town/Resort Havant
Directions Exit the M27 or the A3M motorway at Havant. Follow the A3023 from Havant, turn left into Copse Lane. You will see the sign after being on Hayling Island for approx 1¼ miles.
Acreage 5 **Open** March to November
Access Good   **Site** Level
Sites Available ▲ ⊕ ⊟ **Total** 150
Low Season Band B
High Season Band B
Facilities ƒ ⊠ ♨ ɾ ⊙ ⌐ ⬛ ☎
§ ⊙ ⊟ ⓢ ⚑ ⊟
Nearby Facilities ɾ ✔ ⊥ ⍤ U ⇗ ℛ
⇌ Havant.
Near Portsmouth, Isle of Wight, Singlton Open Air Museum, Chichester, excellent beach, all water sports. £7 plus V.A.T. per unit for 2 people. Storage available. Plunge pool on site.

HAYLING ISLAND
Oven Camping Site, Manor Road, Hayling Island, Hampshire, PO11 0QX.
Tel: 464695 Std: 01705
Nearest Town/Resort Havant.
Directions Exit M27 or the A37 at Havant. Take the A3023 from Havant, approx 3 miles after crossing bridge onto Hayling Island bear right at the roundabout. Site is on the left in 450yds.
Acreage 10 **Open** March to October
Access Good   **Site** Level
Sites Available ▲ ⊕ ⊟ **Total** 330

Low Season Band C
High Season Band C
Facilities ⊞ & ƒ ⊠ ♨ ɾ ⊙ ⌐ ⬛ ☎
§ ⊙ ⊟ ⓣ ♠ ⚑ ⊠ ⊟
Nearby Facilities ɾ ✔ ⊥ ⍤ U ⇗ ℛ
⇌ Havant.
Excellent touring area for Portsmouth, Chichester, New Forest etc. Safe, clean beaches, excellent for water sports. Caravan storage and rallies.

NEW MILTON
Bashley Park, Sway Road, New Milton, Hampshire.
Tel: 612340 Std: 01425
Nearest Town/Resort New Milton.
Directions From A35 Lyndhurst/Bournemouth road, take B3055 signposted Sway. Over crossroads at 2¼ miles. Park is ½ mile on left.
Open March to October
Access Good   **Site** Level
Sites Available ⊕ ⊟ **Total** 400
Low Season Band C
High Season Band C
Facilities & ƒ ⊠ ♨ ɾ ⊙ ⌐ ⬛ ☎
§ ⊙ ⊟ ⓢ ✘ ⓣ ♠ ⚑ ⊠ ⊟
Nearby Facilities ✔ ⊥ ⍤ U ⇗
⇌ New Milton.
New Forest - 2 miles from beach, 10 miles Bournemouth. Own golf course, indoor/outdoor pools and tennis. Many facilities. Rose Award for Excellence and England for Excellence Silver Award.

NEW MILTON
Setthorns Camp Site, Wootton, New Milton, Hampshire, BH25 5UA.
Tel: 283771 Std: 01703
Fax: 283929 Std: 01703
Nearest Town/Resort New Milton
Directions From Brockenhurst take the B3055 to Sway, after 2 miles take an unclassified signposted road to the site.
Acreage 60 **Open** All Year
Access Good   **Site** Level
Sites Available ▲ ⊕ ⊟ **Total** 320
Low Season Band B
High Season Band C
Facilities ƒ ☎ ☜ ⊙ ⓢ ⊟
Nearby Facilities ɾ U
⇌ New Milton

OWER
Green Pastures Farm, Ower, Romsey, Hampshire, SO51 6AJ.
Tel: 814444 Std: 01703
Nearest Town/Resort Romsey.
Directions Site is signposted from A36 and A31 at Ower (exit 2 off M27 - signposted for Salisbury).
Acreage 5 **Open** 15 March to 31 October
Access Good   **Site** Level
Sites Available ▲ ⊕ ⊟ **Total** 45
Low Season Band B
High Season Band B
Facilities ⊞ & ƒ ⊠ ♨ ɾ ⊙ ⌐ ⬛ ☎
§ ⊙ ⊟
Nearby Facilities ɾ ✔ U ℛ
⇌ Romsey.
A grassy site on family run farm, within easy reach of the New Forest. Paultons Park 1 mile, convenient for ferries to Isle of Wight and France, from Portsmouth, Southampton and Lymington. Ample space for children to play. ETB Grading 3 Ticks.

RINGWOOD
The Red Shoot Camping Park, Linwood, Nr. Ringwood, Hampshire BH24 3QT.
Tel: 473789 Std: 01425
Fax: 471558 Std: 01425

Nearest Town/Resort Ringwood.
Directions Fron Ringwood take A338, 2 miles north of Ringwood take right turn signed Moyles Court and Linwood. Follow signs to Linwood.
Acreage 4 **Open** March to October
Access Good   **Site** Lev/Slope
Sites Available ▲ ⊕ ⊟ **Total** 100
Facilities & ƒ ⊠ ♨ ɾ ⊙ ⌐ ⬛ ☎
§ ⊙ ✘ ⚑ ⊟
Nearby Facilities ɾ ✔ U ⇗
⇌ Brockenhurst.
Half hour drive to Bournemouth coast, Salisbury and Southampton. Situated in beautiful part of New Forest. Good pub adjacent. Mountain bike hire. Off peak tariff early and late season.

ROMSEY
Doctors Hill Farm Caravan & Camping Park, Sherfield English, Romsey, Hampshire, SO51 6JX.
Tel: 340402 Std: 01794
Fax: 340402 Std: **01794**
Nearest Town/Resort Romsey.
Directions A31 towards Romsey and Winchester, just before you enter Romsey turn left onto the A27. In 4 miles turn right at Sherfield English crossroads. Park is 600yds on the right.
Acreage 10 **Open** March to October
Access Good   **Site** Lev/Slope
Sites Available ▲ ⊕
Low Season Band B
High Season Band B
Facilities ƒ ⊠ ♨ ɾ ⊙ ⌐ ☎ ⊙ ⊟
Nearby Facilities ɾ ✔ U
Within easy reach of the New Forest and the home of the late Lord Mountbatten. Special dog walk, pitch and putt. Lovely views of the surrounding countryside. Graded 3 Tick Park.

SOUTHBOURNE
Chichester Camping, 345 Main Road, Southbourne, Emsworth, Hants, PO10 8JH.
Tel: 373202 Std: 01243
Nearest Town/Resort Emsworth
Directions
Acreage 3 **Open** January to October
Access Level   **Site** Good
Sites Available ▲ ⊕ ⊟ **Total** 60
Facilities & ƒ ⊠ ♨ ɾ ⊙ ⌐ ⬛ ☎ ⓛ ⊟
Nearby Facilities ɾ ✔ ⊥ ⍤ U ⇗
⇌ Southbourne
500 yards through footpath to beach. ideal touring.

SOUTHSEA
Southsea Leisure Park, Melville Road, Southsea, Hampshire, PO4 9TB.
Tel: 735070 Std: 01705
Fax: **821302** Std: 01705
Nearest Town/Resort Portsmouth
Directions From M27/A27/A3M take southbound A2030 for 4 miles, turn left onto the A288 and follow signs.
Acreage 12 **Open** All Year
Access Good   **Site** Level
Sites Available ▲ ⊕ ⊟ **Total** 185
Low Season Band C
High Season Band C
Facilities ⊞ & ƒ ⊠ ♨ ɾ ⊙ ⌐ ⬛ ☎
§ ⓛ ⊙ ⊟ ⓢ ✘ ⓣ ♠ ⚑ ⊠ ⊟
Nearby Facilities ɾ ✔ ⍤ U
⇌ Portsmouth Harbour
Located beside the beach at the quieter end of historic Portsmouth. Only 10 minutes from cross-channel ferries. Fully equipped, modern touring facilities.

In or Out of Season
you're in for a great time

For your main summer holiday or the perfect out-of-season breakaway this award winning touring park takes some beating. In a New Forest location that's beautiful all year round you'll find fantastic facilities and a very warm welcome.

- Super pitches including waste drainage, electricity, water and Satellite TV hook-up.
- Excellent toilet facilities with FREE hot water and showers.
- Supermarket & Launderette.
- Indoor and outdoor heated swimming pools.
- Multi-gym, Solarium, Steam Room, Sauna, Jacuzzi.
- Superb Restaurant and Inn.
- Horse Riding, fishing, table tennis, pool, adventure playground.

Plus, during main season:
- Barbecues, Brass Band Concerts, Country Dances.
- Pottery and watercolour sessions in the Folkhouse.

Write, phone or fax for FREE colour brochure.
New Forest Country Holidays, Sandy Balls Estate Ltd., Godshill,
Fordingbridge, Hampshire SP6 2JZ.
Tel: (01425) 653042
Fax: (01425) 653067

CADE'S WEST COUNTRY CAMPING, TOURING & MOTOR CARAVAN SITE GUIDE 1997

WICKHAM
Frith Farm Park Frith Lane, Wickham, Hampshire
Tel: 361241 Std: 01703
Nearest Town/Resort Portsmouth
Directions M27 off junction 10. A32 to Alton, 2 miles at roundabout fork left, 400yds turn in to square, straight out back of square (don't turn right) to 'T' junction, turn left ½ mile crossroads turn right, site 300yds on left.
Acreage 4 **Open** Easter to October
Access Good **Site** Gently Sloping
Sites Available ▲ ⌸ ⇌ **Total** 65
Low Season Band A

High Season Band A
Facilities ⓊⒷ ♨ ┌ ☉ ♋ ℟ ♨ ♫ ⦿
Nearby Facilities ┌ ✓
⇌ Fareham
Scenic views, ideal touring, many walks. Near historic towns Portsmouth, Southampton and Winchester. Additional 50 acres to explore.

WINCHESTER
Morn Hill Caravan Club Site, Morn Hill, Alresford Road, Winchester, Hants, SO21 1HL.
Tel: 869877 Std: 01962
Nearest Town/Resort Winchester

Directions From Winchester head east on the B3404, in approx. 3 miles at roundabout (Percy Hobbs Public House) turn left, then first right, site is 200metres. DO NOT enter first entrance but proceed forward to the second entrance and reception.
Acreage 9 **Open** 26th March
Access Good **Site** Level
Sites Available ▲ ⌸ ⇌ **Total** 154
Facilities ♨ ∫ ⓊⒷ ♨ ┌ ☉ ♋ ♫ ⦿ ♣
♨ ♫ ⦿ ⦿
Nearby Facilities ┌ ✓ ∪ ₰
⇌ Winchester
Old Cathedral City of Winchester and near to the New Forest.

PLACES OF INTEREST

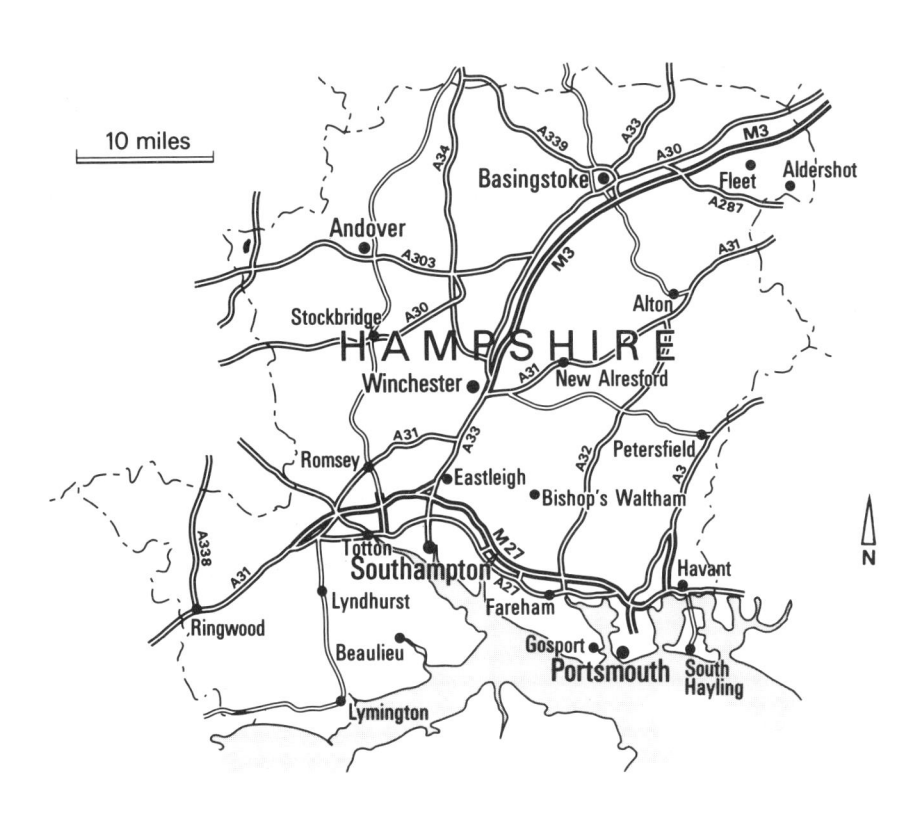

ALDERSHOT
This is an important military centre. The Hero's Shrine has a rockery built of materials taken from fifty-four bombed boroughs and there are several service museums within the town. Basingstoke Canal flows to the North and the parish church displays various monuments and a 15th century tower.
ALDERSHOT

AIRBORNE FORCES MUSEUM : Browning Barracks, Alisons Road, Aldershot, Hampshire, GU11 2BU. Tel : 01252 349619.
Nearest Railway Station : Aldershot. Open : 9am-4.30pm. Last admission 3.45pm. **Special Attractions:** The story of airborne forces from their formation in 1940 to the present day. See the largest collection of airborne weapons and equipment ever put together; also dioramas, briefing models, medals and uniforms.
ALDERSHOT

ROYAL ARMY MEDICAL CORPS MUSEUM : Keogh Barracks, Ash Vale, Aldershot, Hampshire, GU12 5RQ. Tel : 01252 340212. Fax : 01252 340224.
Nearest Railway Station : Ash Vale. Open : Monday to Friday, 8.30am-4pm. Closed weekends and public holidays. **Special Attractions:** The Museum shows the history of the Army Medical Services from 1660 to the present. Includes uniforms, medals, medical equipment and ambulances.

ALRESFORD
THE WATERCRESS LINE : The Railway Station, Alresford, Hampshire, SO24 9JG. Tel : 01962 733810.
Open : Saturdays, Sundays and Bank Holidays, March to October. Tuesdays to Thursdays, June. Daily running: Easter week, early July to early September and last week of October. (Check Timetable). Talking Timetable 01962 734866. **Special Attractions:** Take a "Journey Back in Time" by steam train on the "Watercress Line" in Hampshire. This runs for 10 miles through beautiful countryside between Alresford (7 miles East of Winchester and M3) and Alton (for rail connection to BR). Both towns are just off the A31. The line has steep hills which requires large, powerful steam engines to be used on all trains. Special events throughout the year.

ALTON
CURTIS MUSEUM & ALLEN GALLERY : High Street, Alton, Hants. Tel : 01420 82802. Fax : 01420 84227.
Nearest Railway Station : Alton. Location : Northern end of High Street. Open : Curtis Museum: Tuesday to Saturday 10am-5pm. Allen Gallery: Tuesday to Saturday 10am-5pm. Admission Free. **Special Attractions:** Displays of the local area, ceramics, silver and a changing programme of temporary Exhibitions.

ALTON
JANE AUSTEN'S HOUSE : Chawton, Alton, Hants, GU34 1SD. Tel & Fax : 01420 83262.
Nearest Railway Station : Alton. Location : 1 mile South West of Alton, off the A31 and the A32. Open : 1st March to 31st December (excluding Christmas Day and Boxing Day); January and February, weekends only. 11am-4.30pm. **Special Attractions:** 17th Century home of the novelist Jane Austen from 1809-1817. Contains many items associated with her and her family. Pleasant garden for picnicking, old bakehouse with brick oven and Jane's donkey cart. Refreshments available in village. Bookshop.

ANDOVER
ANDOVER MUSEUM & THE MUSEUM OF THE IRON AGE : 6 Church Close, Andover, Hampshire, SP10 1DP. Tel : 01264 366283. Fax : 01264 339152.
Nearest Railway Station : Andover. Location : Near Town Centre. Open : All year round, 10am-5pm, Tuesday to Saturday for both Museums. Museum of Iron Age only, April to September, Sundays 2pm-5pm. **Special Attractions:** Andover Museum - Displays depict 'The Story of Andover' from its rich archaelogical past to the busy town of today. Museum of Iron Age - This unique Museum tells the story of Danebury, an Iron Age Hill Fort that lies southwest of Andover.

ANDOVER
FINKLEY DOWN FARM PARK : Finkley Down Farm, Andover, Hampshire, SP11 6NF. Tel : 01264 352195.
Nearest Railway Station : Andover Junction. Location : 1.5 miles north of the A303, 2 miles east of Andover. Open : April to the end of October, 10.15am-6pm. Weekends only in October and half term week. **Special Attractions:** The farm has many breeds of farm animals and poultry. Animal activities during the day. Childrens pets, donkeys, ponies, rabbits, etc.. Adventure playground, picnic area and Romany Camp. Rural Bygones light refreshments. Free car park.
ANDOVER

THE HAWK CONSERVANCY : Andover, Hampshire. Tel : 01264 772252. Fax : 01264 773772.
Nearest Railway Station : Andover Junction. Location : Easily reached by car, 3.5 miles west of Andover, fully signposted from the A303. Open : 1st March to the last Sunday in October, from 10.30am daily. Spring and Autumn to 4pm, Summer to 5pm. **Special Attractions:** Largest centre in the south for Birds of Prey from all over the world. Birds are flown completely free at 12 noon, 2pm, 3pm and 4pm daily (weather permitting). Two caravan sites locally. Not to be missed "Valley of the Eagles" demonstration at 2pm, held in "Reg's Downland Meadow", a meadow abundant with wild flowers and grasses. Carousel of Kites at 3pm. New toddlers play area.

BASINGSTOKE
A development area designed to take overspill from London, Basingstoke is a rapidly expanding industrial centre, which includes the headquarters of the AA.

This district has been inhabited from earliest times, although nearby Basing Village claimed greater importance when the construction of the Basingstoke Canal was completed in 1789, and later the railway in 1839. The Canal provided access to the Thames ad London.

An extensive cloth industry had developed by the early 17th Century and some timbered building of this period still survive. One of the town's older buildings is the Church of St Michael and All Angels - this contains work of the 12th, 15th and 16th Century.

Outstanding amongst recently completed buildings is the shopping, sports and recreation complex. The indoor sports centre was opened in 1970 and has facilities for many activities including swimming in two pools. May's Bounty is a cricket ground. Basingstoke is a venue for point to point racing, and a visit to the Willis Museum is recommended.

BASINGSTOKE
BASING HOUSE : Redbridge Lane, Old Basing, Near Basingstoke, Hants. Tel : 01256 467294.
Nearest Railway Station : Basingstoke. Location : North of Junction 6 - M3 Motorway. Open : April to September, Wednesdays to Sundays and Bank Holidays, 2pm-6pm. **Special Attractions:** Ruins of largest private house in Tudor England. Destroyed by Cromwell in the Civil War. Exhibitions tell the story of the house and family. Archaeological work in progress. Beautiful grounds and shop. New reconstruction of a 17th Century formal garden.

BEAULIEU
JOHN MONTAGU BUILDING : Beaulieu, Hants, SO42 7ZN. Tel : 01590 612345. Fax : 01590 612624.
Nearest Railway Station : Brockenhurst. Location : In the heart of the New Forest between Bournemouth and Southampton. Open : Easter to September, 10am-6pm. October to Easter 10am-5pm. (Closed Christmas Day). **Special Attractions:** National Motor Museum and "Wheels" - the legend of the motor car; Palace House and gardens; Beaulieu Abbey and exhibition of monastic life; special features.

BISHOPS WALTHAM
THE OLD GRANARY ART & CRAFT CENTRE : Bank Street, Bishops Waltham, Hampshire, SO32 1BN. Tel : 01489 894595.
Nearest Railway Station : Botley. Location : 10 miles from Winchester, Southampton and Portsmouth. Open : Tuesday to Saturday 10am-4pm, Wednesday 10am-1pm. **Special Attractions:** Various craft workers have workshops such as pottery, picture framing, jewellery, glass engraving, lettered pottery, house plaques, Roman plaques, portrait painting, dried flower arrangements, etc.. Art Gallery by local artists.
BREAMORE

87

HAMPSHIRE

BREAMORE HOUSE & COUNTRYSIDE MUSEUM : Breamore, Near Fordingbridge, Hampshire, SP6 2DF. Tel : 01725 512233. Fax : 01725 512858.
Nearest Railway Station : Salisbury. Location : On the A338 between Salisbury and Fordingbridge. Open : 1st April 1997, 1pm. **Special Attractions:** Fine Elizabethan Manor House with excellent collections of pictures, furniture and needlework. Countryside Museum takes visitors back to when a village was self sufficient. A wonderful afternoon for all the family.

GOSPORT
FORT BROCKHURST : Gunners Way, Elson, Gosport, Hampshire. Tel : 01705 581059.
Nearest Railway Station : Fareham/Portsmouth Hard. Location : A32 Fareham to Gosport road. Open : 1st April to 30th September, 10am-6pm. RAF Exhibition - Weekends and Bank Holidays. (The site closes from 1pm-2pm for lunch). **Special Attractions:** Exhibition and display on Portsmouth fortifications. A massive Victorian fortress surrounded by a wet moat. Tunnels, cells and a variety of wildlife. New RAF Exhibition.

GOSPORT
GOSPORT FERRY LIMITED : South Street, Gosport, Hampshire, PO12 1EP. Tel : 01705 524551.
Nearest Railway Station : Portsmouth Harbour. Location : Junction 11 off M27, A32 into Gosport, follow signs for ferry. Open : Trips arranged to suit school timetable. Harbour cruises last for approximately 1 hour. **Special Attractions:** Tours of Historic Portsmouth Harbour with full live commentary aboard large all-weather vessels. See the ships of the Royal Navy, both Historic and present day. Teachers workpack available.

GOSPORT
SUBMARINE WORLD : Haslar Jetty Road, Gosport, Hampshire. Tel : 01705 529217.
Nearest Railway Station : Portsmouth Harbour. Open : Every day except 24th December to the 1st January. **Special Attractions:** Large 1947 Submarine (guided tour), Holland I (Royal Navy's first submarine), pre-visit audio-visual, x-craft. Museum full of models, photographs and artefacts. Superb new gift shop, cafeteria. Free parking. Accessible by Harbour Boat Tours.

HAVANT
STAUNTON COUNTRY PARK : Middle Park Way, Havant, Hampshire, PO9 5HB. Tel : 01705 453405. Fax : 01705 498156.
Nearest Railway Station : Havant. Location : On the B2149 between the A27 near Portsmouth and the A3M near Petersfield. Open : All Year except Christmas Day and Boxing Day. Summer 10am-5pm, Winter 10am-4pm. **Special Attractions:** Within a 1000 acre Historic Estate lie a Victorian Ornamental Farm and Tropical Glasshouses - A delight to young and old alike. A variety of exotic and rare animals and their babies. Giant water lily and colourful plants fill the glasshouses.

LYMINGTON
This holiday resort and yachting centre is situated on the Lymington River where it flows into the Solent. The Harbour Master's Office of 1833 was once a bath house, and the porch of Pressgang Cottage, a former Inn was the headquarters of an 18th Century pressgang.

A car ferry connects Lymington with the Isle of Wight town, Yarmouth. Much of the church is Georgian and many 18th Century houses still remain. Historian Edward Gibbon was once an MP for the town. A lofty obelisk commemorates Admiral Sir Harry Burrard-Neale, who died in 1840.

LYMINGTON
SPINNERS : Boldre, Lymington, Hampshire, SO41 5QE. Tel : 01590 673347.
Nearest Railway Station : Lymington. Location : Signed off the A337 between Brockenhurst and Lymington. Open : 14th April to 14th September, Wednesday to Saturday (also Sundays in May), 10am-5pm (also at other times by appointment). No entry charge into the Nursery and part of Garden. **Special Attractions:** Woodland garden built by owners without paid labour between 1960 and 1980. Rhododendrons, Azaleas, Magnolias, Japanese Maples, Hydrangeas etc. interplanted with a wide variety of choice woodland and groundcover plants. Adjoining a nursery for less common and rare hardy trees, shrubs and plants.

LYNDHURST
FURZEY GARDENS : Minstead, Near Lyndhurst, Hants, SO43 7GL. Tel : 01703 812464. Fax : 01703 812297.
Nearest Railway Station : Lyndhurst. Location : Off A31 and up lane by Minstead Hall - follow signposts. Open : Daily (except Christmas Day and Boxing Day) 10am-5pm, dusk in Winter. **Special Attractions:** 16th Century Cottage and Will Selwood Gallery displaying work of local craftsmen set in 8 acres of delightful gardens of botanical interest all year. After maintenance all proceeds go to a charity training young people with learning difficulties.

LYNDHURST
NEW FOREST MUSEUM & VISITOR CENTRE : High Street, Lyndhurst, Hampshire, SO43 7NY. Tel : 01703 283914. Fax : 01703 284236.
Nearest Railway Station : Ashurst. Location : In the main car park in Lyndhurst. Open : All year round, 10am-6pm. **Special Attractions:** Multi-projector audio visual show and exhibition telling the story of the New Forest - Its history, characters, traditions and wildlife. Includes the New Forest Embroidery. Free childrens quiz. Gift shop.

OWER
PAULTONS PARK : Ower, Romsey, Hampshire, SO51 6AL. Tel : 01703 814455.
Nearest Railway Station : Southampton. Location : Just off exit 2 M27, at junction A31/A36 between Southampton and Romsey. Open : 10am daily, Mid-March to October. **Special Attractions:** A whole day of fun for all the family. Beautiful gardens, lake, maze, exotic birds, animals and pets corner. Miniature railway. Village Life and Romany Museums, Victorian Watermill. Lots for children - Kids Kingdom, Dinosaurs, Magic Forest, Rabbit Ride. Bumper Boats, Astroglide, Go-Karts, Crazy Golf, Runaway Train and much more. Shops. Restaurants. Great value Family Supersavers.

PETERSFIELD
THE BEAR MUSEUM : 38 Dragon Street, Petersfield, Hampshire, GU31 4JJ. Tel : 01730 265108 (10am-5pm).
Nearest Railway Station : Petersfield. Location : Situated 100yds south from the bottom of Petersfield High Street. Tourist Board signed. Open : Tuesday to Saturday, 10am-5pm. Closed Sunday and Monday. **Special Attractions:** The first museum devoted to Teddy Bears. Now in its 13th year, one of the largest and most interesting collections on public display in Britain. Quality gift shop selling some bears.

PETERSFIELD
BUTSER ANCIENT FARM : Nexus House, Gravel Hill, Waterlooville, Hampshire, PO8 0QE. Tel & Fax : 01705 598838.
Nearest Railway Station : Petersfield. Location : Signposted off the A3, 5 miles south of Petersfield. Open : March to November, 10am-4pm. **Special Attractions:** A representation of an Iron Age farm settlement. Based on archaeological evidence and the focus of an environmental research project.

PETERSFIELD
QUEEN ELIZABETH COUNTRY PARK : Gravel Hill, Horndean, Portsmouth, Hampshire. Tel : 01705 595040. Fax : 01705 592409.
Nearest Railway Station : Petersfield. Location : 4 miles south of Petersfield, 16 miles North of Portsmouth. Park Centre. Open : April to October inclusive, 10am-5.30pm (every day). November to March inclusive, 10am-5.30pm (Weekends only). **Special Attractions:** 1400 acres of woodland and downland with picnic areas, waymarked trails, pony trekking and mountain biking. Facilities include a Visitor Centre with theatre, an exhibition area and a cafe.

PORTSMOUTH

HAMPSHIRE

Portsmouth has been home port for generations of sailors, officers and men, volunteers and "pressed" men since "Nelson was a boy" and beyond.

Frequent bombing raids during the last war caused the demolition of many fine buildings. The City has had to undertake extensive restoration work.

The dockyard cover about 300 acres and includes many 18th Century buildings. Nelson's famous ship "H.M.S. Victory" which was launched originally in 1765 lies here in dry dock. Alongside there is a Naval Museum.

Cumberland Fort dates from 1746 and 1786 and the Eastney Bream - Engine House forms the nucleus of an industrial archaeology museum and the interesting Royal Marines Museum is housed in Eastney Barracks.

Charles Dickens was born at a house in Commercial Road in 1812. His father was a dockyard clerk and the house now contains a museum. Isambard Kingdom Brunel, the great engineer, was also born at Portsmouth in 1806. The Cathedral and the Garrison Church are each bristling with the memories of famous men, and are both worth visiting for there is much to be admired in each.

A car ferry connects with the Isle of Wight and there is also a passenger hovercraft service.

PORTSMOUTH
CHARLES DICKENS BIRTHPLACE : 393 Old Commercial Road, Portsmouth, Hampshire, PO1 4QL. Tel : 01705 827261. Fax : 01705 875276.
Nearest Railway Station : Portsmouth and Southsea. Location : Close to Commercial Road shopping precinct and Sainsburys. By road follow signposting to Charles Dickens coming off the M275 into Portsmouth (look for the symbol [M] on the brown signposts). Open : Daily. April to October, 10am-5.30pm. December to two weeks before Christmas, 10am-4.30pm. Closed 24th, 25th and 26th December. Last admission half hour before closing time. **Special Attractions:** Charles Dickens was born in this house in 1812. It has been restored, decorated and furnished in the Regency style appropriate to his parents. Exhibition room which includes the couch on which he died.

PORTSMOUTH
D-DAY MUSEUM & OVERLORD EMBROIDERY : Clarence Esplanade, Southsea, Hampshire, PO5 3NT. Tel : 01705 827261. Fax : 01705 875276.
Nearest Railway Station : The Hard. Location : By road follow signposting to D-Day Museum from M27/M275 or M27/A2030 into Portsmouth (look for the symbol [M] on the brown signposts). Open : Daily. April to October, 10am-5.30pm. November to March, 10am-4.30pm. Closed 24th, 25th and 26th December. Last admission 1 hour before closing time. **Special Attractions:** The magnificent 'Overlord Embroidery', 34 panels tell the complete story of the D-Day operation with personal Soundalive commentary. Archive film and re-created scenes of life in Wartime Britain 1944, with simulated sound and visual effects. Go through the Airborne drop and board a genuine landing craft to experience the world's largest ever seaborne invasion.

PORTSMOUTH
ROYAL MARINES MUSEUM : Southsea, Eastney, Portsmouth, Hampshire. Tel : 01705 819385. Fax : 01705 838420.
Nearest Railway Station : Portsmouth. Location : Follow signs to Southsea on the A2030 and head towards the seafront, from which the museum is signposted. Open : 10am-5pm, Whitsun to August. 10am-4.30pm, September to May. **Special Attractions:** Take a fascinating journey through time and discover 300 years of action-packed history. Special effect displays, Jungle and Trench Warfare (even a live snake and Scorpions), multi-media cinema, medal room and thousands of treasures and unusual memorabilia. Licensed restaurant and shop.

PORTSMOUTH
SEA LIFE CENTRE, PORTSMOUTH : Clarence Esplanade, Southsea, Portsmouth, Hants. Tel : 01705 875222. Fax : 01705 294443.
Nearest Railway Station : Portsmouth and Southsea. Location : On Southsea Seafront. Open : All year from 10am (except Christmas Day). **Special Attractions:** New for 1995: "The Jelly Lab", an amazing insight into the lifecycle of the Jellyfish, from birth to death. New tropical marine centre and our latest arrivals, the Sea Horses.

PORTSMOUTH
SOUTHSEA CASTLE : Clarence Esplanade, Southsea, Hampshire, PO5 3PA. Tel : 01705 827261. Fax : 01705 875276.
Nearest Railway Station : Portsmouth and Southsea. Location : By road follow signposting to Southsea Castle from the M275 or the M27/A2030 into Portsmouth (look for the symbol [M] on the brown signposts). Open : Daily, April to October, 10am-5.30pm. Weekends only, November to March, 19am-4.30pm. Closed 24th, 25th and 26th December. Last admission half hour before closing time. **Special Attractions:** Built by Henry VIII in 1545 to protect Portsmouth. Featuring 'Life in the Castle' Time Tunnel Experience. Audio-visual show. Tudor, Civil War and Victorian military history displays. Artillery, underground tunnels and home of Fort Cumberland Guard.

PORTSMOUTH
SOUTHSEA MODEL VILLAGE : Lumps Fort, Southsea Seafront, Portsmouth, Hampshire. Tel : 01705 294706.
Location : 1 mile from Southsea Caravan Site, near the pier and canoe lake. Car and coach park next door. Open : 10am to dusk. **Special Attractions:** Doll's house scale buildings and pretty gardens, inside the grounds of a Victorian Fort with scenic views. Garden railway, toy museum, underground tunnels and pottery.

PORTSMOUTH
SPITBANK FORT : Portsmouth Harbour, Hants. Tel : 01329 664286 OR 0831 608383.
Nearest Railway Station : Portsmouth Harbour. Location : The Solent, Portsmouth. Open : Easter to October. Closed on Mondays and Tuesdays (excluding Bank Holidays). **Special Attractions:** A Victorian Fort built in the sea one mile from Portsmouth Harbour. A monumental example of engineering and architecture.

RINGWOOD
NEW FOREST CIDER : Littlemead, Pound Lane, Burley, Ringwood, Hampshire, BH24 4ED. Tel & Fax : 01425 403589.
Nearest Railway Station : Brockenhurst. Location : Burley in the New Forest. Open : Summer, daily 10am-7pm. Winter 10am-Dusk. **Special Attractions:** Traditional Farmhouse Cider makers on a forest commoners holding. Taste and buy draught Scrumpy Cider from the barrels in the cowshed. See the press working during the Autumn period Mid-September to late November (subject to availability of fruit).

RINGWOOD
NEW FOREST OWL SANCTUARY : Crow Lane, Crow, Ringwood, Hampshire, BH24 1EA. Tel : 01425 476487.
Nearest Railway Station : Bournemouth. Location : Signposted with brown tourist signs off the A31 (main trunk road), 1 mile from the centre of Ringwood. Open : 1st March to 5th November, then weekends, Christmas holiday. Summer 10am-5pm, Winter 10am-4pm. **Special Attractions:** Largest collection of Owls in Europe. Flying displays every hour from 10am onwards. Indoor displays to suit all ages. Access for wheelchairs. Cafe, picnic area, car park and shop. Great day out for all the family.

ROCKBOURNE
ROCKBOURNE ROMAN VILLA : Rockbourne, Hampshire, SP6 3PG. Tel : 01725 518541.
Nearest Railway Station : Salisbury. Location : 4 miles west of Fordingbridge off the B3078. 10 miles south of Salisbury. Open : April, May, June and September, weekdays 12pm-6pm, weekends and Bank Holidays 10.30am-6pm. July and August, all days 10.30am-6pm. **Special Attractions:** Remains of the largest known Villa in the South area, discovered in 1942. See the best mosaics,

CADE'S WEST COUNTRY CAMPING, TOURING & MOTOR CARAVAN SITE GUIDE 1997   **89** part of the underfloor heating system and the outline of Villa's forty rooms in original positions. Recently refurbished Museum which displays many fascinating objects found outside and which describe the life of Roman Britons living over 1600 years ago.

ROMSEY
BROADLANDS: Romsey, Hants, SO51 9ZD. Tel: 01794 517888. Nearest Railway Station: Romsey. Location: Off A31 Romsey By-pass. Open: 14th June to 7th September, daily 12noon-5.30pm. Last admission at 4pm. **Special Attractions:** Palladian mansion on banks of River Test famous as the home of Lord Mountbatten. Special attractions include House with its art treasures and mementoes of the famous, Riverside Lawns, Mountbatten Exhibition and spectacular Mountbatten A-V Presentation.

ROMSEY
ROMSEY RAPIDS: Southampton Road, Romsey, Hampshire. Tel: 01794 830333. Information Line: 01794 514202. Nearest Railway Station: Romsey. Location: Next door to Broadlands. Open: 7 days a week from 10am. **Special Attractions:** Swim the exciting rapids, zoom down the 70 metre flume, have fun in the spa pool, plus bubble seats, rain shower, mushroom shower. Also fitness suite, sauna, steam room and jacuzzi. Coffee shop.

ROMSEY
THE SIR HAROLD HILLIER GARDENS & ARBORETUM: Jermyns Lane, Ampfield, Near Romsey, Hampshire, SO51 0QA. Tel: 01794 368787. Fax: 01794 368027. Nearest Railway Station: Romsey. Location: 3 miles north-east of Romsey, signposted off the A31 Romsey to Winchester road. Open: Every day, 10.30am-6pm or dusk if earlier. Closed public and Bank Holidays over Christmas. **Special Attractions:** Beautiful 166 acre gardens, home to one of the best collections of trees and shrubs in the Country. A garden for all seasons, there is something to enjoy here all year round from the flamboyant blossoms of Spring to the magical Winter Witch Hazels.

SOUTHAMPTON
Southampton is an important trans-atlantic port with extensive docks, and a harbour which is noted for its double tide, Southampton achieved City status in 1946.

However, Southampton's roots lie deep in history, being a fortified port under Saxon rule at least one thousand years ago. The Saxon fortifications of earth and timber were replaced in the 13th Century with a tremendous Norman Fortress Castle.

Today, three magnificent gateways - remnants of the Great Castle - still survive. These are the Bar Gate, Westgate and God's House Gate. Each of these structures (up to 60ft thick) have unique embellishments; one is still tied in the elements of the Castle towers and the gallery prison (now a museum).

Other places of interest include The Wool House, which displays massive buttresses and houses a maritime museum, and the Tudor House in Blue Anchor Lane which houses a folk museum with fine examples of skilled craftsmanship and many unusual artefacts. A seaplane which won the Schneider Cup for Britain in 1931 can be seen in the Mitchell Memorial Museum.

Shipping naturally dominates Southampton, throughout the City one is constantly reminded of the importance to the City. There is a memorial to the ill-fated Titanic standing near the modern civic centre, the remains of Holy Rood Church include a 14th Century tower and now serves as a memorial to the Merchant Navy.

Famous natives of Southampton include Lord Jellicoe, Sir John Millais and Isaac Watts.

A car ferry and hovercraft service from Southampton connects to the Isle of Wight.
SOUTHAMPTON

ELING TIDE MILL: The Toll Bridge, Eling, Totton, Southampton, Hampshire, SO40 9HF. Tel: 01703 869575. Nearest Railway Station: Totton. Open: All Year, Wednesday to Sunday, 10am-4pm. **Special Attractions:** The only surviving tide mill to harness natural tidal energy for the regular production of wholemeal flour.

SOUTHAMPTON
LONGDOWN DAIRY FARM: Longdown, Ashurst, Near Southampton, Hampshire, SO40 4UH. Tel: 01703 293326. Fax: 01703 293376. Location: Off the A35 between Lyndhurst and Southampton. Open: Easter to the end of October, daily 10am-5pm. **Special Attractions:** A modern working farm where visitors can watch the afternoon milking, feed and touch the young animals and learn about modern farming methods. Play area, picnic area, refreshment kiosk, video room and a shop. Ample free parking.

SOUTHAMPTON
NEW FOREST NATURE QUEST: Longdown, Ashurst, Southampton, Hampshire, SO40 4UH. Tel: 01703 292408. Fax: 01703 293367. Nearest Railway Station: Ashurst. Open: April to December, daily from 10am. **Special Attractions:** The New Forest Nature Quest is a revolutionary new wildlife attraction allowing visitors to get closer than ever before to nature. British wildlife in their natural habitats. As a Nature Detective you have a privileged peek into the secret world of foxes, badgers, frogs, fish and a host more.

SOUTHAMPTON
NUFFIELD THEATRE: University Road, Southampton, Hants, SO17 1TR. Tel: 01703 671771. Nearest Railway Station: Southampton Parkway. Location: On the University Campus, 3 miles North of the City Centre, half a mile from the A33 Southampton-Winchester road. Open: September to July, evening performances, occasional Saturday matinees. **Special Attractions:** One of the Country's leading repertory theatres which presents a lively mixture of new and old work attracting many famous faces from stage and screen.

SOUTHAMPTON
SOUTHAMPTON HALL OF AVIATION: Albert Road South, Southampton, Hampshire. Tel: 01703 635830. Fax: 01703 223383. Nearest Railway Station: Southampton Central. Open: All Year, Tuesday to Saturday 10am-5pm. Sundays 12pm-5pm. Closed Mondays except Bank Holidays. **Special Attractions:** Depicts the History of Aviation in the Solent area. Tells the story of 26 aircraft companies, including Supermarine, definitive memorial to R. J. Mitchell designer of the Spitfire and Schneider trophy winning aircraft S6B. The largest aircraft on display is the four engined Sandringham Flying Boat. Many exhibits of aircraft, photographs, paintings and models.

SOUTHAMPTON
SOUTHAMPTON CITY MUSEUMS: **Tudor House Museum:** Bugle Street. **The Maritime Museum:** Bugle Street/Town Quay. **'Museum of Archaeology' God's House Tower:** Winkle Street/Town Quay. Tel: 01703 635904. Fax: 01703 339601. Location: All within one area, lower end of town and within a few minutes walk of each other. Open: (In general) 10am-5pm Tuesday to Friday, 10am-4pm Saturday, 2pm-5pm Sunday. **Special Attractions:** Tudor House with Tudor Garden, domestic and social history. Maritime Museum: the story of the White Star Line and the Titanic; Queen Mary, Queen of the Seas. Southampton Wall Walk - walk along some of the finest medieval town walls in England. Information panels tell you about the people who lived in Medieval Southampton, and you can see where they lived and worked. FREE admission to Museums.

STOCKBRIDGE

HOUGHTON LODGE GARDEN : Houghton, Near Stockbridge, Hampshire, SO20 6LQ. Tel : 01264 801177/810502. Fax : 01794 388072.
Nearest Railway Station : Winchester or Andover. Location : 1.5 miles south of the A30 at Stockbridge, on a minor road to Houghton Village. Open : March to September. Saturday and Sunday 10am-5pm. Monday, Tuesday and Friday 2pm-5pm. Other times by appointment. **Special Attractions:** Fine lawns and trees surround this unique 18th Century Cottage Ornee with lovely pastoral views over river and water meadows. Featured in BBC's TV series "The Buccaneers". Traditional Kitchen Garden (Fuchsias a speciality) and Hydroponicum: a living exhibition of HORTICULTURE WITHOUT SOIL and its use WORLDWIDE AND IN SPACE.

WHITCHURCH
WHITCHURCH SILK MILL : 28 Winchester Street, Whitchurch, Hampshire. Tel : 01256 893882.
Nearest Railway Station : Whitchurch. Location : Just off A34 midway between Newbury and Winchester. Open : Tuesday to Sunday, 10.30am-5pm and Bank Holidays. **Special Attractions:** Historic Silk Mill on the River Test. Traditional weaving on Victorian looms for fabrics for TV (Pride and Prejudice) and interior design. Water wheel and garden, gift shop for silk goods and a tea room.

WINCHESTER
Winchester is Hampshire's County's Capital City. Once the habitat and court of Kings and Princes, and for centuries, and ecclesiastical centre almost without equal. In 1079 the present cathedral was begun by Bishop Wakelin. The cathedral was imaginatively modulated in the late 14th Century by the brilliant Bishop of Wykeham. This marvellously crafted building is full of the genius of art, design, sculpture and carving, and reputed to be the most gifted of all the great cathedrals in the United Kingdom. Winchester College was founded by William of Wykeham in 1382, and is one of the oldest public schools in England. Much of the original structure is preserved.

Castle Hall dates from the 13th Century and has been restored and adopted for modern use. One of its main features is the famous Round Table of King Arthur.

Winchester recognizes the contributions of the County's Serving Regiments. The baroque-style Serle's House contains the Hampshire Regimental Museum and the Green Jackets' Regimental Museum is also of interest. The City Museum portrays much of the history and archaeology of Central Hampshire. Winchester is also the place where Jane Austen died in 1817, her house where she died is in College Street.

The Guildhall, the High Street and the County and Cathedral Libraries are other places of interest and beauty, as are the group of buildings known as the Hospital of St Cross.

WINCHESTER
THE GURKHA MUSEUM : Peninsula Barracks, Romsey Road, Winchester, Hants, SO23 8TS. Tel : 01962 842832 (24hr answer phone). Fax : 01962 877597.
Nearest Railway Station : Winchester (5 min walk). Open : Tuesday-Saturday and Bank Holidays and closed the following Tuesday. 10am-5pm, last entry 4.30pm. **Special Attractions:** A fascinating journey from Nepal and across the world, tells the story of the Gurkhas service from 1815 to the present. Life-size dioramas, sound and light shows plus talking figures bring alive the past.

WINCHESTER
MARWELL ZOOLOGICAL PARK : Colden Common, Near Winchester, Hants. Tel : 01962 777406.
Nearest Railway Station : Winchester/Eastleigh. Location : 6 miles South East of Winchester on the B2177 Winchester-Fareham road. Only 5 miles from both the M3 and M27. Open : Every day of the year (except Christmas Day). Hours from 10am. Last admission 5pm or one hour earlier in Winter. The zoo closes at 6pm. **Special Attractions:** Marwell is one of the largest and most interesting collections in Great Britain. It is a registered charity set up to preserve and breed endangered species. The zoo is set in over 100 acres of parkland. There are nearly 1,000 animals to see from all over the world including Giraffe, Rhino, Big Cats, Hippo, Monkeys and always lots of young babies to be seen. Childrens Farmyard, adventure playground, railway, roadtrain. Gift shops and full catering facilities. A visit to Marwell is a must.

ISLE OF WIGHT

ISLE OF WIGHT

ATHERFIELD
Chine Farm Camping Site, Military Road, Atherfield Bay, I.O.W., PO38 2JH.
Tel: 740228 Std: 01983
Nearest Town/Resort Freshwater
Directions East of Freshwater 8 miles on the A3055 Coast Road.
Acreage 5 **Open** May to September
Access Good **Site** Level
Sites Available ▲ ⊕ ⊟ **Total** 80
Low Season Band B
High Season Band B
Facilities 🄵 🆄 ♣ ⌐ ⊙ ❀ ⬚ 🄰 🄿
Nearby Facilities ⌐ ✓
Own private footpath to beach. Sea view. 3¼ miles Blackgang Chine.

BEMBRIDGE
Whitecliff Bay Holiday Park, Hillway, Whitecliff Bay, Bembridge, Isle of Wight, PO35 5PL.
Tel: 872671 Std: 01983
Nearest Town/Resort Sandown
Directions B3395 road to Sandown, follow signposts.

Acreage 15 **Open** April to October
Access Good **Site** Lev/Slope
Sites Available ▲ ⊕ ⊟ **Total** 450
Facilities 🆓 ✓ 🆄 ♣ ⌐ ⊙ ❀ ⬚ 🄰 🄿
S🄴 🄸 🄾 ♠ ✗ ♀ 🄼 ♣ 🄽 ⪡ 🄼
Nearby Facilities ⌐ ✓ ⟂ ♨ ∪ ≀ ℛ
✚ Brading.
Situated in pleasant countryside adjoining Whitecliff Bay with sandy beach. Indoor pool and leisure centre, family owned and managed.

COWES
Comforts Farm Camping Park & Riding School, Comforts Farm, Pallance Road, Northwood, Cowes, Isle of Wight, PO31 8LS.
Tel: 293888 Std: 01983
Nearest Town/Resort Cowes.
Directions From Cowes take the A3020, turn right into The Gates Road at Plessey Radar Site. Turn left into Place Road, after ½ mile bear right into Pallance Road. Farm entrance is on the right after passing Travellers Joy Public House.
Acreage 8¼ **Open** March to October
Access Good **Site** Lev/Slope
Sites Available ▲ ⊕ ⊟ **Total** 50

Low Season Band A
High Season Band B
Facilities 🆓 ✓ 🆄 ♣ ⌐ ⊙ ❀ ⬚ 🄰 🄿
S🄴 🄸 🄾 ♠ ✗ ♀ 🄼 ♣ 🄽
Nearby Facilities ⌐ ✓ ⟂
Horse riding on site.

COWES
Thorness Bay Holiday Park, Thorness, Isle of Wight, PO31 8NJ.
Tel: 523109 Std: 01983
Nearest Town/Resort Newport.
Directions From Fishbourne, follow signs to Newport and turn off roundabout onto dual carriageway following signs for West Cowes then Yarmouth onto the A3054 (Forest Road) for approx 1 mile. Thorness Bay is signposted.
Open April to October
Access Good **Site** Sloping
Sites Available ▲ ⊕ ⊟ **Total** 200
Facilities 🄵 ✓ 🆄 ♣ ⌐ 🄾 S🄴 🄸 🄾 ♠ ✗ ♀ 🄼 ♣ 🄽 ⪡
Nearby Facilities ⌐ ✓ ⟂ ♨ ∪ ≀ ℛ ✚
Pools, riding stables, family club, beaches. On site facilities.

91

ISLE OF WIGHT

COWES
Waverley Park Holiday Centre, Old Road, East Cowes, Isle of Wight, PO32 6AW.
Tel: 293452 Std: 01983
Fax: 200494 Std: 01983
Nearest Town/Resort East Cowes
Directions Signposted from Red Funnell Terminal at East Cowes, ¼ mile.
Open Easter to October
Access Good **Site** Sloping
Sites Available Å ♤ ⊖ **Total** 50
Low Season Band C
High Season Band C
Facilities ∮ ⍰ ⚓ ⌐ ☉ ⌐ ◿ ◻ ☎
♋ ⍰ ⊖ ⚑ ✕ ∇ ⋂ ⋋ ⌸
Nearby Facilities ⌐ ✔ ⊥ ↘ ∪ ⇗ ℛ
⛵ Ryde

FRESHWATER
Heathfield Farm Camping Site Heathfield Road, Freshwater, Isle Of Wight, PO40 9SH
Tel: 752480 Std: 01983
Fax: 752480 Std: 01983
Nearest Town/Resort Freshwater
Directions 2 miles west of Yarmouth ferry port on the A3054.
Acreage 4 **Open** 1st May to 30 September
Access Good **Site** Level
Sites Available Å ♤ ⊖ **Total** 60
Low Season Band B
High Season Band C
Facilities ∮ ⍰ ⚓ ⌐ ☉ ⌐ ☎ ♋ ⊖ ⌸
Nearby Facilities ⌐ ✔ ⊥ ↘ ∪ ⇗ ℛ
Near beach with sea and open country views.

NETTLESTONE
Pondwell Camping and Chalets, Pondwell Hill, Nettlestone, Isle of Wight.
Tel: 612330 Std: 01983
Nearest Town/Resort

Directions Signposted from Wightlink Fishbourne. Take A3054 to Ryde then A3055turning left along B3350 to Seaview. Site is next to Wishing Well Pub.
Acreage 14 **Open** May to September
Access Good **Site** Level
Sites Available Å ♤ ⊖ **Total** 200
Low Season Band A
High Season Band C
Facilities ∮ ⚓ ⍰ ⌐ ☉ ⌐ ◿ ◻ ☎
♋ ⊖ ⚑ ⋂ ⚓ ⊛ ⋈ ⌸
Nearby Facilities ⌐ ✔ ⊥ ↘ ∪ ⇗ ℛ
⛵ Ryde
Set in countryside with scenic views, walking distance to sea.

NEWCHURCH
Southland Camping Park, Winford Road, Newchurch, Isle of Wight.
Tel: 865385 Std: 01983
Fax: 867663 Std: 01983
Nearest Town/Resort Sandown/Shanklin.
Directions Newport to Sandown road A3056/A3055 through Arreton, after Fighting Cocks Public House take the second left. Continue along road for 1 mile, site is on the left.
Acreage 5¾ **Open** Easter to September
Access Good **Site** Level
Sites Available Å ♤ ⊖ **Total** 100
Low Season Band B
High Season Band C
Facilities ⚘ ∮ ⚓ ⍰ ⚓ ⌐ ☉ ⌐ ◿ ◻ ☎
♋ ⍰ ⊖ ⚑ ⋂ ⚓
Nearby Facilities ⌐ ✔ ⊥ ↘ ∪ ⇗ ℛ
⛵ Lake
Sheltered, secluded touring park, generous level pitches. Far reaching views over Arreton Valley. 5 Tick (Excellent) Graded Park.

SANDOWN
Cheverton Copse Caravan & Camping Park, Newport Road, Near Lake, Sandown, Isle of Wight, PO36 0JP.
Tel: 403161 Std: 01983
Fax: 403161 Std: 01983
Nearest Town/Resort Sandown.
Directions On the A3056 Newport/Sandown road, 1¼ miles west of Sandown.
Acreage 1 **Open** May to September
Access Good **Site** Sloping
Sites Available Å ♤ ⊖ **Total** 26
Facilities ∮ ⚓ ⍰ ⌐ ☉ ⌐ ◿ ◻ ☎
♋ ⍰ ⊖ ⚑ ⋂ ⚓ ⋈ ⌸
Nearby Facilities ⌐ ✔ ⊥ ↘ ∪
⛵ Lake
Near to all amenities, ideal for touring with superb views.

SANDOWN
Cheverton Farm Camping Site, Cheverton Farm, Newport Road, Apse Heath, Sandown, Isle of Wight.
Tel: 866414 Std: 01983
Nearest Town/Resort Sandown/Shanklin
Directions Road number 3056, 500 yards Sandown side of Apse Heath.
Acreage 5 **Open** 1st March to 31st October
Access Good **Site** Lev/Slope
Sites Available Å ♤ ⊖ **Total** 60
Low Season Band B
High Season Band B
Facilities ⚘ ∮ ⍰ ⌐ ☉ ⌐ ◿ ◻ ☎
♋ ⍰ ⊖ ⚑ ⋂ ⚓ ☎
Nearby Facilities ⌐ ✔ ⊥ ↘ ∪ ⇗ ℛ
⛵ Sandown.
Near beach, scenic views, country walks.

The ORCHARDS Holiday Caravan & Camping Park

The **only** Caravan Club Appointed site and the **only** Best of British Caravan & Camping Park on the **Isle of Wight**

- Special ferry inclusive package holidays
- Excellent toilet, shower and laundrette facilities
- **Indoor & outdoor swimming pool complex with cafe bar**
- Superb self service shop with off-licence
- Take-away food bar
- Wonderful walking and cycling
- Private coarse fishing
- Small rallies welcome
- Meeting room available

DIAL-A-BROCHURE ON
01983 531331
or write to the Proprietor
Malcolm Q. Peplow
The Orchards, Newbridge, Yarmouth, Isle of Wight, PO41 0TS

Best of British THE CARAVAN CLUB APPOINTED

AA

ISLE OF WIGHT

SANDOWN
Fairway Holiday Park, The Fairway, Sandown, Isle of Wight, PO36 9PS.
Tel: 403462 Std: 01983
Fax: **405713** Std: **01983**
Nearest Town/Resort Sandown.
Directions Off Sandown/Shanklin road, into Fairway at Manor House Hotel, Lake. Approx 1 mile from centre of Sandown.
Acreage 5½ **Open** March to September
Access Good **Site** Level
Sites Available ▲ ⊕ ⊟ **Total** 150
Low Season Band B
High Season Band C
Facilities 🄱 ƒ ⊞ ♨ ⌠ ⊙ ↩ ▣ ☎
♨ ⛋ ✕ ♀ ⋔ ♠ ⋒ ⊟
Nearby Facilities ┌ ⋌ ⌴ ⥿ ∪ ⥼ ⥽ ⥾
⩮ Sandown.
Picturesque location, with many facilities, relaxed, family atmosphere.

SANDOWN
Queen Bower Dairy Caravan Park, Alverstone Road, Queen Bower, Sandown, Isle of Wight.
Tel: 403840 Std: 01983.
Nearest Town/Resort Sandown.
Directions
Acreage 2¼ **Open** May to October
Access Good **Site** Level
Sites Available ⊕ ⊟ **Total** 20
Low Season Band A
High Season Band A
Facilities ⛭ ⊞ ☎ ⟪ ▣
Nearby Facilities ┌ ⋌ ⌴ ⥿ ⥼ ⥽
⩮ Sandown.
Scenic views, ideal touring. Sell our own produced Dairy products (milk and cream). Public telephone ¼ mile.

SHANKLIN
Languard Camping Park, Languard Manor Road, Shanklin, Isle of Wight.
Tel: 867028 Std: 01983
Nearest Town/Resort Shanklin.
Directions A3056 from Newport, ½ mile before Lake Town sign turn right up Whitecross Lane. 400 yards to site.
Acreage 5 **Open** May to September
Access Good **Site** Level
Sites Available ▲ ⊕ ⊟ **Total** 150
Low Season Band B
High Season Band C
Facilities ⛭ ƒ ⊞ ♨ ⌠ ⊙ ↩ ▣ ☎
♨ ⛋ ✕ ♀ ⋔ ♠ ⋒ ⊟
Nearby Facilities ┌ ⋌ ⌴ ⥿ ∪ ⥼ ⥽
⩮ Shanklin.
Marked pitches.

SHANKLIN
Lower Hyde Holiday Village, Shanklin, Isle of Wight, PO37 7LL.
Tel: 866131 Std: 01983
Nearest Town/Resort Shanklin.
Directions Approach Shanklin on the A3020, turn left at the traffic lights, go down the High Street and at Boots turn left into Regent Street. Take the first left, then turn right into Landguard Road. The park is on the left.
Acreage 8 **Open** 31 April to 16 October
Access Good **Site** Level
Sites Available ▲ ⊕ ⊟ **Total** 145
Low Season Band C
High Season Band C
Facilities ƒ ⛭ ⊞ ♨ ⌠ ⊙ ↩ ▣ ☎
♨ ⛋ ✕ ♀ ⋔ ♠ ⋒ ⊟
Nearby Facilities ┌ ⋌ ∪ ⥽
⩮ Shanklin.
Lies within some 55 acres of delightful wooded downland. Just outside Shanklin.

SHANKLIN
Ninham Country Holidays, Shanklin, Isle of Wight.
Tel: 864243 Std: 01983
Fax: **868881** Std: **01983**
Nearest Town/Resort Shanklin.
Directions Signposted off Newport/Sandown road (A3056). Site entrance is ¼ mile west of Safeway's on the left.
Acreage 10 **Open** May to September
Access Very Good **Site** Level
Sites Available ▲ ⊕ ⊟ **Total** 98
Low Season Band A
High Season Band C
Facilities 🄱 ƒ ⛭ ⊞ ♨ ⌠ ⊙ ↩ ▣ ☎
♨ ⛋ ✕ ♀ ⋔ ♠ ⋒ ⋇ ⊟
Nearby Facilities ┌ ⋌ ⌴ ⥿ ∪ ⥼ ⥽
⩮ Shanklin.
Country park setting close to Islands premier seaside resort.

ST. HELENS
Nodes Point Holiday Park, St. Helens, Ryde, Isle of Wight, PO33 1YA.
Tel: 872401 Std: 01983
Nearest Town/Resort
Directions Approach Ryde on the A3054 to join the A3055 in the town. At Bishop Lovett School (on the left), go straight ahead onto the B330 to St. Helens/Bembridge/Nodes Point.
Acreage 16 **Open** 30 April to 1 October
Site Lev/Slope
Sites Available ▲ ⊕ ⊟ **Total** 240
Facilities ƒ ⛭ ⊞ ♨ ⌠ ⊙ ↩ ▣ ☎
♨ ⛋ ✕ ♀ ⋔ ♠ ⋒ ⊟
Nearby Facilities ┌ ⋌ ⌴ ∪
⩮ Ryde.
Within 65 acres of parkland running down to the beach.

VENTNOR
Appuldurcombe Gardens Caravan & Camping Park, Wroxall, Ventnor, I.O.W., PO38 3EP.
Tel: 852597 Std: 01983 Fax: 856225 Std: 01983
Nearest Town/Resort Ventnor.
Directions A3020 from Newport and Shanklin. Turn off at Whitely Bank roundabout.
Acreage 4 **Open** April to October
Access Good **Site** Lev/Slope
Sites Available ▲ ⊕ ⊟ **Total** 100
Facilities ƒ ⊞ ♨ ⌠ ⊙ ↩ ▣ ☎
♨ ⛋ ✕ ♀ ⋔ ♠ ⋒ ⊟
Nearby Facilities ┌ ⌴ ∪ ⥼ ⥽
⩮ Shanklin.
Country setting with a stream. Ideal for walkers and cyclists.

VENTNOR
Undercliff Riviera Caravan Park, Niton Undercliff, Ventnor, Isle of Wight.
Tel: Niton 730268 Std: 01983
Nearest Town/Resort Ventnor.
Directions 4 miles southwest Ventnor A3055.
Acreage 2 **Open** Easter to September
Access Good **Site** Lev/Slope
Sites Available ▲ ⊕ ⊟ **Total** 15
Low Season Band B
High Season Band C
Facilities ⛭ ⊞ ♨ ⌠ ⊙ ↩ ▣ ☎ ⟪ ▣
Nearby Facilities ┌ ⋌ ⌴ ⥿ ∪ ⥼ ⥽
⩮ Shanklin.
Sited in picturesque coastal strip in ground of country house overlooking sea. Site shop in high season only. Stamp for brochure.

YARMOUTH
The Orchards Holiday Caravan & Camping Park, Newbridge, Yarmouth, Isle of Wight, PO41 0TS.
Tel: 531331 Std: 01983 Fax: 531666 Std: 01983
Nearest Town/Resort Yarmouth.
Directions 4 miles east of Yarmouth and 6 miles west of Newport on B3401. Entrance opposite Newbridge Post Office.
Acreage 8 **Open** 22 March to October
Access Good **Site** Lev/Slope
Sites Available ▲ ⊕ ⊟ **Total** 175
Low Season Band A
High Season Band A
Facilities ⛭ ƒ ⊞ ♨ ⌠ ⊙ ↩ ▣ ☎
♨ ⛋ ✕ ♀ ⋔ ♠ ⋒ ⋇ ⊟
Nearby Facilities ┌ ⋌ ⌴ ⥿ ∪
⩮ Lymington.
Good views of the Downs and Solent. Bookings inclusive of car ferries throughout season. Outdoor swimming pool from late May to early September, indoor swimming pool all season. Take-away food and coarse fishing on site. Battery charging, small function/meeting room. Small rallies welcome. Ideal for rambling and cycling.

CADE'S 25 YEARS 1972–1997

CADE'S HAVE BEEN PROVIDING QUALITY INFORMATION FOR THE TOURING HOLIDAYMAKER FOR TWENTY FIVE YEARS

UPADATED ANNUALLY AND WE BELIEVE THE MOST ACCURATE AVAILABLE

PLACES OF INTEREST

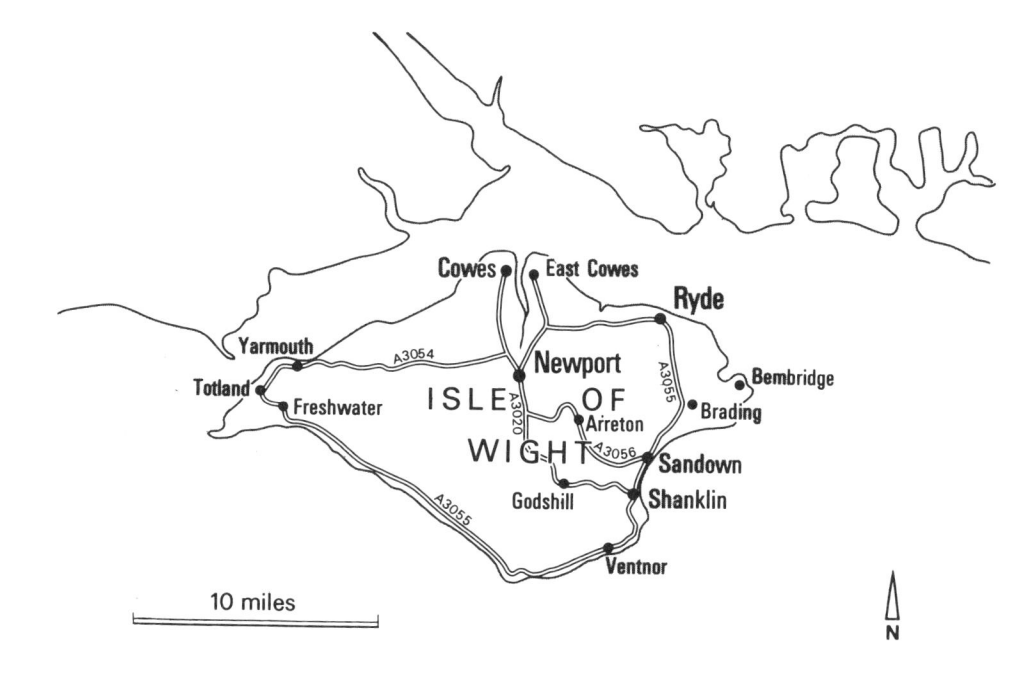

The Isle of Wight is only about 150 square miles in extent and measures only 22 to 23 miles at its two most furthest extremities.

It is reached by ferry, hovercraft and hydrofoil from Lymington, Southampton, and Southsea landing at Yarmouth, Cowes and Ryde respectively. Thousands visit the Island annually, for it has some of the excitement and mystique of going abroad, but with none of the tedium. The journey across the short intervening sea is an event in itself, for children especially.

ARRETON
HASELEY MANOR : Arreton, Near Newport, Isle of Wight, PO30 3AN. Tel : 01983 865420. Fax : 01983 867547. Location : Main Sandown to Newport road. Open : Easter to 31st October, 10am-5.30pm, 7 days per week. **Special Attractions:** The Island's oldest manor, part dating from Circa 1350, audio visual displays and a new herb garden. Craft Village, large Pottery Studio where children can make an Isle of Wight mouse and the home of Island Maid Sweets where you can see them being made. A fun time for all ages and tastes!

BEMBRIDGE
MARITIME MUSEUM : 'The Isle of Wight Shipwreck Centre', Bembridge, Isle of Wight. Tel : 01983 872223. Nearest Railway Station : Ryde. Location : The Museum is in the centre of the Village close to the Harbour and sandy beaches. Open : Every day, Late March to October 10am-5pm. **Special Attractions:** Unique collection of ship models, local history, navigation, shipwrecks, salvage, early diving equipment, Merman, Trinity House, hovercraft, deep water sail, paddle steamers, gift shop. Family and OAP rates.
BRADING

ISLE OF WIGHT WAX MUSEUM : High Street, Brading, Isle of Wight, PO36 0DQ. Tel : 01983 407286. Fax : 01983 402112. Nearest Railway Station : Brading. Open : Summer, 10am-10pm. October to April inc., 10am-5pm. **Special Attractions:** The Chamber of Horrors in the Castle Dungeons. Professor Copperthwaite's Extraordinary Exhibition of Oddities. Morning coffee, afternoon teas and A la Carte menu available at the Bugle Inn alongside. Families welcome.

BRADING
THE LILLIPUT MUSEUM OF ANTIQUE DOLLS & TOYS : High Street, Brading, Isle of Wight. Tel : 01983 407231. Nearest Railway Station : Brading. Open : Daily throughout the year, 9.30am-9.30pm (High Season), 10am-5pm (Winter). **Special Attractions:** Considered one of the finest Dolls' Museum in the U.K., with large collection of toys, and in 1983 was awarded a Certificate of Merit in the British Tourist authorities "Come to Britain" Trophy Competition.

BRADING
MORTON MANOR : Morton Manor, Brading, Isle of Wight, PO36 0EP. Tel : 01983 406168. Nearest Railway Station : Brading. Location : Off the main Sandown to Ryde road (the A3055). Turn at Yarbridge Cross traffic lights. Open : April to October, daily 10am-5.30pm. Closed Saturday. **Special Attractions:** Historic house dating back to 1249, largely rebuilt in 1680. Magnificent gardens, winners of Isle of Wight and Southern England in Bloom 1996, Simply the Best! Vineyard, winery, museum, tearooms and a shop. One all-inclusive admission.

BRADING

NUNWELL HOUSE & GARDENS : Coach Lane, Brading, Isle of Wight, PO36 0JQ. Tel : 01983 407240.
Nearest Railway Station : Brading. Open : 10am-1pm on certain dates in June, July, August and September. Please telephone for exact details. **Special Attractions:** Nunwell reflects 5 centuries of island history. A family home since 1522 with well furbished Jacobean, Georgian and Victorian rooms. Family Military Collection and Home Guard Museum. Kitchen display. Six acres of tranquil gardens with cross-Solent views.

BRIGHSTONE
ISLE OF WIGHT PEARL : Chilton Chine, Military Road, Brighstone, Isle of Wight, PO30 4DD. Tel : 01983 740352.
Location : Situated on the Military Road at Chilton Chine, halfway between the Southern and Western tips of the island. Open : All Year, 10am-5.30pm Monday to Saturday. June to August, 10am-7.30pm weekdays, 10.30am-4.30pm Sundays. **Special Attractions:** Isle of Wight Pearl, a unique insight into the world of pearl jewellery. Prices range from £3.00 to £3,500 so there is a pearl for every pocket. Every visitor has the chance to win a new car, absolutely free! Free entrance and parking for the pearl complex and coffee shop.

COWES
Cowes is a busy port with a good harbour on the River Medina - which separates the town from East Cowes. A ferry and floating bridge connect the two.

It is the chief yachting centre in the country, and the headquarters of the Royal Yacht Squadron is situated in Cowes Castle. The Royal London Yacht Club is also based here.

Thomas Arnold, Headmaster of Rugby School, was born here in 1795. East Cowes Castle was built by John Nash. Steamer and hovercraft services link with the mainland and the building of hovercraft is a local industry. Osborne House was the home of Queen Victoria.

GODSHILL
THE MODEL VILLAGE - GODSHILL : High Street, Godshill, Isle of Wight, PO38 3HH. Tel : 01983 840270. Fax : 01983 840270.
Nearest Railway Station : Shanklin. Location : Centre of Godshill Village. Open : April, May, June, early July and September, 10am-5pm. Late July and August, 10am-6pm, (Saturday to 5.30pm). October 10.30am-4pm. **Special Attractions:** Illuminated in late July and August.

HAVENSTREET
ISLE OF WIGHT STEAM RAILWAY : The Railway Station, Havenstreet, Isle of Wight, PO33 4DS. Tel : 01983 882204.
Nearest Railway Station : Smallbrook Junction. Location : Stations at; Wootton, Havenstreet, Ashey and Smallbrook Junction. Open : Selected days, Mid March to the end of December. Trains generally operate between 10am and 4pm. **Special Attractions:** Genuine Vintage trains and atmosphere. Museum of Island Rail History, garden, picnic area, shop and catering facilities.

NEWPORT
Newport is the administrative and business capital of the Isle of Wight as well as having an estuary harbour which is principally used by pleasure craft. Newport has a prominent part of history, for it was in the Old Town Hall that Charles I negotiated with the fifteen of Cromwell's Parliamentary Commissioners, and concluded the Treaty of Newport, which would have saved his life. However, Charles repudiated his agreement and paid for it with his head. The Town Hall has long since been replaced with the present structure, designed by John Nash and raised in 1816. It has a touch of classical Greece in its ionic columns and clean lines.

Newport's old grammar school was the original schoolroom where Charles I lodged and was used as an audience chamber. Newport's church, founded in 1854 has a 17th Century oak pulpit complete with canopy exquisitely carved and a carrara marble monument dedicated to Princess Elizabeth, daughter of Charles I who died at the tender age of 13. The Memorial dates from 1856 and was commissioned by Queen Victoria from the Italian aristocratic sculptor Baron Marochetti.

Queen Elizabeth I favoured and trusted three of Newport's sons - Doctor Edes, per personal Chaplain, her Doctor, Doctor James, and Thomas Fleming whom she appointed Lord Chief Justice. Lord Fleming presided at the trial of Guy Fawkes and no doubt passed sentence on him.

NEWPORT
ROBIN HILL COUNTRY PARK : Downend, Near Arreton, Newport, Isle of Wight, PO30 2NU. Tel : 01983 527352. Fax : 01983 527347.
Location : 2 miles outside Newport, next to the Hare and Hounds Pub. Open : April to October, Monday to Saturday, 10am-5pm. Last admission 4pm. **Special Attractions:** Robin Hill is an 88 acre park with lots of activities for all the family. Treetop Trail, large wooden panel maze, Duckdown on the Green Play Village, Countryside Centre, 400 metre toboggan run, Hillbilly Slides, Snake Slides, activity course, 9 hole pitch 'n' Putt, Toddlers Labyrinth, football, basketball, Troll Island and Clatter Bridges, amusements and woodland walks. Catering available. New features planned for 1997.

NEWPORT
YAFFORD MILL : Mill Lane, Shorwell, Nr. Newport, Isle of Wight. Tel : 01983 740610/741725.
Location : On Shorwell to Brighstone on the B3399, half a mile from Shorwell turn left. Open : March to December 10am-6pm, November and December weekends only. **Special Attractions:** "Sophie" the Yafford seal. Rare breeds of cattle, sheep, waterfowl. Working water mill, farm museum and narrow gauge railway. Cafe, gift shop, nature trail, childrens playground and picnic areas.

NEWTOWN
THE OLD TOWN HALL - NEWTOWN : Newtown, Nr. Newport, Isle of Wight. Tel : c/o 01983 741052.
Location : Between Newport and Yarmouth, 1 mile north of the A3054. (Bus No.7 or No.35, alight at Barton's Corner). Open : 1st April to end of October, Monday, Wednesday and Sunday, 2pm-5pm. Also Tuesday and Thursday in July and August. **Special Attractions:** The small, tranquil village of Newtown once sent two M.P.'s to Parliament. Collections of pewter and oak furniture. Who were the Fergusons Gang? New exhibition about these mysterious N.T. Benefactors.

RYDE
This well known resort overlooks the Solent and offers excellent sands, bathing and fishing. Views of the mainland are afforded by a nearby hilltop, and regattas are held here. The railway to Shanklin has been electrified, utilizing ex-London Transport rolling stock.

The Norman Ball Collection of veteran and vintage cars exists at the airport.

RYDE
BRICKFIELDS HORSE COUNTRY : Newnham Road, Binstead, Nr. Ryde, Isle of Wight. Tel : 01983 615116/566801. Fax : 01983 562649.
Nearest Railway Station : Ryde. Location : Half a mile from Binstead Village off the A3054 main Newport/Ryde road. Open : All year round, 10am-5pm. Closed 25th and 26th December. **Special Attractions:** Working Shire horses, miniature pony centre, 'Donkeytown' wagon rides, parades. Guided tours of unique carriage collection and heritage museums. Farm Corner, play area, bar and restaurant.

SANDOWN

95

ISLE OF WIGHT-SOMERSET

Sandown has an excellent sandy beach. Culver Cliff prominent chalk formation and the Yarborough Monument stands on Bembridge Down.

The Museum of Wight Geology is an interesting feature of the town and there is a zoo. An airport is situated nearby.

SANDOWN
MUSEUM OF ISLE OF WIGHT GEOLOGY : High Street, Sandown, Isle of Wight, PO36 8AF. Tel : 01983 404344. Fax : 01983 402748. Nearest Railway Station : Sandown. Location : At the junction of Avenue Road and High Street, above the library. Open : Monday to Friday, 9.30am-5.30pm. Saturday, 9.30am-4.30pm. **Special Attractions:** Local geology including rocks and fossils, emphasis on dinosaur bones and skeletons.

SEAVIEW
FLAMINGO PARK : Springvale, Seaview, Isle of Wight, PO34 5AP. Tel : 01983 612153.
Nearest Railway Station : Ryde. Location : Seaview. Open : Easter to end September, 10am-5pm. October, 10.30am-4pm. **Special Attractions:** Hundreds of tame waterfowl which feed from the hand, plus Flamingos, Cranes, Swans, Peacocks, etc. Plant and Bird House, Cold Water Fish Aquarium, waterfalls and fountains. Gift shop and refreshments. So much of nature to see and enjoy. Suitable for all the family. (Don't miss us and don't forget to bring your camera!). Award winners 1989, 1991 & 1992.

SHANKLIN
This popular resort is built partly on cliffs and a lift provides access to the beach. Amenities include excellent sands, bathing, fishing and golf.

The restored 12th Century preserves a fine chest of 1512. An electrified railway from Ryde uses former London Transport Coaches and ends here.

The old village includes the picturesque Crab Inn and delightfully wooden Shankline Chine. A fountain near the Crab Inn carries lines which were written by Longfellow while visiting the Island. Shanklin Down rises to 779 feet and a fine coastal walk can be taken to Luccombe Chine and Branchurch.

VENTNOR
This pleasant resort is built on terraces with a sandy beach below and high downs in the background.

The Empress of Austria and Empress Eugenie of France stayed at Steephill Castle, which was built in 1833, but is now demolished. St Boniface Down is a fine viewpoint rising to 787 feet and is the highest point on the Island.

VENTNOR
ISLE OF WIGHT RARE BREEDS & WATERFOWL PARK : Undercliff Drive (A3055), St Lawrence, Ventnor, Isle of Wight, PO38 1UW. Tel : 01983 852582/855144.
Nearest Railway Station : Shanklin. Location : Main Southern road of Isle of Wight (A3055) between Ventnor and Niton. Bus stops at entrance - Routes 7, 7A and 31. Open : Easter to October 31st, 7 days a week, 10am-5.30pm. Winter opening weekends only, 10am-4pm. **Special Attractions:** One of the largest collections of rare breeds of domestic animals in the U.K. including sheep, cattle, pigs, goats, ponies, Falabella miniature horses, miniature donkeys, deer, llamas and Otters. Over 100 species of waterfowl, poultry including coloured Turkeys and Pheasants, Tropical waterfall house. A Rare Breeds Survival Trust approved park.

VENTNOR
MUSEUM OF SMUGGLING HISTORY : Botanic Garden, Ventnor, Isle of Wight. Tel : 01983 853677.
Nearest Railway Station : Shanklin. Location : 1 mile west of Ventnor on the A3055. Open : Easter to the end of September, 10am-5.30pm daily.

WOOTTON
BUTTERFLY WORLD & FOUNTAIN WORLD : Staplers Road, Wootton, Isle of Wight. Tel : 01983 883430.
Neareast Railway Station : Ryde Esplanade. Location : Mid-way between Wootton and Newport on the alternative Wootton Common/Staplers road. Open : Good Friday to October 31st. **Special Attractions:** Butterfly World is a beautiful covered garden filled with large exotic butterflies on the wing. Fountain World has an Italian and a Japanese garden plus water features and huge fish.

YARMOUTH
CHESSELL POTTERY : Chessell, Nr. Yarmouth, Isle of Wight, PO41 0UE. Tel : 01983 531248. Fax : 01983 531210.
Location : Shalcombe, near Brook, on the main Newport to Freshwater road. Open : April to October - Monday to Saturday 9am-5.30pm, Sunday 10am-5.30pm. November to March - Monday to Saturday 9am-5.30pm. **Special Attractions:** Porcelain making and decorating, studios, factory shop. Gallery for original pictures and individual studio pottery. Technical display. Historical display showing early pieces of Chessell pottery. Light refreshments.

SOMERSET

BRIDGWATER
Mill Farm Caravan & Camping Park, Fiddington, Bridgwater, Somerset, TA5 1JQ.
Tel: 732286 Std: 01278
Nearest Town/Resort Bridgwater.
Directions Leave M5 at junction 23 or 24, take A39 west for 6 miles. Turn right to Fiddington, then follow camping signs.
Acreage 12 **Open** All year
Access Good **Site** Level
Sites Available A ⊕ ⊞ **Total** 250
Low Season Band B
High Season Band C
Facilities f ⊞ ♣ ┌ ⊙ ╼ ▣ ◯ ☏
⚲ ⊙ ☎ ✕ ▯ ♠ ↺ ⋇ ⊟
Nearby Facilities ┌ ✔ ↘ ∪ ⇗ ℛ
⇌ Bridgwater.
Free boating, canoe and trampoline hire on site. Walking, riding, fishing. Quantock Hills 2 miles. Beach 4 miles. Exmoor, Cheddar Gorge, Wookey Caves within easy reach. Tourist Information Room. Free swimming and paddling pools. Children's pony rides on site. Off licence, large sandpit, Splash Pool. Holiday cottage to let.

BRIDGWATER
The Fairways International Touring Caravan & Camping Park, Bath Road, Bawdrip, Bridgwater, Somerset, TA7 8PP.
Tel: 685569 Std: 01278
Nearest Town/Resort Bridgwater
Directions 3¼ miles on Glastonbury side of Bridgwater. 1½ miles off M5 junction 23 at junction A39 and B3141.
Acreage 5¾ **Open** 1st March to 15th Nov
Access Good **Site** Level
Sites Available A ⊕ ⊞ **Total** 200
Low Season Band B
High Season Band C
Facilities ⚿ f ⊞ ♣ ┌ ⊙ ╼ ▣ ◯ ☏
⚲ ⊙ ☎ ▯ ♠ ↺ ⊟
Nearby Facilities ┌ ✔ ↘ ∪ ⇗ ℛ
⇌ Bridgwater
Ideal for touring Somerset. Off Licence. "Loo of the Year" Award Winner 1994 & 1995.

BURNHAM ON SEA
Burnham On Sea Sports Club, Stoddens Road, Burnham-on-Sea, Somerset.
Tel: 751235 Std: 01278
Nearest Town/Resort Burnham On Sea
Directions M5 junction 22 follow brown signs over roundabout at next roundabout exit right signposted Middle Burnham. After 600yds fork left, entrance on right over cattle grid approx 300 yds.
Acreage 23 **Open** All Year
Access Good **Site** Level
Sites Available A ⊕ ⊞ **Total** 20
Low Season Band A
High Season Band B
Facilities f ⊞ ☏ l₂ ❋ ◯ ⊞ ✦ ⋈ ⊟
Nearby Facilities ┌ ✔ ↯ ∪ ⇗ ℛ
⇌ Highbridge
Ideal base for touring West Country. A small, wuiet park. 1 mile from the town centre and beach.

CADE'S

Northam Farm

BREAK SANDS
Camping and Caravan Park
Where the sea meets the countryside

The first-class facilities at Northam Farm include: a superloo block with showers, facilities for the disabled. Launderette and public telephone, clean and spacious dish-washing area, swings and slide, and fishing in well-stocked pond. Self-service shop plus gas sales.

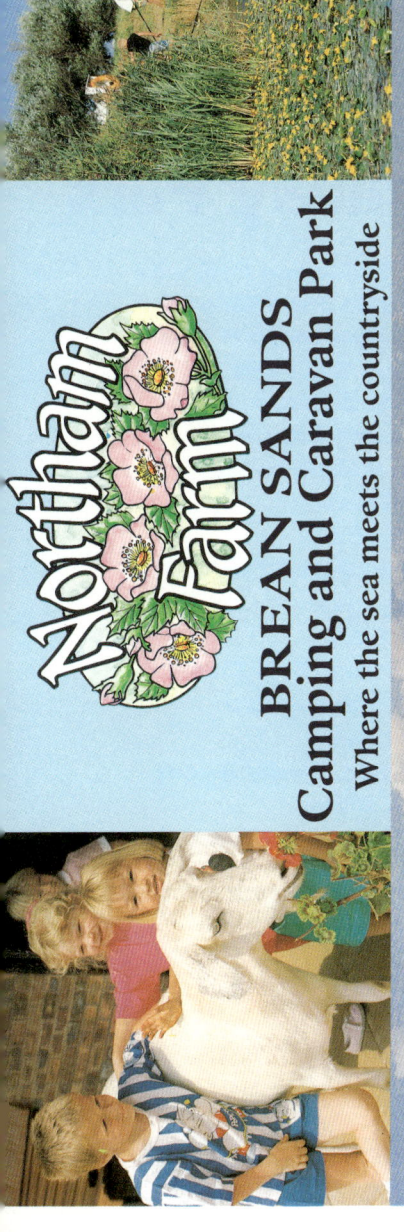

The park has a 'natural' feel and is an ideal base from which to explore the West Country. It is adjacent to 7 miles of safe, sandy beach with horse riding available. Central for children's amusements and night life.

A friendly welcome awaits you at Northam Farm.
For our full colour brochure please contact:
Mr. and Mrs. M. Scott and family,
Northam Farm Camping and Caravan Park, Brean,
Near Burnham-on-Sea, Somerset, TA8 2SE.
Telephone: (0278) 751244/751222.
(½ mile past Brean Leisure Park on right-hand side.)

Burnham-on-Sea Holiday Village
Somerset

Burnham-on-Sea Holiday Village, Marine Drive, Burnham-on-Sea Somerset, TA8 1LA

TOURERS / MOTOR CARAVANS / TENTS / STATIC CARAVANS

A Great Family holiday Park

- Indoor Swimming Pool with Waterchute and Whirlpool
- Heated Outdoor Pool with Extensive Sun Patio
- Solarium, Gymnasium
- Amusement Arcade
- Private Fishing Lakes
- Tennis Courts
- Bicycle Hire
- Pitch and Putt, Crazy Golf
- Bowling green
- Games Field
- Bradley Bear Kids Club
- Teen Challenge Club
- Cabaret Acts
- Live Music, Family Discos
- Bumper Bingo
- Cafe, Restaurant, Takeaway Food

Call now for further details and your free colour brochure

Lo-call Rate 01278 783391 7 Days 24 Hrs

or see your local travel agents

Cades

A BRITISH HOLIDAYS TOURING PARK

HOLIDAYS FOR ALL AGES AT...

Pitches for Tourers, Tents & Motor Homes

Entertainment Day & Night

Holiday Caravans for Hire & Sale

Only a sand dune away from the sea

Indoor & Outdoor Pool Complex

Special Offers for Children & Over 50's

Holiday Resort UNITY

At Unity Farm, Coast Road, Brean Sands, Somerset TA8 2RB
☎ Telephone: 01278 751235, Fax: 01278 751539

Do you know a Park with more facilities?

SOMERSET

BURNHAM-ON-SEA
Diamond Farm Caravan & Touring Park, Diamond Farm, Weston Road, Brean, Nr Burnham-on-Sea, Somerset.
Tel: 751263 Std: 01278
Nearest Town/Resort Burnham-on-Sea
Directions M5 junction 22, follow signs to Brean, ½ mile past leisure park turn right to Lympsham/Weston-super-Mare. Diamond Farm is 800yds on the left hand side.
Acreage 6 **Open** April to 15 October
Access Good   **Site** Level
Sites Available A ♛ ♚ **Total** 100
Facilities &c ƒ ♠♣ ♦ ɾ ⊙ ↵ ⍰ ⌂ ☕
♕ ⊙ ☒ ✕ ⏃ ⍟ 🎲
Nearby Facilities ɾ ⏊ ↘ ⌇ ⌲ ⏊
⋕ Weston-super-Mare
A quiet, family site alongside River Axe and only 800yds from the beach. Fishing and horse riding on site.

BURNHAM-ON-SEA
Holiday Resort Unity at Unity Farm, Coast Road, Brean Sands, Somerset.
Tel: 751235 Std: 01278
Fax: **751539** Std: **01278**
Nearest Town/Resort Burnham-on-Sea.
Directions Leave M5 at junction 22. Follow signs for Berrow and Brean, site on right 4½ miles from M5.
Acreage 150 **Open** Easter to October
Access Good   **Site** Level
Sites Available A ♛ ♚ **Total** 600
Low Season Band A
High Season Band C
Facilities ⌂ &c ƒ ♠♣ ♦ ɾ ⊙ ↵ ⍰ ⌂ ☕
♕ ⍰ ⊙ ☒ ✕ ⏃ ⍟ 🎲
Nearby Facilities ɾ ⌲ ⏊ ↘ ∪ ⌇ ⌲ ⊁
⋕ Weston-super-Mare.
200yds from 7 mile beach, own leisure centre with 30 fun fair attractions, pool complex with 3 giant water slides, 18 hole golf course, lake for fishing, horse riding and 10 Pin Bowling. Family entertainment - end of Mayto end of Sept. Special offers for young families and OAPs in June and Sept.

BURNHAM-ON-SEA
Northam Farm Caravan and Touring Park, Brean, Nr. Burnham-on-Sea, Somerset.
Tel: 751244/751222 Std: 01278
Fax: **751150** Std: **01278**
Nearest Town/Resort Burnham-on-Sea.
Directions M5 Junction 22. Follow signs to Brean, ¼ mile past Leisure Park on righthand side.
Acreage 20 **Open** Easter to October
Access Good   **Site** Level
Sites Available A ♛ ♚ **Total** 350
Facilities &c ƒ ♠♣ ♦ ɾ ⊙ ↵ ⍰ ⌂ ☕
♕ ⍰ ⊙ ☒ ✕ ⏃ ⍟ 🎲
Nearby Facilities ɾ ⌲ ⏊ ↘ ∪ ⌇ ⌲
⋕ Weston-super-Mare.
Ideal base for seeing Somerset. 200 metres to safe sandy beach. Family entertainment within east walking distance. Excellent facilities, fishing lake on park. Take-away food.

BURNHAM-ON-SEA
Southfield Farm Caravan Park, Brean, Nr. Burnham-on-Sea, Somerset TA8 2RL.
Tel: 751233 Std: 01278
Nearest Town/Resort Burnham-on-Sea.
Directions 4 miles north along coast road from Burnham-on-Sea (well signposted). Site is in Brean village.
Acreage 10 **Open** Spring Bank Holiday to September
Access Good   **Site** Level
Sites Available A ♛ ♚
Low Season Band A
High Season Band B

Facilities &c ⌂ ɾ ⊙ ↵ ♚ ♕ ⌂ ☕ ♕ ⍰ ⊙ ☒
Nearby Facilities ɾ ⌲ ⏊ ∪ ⌲ ⌲
⋕ Weston-super-Mare.
Adjacent beach, good centre for touring Somerset. Local entertainments nearby.

BURNHAM-ON-SEA
Warren Farm Touring Park, Brean Sands, Burnham-on-Sea, Somerset, TA8 2RP.
Tel: 751227 Std: 01278
Nearest Town/Resort Burnham-on-Sea.
Directions Leave M5 at junction 22, follow signs to Burnham-on-Sea, Berrow and Brean on the B3140. Site is 1¼ miles past the leisure centre.
Acreage 50 **Open** April to Mid October
Access Good   **Site** Level
Sites Available A ♛ ♚ **Total** 500
Low Season Band B
High Season Band C
Facilities &c ƒ ♠♣ ♦ ɾ ⊙ ↵ ⍰ ⌂ ☕
♕ ⍰ ⊙ ☒ ✕ ⏃ ⍟ 🎲
Nearby Facilities ɾ ⌲ ⏊ ∪ ⌲
⋕ Weston-super-Mare.
Flat, grassy, family park with excellent facilities. 100 metres from 5 miles of sandy beach.

CHARD
Alpine Grove Touring Park, Forton, Chard, Somerset, TA20 4HD.
Tel: 63479 Std: 01460
Nearest Town/Resort Chard.
Directions Turn left off the A30 Crewkerne to Chard road onto the B3167 (Axminster). In 1½ miles at the crossroads turn right onto the B3162 signposted Forton. Site is on the right in about ½ mile.
Acreage 7½ **Open** Easter to End September
Access Good   **Site** Level
Sites Available A ♛ ♚ **Total** 40
Low Season Band B
High Season Band C
Facilities ⌂ ƒ ♠♣ ɾ ⊙ ↵ ⌂ ☕
⊙ ♕ ⍰
Nearby Facilities ɾ ⌲
⋕ Axminster
Quiet, peaceful, woodland site with mature oak trees and Rhododendrons. Numerous places of interest to visit nearby. Shingle and sandy beach 11 miles.

CHARD
Snowdon Hill Farm, "The Beeches", Catelgate Lane, Wambrook, Chard, Somerset.
Tel: 63213/66828 Std: 01460
Nearest Town/Resort Chard
Directions Just off main A30 Chard to Exeter road.
Acreage 3 **Open** April to November
Access Good   **Site** Level
Sites Available A ♛ ♚ **Total** 5
Low Season Band A
High Season Band A
Facilities ☕ ⍰
Nearby Facilities ɾ ⌲ ∪
⋕ Axminster
25 minutes to coast, 4 miles to wildlife park at Cricket St. Thomas, ideal touring, scenic views. Lovely country walks, good food at local pubs. Swimming pool in Chard 1 mile away.

CHARD
South Somerset Holiday Park, The Turnpike, Howley, Chard, Somerset, TA20 3EA.
Tel: 62221/66036 Std: 01460
Nearest Town/Resort Chard

Directions 3 miles west of Chard on the A30.
Acreage 7 **Open** All Year
Access Good   **Site** Level
Sites Available A ♛ ♚ **Total** 110
Low Season Band B
High Season Band C
Facilities &c ƒ ♠♣ ♦ ɾ ⊙ ↵ ⍰ ⌂ ☕
⊙ ☒ ⍰ 🎲
Nearby Facilities ɾ ⌲ ∪ ⌲
⋕ Crewkerne
Scenic views and ideal touring.

CHEDDAR
Broadway House Holiday, Touring Caravan & Camping Park, Cheddar, Somerset.
Tel: 742610 Std: 01934
Nearest Town/Resort Cheddar Gorge.
Directions Exit 22 (M5) 8 miles. Follow brown tourist signs for Cheddar Gorge. We are midway between Cheddar and Axbridge on the A371.
Acreage 25 **Open** March to November
Access Good   **Site** Level
Sites Available A ♛ ♚ **Total** 400
Low Season Band A
High Season Band C
Facilities &c ƒ ♠♣ ♦ ɾ ⊙ ↵ ⍰ ⌂ ☕
♕ ⍰ ⊙ ☒ ✕ ⏃ ⍟ 🎲
Nearby Facilities ɾ ⌲ ∪ ⌲ ⊁
⋕ Weston-super-Mare.
Centrally situated in wonderful touring area, i.e. Wells, Bristol and Weston-super-Mare.

CHEDDAR
Bucklegrove Caravan and Camping Park, Rodney Stoke, Cheddar, Somerset, BS27 3UZ.
Tel: 870261 Std: 01749
Nearest Town/Resort Wells/Cheddar
Directions Midway Between Wells and Cheddar on the A371.
Open March to November
Access Good   **Site** Lev/Slope
Sites Available A ♛ ♚ **Total** 125
Low Season Band B
High Season Band C
Facilities &c ƒ ♠♣ ɾ ⊙ ↵ ⍰ ⌂ ☕
♕ ⍰ ⊙ ♕ ⏃ 🎲
Nearby Facilities ɾ ⌲ ⏊ ↘ ∪ ⌲ ⊁
⋕ Weston super Mare
Ideal touring centre at foot of Mendip Hills, scenic views, walking.

CHEDDAR
Church Farm Caravan & Camping Park, Church Street, Cheddar, Somerset, BS27 3RF.
Tel: 743048 Std: 01934
Nearest Town/Resort Cheddar/Weston-super-Mare
Directions On the main A371 take the first turning on the right past the church.
Acreage 6 **Open** March to October
Access Good   **Site** Level
Sites Available A ♛ ♚ **Total** 144
Low Season Band B
High Season Band B
Facilities ⌂ ƒ ♠♣ ɾ ⊙ ↵ ⍰ ⌂ ☕
♕ ⍰ 🎲
Nearby Facilities ɾ ⌲ ∪ ⊁
The River Yeo runs through the site, ideal for children to paddle in and fishing. Only a 3 minute walk to the village shops and pubs, 10-15 minute walk away from Cheddar Gorge and Caves.

100   CADE'S WEST CUONTRY CAMPING, TOURING & MOTOR CARAVAN SITE GUIDE 1997

Warren Farm Touring Park

Brean Sands – for your seaside holiday in Somerset

- Private path to five miles of sandy beach
- Panoramic views of the Mendips
- Fully equipped, modern facility blocks
- Electric hook-ups
- Children's play areas and pets' corner
- Shop and café take-away
- Lounge bars and restaurant adjoining the park

Send or telephone for a colour brochure

Warren Farm Caravan and Camping Park
Brean Sands, Nr Burnham-On-Sea, Somerset TA8 2RP
Telephone: 01278 751227

SOMERSET

CHEDDAR
Froglands Farm Caravan and Camping Park, Froglands Farm, Cheddar, Somerset.
Tel: 742058 Std: 01934
Nearest Town/Resort Cheddar/Weston-super-Mare
Directions On main A371, 150yds past village church.
Acreage 4 **Open** Easter to October
Access Good **Site** Level
Sites Available ▲ ♣ ♞ **Total** 68
Low Season Band B
High Season Band B
Facilities 🕮 ƒ ⚿ 🅆 ♨ ┍ ⊙ ⌐ ◪ ◎ ♚
🕿 🛈 ⬤ ⊡
Nearby Facilities ┍ ✔ ⊥ ∪
⇝ Weston-super-Mare
Walking distance, village shops, pubs, Gorge and Caves.

CHEDDAR
Splott Farm, Blackford, Near Wedmore, Somerset, BS28 4PD.
Tel: 641522 Std: 01278
Nearest Town/Resort Burnham-on-Sea/Cheddar
Directions Leave M5 at junction 22, 2 miles to Highbridge, take B3139 Highbridge/Wells road, about 5 miles.
Acreage 4¼ **Open** March to September
Access Good **Site** Gentle Slope
Sites Available ▲ ♣ ♞ **Total** 20
Low Season Band A
High Season Band A
Facilities 🕮 ┍ ⊙ ♚ 🛈 ▯ ❋
Nearby Facilities ┍ ✔ ⊥ ❦ ∪ ∂ ♃ ➹
⇝ Highbridge
Views of Mendip Hills (and Quantocks), very peaceful site, ideal touring. Weston-super-Mare, Wells, Cheddar, Burnham-on-Sea, Wookey. Very rural area.

DULVERTON
Exmoor House Caravan Club Site, Dulverton, Somerset, TA22 9HL.
Tel: 323268 Std: 01398
Nearest Town/Resort Tiverton
Directions From M5 junction 27 take the A361, roundabout at Tiverton turn right onto the A396 to Exbridge. Fork left onto the B3222 at Dulverton turn left between the bridge and The Bridge Inn, site is 150 metres.
Acreage 3½ **Open** Late March to Early January
Access Good **Site** Level
Sites Available ♣ ♞ **Total** 60
Facilities 🕮 ♨ ┍ ⊙ ⌐ ◎ ♚ 🛈 ⬤ ⊡
Nearby Facilities ✔ ∪
⇝ Taunton
In centre of the village of Dulverton, ideal for touring Exmoor.

DULVERTON
Lakeside Touring Caravan Park, Higher Grants, Exbridge, Dulverton, Somerset, TA22 9BE.
Tel: 324068 Std: 01398
Nearest Town/Resort Dulverton
Directions Leave the M5 junction 27. Take the A361 towards Barnstaple, turn right onto A396 at first roundabout. Turn left at the next roundabout, straight on at the Black Cat and stay on the A396. Park is 3 miles on the left hand side.
Acreage 4 **Open** 1 March to 31 October
Access Good **Site** Lev/Slope
Sites Available ♣ ♞ **Total** 50
Low Season Band B
High Season Band C
Facilities 🕮 ȵ ƒ ⚿ 🅆 ♨ ┍ ⊙ ⌐ ◪ ◎ ♚
▯ ⬤ ✖ ⊡

Nearby Facilities ✔ ⊥ ∪
Lovely views, ideal for touring Exmoor. Dog walking field.

EAST BRENT
Dulhorn Farm Holiday Park, Weston Road, Lympsham, Weston-super-Mare, North Somerset, BS24 0JQ.
Tel: 750298 Std: 01934
Fax: 750913 Std: 01934
Nearest Town/Resort
Directions From Weston-super-Mare take the A370 Bridgwaier road. Site is on the right approx 4½ miles. From the M5 junction 22 take the A38 for Bristol, at the second island bear left, A370 Weston-super-Mare, site is on the left.
Acreage 1½ **Open** March to October
Access Good **Site** Level
Sites Available ▲ ♣ ♞ **Total** 45
Low Season Band A
High Season Band B
Facilities ƒ 🅆 ♨ ┍ ⊙ ♚ 🛈 ⬤ ▯ ⊡
Nearby Facilities ┍ ✔ ∪ ∂ ➹
⇝ Weston-super-Mare

EXFORD
Downscombe Farm campsite, Downscombe Farm, Exford, Nr. Minehead, Somerset, TA24 7NP.
Tel: 831239 Std: 01643
Nearest Town/Resort Porlock
Directions 1 mile from Exford. Take the Porlock road, after ½ mile fork left, after ½ mile campsite is on the left.
Acreage 10 **Open** April to October
Access Good **Site** Level
Sites Available ▲ ♣ ♞ **Total** 60
Low Season Band B
High Season Band B
Facilities 🅆 ♨ ┍ ⊙ ♚ 🛈 ⊡
Nearby Facilities ∪
⇝ Taunton
Very peaceful site beside the River Exe. Level meadows with wooded hills either side

EXFORD
Westermill Farm, Exford, Minehead, Somerset, TA24 7NJ.
Tel: 831238 Std: 01643
Fax: **831660** Std: **01643**
Nearest Town/Resort Exford.
Directions Leave Exford on Porlock Road. After ½ mile fork left. Continue for 2 miles past another campsite until "Westermill" seen on tree, fork left.
Acreage 6 **Open** End March to End Oct
Access Poor **Site** Level
Sites Available ▲ ♣ ♞ **Total** 60
Low Season Band C
High Season Band C
Facilities 🅆 ♨ ┍ ⊙ ⌐ ◎ ♚
🕿 🛈 ⬤ ⊡ ⊡
Nearby Facilities ✔ ∪
⇝ Taunton
Beautiful, secluded site beside a river. Fascinating 500 acre farm with Waymarked walks. Centre Exmoor National Park. Log cottages and farmhouse cottage for hire.

GLASTONBURY
The Old Oaks Touring Park, Wick Farm, Wick, Glastonbury, Somerset, BA6 8JS.
Tel: 831437 Std: 01458
Nearest Town/Resort Glastonbury
Directions A361 2 miles from town centre left at signpost Wick 1 Mile.
Acreage 2½ **Open** March to October
Access Good **Site** Lev/Slope
Sites Available ▲ ♣ ♞ **Total** 40
Low Season Band C
High Season Band C

Facilities & ƒ 🕮 ♨ ┍ ⊙ ⌐ ◪ ◎ ♚
🕿 🛈 ⬤ ⬤ ♞ ⊡
Nearby Facilities ✔ ✗
⇝ Castle Cary
A family run park offering excellent centrally heated facilities in an outstanding environment.

ILMINSTER
Thornleigh Caravan Park, Hanning Road, Horton, Ilminster, Somerset, TA19 9QH.
Tel: 53450 Std: 01460
Fax: **53450** Std: **01460**
Nearest Town/Resort Ilminster
Directions A303 West Ilminster, take the A358 signposted Chard. ½ mile turn right signposted Horton and Broadway. Site on the left opposite the filling station, ¾ mile.
Acreage 1¼ **Open** March to October
Access Good **Site** Level
Sites Available ▲ ♣ ♞ **Total** 20
Low Season Band B
High Season Band B
Facilities ƒ 🕮 ♨ ┍ ⊙ ♚ 🛈 ⊡
Nearby Facilities ┍
⇝ Crewkerne
Flat site, ideal for touring Somerset and Devon. Sauna and solarium on site. 6 miles to Cricket St Thomas Wildlife Park twinned with Crinkley Bottom. New shower block for 1997. Holiday chalet also to let.

LANGPORT
Crest Leisure Caravan Park, Bowden, Langport, Somerset, TA10 0DD.
Tel: 250553 Std: 01458
Nearest Town/Resort Langport
Directions On the A375, 1¼ miles north of Langport towards Bowdens. Plenty of caravan signs.
Acreage 5 **Open** March to November
Access Good **Site** Level
Sites Available ▲ ♣ ♞ **Total** 30
Facilities ƒ 🕮 ♨ ┍ ⊙ ⌐ ◪ ◎ ♚
🕿 🛈 ⬤ ⊡
Nearby Facilities ✔ ∪
⇝ Taunton/Yeovil
Park with shaded areas from woods. Level ground with good drainage. Swimming nearby.

MARTOCK
Southfork Caravan Park, Parrett Works, Martock, Somerset, TA12 6AE.
Tel: 825661 Std: 01935
Nearest Town/Resort Martock/Yeovil.
Directions Situated 2 miles north west of A303 (between Ilchester and Ilminster). From A303 east of Ilminster, at roundabout take first exit signposted South Petherton and follow camping signs. From A303 west of Ilchester, after Cartgate roundabout (junction with A3088 to Yeovil) take exit signposted Martock and follow camping signs.
Acreage 2 **Open** All Year
Access Good **Site** Level
Sites Available ▲ ♣ ♞ **Total** 30
Low Season Band B
High Season Band B
Facilities ƒ 🕮 ♨ ┍ ⊙ ⌐ ◪ ◎ ♚
🕿 🛈 ⬤ ▯ ⊡
Nearby Facilities ┍ ✔ ✗
⇝ Yeovil
Set in beautiful countryside by River Parrett. Numerous places of interest nearby for all age groups. Ideal base for touring.

MINEHEAD
Blue Anchor Park, Blue Anchor, Nr. Minehead, Somerset, TA24 6JT.
Tel: 821360 Std: 01643

102   CADE'S WEST CUONTRY CAMPING, TOURING & MOTOR CARAVAN SITE GUIDE 1997

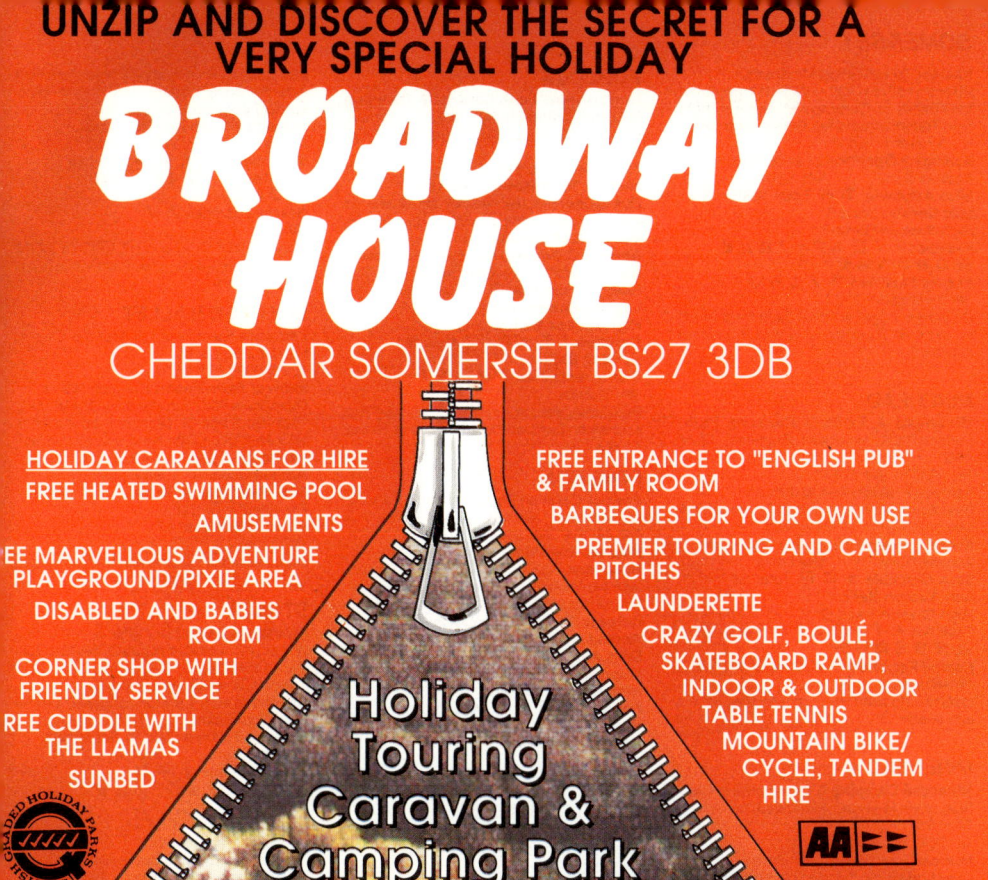

UNZIP AND DISCOVER THE SECRET FOR A VERY SPECIAL HOLIDAY

BROADWAY HOUSE

CHEDDAR SOMERSET BS27 3DB

<u>HOLIDAY CARAVANS FOR HIRE</u>
FREE HEATED SWIMMING POOL
AMUSEMENTS
FREE MARVELLOUS ADVENTURE PLAYGROUND/PIXIE AREA
DISABLED AND BABIES ROOM
CORNER SHOP WITH FRIENDLY SERVICE
FREE CUDDLE WITH THE LLAMAS
SUNBED

FREE ENTRANCE TO "ENGLISH PUB" & FAMILY ROOM
BARBEQUES FOR YOUR OWN USE
PREMIER TOURING AND CAMPING PITCHES
LAUNDERETTE
CRAZY GOLF, BOULÉ, SKATEBOARD RAMP, INDOOR & OUTDOOR TABLE TENNIS
MOUNTAIN BIKE/CYCLE, TANDEM HIRE

Holiday Touring Caravan & Camping Park

BRITISH GRADED HOLIDAY PARKS

AA

RAC APPOINTED

ACTIVITY PROGRAMME-ARCHERY, RIFLE SHOOTING, ABSEILING, CAVING, CANOEING, PLUS PRIVATE THREE ACRE FISHING LAKE

TEL: 01934 742610   FAX: 01934 744950

SOMERSET

Nearest Town/Resort Minehead
Directions From A39 at Williton, travel west for 4 miles to Carhampton and turn right onto B3191 signposted Blue Anchor. Park is 1¼ miles on right.
Acreage 5 **Open** March to October
Access Good **Site** Level
Sites Available ♣ ♣ **Total** 103
Low Season Band B
High Season Band C
Facilities ⊙ ∫ ⊞ ♣ Γ ⊙ ⌐ ▲ ◘ ♠
♨ ⓞ ♠ ♫ ♀ ⋈ ⊡
Nearby Facilities Γ ✓ ⊥ ⋆ U ≠ ℛ
⟲ Minehead
On waters edge, an ideal base from which to explore Exmoor and this beautiful coastline.

MINEHEAD

Minehead & Exmoor Caravan Park, Porlock Road, Minehead, Somerset, TA24 8SN.
Tel: 703074 **Std:** 01643
Nearest Town/Resort Minehead.
Directions Main A39 offically signposted 1 mile from centre of Minehead.
Acreage 2 **Open** March to 1 November
Access Good **Site** Level
Sites Available ▲ ♣ ♣ **Total** 50
Low Season Band B
High Season Band B
Facilities ⊙ ∫ ⚡ ⊞ ♣ Γ ⊙ ⌐ ▲ ◘ ♠
♨ ⓞ ♠ ♫ ♀ ⊡
Nearby Facilities Γ ✓ ⊥ ⋆ U ≠ ℛ ⋆
⟲ Minehead.
Ideal touring site 1 mile from Minehed centre and beach.

MINEHEAD

Minehead Camping & Caravanning Club Site, North Hill Road, Minehead, Somerset, TA24 5SF.
Tel: 704138 **Std:** 01643
Nearest Town/Resort Minehead
Directions From the town centre go towards the sea front, turn left into Blenheim Road, left into Martlett Road, left around the War Memorial into St Michaels Road. Go past the church into Moor Road and the site is on the right.
Acreage 3¾ **Open** 3 November to 31 October
Site Sloping
Sites Available ▲ ♣ **Total** 60
Facilities ⊞ ♣ Γ ⌐ ▲ ♠ ⊞ ⊡
Nearby Facilities
Views over Blue Anchor Bay, good for walking. West Somerset Steam Railway, Exmoor, Carriage Driving Championships and a Cycling Festival.

MINEHEAD

Totterdown Farm Camp Site, Mr & Mrs B.T. Halse, Totterdown Farm, Timberscombe, Minehead, Somerset, TA24 7TA.
Tel: 841317 **Std:** 01643
Nearest Town/Resort Minehead.
Directions Take the A396 Tiverton Road from Dunster for 2 miles. Farm in layby on the left before Timberscombe Village.
Acreage 8 **Open** Mid July to Mid September
Access Good **Site** Level
Sites Available ▲ ♣ ♣ **Total** 15
Facilities ⊞ ⓛ ⊡
Nearby Facilities Γ ✓ ⊥ ⋆ U
⟲ Taunton.
Quiet, rural site with beautiful views of Exmoor. Near the River Avil. 1 mile from Dunster Castle and 6 miles from Minehead beach.

PORLOCK

Burrowhayes Farm Caravan & Camping Site and Riding Stables, West Luccombe, Porlock, Nr. Minehead, Somerset, TA24 8HU.
Tel: 862463 **Std:** 01643
Nearest Town/Resort Minehead.
Directions 5 miles west of Minehead on A39, left hand turning to West Luccombe, site [3] mile on the right.
Acreage 8 **Open** 15 March to 31 October
Access Good **Site** Lev/Slope
Sites Available ▲ ♣ ♣ **Total** 140
Low Season Band B
High Season Band C
Facilities ∫ ⊞ ♣ Γ ⊙ ⌐ ▲ ◘ ♠
♨ ⓘ ⓞ ♠ ⊡
Nearby Facilities Γ ✓ ⊥ ⋆ ℛ
⟲ Taunton.
Real family site set in glorious National Trust scenery on Exmoor. Ideal for walking. Riding on site.

PORLOCK

Porlock Caravan Park, Highbank, Porlock, Nr. Minehead, Somerset, TA24 8NS.
Tel: 862269 **Std:** 01643
Nearest Town/Resort Minehead.
Directions A39 from Minehead to Lynton, take the B3225 in Porlock to Porlock Weir. Site signposted.
Acreage 3½ **Open** Mid March to October
Access Good **Site** Level
Sites Available ▲ ♣ ♣ **Total** 40
Low Season Band B
High Season Band B
Facilities ∫ ⊞ ♣ Γ ⊙ ⌐ ▲ ◘ ♠
♨ ⓘ ⓞ ♠ ⊡
Nearby Facilities Γ ✓ ⋆ U ℛ
⟲ Taunton.
Scenic views, Ideal touring and walking.

SHEPTON MALLET

Greenacres Camping, Barrow Lane, North Wootton, Nr. Shepton Mallet, Somerset, BA4 4HL.
Tel: 890497 **Std:** 01749
Nearest Town/Resort Wells
Directions From Wells take the A39, turn left at Brownes Garden Centre. Site signposted in the village.
Acreage 4¼ **Open** April to October
Site Level
Sites Available ▲ ♣ **Total** 30
Facilities ⊞ ♣ Γ ⊙ ⌐ ▲ ◘ ♠ ⋈ ⊡
Nearby Facilities Γ ✓ U ℛ
⟲ Castle Cary
An award winning family site. Peacefully set within sight of Glastonbury Tor.

SHEPTON MALLET

Manleaze Caravan Park, Cannards Grave, Shepton Mallet, Somerset.
Tel: 342040 **Std:** 01749
Nearest Town/Resort Shepton Mallet
Directions 1 mile south of Shepton Mallet on A371.
Acreage ¾ **Open** All Year
Access Good **Site** Level
Sites Available ▲ ♣ ♣ **Total** 25
Low Season Band A
High Season Band A
Facilities ∫ ⊞ ♣ Γ ⊙ ♠ ◘ ⊡
Nearby Facilities Γ ⋆
⟲ Castle Cary

SHEPTON MALLET

Old Down Caravan & Camping Park, Emborough, Bath, Somerset, BA3 4SA.
Tel: 232355 **Std:** 01761
Nearest Town/Resort Midsomer Norton.
Directions From Shepton Mallet take the A37 towards Bristol, after 6 miles turn right onto the B3139. Site is on the right opposite Old Down Inn.
Acreage 4 **Open** April to October
Access Good **Site** Level
Sites Available ▲ ♣ ♣ **Total** 25
Facilities ⊠ ∫ ⊞ ♣ Γ ⊙ ⌐ ♠
♨ ⓘ ⓞ ♠ ⊡
Nearby Facilities Γ ✓
⟲ Bath
A level field with an ancient oak tree as the centre-piece of a large recreation area. Ideal touring centre.

SHEPTON MALLET

Phippens Farm, Stoke St. Michael, Oakhill, Nr. Bath, Somerset.
Tel: 840395 **Std:** 01749
Nearest Town/Resort Shepton Mallet.
Directions A367 Bath/Shepton Mallet road. Turn into Stoke St. Michael village, top of Oakhill sit on right hand side (1½ miles).
Acreage 7 **Open** Easter to September
Access Good **Site** Level
Sites Available ▲ ♣ ♣
Facilities ∫ ⊙ ⓘ
Nearby Facilities
⟲ Frome
Good touring area. Longleat, Bath, Cheddar, Wookey Hole, Bristol, Wells, etc.

STREET

Bramble Hill Camping Site, Bramble Hill, Walton, Nr. Street, Somerset, BA16 9RQ.
Tel: 442548 **Std:** 01458
Nearest Town/Resort Street
Directions A39 1 mile from Street, 2 miles from Glastonbury.
Acreage 3½ **Open** April to September
Access Good **Site** Level
Sites Available ▲ ♣ ♣
Facilities ∫ ⊞ ♣ Γ ⊙ ⌐ ▲ ◘ ♠
ⓘ ♠ ✕ ⓞ ♠ ⊡
Nearby Facilities Γ ✓ U
⟲ Castle Cary/Taunton
Quiet site. Caravan storage also available. Ideal site for visiting Clarks Village - 1 mile.

TAUNTON

Ashe Farm Caravan & Camp Site, Ashe Farm, Thornfalcon, Taunton, Somerset TA3 5NW.
Tel: 442567 **Std:** 01823
Fax: 443772 **Std:** 01823
Nearest Town/Resort Taunton.
Directions 4 miles southeast Taunton on A358, turn right at 'Nags Head' towards West Hatch, ¼ mile on right.
Acreage 7 **Open** April to October
Access Good **Site** Level
Sites Available ▲ ♣ ♣ **Total** 30
Low Season Band B
High Season Band B
Facilities ∫ ⊞ ♣ Γ ⊙ ⌐ ▲ ♠
♨ ⓘ ⓞ ♠ ♫ ⊡
Nearby Facilities Γ ✓ U ℛ
⟲ Taunton.
Ideal touring centre, easy reach of Quantock and Blackdown Hills.

TAUNTON

Holly Bush Park, Culmhead, Taunton, Somerset, TA3 7EA.
Tel: 421515 **Std:** 01823
Fax: 421885 **Std:** 01823
Nearest Town/Resort Taunton
Directions From Taunton follow signs for the Racecourse and Corfe on the B3170, 3½ miles from Corfe turn right at crossroads towards Wellington. Turn right at the next T-Junction, site is 200yds on the left.
Acreage 2¼ **Open** All Year

104 CADE'S WEST CUONTRY CAMPING, TOURING & MOTOR CARAVAN SITE GUIDE 1997

SOMERSET

Access Good　　　　Site Level
Sites Available ▲ ⌑ ⌑ Total 40
Low Season Band B
High Season Band B
Facilities ⌑ ⌑ ⌑ ⌑ ⌑ ⌑ ⌑ ⌑
⌑ ⌑ ⌑ ⌑
Nearby Facilities ⌑ ⌑ ∪ ⌑
⌑ Taunton.
Area of Outstanding Natural Beauty.

WATCHET

Doniford Bay Holiday Park, Watchet, Somerset, TA23 0TJ.
Tel: 632423 Std: 01984
Nearest Town/Resort Watchet
Directions Leave the M5 at exit 24. Follow Minehead signs on the A39 until you reach West Quantoxhead. Fork right after St. Audries Garage to Doniford Bay, the park is signposted.
Acreage 5 **Open** 26 March to 8 October
Site Sloping
Sites Available ▲ ⌑ ⌑ Total 120
Facilities ⌑ ⌑ ⌑ ⌑ ⌑ ⌑ ⌑ ⌑ ⌑
⌑ ⌑ ⌑ ⌑ ⌑ ⌑ ⌑ ⌑
Nearby Facilities ⌑ ∪ ⌑
⌑ Taunton
Overlooking the sea.

WELLINGTON

Cadeside Caravan Club Site, Nynehead Road, Wellington, Somerset, TA21 9HN.
Tel: 663103 Std: 01823
Nearest Town/Resort Wellington.
Directions Leave M5 at junction 26 (signposted Wellington), at roundabout in ¾ mile turn onto the B3187 (signposted Wellington). In ¾ mile turn right at signpost Nynehead and Poole. Site is on the right within 80yds.
Acreage 4¾ **Open** 26 March to 29 September
Access Good　　　　Site Level
Sites Available ⌑ ⌑ Total 60
Low Season Band A
High Season Band B
Facilities ⌑ ⌑ ⌑ ⌑ ⌑
⌑ Taunton
Nearby Facilities
Walking and cycling on the Quantocks and Blackdown Hills. Ideal for touring Wells, Glastonbury and Cheddar. Good days out to the beaches at Minehead on the West Coast and Sidmouth, Lyme Regis, etc. on the South Coast.

WELLS

Chewton Cheese Dairy, Priory Farm, Chewton Mendip, Bath, BA3 4NT.
Tel: 241666 Std: 01761
Fax: **241202** Std: **01761**
Nearest Town/Resort Wells
Directions On A39 6 miles north east of Wells.
Open All Year
Access Good　　　　Site Level
Sites Available ▲ ⌑ ⌑ Total 25
Low Season Band B
High Season Band B
Facilities ⌑ ⌑ ⌑ ⌑ ⌑ ⌑
⌑ ⌑ ⌑ ⌑
Nearby Facilities ⌑ ⌑ ∪ ⌑
⌑ Bath
Cheese dairy on site, wooded picnic area and gardens, ideal for visiting Wells, Bath, Cheddar and Mendip Hills.

WELLS

Ebborlands Camping Grounds, Ebborlands Farm, Wookey Hole, Nr Wells, Somerset.
Tel: 672550 Std: 01749
Fax: **672550** Std: **01749**
Nearest Town/Resort Wells
Directions Wells - Unclassified road to Wookey Hole, approx 2 miles.

Acreage 2 **Open** April to October
Access Good　　　　Site Sloping
Sites Available ▲ ⌑ ⌑ Total 20
Low Season Band B
High Season Band B
Facilities ⌑ ⌑ ⌑ ⌑
Nearby Facilities ⌑ ⌑ ⌑ ∪ ⌑ ⌑
⌑ Castle Cary
Near Wookey Hole Caves and Mendip Hills.

WELLS

Homestead Park, Wookey Hole, Wells, Somerset.BA5 1BW
Tel: 673022 Std: 01749
Nearest Town/Resort Wells.
Directions Leave Wells by A371 towards Cheddar, turn right for Wookey Hole. Site 1¼ miles on left in village.
Acreage 2 **Open** Easter to October
Access Good　　　　Site Level
Sites Available ▲ ⌑ ⌑ Total 55
Low Season Band C
High Season Band C
Facilities ⌑ ⌑ ⌑ ⌑ ⌑ ⌑ ⌑ ⌑ ⌑
Nearby Facilities ⌑ ⌑ ∪
⌑ Bristol/Bath
Sheltered on bank of River Axe, Wookey Hole Caves, National Trust Area, Mendip Hills, walking, climbing. Leisure centre nearby.

WELLS

Mendip Heights Camping & Caravan Park, Priddy, Wells, Somerset, BA5 3BP.
Tel: 870241 Std: 01749
Fax: **870241** Std: **01749**
Nearest Town/Resort Wells.
Directions On A39 north from Wells, turn left at Green Ore crossroads onto B3135 towards Cheddar and follow campsite signs.
Acreage 4¼ **Open** March to 15 November
Access Good　　　　Site Level
Sites Available ▲ ⌑ ⌑ Total 90
Facilities ⌑ ⌑ ⌑ ⌑ ⌑ ⌑ ⌑ ⌑
⌑ ⌑ ⌑ ⌑ ⌑
Nearby Facilities ⌑ ⌑ ⌑ ⌑ ⌑ ⌑
⌑ Bristol/Bath/Weston-super-Mare
Peaceful, rural park in an area of outstanding natural beauty. Ideal for touring and walking. Near Cheddar, Wookey Hole and Wells. Activities available - see our main advertisement.

WELLS

Ye Olde Punch Bowl Inn & Restaurant, Henton, Wells, Somerset, BA5 1PD.
Tel: 672212 Std: 01749
Nearest Town/Resort Wells
Directions 3 miles from Wells on B3139 to Wedmore/Burnham on Sea. Park is on the right hand side just as you enter the village. Midway between Wells and Wedmore exit M5 junction 22.
Acreage 1 **Open** Easter to End September
Access Good　　　　Site Level
Sites Available ⌑ ⌑ Total 5
Low Season Band A
High Season Band A
Facilities ⌑ ⌑ ⌑ ⌑ ⌑
Nearby Facilities ⌑ ⌑ ∪ ⌑
Central for Cheddar 8 miles. 12 miles to Wookey Hole Caves and coast. Open views from site of the Mendip Hills and Cheddar Valley with a small stream. Pub and Restaurant open: Evenings Wednesday to Sunday inclusive and for Sunday Lunch also all week Bank Holiday weekends. Toilets open during pub opening hours only, advised own on board toilet. Small fee for awnings.

WEST LYDFORD

Rose Fair Touring Park, Fair Place, West Lydford, Somerset, TA11 7DN.
Tel: 240490/240234 Std: 01963

Nearest Town/Resort Castle Cary/Shepton Mallet
Directions From Shepton Mallet take the A37 directly to West Lydford (approx 7 miles).
Acreage 3 **Open** Easter to October
Access Good　　　　Site Level
Sites Available ▲ ⌑ ⌑ Total 150
Low Season Band B
High Season Band C
Facilities ⌑ ⌑ ⌑ ⌑ ⌑ ⌑ ⌑
⌑ ⌑ ⌑ ⌑
Nearby Facilities ⌑ ⌑ ∪
⌑ Castle Cary
Very close to Royal bath and West Showground/Glastonbury Tor. Local fishing on the River Brue. Taunton town and races, Cheddar Caves, Wells cathedral, Street Village shopping centre and Cricket St. Thomas. Jet-skiing nearby.

WILLITON

Home Farm Holiday Centre, St. Audries Bay, Williton, Somerset.
Tel: 632487 Std: 01984
Fax: **634687** Std: **01984**
Nearest Town/Resort Williton / Watchet
Directions Leave M5 at Junction 23, follow A39 towards Minehead for 17 miles. At West Quantoxhead take first right turn after St. Audries Garages (signposted Blue Anchor, Doniford and Watchet) B3191 take first right turning in ½ mile to our drive.
Open All Year
Access Good　　　　Site Terraced
Sites Available ▲ ⌑ ⌑ Total 30
Low Season Band B
High Season Band B
Facilities ⌑ ⌑ ⌑ ⌑ ⌑ ⌑ ⌑ ⌑ ⌑
⌑ ⌑ ⌑ ⌑ ⌑ ⌑
Nearby Facilities ⌑ ⌑ ∪
⌑ Taunton.
Private beach, good base for touring Exmoor. West Somerset Railway - 2 miles.

WINSFORD

Halse Farm Caravan & Tent Park, Halse Farm, Winsford, Minehead, Somerset, TA24 7JL.
Tel: 851259 Std: 01643
Fax: **851259** Std: **01643**
Nearest Town/Resort Dulverton.
Directions Turn off the A396 (Tiverton to Minehead road) to Winsford. In Winsford take small road in front of Royal Oak Inn. 1 mile up hill and over cattle grid, our entrance is immediately on the left.
Acreage 3 **Open** March to End October
Access Good　　　　Site Level
Sites Available ▲ ⌑ ⌑ Total 44
Low Season Band B
High Season Band B
Facilities ⌑ ⌑ ⌑ ⌑ ⌑ ⌑ ⌑ ⌑ ⌑
⌑ ⌑ ⌑ ⌑
Nearby Facilities ⌑ ∪
⌑ Taunton
In Exmoor National Park, on working farm with beautiful views. For those who enjoy peaceful countryside. New heated toilet block and FREE showers.

WIVELISCOMBE

Bouchers Farm Camping Site, Bouchers Farm, Waterrow, Wiveliscombe, Taunton, Somerset.
Tel: 623464 Std: 01984
Nearest Town/Resort Wiveliscombe.
Directions 10 miles west Taunton on B3227 First left after Waterrow.
Acreage 4 **Open** 1 April to 1 October
Access Good　　　　Site Level
Sites Available ▲ ⌑ ⌑ Total 100
Facilities ⌑ ⌑ ⌑
Nearby Facilities ⌑ ∪ ⌑
⌑ Taunton.
Alongside river with scenic views. £3 per night, tent or caravan.

SOMERSET
PLACES OF INTEREST

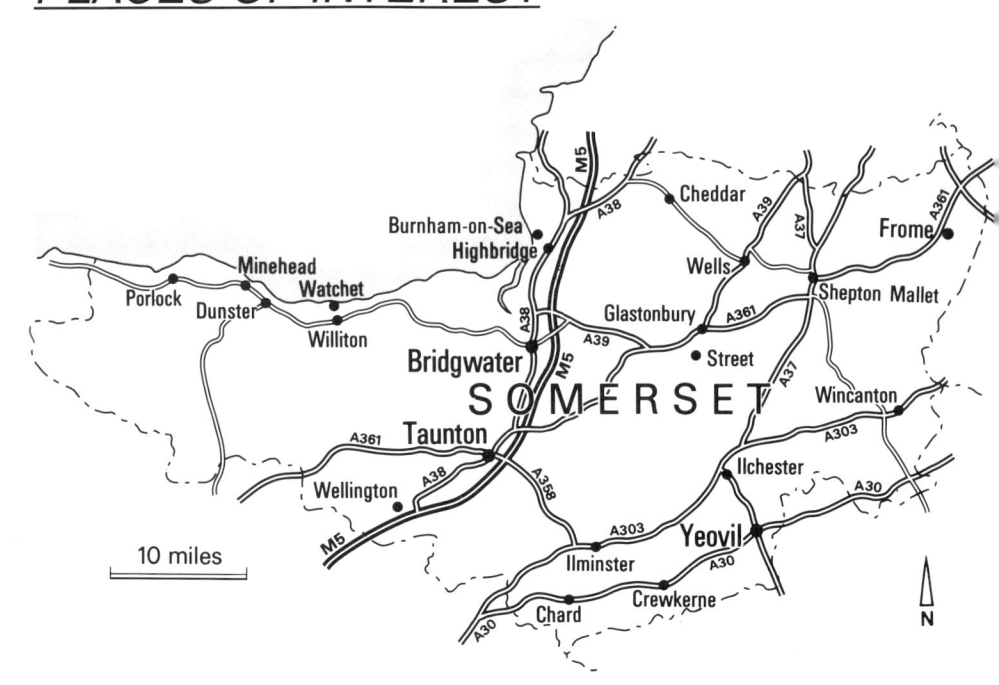

SOMERSET

AXBRIDGE
KING JOHN'S HUNTING LODGE : The Square, Axbridge, Somerset. Tel : 01934 732012. Fax : 01278 444076.
Nearest Railway Station : Weston-super-Mare. Location : In the centre of Axbridge. Open : Easter to the end of September, daily 2pm-5pm. **Special Attractions:** Late medieval merchant's house, restored by the National Trust and now housing Axbridge Museum with its fascinating collection of local archaeology and history items. Admission FREE.

BRIDGWATER
Bridgwater is a market and industrial town on the River Parrett. The rebel Duke of Monmouth was proclaimed King here in 1685 before his forces were defeated at nearby Sedgemoor. He surveyed the field from the tower, decorated and perpendicular St Mary's Church which still stands today and contains good examples of screenwork.

The one time house of Admiral Blake is now a museum and Water Gate House is a reminder of the old 13th Century Castle. A nuclear power station which has guided tours has been built at Hinkley Point on Bridgwater Bay.

BRIDGWATER
ADMIRAL BLAKE MUSEUM : Blake Street, Bridgwater, Somerset, TA6 3NB. Tel : 01278 456127. Fax : 01278 444076.
Nearest Railway Station : Bridgwater. Location : In the centre of Bridgwater, next to Blake Gardens. Open : 2nd January to December. **Special Attractions:** Local history museum located in the reputed birth place of Robert Blake, General at Sea (1598-1657). Artifacts from Blake's family etc. Full display of the Battle of Sedgemoor in 1685 also displays on the Monmouth Rebellion (1685) and archaeology. Industrial history of Bridgwater, shipping and docks. Art and temporary exhibitions.

BRIDGWATER
COLERIDGE COTTAGE : Nether Stowey, Near Bridgwater, Somerset.
Location : At West end of Nether Stowey, on South side of A39, 8 miles West of Bridgwater. Open : April to October, Tuesday to Thursday and Sunday, 2pm-5pm. **Special Attractions:** Here Samuel Taylor Coleridge lived from 1797 to 1800 and wrote The Ancient Mariner. National Trust Members FREE.

BRIDGWATER
MOORLYNCH VINEYARD : Moorlinch, Bridgwater, Somerset, TA7 9DD. Tel : 01458 210393. Fax : 01458 210247.
Nearest Railway Station : Bridgwater. Location : Off the A39 Bridgwater to Glastonbury road and the A361 Taunton to Glastonbury road. (M5 junction 23). Open : Easter week and May to September. Tuesday to Saturday 10.30am-5pm, Sunday 12pm-5pm, Bank Holiday Mondays 10.30am-5pm. **Special Attractions:** 16 acre vineyard growing and producing still and sparkling English wine. Winery, Visitor Centre and Video. Self-guided individual tours and guided group tours with tastings. Idyllic country setting. Wine shop and restaurant.

BURNHAM-ON-SEA
Burnham-on-Sea is a popular resort with miles of sandy beach providing access for bathing. Wide views over Bridgwater Bay, part of which is now a natural nature reserve and can be enjoyed from here.

The church has a white marble alter which was originally carved for the Chapel of Whitehall Palace by Grinling Gibbons. The alter was first moved to Hampton Court and then to Westminster Abbey. George IV disposed of it to Bishop King of Rochester, who was then Vicar of Burnham in 1830.

SOMERSET

BURNHAM-ON-SEA
BREAN DOWN BIRD GARDEN : Brean Down, Burnham-on-Sea, Somerset, TA8 2RS. Tel : 01278 751209.
Nearest Railway Station : Weston-Super-Mare/Highbridge. Location : Brean Down. Open : March to October, 9am-5pm. **Special Attractions:** Many different species of birds from all over the world. Cafe/restaurant and Gift Shop.

BURNHAM-ON-SEA
BREAN LEISURE PARK : Brean Sands, Burnham-on-Sea, Somerset. Tel : Brean Down 01278 751595.
Location : Signposted from Junction 22 M5 (4 1/4). Open : Weekends from Easter and daily, end of May-end of September. Telephone for opening times out of school holidays. Free admission - Pay to ride - Car Park £1.00. **Special Attractions:** Family fun park with over 30 attractions 200 yards from a 7 mile beach. Roller Coaster, pool complex with aquaslides, fun fair, 18 hole golf course, bars with evening cabaret and family entertainment. Open air market on Mondays in the high season, car boot sales on Sundays. Caravan and Camping facilities.

BURNHAM-ON-SEA
SECRET WORLD : New Road, East Huntspill, Highbridge, Somerset, TA9 3PZ. Tel & Fax : 01278 783250.
Nearest Railway Station : Highbridge. Location : Tourist Board signposted to Secret World and Visitor Centre on the A38 Highbridge to Bridgwater road. Open : Every day 10am-6pm. **Special Attractions:** Secret World is a badger and wildlife rescue centre set in the surroundings of a traditional farm. Winner of ITV's Animal Country award and stars of "Nature Detectives". Badger observation sett, tremendous variety of wildlife farm animals and displays. Somersets Visitor Centre, farmhouse, tea rooms, adventure playground. Super day out rain or shine.

CASTLE CARY
CASTLE CARY VINEYARD : Honeywick House, Hadspen, Castle Cary, Somerset. Tel : Castle Cary 01963 351773.
Nearest Railway Station : Castle Cary. Location : Half mile East of Castle Cary. Open : Weekdays 10am-6pm. Sunday Noon-3pm. Vineyard open 1st May-30th September. Vineyard shop open all year. **Special Attractions:** The vineyard is situated on the Southern slopes of a picturesque fold in the hills Just off the A371. No entry charge. Wine, cider and associated items sold in the shop. Free tasting.

CHARD
CHARD & DISTRICT MUSEUM : Godworthy House, High Street, Chard, Somerset, TA20 1QL. Tel : 01460 65091.
Nearest Railway Station : Crewkerne or Axminster. Open : Early May to late October. Monday to Saturday 10.30am-4.30pm, plus Sundays in July and August. **Special Attractions:** History of Chard. John Stringfellow - Pioneer of powered flight, James Gillingham's early artificial limbs, Margaret Bondfield - first woman Cabinet Minister. Reconstructed blacksmith's, carpenter's and wheelwright's shops. Victorian schoolroom and kitchen, cider and dairy exhibitions and a 1940's garage. Agricultural machinery, implements and wagons. Lace making machines and a small costume gallery.

CHARD
FERNE ANIMAL SANCTUARY : Wambrook, Chard, Somerset, TA20 3DH. Tel & Fax : 01460 65214.
Nearest Railway Station : Crewkerne. Location : Signposted on the A30 Chard to Honiton road. Open : April to September. Wednesday, Saturday, Sunday and all Bank Holidays within that period, 2pm-5pm. **Special Attractions:** Over 300 animals are at home in 51 acres of beautiful Somerset countryside. See our vintage farm machinery, nature trail, dragonfly pools and conservation area. Visit our gift shop and tea room. Well equipped education centre for the use of visiting groups. Cat and dog adoption schemes. Facilities for the dsiabled.

CHARD
HORNSBURY MILL : Eleighwater, Near Chard, Somerset, TA20 3AQ. Tel & Fax : 01460 63317.
Nearest Railway Station : Crewkerne. Location : On the A358 Taunton to Lyme Regis road. **Special Attractions:** Working watermill set in 5 acres of lakeside gardens with a museum. Licensed restaurant, full bar facilities, en suite bedrooms, conference suite, plus the Lakeside Suite, a 100 seater room for weddings and dinner dances.

CHEDDAR
THE CHEDDAR GORGE CHEESE COMPANY : The Cliffs, Cheddar, Somerset, BS27 3QA. Tel : 01934 742810. Fax : 01934 741020.
Nearest Railway Station : Weston-super-Mare. Location : At the foot of Cheddar Gorge. Open : 17th March to the end of April, 10am-4pm (last admission 3pm). 1st May to the end of October, 10a-6pm (last admission 4.30pm). **Special Attractions:** Rural village with the last remaining cheese dairy in Cheddar. Some village highlights to see: Candleworks, spinner and lacemaker, village pottery, fudge kitchen, Legbender Cider Barn, conservatory restaurant.

CHEDDAR
MONKEYS CHILDRENS PLAY CENTRE : Tweentown, Cheddar, Somerset, BS27 3JE. Tel : 01934 742270/712304.
Nearest Railway Station : Weston-super-Mare. Location : 100yds from the bottom of Cheddar Gorge on the road to Axbridge. Open : Daily during school holidays, 10.30am-5.30pm. After school, 3.30pm-5.30pm. Every Saturday and Sunday. Special day for Under Fives during term time. **Special Attractions:** Indoor adventure play area, ball pond, bouncy castle, slides, climbing structure and soft play. Cafeteria and party room. No time limits. Great fun whatever the weather. Age limit 11 years. Snooker available for adults. Large car park.

CHEWTON MENDIP
CHEWTON CHEESE DAIRY : Priory Farm, Chewton Mendip, Bath, Somerset, BA3 4NT. Tel : 01761 241666. Fax : 01761 241202.
Location : Off main Bristol-Wells road (A39) on the Wells side of Chewton Mendip. Near the historic cities of Bath and Wells and close to Cheddar Gorge. Open : Cheese making every day except Sunday and Thursday. Farm shop and Restaurant open every day. **Special Attractions:** Visitors can watch chessemakers at work in a working farmhouse Cheese Dairy, where traditional Cheddar Cheese is made most days. Licensed Restaurant offering Farmhouse Lunches and Cream Teas. Wooded 25-van Caravan Site, Gardens.

FROME
Frome pronounced "FROOME" has as its main industry the manufacture of cloth and carpets. It is criss-crossed by steep narrow streets and its well-restored richly decorated church contains numerous chapels. Cheap Street has a central water-course running down the middle of the road and the Bluecoat School dates from about 1720. Old almshouses stand by a bridge spanning the River Frome - most of the old houses here date from the 18th Century. Orchardleigh Park has a Victorian Mansion.

An Island in the lake has a small interesting restored church, particularly notable for its examples of ancient glass and fine priest's doorway.

GLASTONBURY
According to legend, Joseph of Arimathea landed on the Somerset coast with the holy Grail and made his way inland to Glastonbury. He and his followers reached Wearyall Hill on Christmas morning, where he stuck his staff in the ground while he rested. The staff took root and flowered, a sign that his travels were over, and that he should find a religious house. St Patrick is said to have retired here and been adopted as Abbot in the 5th Century. Even more legends tell how King Arthur lived here and was buried with his wife Guinevere on the Isle of Avalon.

SOMERSET

Glastonbury is also famous for its Abbey, little of its early history is actually known, but is was probably of Celtic origin with Saxon additions. The Abbey had a difficult history, destroyed by fire, rebuilt and later partly dismantled by marauding armies. Remains of the Abbey now comprise St Mary's Chapel, the Abbey Church and the Monastic buildings. St Mary's Chapel is a beautiful ruined shell with an underground Chapel to St Joseph beneath it. The Abbey Tithe Barn and Museum with the famous flowering Glastonbury Thorn Tree which flowers at Christmas against horticulture theory are well worth visiting.

Close to the Abbey is a hill called the Tor, a pyramid in shape and crowned by the nun of the tower. The Tor is reputed to be the burial place of a number of early Abbots. It is a prominent landmark virtually unscalable in Winter, but in Summer a relatively easy climb giving extensive and impressive panoramic views.

Glastonbury is also famous for its Summer festival. The Glastonbury Festival usually takes place in July and is the venue for open air rock and folk concerts. These concerts are also the meeting place for many diverse travellers who take the opportunity to display their cultural, spiritual and socially ethnic ideas and values.

GLASTONBURY
GLASTONBURY ABBEY : Abbey Gatehouse, Magdalene Street, Glastonbury, Somerset, BA6 9EL. Tel : 01458 832267. Nearest Railway Station : Bath, Bristol or Taunton. Location : Signposted from the M5 junction 23 and off the A303 at Podimore crossroads. Approximately 7 miles from Wells. Open : 9.30am-6pm (or dusk if earlier). Opens at 9am in June, July and August. **Special Attractions:** Traditionally the oldest Christian sanctuary in the British Isles and the legendary burial place of King Arthur. The ruins of the Abbey, The Holy Thorn, the modern museum and shop all in 36 acres of glorious parkland make Glastonbury a 'must' for any visit to the West Country.

GLASTONBURY
GLASTONBURY TRIBUNAL : High Street, Glastonbury, Somerset, BA6 9DP. Tel : 01458 832954/832949. Fax : 01458 832949. Nearest Railway Station : Castle Cary. Location : In the main High Street. Open : 7 days a week, all year round. **Special Attractions:** Building houses the museum of the remains from the lake villages (Iron Age). Building is also used as the Tourist Information Centre.

GLASTONBURY
PEAT MOORS VISITOR CENTRE : Shapwick Road, Westhay, Near Glastonbury, Somerset, BA6 9TT. Tel : 01458 860697. Location : Between the villages of Shapwick and Westhay, not far from the M5. Open : April to October, every day 10am-4.30pm. November to March by appointment only. **Special Attractions:** Natural History of Somerset Levels, Peat Industry, archaeology, including reconstruction of Glastonbury Lake Village and trackways dating back to 4000BC. Ancient craft demonstrations on weekends.

GLASTONBURY
SOMERSET RURAL LIFE MUSEUM : Abbey Farm, Chilkwell Street, Glastonbury, Somerset, BA6 8DB. Tel & Fax : 01458 831197. Nearest Railway Station : Castle Cary (11 miles). Open : Easter to the 31st October, Tuesday to Friday and Bank Holiday Mondays 10am-5pm, weekends 2pm-6pm. 1st November to Easter, Tuesday to Friday 10am-5pm, Saturday 11am-4pm. Closed Good Friday. **Special Attractions:** Displays and collections of social and domestic life in a Victorian farm and medieval Abbey Barn. Original farmhouse kitchen, cider and cheese making equipment and the illustrated life story of a Victorian farm labourer. Temporary exhibitions, special events, craft demonstrations and farming activities. Tea room in the Summer only and museum shop.

HIGHBRIDGE
ALSTONE WILDLIFE PARK : Alstone Road, Highbridge, Somerset, TA9 3DT. Tel : 01278 782405. Fax : 01278 792288. Nearest Railway Station : Highbridge. Location : Signposted on the main A38 Highbridge to Bridgwater road. Open : Easter to 31st October, 10am-6pm. **Special Attractions:** Walk with and hand-feed the heard of Red Deer. Meet Theadore the very friendly Camel, Horatio the Billy Goat Gruff, Ollie the amusing Emu, Harriet and the Pot Bellied Pig family. Mini ponies, Barn Owls, Eagle Owls and many more. Picnic area.

HIGHBRIDGE
"THE BUNKER" UNDERGROUND MILITARY MUSEUM : Highbridge, Somerset. Tel : 01934 629000. Nearest Railway Station : Highbridge. Open : Summer, every day except Wednesday, 10am-4pm. Winter, weekends only. **Special Attractions:** A large assortment of World War I and World War II memorabilia. Military weapons, Anderson shelter, uniforms, wreckage from a B.17 flying fortress, Sirens, badges, medals, WWI trench. Blitz Room, escape tunnel, Radio Room, bunker and much more.

ILMINSTER
BARRINGTON COURT & GARDENS (NATIONAL TRUST) : Barrington Court, Barrington, Near Ilminster, Somerset, TA19 0NQ. Tel : 01460 241938. Nearest Railway Station : Taunton. Location : 5 miles north east of Ilminster in the village of Barrington. Open : 22nd March to 31st October 1997, 11am-5.30pm daily except Friday. **Special Attractions** : Elizabethan house set in Gertrude Jekyll inspired gardens. Gift shop and restaurant. National Trust property.

ILMINSTER
PERRY'S CIDER MILLS : Dowlish Wake, Ilminster, Somerset. Tel : Ilminster 01460 52681. Nearest Railway Station : Crewkerne/Taunton. Location : 2 miles from Ilminster off the A303, 5 miles from Chard off the A30 and the A358. Open : All year, weekdays 9am-1pm and 1.30pm-5.30pm, Saturdays 10am-1pm and 1.30pm-4.30pm. Sundays 10am-1pm. **Special Attractions:** Quality traditional cider which may be tasted before buying. Museum of farm tools, photographic displays. Cider making can be seen in Autumn. **Shop** selling Cider made at the Cider Mills, Somerset Cider Brandy, Stone Jars, interesting and unusual pottery and gifts, Terracotta, garden tubs. Set in attractive village with packhorse bridge and historic church. Excellent facilities for food nearby. FREE ENTRY.

MINEHEAD
Good sands, bathing and a small harbour help to make this resort popular with holiday makers. Fisherman's Chapel dates from 1630, old almshouses exist in Market House Lane and a model village can be seen on the seafront. Blenheim Gardens are to be much admired and the picturesque old village includes the church which displays a lofty perpendicular tower and fine carved screen.

Minehead makes a good centre for touring Exmoor and the Brendan Hills. A curious Hobby-Horse dance is performed on May Day.

MINEHEAD
WEST SOMERSET RAILWAY : The Railway Station, Minehead, Somerset, TA24 5BG. Tel : 01643 704996. 24-Hour Talking Timetable - Tel : 01643 707650. Fax : 01643 706349. Location : On sea front, 5 minutes walk from Somerset World. **Special Attractions:** Britain's longest preserved railway running trains over the 20 miles from Minehead through stunning scenery and the Quantock Hills via Dunster, Blue Anchor, Washford, Watchet, Williton, Stogumber and Crowcombe to Bishops Lydeard with bus connections to Taunton. Visitors Centre and model railways at Bishops Lydeard, GW Museum at Blue Anchor, S&D Museum at Washford, Diesel and Electric Group Depot at Williton.

CADE'S WEST CUONTRY CAMPING, TOURING & MOTOR CARAVAN SITE GUIDE 1997

SOMERSET

PORLOCK
BOSSINGTON BIRDS OF PREY & FARM PARK : Allerford, Near Porlock, Somerset, TA24 8HJ. Tel : 01643 862816.
Nearest Railway Station : Taunton. Location : 5 miles west of Minehead off the A39, turn right through Allerford Village, we are 0.75 miles on the left hand side. Open : March to October, 10.30am-5pm. **Special Attractions:** Unique bird of prey and farm park where visitors can intermingle with tame animals set in 15th Century farmyards in Exmoor National Park. Twice daily flying displays, animal handling, feeding, pony rides and farmhouse. Refreshments and a gift shop.

RODE
RODE BIRD GARDENS : Rode, Somerset, BA3 6QW. Tel : Frome 830326 STD 01373, Catering Department 01373 830585.
Location : Turn off the A36 at the Red Lion, Woolverton (10 miles South of Bath). Open : Summer 10am-6pm. Winter 10am-Dusk. Last admittance 1 hour before closing time (closed Christmas Day). Prices of admission available on application. Car park. **Special Attractions:** In 17 acres, hundreds of brilliant exotic birds in lovely natural surroundings - woodlands, flower gardens, ornamental lake, Clematis Collection, Childrens play area, information centre and souvenir shop. During the Summer months there is a licensed cafeteria (Winter - light refreshments). Pets Corner and garden sales. Woodland Steam Railway, Easter to October (weather permitting). Sorry, no dogs. Children must be accompanied by an adult.

SHEPTON MALLET
PILTON MANOR VINEYARD : Pilton, Shepton Mallet, Somerset, BA4 4BE. Tel : 01749 890325. Fax : 01749 850262.
Nearest Railway Station : Castle Cary. Location : On A361 Shepton Mallet-Glastonbury road. Open : 11am-5pm daily for wine sales, June to September.

SHEPTON MALLET
WOOTTON VINEYARD : North Wootton, Shepton Mallet, Somerset. Tel : Pilton 01749 890359.
Nearest Railway Station : Castle Cary. Location : 3 miles South West of Wells, 3 miles South East of Shepton Mallet. Vineyard Open : Weekdays 10am-1pm then 2pm-5pm, particularly June to September. **Special Attractions:** The vineyard is set in a beautiful and remote valley. The winery is housed in clay tiled farm buildings some 300 years old. No entry charge. Wine and cider wine may be bought at the winery. Also "Somerset Eau De Vie De Vin", the first and only made in England.

SOUTH PETHERTON
EAST LAMBROOK MANOR GARDEN : East Lambrook, Nr. South Petherton, Somerset, TA13 5HL. Tel : 01460 240328. Fax : 01460 242344.
Nearest Railway Station : Yeovil Junction. Open : 1st March to 31st October, Monday to Saturday, 10am-5pm. **Special Attractions:** Grade 1 listed garden and plant nursery.

STREET
CLARKS VILLAGE - FACTORY SHOPPING : Farm Road, Street, Somerset, BA16 0BB. Tel : 01458 840064. Fax : 01458 841132.
Nearest Railway Station : Castle Cary. Location : 15 minutes from junction 23 of the M5, 40 minutes from Bath and 25 minutes from Taunton. Close to Glastonbury. Open : Every day (except Christmas Day), Monday to Saturday 9am-6pm (5.30pm in Winter), Sunday 11am-5pm. **Special Attractions:** Over 40 famous name shops including Laura Ashley, Monsoon, Black & Decker, Clarks, Wrangler, Denby, Dartington and many more - All selling direct to the public at big discounts. Plus beautiful, landscaped setting, working pottery and artist studio, restaurants, take-aways and play areas.

TAUNTON
In 1640, Taunton was one of the few towns that declared and steadfastly maintained allegiance to the Puritans. It was under siege from Royalist forces for a full year (1645-1646) and the defence was led by prominent Parliamentary leader, Admiral Blake. Though much of the town was destroyed, and food was down to the last pig, the town held out until relieved by General Fairfax.

Taunton is the centre for the cider brewing industry, its raw fruit being grown in massive quantities in the fertile Vale of Taunton. Somerset cider has a well proven reputation for being very powerful and should be drunk with extreme caution by those unfamiliar with it. By contrast, it seems to be regarded as "Mother's Milk" by Somerset folk upon whom it appears to have little effect. There is a curious old custom - that of wassailing the apple trees - which takes place at Norton Fitzwarren, on the 16th January each year. Well worth a visit to discover the details of which there is insufficient space to relate here. Taunton itself, has much to offer for the visitor in its Georgian Terraces, a busy market and excellent modern shopping facilities. The rural district offices was formerly a thatched lepers' hospital. The partly 12th Century Castle contains a museum and was the scene of Judge Jeffrey's Bloody Assizes after the 1685 Battle of Sedgemoor.

St Mary's and St James's Churches are each notable, the former for the fact that in the mid 19th Century it was in such a state of dilapidation that it was taken down and rebuilt exactly as before - a remarkable achievement. The latter Church also had to have its tower rebuilt, but inside it has an interesting pulpit decorated on one panel with comely mermaids.

TAUNTON
BEE WORLD & ANIMAL CENTRE : Near Stogumber Station, Stogumber, Taunton, Somerset, TA4 3TR. Tel : 01984 656545.
Nearest Railway Station : Taunton. Location : Off the A358 Taunton to Williton road, signposted with brown tourist signs. 1.5 miles from the A358 next to Stogumber Station - West Somerset Railway. Open : Easter to the end of October, 10am-6pm (dusk if earlier). Last admission 5pm during Summer. **Special Attractions:** Bee Displays - all behind glass. Video showing the extraction of honey and candle making. Rare and minority breed animals, hands-on experience with rabbit cuddles, animal feeding and Shetland Pony rides. Wild flower walk beside the stream, adventure play area with sand pit and swings. Shop selling honey, wax products, souvenirs and gifts. Restaurant.

TAUNTON
BLAZES, THE FIRE MUSEUM : Sandhill Park, Bishops Lydeard, Taunton, Somerset, TA4 3DF. Tel : 01823 433939. Fax : 01823 433964.
Nearest Railway Station : Taunton BR. Location : The entrance to Sandhill Park is 100 yards from the West Somerset Railway Station at Bishops Lydeard. Open : Easter to 15th December, 10am-6pm, closed Mondays outside the high season (Mid July to September). **Special Attractions:** Situated in a magnificent Grade II Listed Mansion, Blazes offers not only fire engines but an entertaining and enjoyable experience. Fire through the ages, its benefits and comforts. Fire in nature, fire in industry and fire in transport from Roman times to the 21st century.

TAUNTON
FYNE COURT : Broomfield, Bridgwater, Somerset, TA5 2EQ. Tel : 01823 451587.
Nearest Railway Station : Taunton. Location : 6 miles North East of Taunton. Open : All year round, 9am-6pm, 7 days per week. **Special Attractions:** Nature Reserve with nature trails, woodland walks, picnic areas, exhibitions, information centre and a shop. Headquarters of the Somerset Wildlife Trust.

TAUNTON
SHEPPY'S CIDER FARM CENTRE (R.J.SHEPPY & SON) : Three Bridges, Bradford-on-Tone, Taunton, Somerset, TA4 1ER. Tel : 01823 461233. Fax : 01823 461712.
Nearest Railway Station : Taunton. Location : On A38 midway between Taunton and Wellington. M5 Motorway turn off Junction 26. Open : Monday to Saturday, 8.30am-6pm. Sundays (Easter to Christmas), 12noon-2pm only. **Special Attractions:** Plenty of room to pull in cars and caravans. Farm and Cider Museum, press room, orchards, etc. Purchase of cider and other goods.

CADE'S WEST COUNTRY CAMPING, TOURING & MOTOR CARAVAN SITE GUIDE 1997

SOMERSET

Video room, farm trails, cider tasting before purchasing. Licensed tea room open in season for teas, coffee, snacks, light lunches and afternoon cream teas. Childrens play area.

TAUNTON
SOMERSET COUNTY MUSEUM : Taunton Castle, Castle Green, Taunton, Somerset. Tel : 01823 320201. Fax : 01823 320229. Nearest Railway Station : Taunton. Location : Alongside bus station in centre of Taunton. Open : Tuesday to Saturday 10am-5pm. **Special Attractions:** Fine collection of antiquities, toys, dolls, military relics, silver, pottery, glass.

TAUNTON
SOMERSET CRICKET MUSEUM : 7 Priory Avenue, Taunton, Somerset, TA1 1XX. Tel : 01823 275893. Nearest Railway Station : Taunton. Location : Within Somerset County Cricket Ground. Open : April to October, Monday to Friday, 10am-4pm. **Special Attractions:** Display of cricket memorabilia, housed in a historic priory barn.

WATCHET
TROPIQUARIA : Washford Cross, Watchet, Somerset. Tel & Fax : 01984 640688. Nearest Railway Station : Washford. Location : On A39 between Williton and Minehead. Open : Easter-end of October, 10am-5pm. Open Winter weekends and school Holidays. Closed December 1st-26th. **Special Attractions:** Exotic indoor tropical jungle with rainforest plants, snakes. spiders, turtles, tree frogs, lizards and free flying birds. Aquarium with freshwater fish and tropical marines. Shadowstring Puppet Theatre during the season. Cafe and gift shop. Picnic areas and mature gardens. Also "Wireless in the West" Museum.

WINCANTON
ROSIES CIDER : Lawrence Hill, Wincanton, Somerset, BA9 8AB. Tel : 01963 32457. Nearest Railway Station : Templecombe. Location : 1 mile South West of Wincanton, 4 miles North of Templecombe on A371. Open : Monday to Saturday, 9am-5.30pm. **Special Attractions:** Located in an Antique Bric-A-Brac shop. You are invited for a FREE taste of Somerset Cider and Apple Juice. We also sell the famous Somerset Royal Cider Brandy, Country Wines, local White Wine, preserves and small souvenirs.

YEOVIL
Yeovil is well known for manufacturing glass and cheese, but the town has a diversified and commercial base. It has continued to develop its traditional glove making industry and has been for some years the home of a major helicopter constructor. It is also an important market centre, holding agriculture markets on Mondays and Fridays. In keeping with the aircraft emphasis at Yeovil, proper, is the huge Fleet Air Arm Base at Yeovilton nearby.

Interesting features of the town are the excavated foundations of the original Roman Villa around which the town grew - the old surviving houses in the town are built in the local distinctive Ham Stone, a grey/gold colour in its unweathered state. Newton Sumarville, a very lovely old house built in 1612, stands in a park through which the River Yeo flows. Hendford Manor Hall houses the Borough Museum.

The Parish Church of St John the Baptist built in the late 14th Century, is one of the rare churches to have been built consistently in this one style - the perpendicular, and is extremely rare in the architect's use of window space. It is constructed in Ham Stone, and the windows light the interior so well and are so distinctive in their proportions that the church has earned the sobriquet of "The Lantern of the West".

YEOVIL
HAYNES MOTOR MUSEUM : Sparkford, Nr. Yeovil, Somerset, BA22 7LH. Tel : 01963 440804. Nearest Railway Station : Castle Cary. Location : 6 miles north of Yeovil on the A359. Open : All Year, 7 days a week. Summer 9.30am-5.30pm, Winter 10am-4pm.

HAYNES MOTOR MUSEUM

THE UK'S MOST EXTENSIVE COLLECTION OF MOTOR VEHICLES FROM AROUND THE WORLD

- FROM THE CLASSIC TO THE EXOTIC, OVER 250 FASCINATING CARS
- RESTORATION WORKSHOP
- FREE VIDEO CINEMA
- PIT STOP CAFE AND PICNIC AREA
- BOOKSHOP AND GIFT SHOP
- CHILDRENS THEMED PLAY AREA
- NEW EXHIBITION HALL FOR 1997

Keeping the spirit of motoring alive!

Open 9.30 to 5.30 (10.00 to 4.00 Winter) 7 days a week. Situated just off the A303 at Sparkford, Somerset. Tel (01963) 440804. The Haynes Motor Museum is a charitable Trust No 292048

---

110   *CADE'S WEST CUONTRY CAMPING, TOURING & MOTOR CARAVAN SITE GUIDE 1997*

SOMERSET-WILTSHIRE

YEOVILTON
FLEET AIR ARM MUSEUM : Royal Naval Air Station, Yeovilton, Ilchester, Somerset, BA22 8HT. Tel : 01935 840565. Fax : 01935 840181.
Nearest Railway Station : Yeovil. Location : Just off the A303/A37 on the B3151 near Ilchester. Open : Daily (except 24th to 26th December), 10am-5.30pm (4.30pm in Winter). **Special Attractions:** One of the World's finest aviation museums with over 40 historic aircraft including Concorde and hundreds of models, uniforms, documents and other memorabilia. Realistic displays and special effects bring to life such exhibitions as WWI, WWII, Wrens, Korea and Harrier. A new exhibition is the spectacular Aircraft Carrier Exhibition, recreating life aboard ship including the flight deck and experience chamber. Simulator, adventure playground, two licensed restaurants, mother and baby room, gift shop, access and facilities for the disabled, free parking - caravans welcome.

WILTSHIRE

CALNE
Blackland Lakes Holiday & Leisure Centre, Stockley Lane, Calne, Wiltshire, SN11 0NQ.
Tel: 813672 Std: 01249
Fax: **813672** Std: **01249**
Nearest Town/Resort Calne
Directions Signposted east of Calne from the A4.
Acreage 17 **Open** All Year
Access Good   **Site** Mostly Level
Sites Available ▲ ⊞ ⊟ **Total** 180
Low Season Band C
High Season Band C
Facilities ∆ ∮ ⌂ ♨ ୮ ⊙ ⊣ ⬚ ⬚ ♥
🆂 ⊙ 🅿 ⊞ ⩓ ⌂ ⩘ 🅿
Nearby Facilities ୮ ⩘ U ℛ
≠ Chippenham
Rural, natural, scenic, sheltered paddocks. 3 small lakes for super coarse fishing. 20 x 10m covered swimming pool. Catering and licensed bar for groups. 120 electric hookups (increased supply for 1997 - mostly 10 amp). 15 Super Pitches.

CHIPPENHAM
Piccadilly Caravan Site, Folly Lane West, Lacock, Chippenham, Wiltshire, SN15 2LP.
Tel: Lacock 730260 Std: 01249
Nearest Town/Resort Chippenham/Melksham.
Directions Turn right off A350 Chippenham/Melksham Road,5 miles south of Chippenham, close to Lacock. Signposted to Gastard (with caravan symbol), site is after the Nurseries.
Acreage 2½ **Open** April to October
Access Good   **Site** Level
Sites Available ⊞ ⊟ **Total** 40
Low Season Band B
High Season Band B
Facilities ∮ ⌂ ♨ ୮ ⊙ ⊣ ⬚ ⬚ ♥
⩓ ⊙ ⬚ ⩘ 🅿
Nearby Facilities ୮ ⩘ U
≠ Chippenham.
Close National Trust village of Lacock. Ideal touring centre.

DEVIZES
Bell Caravan and Camping Site, Andover Road, Lydeway, Devizes, Wiltshire, SN10 3PS.
Tel: 840230 Std: 01380
Nearest Town/Resort Devizes.
Directions 3 miles south east of Devizes on Andover A342 road.
Acreage 3 **Open** April to 1 October
Access Good   **Site** Level
Sites Available ▲ ⊞ ⊟ **Total** 30
Low Season Band B
High Season Band B
Facilities ∮ ⌂ ♨ ୮ ⊙ ⊣ ⬚ ⬚ ♥
🆂 ⊙ 🅿 ⊞ ⩓ ⌂ ⩘ 🅿
Nearby Facilities
≠ Pewsey.
Ideal touring, Stonehenge, Avebury and Bath. Off License.

DEVIZES
Lakeside, Rowde, Devizes, Wiltshire.
Tel: 722767 Std: 01380
Nearest Town/Resort Devizes.
Directions 1 mile from Devizes on A342 towards Chippenham.
Acreage 6¼ **Open** April to October
Access Good   **Site** Level
Sites Available ▲ ⊞ ⊟ **Total** 55
Facilities ∆ ∮ ⌂ ♨ ୮ ⊙ ⊣ ⬚ ♥
⩓ ⊞ ⊙ 🅿
Nearby Facilities ୮ ⩘ U ℛ
≠ Chippenham.
Pub within 500yds, restaurant and bar food. Well stocked, 2 acre fishing lake on site.

MALMESBURY
Burton Hill Caravan and Camping Park, Arches Lane, Burton Hill, Malmesbury, Wiltshire.
Tel: 822585/822367 Std: 01666
Fax: **822585** Std: **01666**
Nearest Town/Resort Malmesbury.
Directions Turn off the A429 Chippenham road into Arches Lane, opposite Malmesbury Hospital. ½ mile south of Malmesbury.
Acreage 1½ **Open** April to November
Access Good   **Site** Level
Sites Available ▲ ⊞ ⊟ **Total** 30
Low Season Band B
High Season Band B
Facilities ∮ ⌂ ♨ ୮ ⊙ ⊣ ⬚ ♥
Nearby Facilities ୮ ⩘
≠ Malmesham.
A quiet site on the edge of Cotswolds. Dogs welcome. Tourist Board Grading 3 Ticks.

MARLBOROUGH
Hill-View Caravan Park, Oare, Marlborough, Wiltshire.
Tel: 563151 Std: 01672
Nearest Town/Resort Marlborough.
Directions On A345, 6 miles south of Marlborough on Pewsey/Amesbury road.
Open Easter to September
Access Good   **Site** Level
Sites Available ▲ ⊞ ⊟ **Total** 10
Facilities ∮ ⌂ ♨ ୮ ⊙ ♥ 🅿
Nearby Facilities U
≠ Pewsey.
Place of historic interest and scenic views. SAE for enquiries. Graded 4 Ticks. Booking is advisable.

MARSTON MEYSEY
Second Chance Caravan Park, Marston Meysey, Wiltshire, SN6 6SN.
Tel: 810675 Std: 01285
Nearest Town/Resort Cricklade.
Directions Between Swindon and Cirencester on the A419. Turn off the Fairford signpost and caravan park signs. Proceed approx. 3 miles then turn left at the Castle Eaton signpost. We are on the left.
Acreage 2 **Open** March to November
Access Good   **Site** Level

Sites Available ▲ ⊞ ⊟ **Total** 26
Low Season Band B
High Season Band B
Facilities ⊟ ∮ ⌂ ♨ ୮ ⊙ ⊣ ⬚ ♥ 🅿
Nearby Facilities ୮ ⊥ ⩘ ⩘
≠ Swindon
Riverside location, private fishing and access for your own canoe, to explore upper reaches of Thames. Ideal base for touring the Cotswolds. A.A. 2 Pennants.

NETHERHAMPTON
Coombe Caravan Park, Coombe Nurseries, Race Plain, Netherhampton, Salisbury, Wilts, SP2 8PN.
Tel: 328451 Std: 01722
Nearest Town/Resort Salisbury
Directions Take A36-A30 Salisbury - Wilton road, turn off at traffic lights onto A3094 Netherhampton - Stratford Tony road, cross on bend following Stratford Tony road, 2nd left behind racecourse, site on right, signposted.
Acreage 3 **Open** All Year
Access Good   **Site** Level
Sites Available ▲ ⊞ ⊟ **Total** 48
Low Season Band B
High Season Band B
Facilities ∮ ⌂ ♨ ୮ ⊙ ⊣ ⬚ ♥
🆂 ⊙ ⬚ 🅿
Nearby Facilities ୮ U ℛ
≠ Salisbury
Adjacent to racecourse (flat racing), ideal touring, lovely views.

ORCHESTON
Stonehenge Touring Park, Orcheston, Near Shrewton, Wiltshire.
Tel: 620304 Std: 01980
Fax: **621121** Std: **01980**
Nearest Town/Resort Salisbury
Directions On A360 11 miles Salisbury, 11 miles Devizes.
Acreage 2 **Open** All Year
Access Good   **Site** Level
Sites Available ▲ ⊞ ⊟ **Total** 30
Low Season Band B
High Season Band C
Facilities ∮ ⌂ ♨ ୮ ⊙ ⊣ ⬚ ♥
🆂 ⊙ 🅿 ⩓ ⊞ 🅿
Nearby Facilities ୮ ⩘ U
≠ Salisbury.
Stonehenge 5 miles, Salisbury plain, easy reach Bath and the New Forest. AA 3 Pennants and BGHP 4 ticks. Take Away Food.

TILSHEAD
Brades Acre, Tilshead, Salisbury, Wiltshire. SP3 4RX
Tel: Shrewton 620402 Std: 01980
Nearest Town/Resort Salisbury/Devizes.
Directions A360, 10 miles to Devizes, 13 miles to Salisbury.
Acreage 1½ **Open** All Year
Access Good   **Site** Level
Sites Available ▲ ⊞ ⊟ **Total** 35
Low Season Band B
High Season Band C

SOMERSET

Facilities ⬛ ƒ ⬛ ♨ ┌ ⊙ ⌐ ◯ ☰
⌶ ◯ ⬛ ✕ ⎕
Nearby Facilities ┌ ✔ ∪ ♪
⌮ Salisbury.
Touring for Stonehenge, Salisbury Cathedral, Wilton and Longleat Houses. Avebury, Orcheston riding.

WARMINSTER
Longleat Caravan Club Site, Warminster, Wiltshire, BA12 7NL.
Tel: 844663 Std: 01985
Nearest Town/Resort Warminster.
Directions From Warminster and the A36, follow signs for Longleat House (NOT Safari Park) then Caravan Club Pennant signs within the Estate.
Acreage 14 **Open** Easter to End October
Access Good   **Site** Level
Sites Available ⬛ ⊟ **Total** 150
Low Season Band B
High Season Band C
Facilities ƒ ⚿ ⬛ ♨ ┌ ⊙ ⌐ ☰
⚲ ⎗ ◯ ♨ ⎕ ⎕

PLACES OF INTEREST

Nearby Facilities ┌ ✔ ⊥ ∪
⌮ Warminster.
Within the Longleat Estate. Near the National Trust Stourhead Gardens.

WESTBURY
Woodland Park, Brokerswood, Nr. Westbury, Wiltshire, BA13 4EH.
Tel: 822238 Std: 01373
Fax: **858474** Std: **01373**
Nearest Town/Resort Westbury/Trowbridge.
Directions 4 miles Westbury, 5 miles Trowbridge, 5 miles Frome, left off A361 Southwick onto unclassified 1¼ miles on left, turn at Standerwick on A36.
Acreage 1 **Open** All Year
Access Good   **Site** Level
Sites Available ⬛ ⊟ **Total** 30
Facilities ƒ ⬛ ♨ ┌ ⊙ ⌐ ☰
⚲ ⬛ ✕ ⎕ ⎕
Nearby Facilities ┌ ✔ ∪
⌮ Westbury.
Site adjoins an 80 acre area of forest open to the public together with a museum, lake, Narrow Gauge Railway, etc.

WHITEPARISH
Hillcrest Campsite, Southampton Road, Whiteparish, Nr Salisbury, Wilts, SP5 2QW.
Tel: 884471 Std: 01794
Nearest Town/Resort Salisbury
Directions 8 miles from Salisbury on A36. Travelling towards Southampton, one mile from A27 junction at Brickworth Garage on left.
Acreage 3 **Open** All Year
Access Good   **Site** Lev/slop
Sites Available ⚐ ⬛ ⊟ **Total** 35
Low Season Band C
High Season Band C
Facilities ⬛ ƒ ⬛ ♨ ┌ ⊙ ⌐ ◯ ☰
⌶ ◯ ⬛ ⎕
Nearby Facilities ┌ ✔ ∪
⌮ Salisbury
Central to Salisbury, Winchester, New Forest. Ideal for overnight stop before channel crossing.

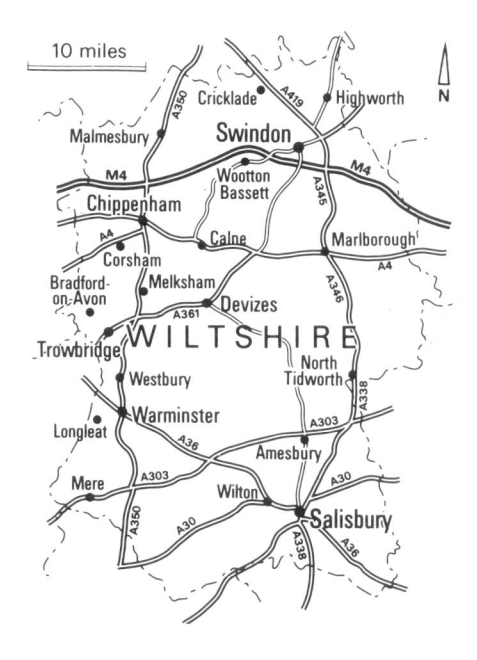

WILTSHIRE

AMESBURY
CHOLDERTON RARE BREEDS FARM PARK : Amesbury Road, Cholderton, Salisbury, Wiltshire. Tel : 01980 629438. Nearest Railway Station : Grateley. Location : Signed from junction A303/A338. 8 miles west of Andover, 3 miles east of Stonehenge. Open : End of March to the end of October, daily, 10am-6pm. **Special Attractions:** Learn about, touch and feed endangered breeds of farm animals. In a picturesque setting. Visit Rabbit World, probably the largest collection of breeds in England, meet the Shire horse, sit with the three little piglets and mix with the friendly pygmy goats. Undercover sheep and poultry unit. See the unique pig races at weekends and school holidays. Gardens, orchards, superb views, picnic areas, water gardens, nature trail, play areas, restaurant and shop.

BRADFORD-ON-AVON
IFORD MANOR GARDENS : Iford Manor, Bradford-on-Avon, Wiltshire, BA15 2BA. Tel : 01225 863146. Fax : 01225 862364. Nearest Railway Station : Freshford Halt. Location : 7 miles south of Bath off the A36, 1 mile from Bradford-on-Avon. Open : 2pm-5pm. April to Easter, Sunday and Monday. May to September, daily except Monday and Friday. October, Sunday only. **Special Attractions:** An enchanted garden in the Italian style, with colonnades and terraces, cloister and casita, statues and ponds. It was once the home of Harold Peto, the architect and landscape gardener, and designed between 1898 and 1933.

CALNE
ATWELL-WILSON MOTOR MUSEUM : Downside Stockley Lane, Calne, Wiltshire, SN11 0NF. Tel : 01249 813119. Nearest Railway Station : Chippenham. Location : Just off the A4 out of Calne towards Marlborough. Open : 1st April-31st October, Monday to Thursday 10am-5pm, Sundays 11am-5pm. 1st November-31st March, Monday to Thursday, 10am-4pm, Sundays 11am-4pm. **Special Attractions:** The most surprising things turn up in unexpected places. There is something for every motor enthusiast here at the Atwell-Wilson Motor Museum. Compare the mighty Rolls Royce and Cadillacs to the diminuture but elegant little Singer, and the Jaguar Daimlers to one of the best model "T" Fords in the West - plus many more. Antique childrens play equipment, fully restored.

WILTSHIRE

CALNE
BOWOOD HOUSE & GARDENS : Calne, Wiltshire, SN11 0LZ. Tel : 01249 812102. Fax : 01249 821757.
Nearest Railway Station : Chippenham. Location : Off the A4, midway between Calne and Chippenham in Derry Hill Village. Caravan site (by prior booking only) on the A342 midway between Derry Hill and Sandy Lane villages. Open : 22nd March to 2nd November. **Special Attractions:** Robert Adam House, paintings, watercolours and costumes. Huge adventure playground for 12 years old and under. Garden centre, licensed restaurant and Garden Tea Rooms.

CHIPPENHAM
A pleasant River Avon town of great age, built mostly of natural stone. Fine old houses can be seen on St Mary's Street and most of the old Town Hall dates from the 15th Century.

The 15th Century Church houses an old chest and displays a striking modern window. Ivy House dates from 1730 and Sheldon's Manor from the 14th to 16th Century.

Chippenham is now a developing industrial town, particularly important for food processing and supplying products to the railway industry.

CHIPPENHAM
SHELDON MANOR : Chippenham, Wiltshire, SN14 0RG. Tel : 01249 653120. Fax : 01249 461097.
Nearest Railway Station : Chippenham. Location : 1.5 miles west of Chippenham, signposted from the A350 (Chippenham By-Pass); A420; A4 Eastbound. M4 junction 17 4 miles. Open : Easter Day (30th March) to 5th October. Sundays to Thursdays and Bank Holidays 12.30pm-6pm. House opens at 2pm. **Special Attractions:** Award winning plantagenet Manor House - "Top of the Top Twenty" - with many treasures inside and out. Beautiful gardens with a profusion of old fashioned roses. "The Great House" in "Persuasion" where Jane Austen's characters dined and danced. Distinguished catering, all home made.

CHIPPENHAM
YELDE HALL MUSEUM : The Market Place, Chippenham, Wiltshire, SN15 3BT. Tel : 01249 653145. Fax : 01249 443145.
Nearest Railway Station : Chippenham. Location : Station Hill, Chippenham. Open : March to October, 10am-12pm and 2pm-4.30pm. **Special Attractions:** Museum containing mostly social History items from Chippenham and its immediate surroundings. These include items depicting Chippenhams agricultural and industrial History and a large collection of photographs which show the changes which have occurred in the development of the town.

DEVIZES
BROADLEAS GARDENS, CHARITABLE TRUST LTD. : Broadleas, Devizes, Wilts. Tel : 01380 722035.
Location : 1 mile south of centre of Devizes on the A360 Salisbury road. Open : Sunday, Wednesday and Thursday, 2pm-6pm, April to October. **Special Attractions:** Over 8 acres of beautiful garden with unusual trees and shrubs. Rhododendrums, Magnolias and Perennials in profusion. Own plants propagated for sale.

DEVIZES
DEVIZES MUSEUM : 41 Long Street, Devizes, Wiltshire, SN10 1NS. Tel : 01380 727369. Fax : 01380 722150.
Open : All year, Monday to Saturday, 10am-5pm. Admission charge, concessions. FREE day Monday. Telephone for party bookings. **Special Attractions:** Outstanding archaeology collection including Bronze Age Gallery and Stonehenge barrow finds. Also local and recent history, art gallery and Natural History displays.

MALMESBURY
A pleasant hill top town above the River Avon, Malmesbury was the burial ground 1,000 tears ago where the first King of England Athelston was buried. Here also, is the remains of the great Norman Malmesbury Abbey, the nave of which was converted to the current church. The Abbey is rich in architectural detail and sculptures worth seeing, and has four tremendous columns of an illuminated Bible created by Malmesbury Monks circa 1400, as well as other unusual treasures.

The brilliant Saxon Scholar, Adhelm was trained at Malmesbury and himself founded a school here and also the church at Bradford on Avon.

The medieval historian, William of Malmesbury, was also a distinguished Scholar, who among other works wrote biographies of the Saints, Anselm, Bunston and Wulfston. His style was anecdotal and his works are enlivened with many strange and humorous stories.

SALISBURY
Salisbury, Wiltshire's famous city is best renowned for its Cathedral - Salisbury Cathedral was designed by Bishop Richard Poore and his Canon, Elias de Pereham. It was commenced in 1220 and consecrated in 1258. The Spire designed by Richard Farley is 404 feet high, has two walls, two feet thick at the base and was constructed so that the scaffolding was left intact inside to provide added strength. The Spire weighs 6400 tons and was added to the building circa 1300.

The Cathedral is a glorious building, as are the group of harmonizing buildings around it, for example, the Chapter House, Bishop's Place and the Deanery. The Cathedral's Library is recognized as one of the finest and has over 8,000 books, including a copy of the Magna Carta and over 100 books dating from the 16th Century.

There are many other fine buildings in Salisbury including the Hall of the Shoemakers Guild, the Museum, George Inn, St Thomas's Church and Hornham Mill.

A famous view across the Avon to the Cathedral can be enjoyed from the bridge.

SALISBURY
FARMER GILES FARMSTEAD : Teffont, Salisbury, Wiltshire, SP3 5QY. Tel : 01722 716338.
Nearest Railway Station : Salisbury. Location : Just off the A303 London to Exeter road at Teffont. 11 miles west of Salisbury and 12 miles south west of Stonehenge. Open : 22nd March to 2nd November, 10.30am-6pm daily and every weekend throughout the Winter. **Special Attractions:** A fun filled countryside adventure based on the unique magic of a working dairy farm. Beech Belt Nature Trail, rare breeds, ponies, donkeys and goats. Bottle feed lambs or hand milk a friendly cow. Watch the Friesian herd being milked. Relax by the ponds, windpump and waterfall near the vineyard. Eat in our spacious licensed restaurant and browse through the exhibitions and gift shop. Please enquire about our many special events which include activities as diverse as sheep shearing and model aircraft flying.

SALISBURY
SALISBURY CATHEDRAL : 6 The Close, Salisbury, Wiltshire, SP1 2EF. Tel : 01722 328726. Fax : 01722 323769.
Nearest Railway Station : Salisbury. Location : Near the A30, A303 and M3. Open : Daily 8am-6.30pm. Mid-May to mid-September, 8am-8.15pm). **Special Attractions:** Built between 1220 and 1258, Salisbury Cathedral is a superb example of medieval architecture, and its spire at 404 feet (123 metres) is the tallest in England. An original Magna Carta is regularly on view. Regular tours of the Cathedral, Tower and West Front. Free 'trails' for children. For enquiries please telephone the Visitors' Office on the above number.

SALISBURY
SALISBURY & SOUTH WILTSHIRE MUSEUM : The King's House, 65 The Close, Salisbury, Wiltshire, SP1 2EN. Tel : 01722 332151. Fax : 01722 325611.
Nearest Railway Station : Salisbury. Location : In Salisbury Cathedral Close. Open : All year, Monday to Saturday, 10am-5pm. Sundays in July and August and Salisbury Festival 2pm-5pm. **Special Attractions:** Splendid galleries in a Grade I listed building -

CADE'S WEST COUNTRY CAMPING, TOURING & MOTOR CARAVAN SITE GUIDE 1997   113

WILTSHIRE

Stonehenge, Early Man, Salisbury and The Giant, Pitt Rivers Collection, pre-N.H.S. Surgery, ceramics, pictures, Wedgwood Room, costume, lace and embroidery. Coffee Shop. Gift shop. Winner of six major awards including Special Judges Award Museum of the Year and England for Excellence. Major 1997 exhibition - "Teddy Bears and Soft Toys", 21st June to 27th September. Entrance tickets give unlimited visits throughout the calendar year.

SALISBURY
WILTON HOUSE : Wilton, Salisbury, Wiltshire, SP2 0BJ. Tel : 01722 743115. Fax : 01722 744447.
Nearest Railway Station : Salisbury. Open : 24th March to 2nd November 1997, 7 days a week, 11am-6pm. Last admission 5pm. **Special Attractions:** Home of the Earls of Pembroke for 450 years. 17th Century Double and Single Cube Rooms designed by Inigo Jones. Fabulous private art collection. Introductory film narrated by Anna Massey, plus Tudor Kitchen, Victorian Laundry, Water Garden, landscaped parkland and adventure playground. Restaurant. Woodland walk. Now home to "The Wareham Bears" - some 200 miniature, dressed teddies with their own house and stables.

SWINDON
Wiltshire's biggest and fastest growing town, its growth has been phenomenal considering that only 100 years ago it was a village of only 500 families. Its first stimulus was the decision of Daniel Gooch, Superintendent of the Great Western Railway to build the railway works that now covers 323 acres. Though the works still thrive, Swindon has attributed other industry and thousands of families from London, as part of its own development plan which formed its second great stimulus. It has a fine Railway Museum, as well as interesting conventional museums. It has an excellent reservoir called Coate Water, 72 acres in extent plus a small lake nearby which is a bird sanctuary. Coate Farm, the birth place of Richard Jeffries in 1845, now serves as a museum.

SWINDON
THE GREAT WESTERN RAILWAY MUSEUM : 34 Faringdon Road, Swindon, Wiltshire, SN1 5BJ. Tel : 01793 493189. Fax : 01793 484073.
Nearest Railway Station : Swindon. Open : Monday to Saturday 10am-5pm, Sunday 2pm-5pm. Last admission 4.30pm. **Special** Attractions: Set in a converted Wesleyan Chapel in the heart of Brunel's railway village, the GWR Museum celebrates "Gods Wonderful Railway" through its rich collection of exhibits and distinctive locomotives including "North Star" and "King George V". Also features life and works of Brunel and the growth of Swindon works.

SWINDON
LYDIARD PARK : The House, Lydiard Park, Lydiard Tregoze, Swindon, Wilts, SN5 9PA. Tel : 01793 770401.
Nearest Railway Station : Swindon. Location : 4 miles west of Swindon centre, just off junction 16 on M4. Open : Monday to Saturday, 10am-1pm then 2pm-5.30pm. Sunday, 2pm-5.30pm. Early closing, November to February inclusive, 4pm. **Special Attractions:** Beautiful Georgian house set in country parkland. State Rooms contain elegant plaster work, fine furnishings and portraits. Fascinating painted window and artistic works of Lady Diana Spencer - Lady of the Manor in the 18th Century. Adjacent church of St Marys contains superb monuments. Cafe and visitors centre in the grounds.

SWINDON
RAILWAY VILLAGE MUSEUM : 34 Faringdon Road, Swindon, Wiltshire, SN1 5BJ. Tel : 01793 493189. Fax : 01793 484073.
Nearest Railway Station : Swindon. Open : Monday to Saturday 10am-5pm, Sunday 2pm-5pm. Last admission 4.30pm. Closed 1pm-2pm. **Special Attractions:** Enhance the Great Western Experience by visiting the restored railway cottage in Brunel's railway village. One of the last cottages to have been built in the 1860's, this 'Foremans House' has many original fittings including gas lighting and period furniture.

WESTBURY
THE WOODLAND PARK : Brokerswood, Westbury, Wiltshire, BA13 4EH. Tel : 01373 822238. Fax : 01373 858474.
Nearest Railway Station : Westbury. Location : Off the A36 Bath to Salisbury road, turn at Standerwick, 1.5 miles Southwick. Open : All Year. **Special Attractions:** Camping and caravan sites attached to an 80 acre country park with a museum, lake, two adventure playgrounds, indoor soft play, narrow gauge railway, picnic area and BBQ sites.

Our other titles include:-

- CADE'S CAMPING, TOURING & MOTORCARAVAN SITE GUIDE 1997 *(Nationwide)*

- CADE'S CAMPING, TOURING & MOTOR CARAVAN SITE GUIDE TO FRANCE

- CADE'S SELF CATERING CARAVAN & CHALET PARKS

- Watch out for other titles during 1997

MONEY OFF VOUCHERS

CADE'S — FIFTY PENCE	CADE'S — FIFTY PENCE
WEST COUNTRY CARAVAN & CAMPING SITE GUIDE 1997 PRESENT THIS VOUCHER TO THE SITE OPERATOR WHEN PAYING TO RECEIVE A FIFTY PENCE DISCOUNT PER VOUCHER PER NIGHT. SEE CONDITIONS OVERLEAF. VALID UNTIL 31-12-97	**WEST COUNTRY CARAVAN & CAMPING SITE GUIDE 1997** PRESENT THIS VOUCHER TO THE SITE OPERATOR WHEN PAYING TO RECEIVE A FIFTY PENCE DISCOUNT PER VOUCHER PER NIGHT. SEE CONDITIONS OVERLEAF. VALID UNTIL 31-12-97
CADE'S — FIFTY PENCE	CADE'S — FIFTY PENCE
WEST COUNTRY CARAVAN & CAMPING SITE GUIDE 1997 PRESENT THIS VOUCHER TO THE SITE OPERATOR WHEN PAYING TO RECEIVE A FIFTY PENCE DISCOUNT PER VOUCHER PER NIGHT. SEE CONDITIONS OVERLEAF. VALID UNTIL 31-12-97	**WEST COUNTRY CARAVAN & CAMPING SITE GUIDE 1997** PRESENT THIS VOUCHER TO THE SITE OPERATOR WHEN PAYING TO RECEIVE A FIFTY PENCE DISCOUNT PER VOUCHER PER NIGHT. SEE CONDITIONS OVERLEAF. VALID UNTIL 31-12-97
CADE'S — FIFTY PENCE	CADE'S — FIFTY PENCE
WEST COUNTRY CARAVAN & CAMPING SITE GUIDE 1997 PRESENT THIS VOUCHER TO THE SITE OPERATOR WHEN PAYING TO RECEIVE A FIFTY PENCE DISCOUNT PER VOUCHER PER NIGHT. SEE CONDITIONS OVERLEAF. VALID UNTIL 31-12-97	**WEST COUNTRY CARAVAN & CAMPING SITE GUIDE 1997** PRESENT THIS VOUCHER TO THE SITE OPERATOR WHEN PAYING TO RECEIVE A FIFTY PENCE DISCOUNT PER VOUCHER PER NIGHT. SEE CONDITIONS OVERLEAF. VALID UNTIL 31-12-97
CADE'S — FIFTY PENCE	CADE'S — FIFTY PENCE
WEST COUNTRY CARAVAN & CAMPING SITE GUIDE 1997 PRESENT THIS VOUCHER TO THE SITE OPERATOR WHEN PAYING TO RECEIVE A FIFTY PENCE DISCOUNT PER VOUCHER PER NIGHT. SEE CONDITIONS OVERLEAF. VALID UNTIL 31-12-97	**WEST COUNTRY CARAVAN & CAMPING SITE GUIDE 1997** PRESENT THIS VOUCHER TO THE SITE OPERATOR WHEN PAYING TO RECEIVE A FIFTY PENCE DISCOUNT PER VOUCHER PER NIGHT. SEE CONDITIONS OVERLEAF. VALID UNTIL 31-12-97
CADE'S — FIFTY PENCE	CADE'S — FIFTY PENCE
WEST COUNTRY CARAVAN & CAMPING SITE GUIDE 1997 PRESENT THIS VOUCHER TO THE SITE OPERATOR WHEN PAYING TO RECEIVE A FIFTY PENCE DISCOUNT PER VOUCHER PER NIGHT. SEE CONDITIONS OVERLEAF. VALID UNTIL 31-12-97	**WEST COUNTRY CARAVAN & CAMPING SITE GUIDE 1997** PRESENT THIS VOUCHER TO THE SITE OPERATOR WHEN PAYING TO RECEIVE A FIFTY PENCE DISCOUNT PER VOUCHER PER NIGHT. SEE CONDITIONS OVERLEAF. VALID UNTIL 31-12-97

MONEY OFF VOUCHERS

CONDITIONS OF USE
Vouchers will only redeemed by those sites featuring a £ symbol in their county entry. Presentation of this voucher to the Site Operator at the time of paying your balance will entitle you to a fifty pence discount per voucher, per night (only one voucher per night). Vouchers may be used in multiples i.e. five vouchers presented for a five night stay will entitle you to a discount of £2.50.

A CADE'S WEST COUNTRY CARAVAN & CAMPING SITE GUIDE 1997 EDITION must be presented at the time of payment. Vouchers are valid for accommodation only. Vouchers may not be exchanged for cash. Valid until 31-12-97.

CONDITIONS OF USE
Vouchers will only redeemed by those sites featuring a £ symbol in their county entry. Presentation of this voucher to the Site Operator at the time of paying your balance will entitle you to a fifty pence discount per voucher, per night (only one voucher per night). Vouchers may be used in multiples i.e. five vouchers presented for a five night stay will entitle you to a discount of £2.50.

A CADE'S WEST COUNTRY CARAVAN & CAMPING SITE GUIDE 1997 EDITION must be presented at the time of payment. Vouchers are valid for accommodation only. Vouchers may not be exchanged for cash. Valid until 31-12-97.

CONDITIONS OF USE
Vouchers will only redeemed by those sites featuring a £ symbol in their county entry. Presentation of this voucher to the Site Operator at the time of paying your balance will entitle you to a fifty pence discount per voucher, per night (only one voucher per night). Vouchers may be used in multiples i.e. five vouchers presented for a five night stay will entitle you to a discount of £2.50.

A CADE'S WEST COUNTRY CARAVAN & CAMPING SITE GUIDE 1997 EDITION must be presented at the time of payment. Vouchers are valid for accommodation only. Vouchers may not be exchanged for cash. Valid until 31-12-97.

CONDITIONS OF USE
Vouchers will only redeemed by those sites featuring a £ symbol in their county entry. Presentation of this voucher to the Site Operator at the time of paying your balance will entitle you to a fifty pence discount per voucher, per night (only one voucher per night). Vouchers may be used in multiples i.e. five vouchers presented for a five night stay will entitle you to a discount of £2.50.

A CADE'S WEST COUNTRY CARAVAN & CAMPING SITE GUIDE 1997 EDITION must be presented at the time of payment. Vouchers are valid for accommodation only. Vouchers may not be exchanged for cash. Valid until 31-12-97.

CONDITIONS OF USE
Vouchers will only redeemed by those sites featuring a £ symbol in their county entry. Presentation of this voucher to the Site Operator at the time of paying your balance will entitle you to a fifty pence discount per voucher, per night (only one voucher per night). Vouchers may be used in multiples i.e. five vouchers presented for a five night stay will entitle you to a discount of £2.50.

A CADE'S WEST COUNTRY CARAVAN & CAMPING SITE GUIDE 1997 EDITION must be presented at the time of payment. Vouchers are valid for accommodation only. Vouchers may not be exchanged for cash. Valid until 31-12-97.

CONDITIONS OF USE
Vouchers will only redeemed by those sites featuring a £ symbol in their county entry. Presentation of this voucher to the Site Operator at the time of paying your balance will entitle you to a fifty pence discount per voucher, per night (only one voucher per night). Vouchers may be used in multiples i.e. five vouchers presented for a five night stay will entitle you to a discount of £2.50.

A CADE'S WEST COUNTRY CARAVAN & CAMPING SITE GUIDE 1997 EDITION must be presented at the time of payment. Vouchers are valid for accommodation only. Vouchers may not be exchanged for cash. Valid until 31-12-97.

CONDITIONS OF USE
Vouchers will only redeemed by those sites featuring a £ symbol in their county entry. Presentation of this voucher to the Site Operator at the time of paying your balance will entitle you to a fifty pence discount per voucher, per night (only one voucher per night). Vouchers may be used in multiples i.e. five vouchers presented for a five night stay will entitle you to a discount of £2.50.

A CADE'S WEST COUNTRY CARAVAN & CAMPING SITE GUIDE 1997 EDITION must be presented at the time of payment. Vouchers are valid for accommodation only. Vouchers may not be exchanged for cash. Valid until 31-12-97.

CONDITIONS OF USE
Vouchers will only redeemed by those sites featuring a £ symbol in their county entry. Presentation of this voucher to the Site Operator at the time of paying your balance will entitle you to a fifty pence discount per voucher, per night (only one voucher per night). Vouchers may be used in multiples i.e. five vouchers presented for a five night stay will entitle you to a discount of £2.50.

A CADE'S WEST COUNTRY CARAVAN & CAMPING SITE GUIDE 1997 EDITION must be presented at the time of payment. Vouchers are valid for accommodation only. Vouchers may not be exchanged for cash. Valid until 31-12-97.

CONDITIONS OF USE
Vouchers will only redeemed by those sites featuring a £ symbol in their county entry. Presentation of this voucher to the Site Operator at the time of paying your balance will entitle you to a fifty pence discount per voucher, per night (only one voucher per night). Vouchers may be used in multiples i.e. five vouchers presented for a five night stay will entitle you to a discount of £2.50.

A CADE'S WEST COUNTRY CARAVAN & CAMPING SITE GUIDE 1997 EDITION must be presented at the time of payment. Vouchers are valid for accommodation only. Vouchers may not be exchanged for cash. Valid until 31-12-97.

CONDITIONS OF USE
Vouchers will only redeemed by those sites featuring a £ symbol in their county entry. Presentation of this voucher to the Site Operator at the time of paying your balance will entitle you to a fifty pence discount per voucher, per night (only one voucher per night). Vouchers may be used in multiples i.e. five vouchers presented for a five night stay will entitle you to a discount of £2.50.

A CADE'S WEST COUNTRY CARAVAN & CAMPING SITE GUIDE 1997 EDITION must be presented at the time of payment. Vouchers are valid for accommodation only. Vouchers may not be exchanged for cash. Valid until 31-12-97.

MONEY OFF VOUCHERS

CADE'S — FIFTY PENCE	CADE'S — FIFTY PENCE
WEST COUNTRY CARAVAN & CAMPING SITE GUIDE 1997 PRESENT THIS VOUCHER TO THE SITE OPERATOR WHEN PAYING TO RECEIVE A FIFTY PENCE DISCOUNT PER VOUCHER PER NIGHT. SEE CONDITIONS OVERLEAF. VALID UNTIL 31-12-97	**WEST COUNTRY CARAVAN & CAMPING SITE GUIDE 1997** PRESENT THIS VOUCHER TO THE SITE OPERATOR WHEN PAYING TO RECEIVE A FIFTY PENCE DISCOUNT PER VOUCHER PER NIGHT. SEE CONDITIONS OVERLEAF. VALID UNTIL 31-12-97
WEST COUNTRY CARAVAN & CAMPING SITE GUIDE 1997 PRESENT THIS VOUCHER TO THE SITE OPERATOR WHEN PAYING TO RECEIVE A FIFTY PENCE DISCOUNT PER VOUCHER PER NIGHT. SEE CONDITIONS OVERLEAF. VALID UNTIL 31-12-97	**WEST COUNTRY CARAVAN & CAMPING SITE GUIDE 1997** PRESENT THIS VOUCHER TO THE SITE OPERATOR WHEN PAYING TO RECEIVE A FIFTY PENCE DISCOUNT PER VOUCHER PER NIGHT. SEE CONDITIONS OVERLEAF. VALID UNTIL 31-12-97
WEST COUNTRY CARAVAN & CAMPING SITE GUIDE 1997 PRESENT THIS VOUCHER TO THE SITE OPERATOR WHEN PAYING TO RECEIVE A FIFTY PENCE DISCOUNT PER VOUCHER PER NIGHT. SEE CONDITIONS OVERLEAF. VALID UNTIL 31-12-97	**WEST COUNTRY CARAVAN & CAMPING SITE GUIDE 1997** PRESENT THIS VOUCHER TO THE SITE OPERATOR WHEN PAYING TO RECEIVE A FIFTY PENCE DISCOUNT PER VOUCHER PER NIGHT. SEE CONDITIONS OVERLEAF. VALID UNTIL 31-12-97
WEST COUNTRY CARAVAN & CAMPING SITE GUIDE 1997 PRESENT THIS VOUCHER TO THE SITE OPERATOR WHEN PAYING TO RECEIVE A FIFTY PENCE DISCOUNT PER VOUCHER PER NIGHT. SEE CONDITIONS OVERLEAF. VALID UNTIL 31-12-97	**WEST COUNTRY CARAVAN & CAMPING SITE GUIDE 1997** PRESENT THIS VOUCHER TO THE SITE OPERATOR WHEN PAYING TO RECEIVE A FIFTY PENCE DISCOUNT PER VOUCHER PER NIGHT. SEE CONDITIONS OVERLEAF. VALID UNTIL 31-12-97
WEST COUNTRY CARAVAN & CAMPING SITE GUIDE 1997 PRESENT THIS VOUCHER TO THE SITE OPERATOR WHEN PAYING TO RECEIVE A FIFTY PENCE DISCOUNT PER VOUCHER PER NIGHT. SEE CONDITIONS OVERLEAF. VALID UNTIL 31-12-97	**WEST COUNTRY CARAVAN & CAMPING SITE GUIDE 1997** PRESENT THIS VOUCHER TO THE SITE OPERATOR WHEN PAYING TO RECEIVE A FIFTY PENCE DISCOUNT PER VOUCHER PER NIGHT. SEE CONDITIONS OVERLEAF. VALID UNTIL 31-12-97

CADE'S WEST COUNTRY CAMPING, TOURING & MOTOR CARAVAN SITE GUIDE 1997

MONEY OFF VOUCHERS

CONDITIONS OF USE
Vouchers will only redeemed by those sites featuring a ⓒ symbol in their county entry. Presentation of this voucher to the Site Operator at the time of paying your balance will entitle you to a fifty pence discount per voucher, per night (only one voucher per night). Vouchers may be used in multiples i.e. five vouchers presented for a five night stay will entitle you to a discount of £2.50.

A CADE'S WEST COUNTRY CARAVAN & CAMPING SITE GUIDE 1997 EDITION must be presented at the time of payment. Vouchers are valid for accommodation only. Vouchers may not be exchanged for cash. Valid until 31-12-97.

CONDITIONS OF USE
Vouchers will only redeemed by those sites featuring a ⓒ symbol in their county entry. Presentation of this voucher to the Site Operator at the time of paying your balance will entitle you to a fifty pence discount per voucher, per night (only one voucher per night). Vouchers may be used in multiples i.e. five vouchers presented for a five night stay will entitle you to a discount of £2.50.

A CADE'S WEST COUNTRY CARAVAN & CAMPING SITE GUIDE 1997 EDITION must be presented at the time of payment. Vouchers are valid for accommodation only. Vouchers may not be exchanged for cash. Valid until 31-12-97.

CONDITIONS OF USE
Vouchers will only redeemed by those sites featuring a ⓒ symbol in their county entry. Presentation of this voucher to the Site Operator at the time of paying your balance will entitle you to a fifty pence discount per voucher, per night (only one voucher per night). Vouchers may be used in multiples i.e. five vouchers presented for a five night stay will entitle you to a discount of £2.50.

A CADE'S WEST COUNTRY CARAVAN & CAMPING SITE GUIDE 1997 EDITION must be presented at the time of payment. Vouchers are valid for accommodation only. Vouchers may not be exchanged for cash. Valid until 31-12-97.

CONDITIONS OF USE
Vouchers will only redeemed by those sites featuring a ⓒ symbol in their county entry. Presentation of this voucher to the Site Operator at the time of paying your balance will entitle you to a fifty pence discount per voucher, per night (only one voucher per night). Vouchers may be used in multiples i.e. five vouchers presented for a five night stay will entitle you to a discount of £2.50.

A CADE'S WEST COUNTRY CARAVAN & CAMPING SITE GUIDE 1997 EDITION must be presented at the time of payment. Vouchers are valid for accommodation only. Vouchers may not be exchanged for cash. Valid until 31-12-97.

CONDITIONS OF USE
Vouchers will only redeemed by those sites featuring a ⓒ symbol in their county entry. Presentation of this voucher to the Site Operator at the time of paying your balance will entitle you to a fifty pence discount per voucher, per night (only one voucher per night). Vouchers may be used in multiples i.e. five vouchers presented for a five night stay will entitle you to a discount of £2.50.

A CADE'S WEST COUNTRY CARAVAN & CAMPING SITE GUIDE 1997 EDITION must be presented at the time of payment. Vouchers are valid for accommodation only. Vouchers may not be exchanged for cash. Valid until 31-12-97.

CONDITIONS OF USE
Vouchers will only redeemed by those sites featuring a ⓒ symbol in their county entry. Presentation of this voucher to the Site Operator at the time of paying your balance will entitle you to a fifty pence discount per voucher, per night (only one voucher per night). Vouchers may be used in multiples i.e. five vouchers presented for a five night stay will entitle you to a discount of £2.50.

A CADE'S WEST COUNTRY CARAVAN & CAMPING SITE GUIDE 1997 EDITION must be presented at the time of payment. Vouchers are valid for accommodation only. Vouchers may not be exchanged for cash. Valid until 31-12-97.

CONDITIONS OF USE
Vouchers will only redeemed by those sites featuring a ⓒ symbol in their county entry. Presentation of this voucher to the Site Operator at the time of paying your balance will entitle you to a fifty pence discount per voucher, per night (only one voucher per night). Vouchers may be used in multiples i.e. five vouchers presented for a five night stay will entitle you to a discount of £2.50.

A CADE'S WEST COUNTRY CARAVAN & CAMPING SITE GUIDE 1997 EDITION must be presented at the time of payment. Vouchers are valid for accommodation only. Vouchers may not be exchanged for cash. Valid until 31-12-97.

CONDITIONS OF USE
Vouchers will only redeemed by those sites featuring a ⓒ symbol in their county entry. Presentation of this voucher to the Site Operator at the time of paying your balance will entitle you to a fifty pence discount per voucher, per night (only one voucher per night). Vouchers may be used in multiples i.e. five vouchers presented for a five night stay will entitle you to a discount of £2.50.

A CADE'S WEST COUNTRY CARAVAN & CAMPING SITE GUIDE 1997 EDITION must be presented at the time of payment. Vouchers are valid for accommodation only. Vouchers may not be exchanged for cash. Valid until 31-12-97.

CONDITIONS OF USE
Vouchers will only redeemed by those sites featuring a ⓒ symbol in their county entry. Presentation of this voucher to the Site Operator at the time of paying your balance will entitle you to a fifty pence discount per voucher, per night (only one voucher per night). Vouchers may be used in multiples i.e. five vouchers presented for a five night stay will entitle you to a discount of £2.50.

A CADE'S WEST COUNTRY CARAVAN & CAMPING SITE GUIDE 1997 EDITION must be presented at the time of payment. Vouchers are valid for accommodation only. Vouchers may not be exchanged for cash. Valid until 31-12-97.

CONDITIONS OF USE
Vouchers will only redeemed by those sites featuring a ⓒ symbol in their county entry. Presentation of this voucher to the Site Operator at the time of paying your balance will entitle you to a fifty pence discount per voucher, per night (only one voucher per night). Vouchers may be used in multiples i.e. five vouchers presented for a five night stay will entitle you to a discount of £2.50.

A CADE'S WEST COUNTRY CARAVAN & CAMPING SITE GUIDE 1997 EDITION must be presented at the time of payment. Vouchers are valid for accommodation only. Vouchers may not be exchanged for cash. Valid until 31-12-97.

Burnham-on-Sea Holiday Village Somerset

Burnham-on-Sea Holiday Village,
Marine Drive, Burnham-on-Sea,
Somerset

GREAT ACTIVITIES ALL THE FAMILY WILL ENJOY

KIDS AND TEEN CLUBS

GREAT ENTERTAINMENT AND THEME WEEKENDS

GREAT VALUE HOLIDAYS

SAVE 10%

WHEN YOU BOOK AND STAY WITH US ANYTIME DURING 1997

OFF YOUR ACCOMMODATION OR CARAVAN PITCH

3, 4 AND 7 NIGHT BREAKS AVAILABLE

CALL NOW FOR YOUR FREE COLOUR BROCHURE QUOTE 'CADES'

LO-CALL RATE 24 HOURS - 7 DAYS

0345 508 508

OR SEE YOUR LOCAL TRAVEL AGENT

BRITISH HOLIDAYS INTRODUCTORY OFFER - 10% DISCOUNT

*Book a Holiday at Burnham-on-Sea Holiday Village, present this voucher when paying to receive 10% off the cost of the accommodation - valid until 31st December 1997 - vouchers must be presented with payment, are not exchangeable for cash, subject to availability and the conditions as shown in the current British Holidays Brochure, cannot be used in conjunction with any other offer, not valid for use over Bank Holiday periods and non-transferable.

'Cades'

Book and Stay with us, present the attached voucher and we'll give you a 10% discount off the cost of your accommodation - call for full qualifying details.

0345 508 508

LO-CALL 24 HOURS 7 DAYS A WEEK **0345 508 508** OR SEE YOUR LOCAL TRAVEL AGENT

A BRITISH HOLIDAYS PARK

'Cades'

NOTES